Smoke and Mirrors

The Rise and Fall of a Serial Antipreneur

Written by

Mike James

This second edition
Published in 2022 by
Mike James

Cover Art by Trevor Storey

www.colecochameleon.org

Kickstarter Backers

On October 6, 2020 the Kickstarter campaign to bring this book to life began and we reached our £1,400 funding goal in less than 48 hours, achieving an amazing final total of 253 backers with pledges reaching £5,108 by November 6, 2020.

The paperback version of the book was the result of high demand and a successful Stretch Goal of £3,500 which we easily surpassed.

THE PEOPLE BELOW PLEDGED ENOUGH TO BE NAMED IN THE BOOK AND THEY PLAYED A HUGE PART IN MAKING IT A REALITY.

WE THANK THEM FOR THEIR VALUED SUPPORT

Carey Clanton

Steve Rasmussen

Ken J

Greg Polander

Joe Guadarrama

Nick DiPalma

Matthew Kile

Peter Gibbs

Josh Jacobson

Matson

Aaron Hickman

Paul Nurminen

Robert McEvoy

Sean Robinson

Kevin Otto Nielsen

William Olds

Fabrizio Pedrazzini

Neil Dixon

John Rice

Pix

Jürgen Bloß

Scott Schreiber

Heinlein's Razor:

Never attribute to malice that which can be adequately explained by stupidity, but don't rule out malice.

Scott Schreiber

(September 4, 2016):

Antipreneur is a more accurate term than entrepreneur.

Mike James

(October 4, 2011):

Remember your friends on the way up,

because they'll not forget you on the way down.

Mike Kennedy

(October 4, 2011):

This would make a hell of a documentary, man.

You could make this very entertaining.

Godwin's Law:

As an online discussion grows longer, the probability of a comparison involving Nazis or Hitler approaches; that is, if an online discussion (regardless of topic or scope) goes on long enough, sooner or later someone will compare someone or something to Adolf Hitler or his deeds, the point at which effectively the discussion or thread often ends.

Contents

Foreword

by Mike James

When I sat down to write this book, I didn't sit down to write this book. I didn't even know if it was a book. I knew there was a story to tell, at the very least a factual documentation of the rise and fall of Mike Kennedy, but I didn't just want to write a factual documentation of events. What I didn't realize until I had started writing was that there is also a story between the lines and that is what I wanted to write.

The majority of people who will read this book will be a part of the video game community because, like it or not, the story barely broke out beyond the realms of that community. For those of us involved or following along, it became all-encompassing at times, but it was, at best, a small group of people in a niche audience that were aware of it.

What I realized as I began to write was that there was also a human story, the story of a man who followed his dreams and lost his way. The story of a man who set out on a journey and picked up fellow travelers along the way, some of them disingenuous, some of them with Mike's best interests at heart, but all of them along for the ride, and we will examine Mike's inability or unwillingness to notice the difference.

Throughout the following pages you will join Mike on his journey from innocent gamer to pantomime villain or true pariah, depending on your opinion. You will have to decide. Some people will come out of this book in a better light than others, some will come out of it with their integrity and reputation intact, others will not. This is not an opinion piece, it is a factual representation of events, but having said that, the facts will lead us to some inevitable conclusions.

I hope and believe that the book has appeal beyond the realms of the gaming community as I truly believe it is a valid study of the human condition and its foibles, a study of one man's blindness to the folly of his endeavors and a study of those willing to help and those seeking to hinder him.

Though I was a passenger on the bus as it left the station, before joining others under it, as it began to gather speed before careering out of control as the wheels began to wobble and the inevitable crash happened, I certainly did not look back at the wreckage with any satisfaction. I wasn't, to use an analogy, an ambulance chaser, in fact, on more than one occasion, I was the ambulance offering assistance.

Even after the last wisps of smoke had left the long burned out wreckage, I would have willingly gone back to that station and stopped Mike from boarding. By the end of the book however, you will realize that Mike had his ticket and he was always going to take that ride, wherever it may lead.

Mike James (UKMike)

1: Hey Everybody It's Socalmike

Mike Kennedy (SoCalMike) came across as a happy go lucky kind of guy, the kind of guy that you instantly liked and wanted to like. He worked in sales which seemed to suit his upbeat personality and he had an ability to inspire confidence and he gave you the feeling that he really was personally enthusiastic about whatever the topic for discussion may be.

Mike Kennedy was born in Omaha, Nebraska on November 20, 1969, and his family still reside there. He discovered video games, like most people of his generation, in the very early days of the industry, the mid 1970's, and again, like most people his age, it was with a home Pong console and Mike's was bought by a relative as a Christmas present, probably by his Grandfather who worked at Sears.

Pong consoles were very popular in this era and were simply a home version of the Atari arcade game of the same name that had hit the arcades in 1972 after Al Alcorn created the game as a training exercise. A test unit was put on location at a local bar called Andy Capp's Tavern in August 1972 to see how popular it was and within a few days Al had a phone call to let him know that it had broken. In fact, it wasn't broken, the unit had proven so popular that the coin box had simply filled up and could not take any more coins. This was the true birth of the coin operated Arcade era.

Atari engineer Harold Lee proposed a home version that would connect to a television set and he worked with Alcorn to develop a unit that was based on the same technology used in the arcade game. Their final unit was ready in 1974 and they contacted the Sears Sporting Goods department after they had seen a Magnavox Odyssey advertisement in the sporting goods section of its catalogue. Tom Quinn of Sears offered Atari an exclusive deal, but Atari felt that they would get a better deal elsewhere and took their unit to the New York Toy Fair where it received a lukewarm reception.

With their tail between their legs they went back to Sears and took a demo unit to Chicago before signing a deal that would see them available in stores from 1975. Soon after, other companies began to produce their own versions, known as clones, as the Atari version sold through Sears was officially called the "Sears Tele-Game." Mike is unsure of exactly which unit he had back then as he has no pictures of it from the time to look back at, but he thinks it was most likely a Sears Tele-Game as his Grandfather worked for the company and the family would often receive Sears gifts for Christmas and birthdays. He did however spend lots of his time playing on it and that is what started his life-long love of video games.

His next system was an Atari VCS, sometimes referred to as the Atari 2600, and he picked up lots of games for it over time, either with his pocket money or as gifts for birthdays and Christmas. His favorite games on the Atari VCS were Kaboom, Adventure, Dodgem, Fast Food, Pitfall 2, Jawbreaker and Frostbite, he even remembers the day that he got Kaboom as a gift, before he even had his console.

There was a grocery store near his childhood home that also sold video games, back then many outlets from book stores to grocery stores would have a carousel display that was full of videogame cassettes and diskettes for the various current computers and consoles. In the grocery store Mike saw the tell-tale pink box that belonged to Kaboom and he begged his Mother to buy it for him, knowing that he was getting an Atari for his birthday. She let him have it and he would take it to his friends' houses to play it until he got his own system soon after. He loved the game so much that he would later use the nickname "Kaboomer" on several video game forums.

By the time Mike was attending Junior High School, as luck would have it during his 7th and 8th grade, they had just completed work on their new Computer Lab that boasted over 20 TRS-80 Model III's. These were manufactured by Tandy Corporation from 1977 until 1981 and sold over 100,000 units. The name "TRS" comes from a combination of the names Tandy and Radio Shack who sold them. These were not a video game console but a fully-fledged microcomputer, complete with a full "QWERTY" keyboard, disk drive and monitor, which was actually a modified black and white television. By 1979, the TRS-80 had the largest software library of any microcomputer available and outsold its main rival, the Apple 2 series, by 500%.

Mike wasted no time in familiarizing himself with this new technology and was one of many students who would be eager to stay behind after school had finished to go along to the lab and play on these wonderful new machines. So much so that he joined the school computer club and started playing around with the computers and learning more about them. He also found another of his favorite games there, the classic Oregon Trail. As well as at school, Mike had access to computers at home, including a Timex Sinclair, a Commodore 64 and, when he got to High School, his favorite computer of the time, his Apple 2c with its green, monochrome monitor. Mike's favorite games for the Apple that he kept throughout his High School years were Castle Wolfenstein, Choplifter, Biolstoad and Critical Mass.

Mike even wrote some primitive games for his Sinclair, including one that he was particularly proud of where you placed bets on the outcome of a race between sailing boats. The boats would be made up of the graphics provided on the Sinclair keys rather than using pixels and the boats would race from one side of the screen to the other, with the winner being determined randomly. At this stage Mike was using computers much more than consoles for games and would often have friends over so they could have sleep overs and play marathon games of Archon, M.U.L.E., Temples of

Apshai, Beach Head and the popular Infocom text adventure games like Seven Cities of Gold.

Outside of school and home Mike would visit Millard's local arcades, in particular one called Yada's, which was his favorite, and he spent hour after hour there in that *"vibrant, noisy place that always had a good smell of pizza and popcorn coming from the small snack bar."* He also remembers;

> *"the sounds that emanated from that place as I was opening the door and about to step in: a mixed-up symphony of arcade theme songs and attract screens all greeting me and wanting my attention (and my quarters). It was magical."*

The first arcade game that he remembers playing is Midway's Stunt Pilot which is a 1971 Electro-Mechanical game where you control an airplane that flies around a black light environment. The aim of the game is to fly under the St. Louis Arch and avoid other obstacles. If you crashed your plane, there would be an ambulance that came out with its lights flashing as it drove around. The game has to be seen to be believed as the backgrounds and the environment are made with physical landscapes rather than just computer graphics and look absolutely amazing, even more so to a young Mike Kennedy who had never seen anything like it before.

His favorite games to play at Yada's arcade were Cinematronic's 1980 vector game Star Castle, Atari's 1980 games Missile Command and Battlezone, Sega's 1980 game Carnival and their 1981 game Astro Blaster. It was also at Yada's that Mike saw the 1980 Midway game Pac-Man, which he played, and watched others play, so much that he learned the game's patterns and could routinely progress through the game to the 9th key before the pattern changed. The Pac-Man ghosts are programmed in such a way that their movements can be predicted and that can be used to the player's advantage in avoiding them or eating them after swallowing the power pills. Mike also loved to meet his friends at Yada's and the other arcades of Millard such as Western Bowl, Dragons Lair, Skateland, Peony Park Arcade, WC Franks Millard Plaza, Showbiz Pizza, Happy Joes Pizza and Kart Ranch where they would hang out, play games and eat pizza, much like kids all across America were doing at the time.

Back at home while most of his peers owned the NES (Nintendo Entertainment System) Mike went the other way and got a Sega Master System which he loved, followed by a Sega Genesis which again, he loved, but he realized that he had been limiting himself to the one system and would have the typical playground arguments of the day over which was better, Nintendo or Sega, and while in general he preferred the Sega systems and game libraries, he had his head turned by the 1994 Super Nintendo game Donkey Kong Country developed by Rare. Pretty soon after its release he owned a Super Nintendo.

These were Mike's core gaming years and, like most people his age, there were other consoles to follow such as the Nintendo 64, Atari Jaguar, Atari Lynx, Sega Game Gear, Nintendo Game Boy, Sega Dreamcast, Nintendo Gamecube, Sony PlayStation, Microsoft Xbox and Sony PlayStation 2 but again, like most people, when Mike closes his eyes and thinks of his childhood and the games he played, it is the earlier systems that he remembers most fondly.

Mike continued his schooling at Millard South High School, graduating in the Class of 88 before attending Creighton University from 1989 to 1990 and later the University of Nebraska at Omaha from 1991 to 1994, the same University that his father had attended before him.

As a teenager Mike would spend a lot of time up at Lewis and Clark Lake along with his then girlfriend Tricia and they would follow their shared passion for sailing as well as for each other. Lewis and Clarke Lake sits on the Missouri River at Yankton, South Dakota which is on the border between Nebraska and South Dakota, a short drive from Omaha. It is actually a reservoir that is approximately 25 miles long with a surface area of 31,000 acres. The area was also popular with campers and Mike and Tricia continued this love of camping for many years, frequently traveling and camping in their silver Airstream. As teenagers the two of them would race each other in sailing boats up and down the lake as they spent long summers there, another hobby that they continued to enjoy on board their yacht, Hula Girl, sailing the 22 miles from its mooring at Dana Point to Catalina Island.

While Tricia was studying at Creighton University, Mike would often make the journey over to spend time with her and there are pictures of Mike in her dorm room playing Tetris and Super Mario Land on his Game Boy with headphones plugged in to capture the great stereo sound that the unit had. The two of them were eventually married on December 26, 1992, having met when they were just eight years old.

As well as sailing, the two of them shared a passion for their local college football team, the Nebraska Cornhuskers and they would try to go to every game. The Cornhuskers is the team of the University of Nebraska and located in Lincoln, Nebraska at the Memorial Stadium and Mike and Tricia would go to games wearing their team colors of Scarlet and Cream. The team began playing competitive games in 1890 and Mike and Tricia still go to games when they can, in recent years, usually when the Cornhuskers are playing a California team as the two of them moved out from Nebraska to Southern California in 1999.

The move to the warmer climate allowed Mike to almost continually wear his favorite attire of shorts or jeans and retro gaming T-Shirt, showing a glimpse of his Fred Flintstone tattoo. It also allowed him to rekindle his love affair with gaming, and in particular, retro gaming.

Southern California is well known for its swap meets and Mike would visit them every weekend hoping to pick up cheap games and consoles, a lot of which he would simply never have seen in Nebraska. With Silicon Valley not too far away he was surprised by some of the cool hardware that he would see and he would want to buy it all, and over time he did build up quite a collection of interesting items.

In addition to the swap meets, Mike had begun using eBay in 1997 and before he knew it he had filled his garage, which he also used as a home office, with lots of retro items that he simply didn't need and he found himself having to make difficult decisions about what to keep and what to sell. He decided that he would only keep either the things that he had owned as a child or the things that he had wanted as a child but never got, and he went about selling the rest of his collection on eBay. The profit he made on these sales after picking the items up at swap meets for rock bottom prices and then selling them on eBay at a premium meant that he literally had a collection of items he wanted that had effectively cost him nothing.

One day in 2002, at a swap meet, Mike found an arcade cab and he had to own it. It was the 1981 Exidy game "Venture" and it was only $75 so he took it home with him and began his collection of arcade and pinball machines. As he only had a single garage which also served as his home office, he had limited space for them but generally he rotated a collection of a dozen or so arcade machines. The ones he generally kept were his M.A.M.E. (Multiple Arcade Machine Emulator) cabinet, Atari Battlezone, Atari Video Pinball, Midway Stunt Pilot and the Williams Taxi pinball. He had carpeted his arcade with black light carpet, fitted a laser star projector, an iPod jukebox and various black light and 80's movie posters. He kept a small desk for his work from home job but it was full of Apple, Commodore, and other classic computers with barely enough room for his work laptop. His favorite arcade game, and one that he never wanted to part with, was his Midway Stunt Pilot which he bought from eBay for $400.

Mike did own some modern day systems including a Nintendo DS, a Nintendo Wii and a Sony PlayStation 3, though he does not feel the same passion for those as he does for the old, retro systems. He also played a lot of games on his iPhone and is encouraged by the stream of good games he has found for the system. However, he feels that each console generation has massive highs and massive lows, though this could be said of most eras really, they all had very good and very bad games but he describes the current era as *"an awesome time to be a gamer"* and then expounds upon that with *"Has there ever been a "not awesome" time to be a gamer? I think not."*

Mike was surrounded by these arcade machines, retro systems and collectibles as he carried out his day job which was South West Regional Sales Engineer for Creform Corporation, a manufacturer of material handling products, a position he had held since July 2005. Mike looked after customers in the Southern California area and occasionally travelled around the state and beyond to meet with customers and suppliers. Once he finished his work day at 5pm, and often before, he would hit the gaming forums and chat with like-minded collectors and players and this is how Mike met most of the people he knows in and around the hobby, a hobby that he wanted to turn it into a career.

"I just want to quit my day job and work in gaming, as an ideas man" was his aim and we will go on that journey with Mike to see if he achieves it, but is it a wise aim? Should hobbies remain just that, hobbies, to be enjoyed in free time?

If we look at the definition of "hobby" oxforddictionaries.com describes it as:

"An activity done regularly in one's leisure time for pleasure."

Dictionary.com goes one step further in its definition:

> *"An activity or interest pursued for pleasure or relaxation and not as a main occupation."*

Mike isn't the only person to have attempted that transition but is it a good idea? The video game industry is full of people who love what they do, as are all industries, but it is a fine line between loving what you do for a living and making a living doing what you love. It is equally true that there is little or no place for a guy with only ideas. A programmer or artist with ideas has a place at the table, and virtually all talent at the table has ideas, so there is almost never a place at the table for an individual bringing no talent but telling others what they should do with theirs. This would be the rope that Mike dangled from over the edge of the cliff as he possessed neither the talent or the funding to create his empire. He had to use the time and talents of others until, finally, that rope snapped.

The saying goes: *"If you find a career you love, you'll never work a day in your life"* and while it has been attributed to everybody from Confucius to Marc Anthony, it certainly contains a grain of truth. Getting out of bed every morning to go to a job you hate is no way to start the day and just making that simple change in your life makes a huge difference to your health and well-being. Some people are lucky enough to never have those Monday morning blues or, worse still, the Sunday evening blues and everybody should aim to pursue a career in a field they love and why wouldn't you? You spend your years in school, college, university and any other establishment you care to attend, learning your way to pass exams and equipping yourself with the qualifications to follow the path you set yourself on, presumably choosing the subjects that you find interesting, which makes studying for them much easier and enjoyable, and makes you want to learn more about them. Enthusiasm for your chosen subject and an enjoyment of studying and the learning process is a wonderful thing to experience and that yearning for knowledge increases as we get older, however, that yearning for knowledge and the enjoyment of a chosen subject is very different from a hobby.

The early days of Atari for example, where the pioneers of the industry were programming games like Yar's Revenge, Pitfall, Kaboom and Dragster. Those programmers would eat, sleep and live their games as they went through the whole process of design, programming and packaging. The programmers of these early games, David Crane, Rob Zdybel and Howard Scott Warshaw, to name a few, would go to work when they wanted to program and would work for days on end, sometimes sleeping in the office between sessions, not only because they would lose track of time once their fingers hit the keyboard, but because they loved what they did. They were dedicated programmers and it didn't really matter that they were programming games. To many programmers, the same problems and solutions exist whatever they are working on, they are writing code that solves a problem and it doesn't really matter what that problem is, the mental process for solving that problem and the code used to solve that problem are one and the same.

However, for the hobby coder the scenario is very different. There is a huge void between sitting at home and tinkering with code to make a ball bounce across the screen and sitting in an office having to write a program to control the temperature in a nuclear reactor or writing the code that makes a heat seeking missile seek heat. The pressures are poles apart and the experience is a very different one. You also have to consider what skills you bring with you. To be a programmer for example you have to solve problems, usually complex problems, to be an ideas man you have to have ideas. If you have none of the skills necessary to bring those ideas to fruition though, you need a team around you who can. The problem is, once the team have that idea, they don't need you anymore. They go away and make that idea a reality and you have no further purpose until you come up with the next idea and if your ideas aren't original or are somebody else's, what purpose do you serve at all?

The other problem with making a hobby a career is that you can easily lose sight of what is realistic, what is practical and what is actually a good or a bad idea. Your judgement becomes somewhat clouded as your passion can easily take over as you chase unrealistic dreams. What is hard to gauge is whether your enthusiasm for your idea is limited to yourself or if there is actually a market for it. You could come up with an idea for what you think is a fabulous product but will it sell? Do other people share the enthusiasm for it or not?

I will give the example of a solution to a problem that we all face almost every day of our lives. That of making a cup of tea. You make a cup of tea, you pour boiling water into a mug that contains a teabag and you stir it to help it infuse properly and make a nice strong cup of tea. Once the tea is brewed and you need to remove the teabag from the cup, you use a spoon, you scoop the teabag up, squeeze it slightly against the side of the cup and then carry it from the mug to the waste bin, probably dripping tea all the way as the teabag overhangs the sides of the spoon.

Wouldn't it be fantastic if there was a device that would allow you to stir the tea, squeeze the teabag over the mug and then allow you to carry it to the bin without dripping tea as you do so? There have been countless people and companies bringing such a product to market, all of them have a great case, they all have a problem that needs solving and they all come up with a solution that solves it, but do they sell? No. The public at large just keep on using a teaspoon and will keep on using a teaspoon until the teabag is a thing of the past. It's a problem certainly, but is it a problem that needs solving?

In the minds of inventors who design these products, yes, and each one thinks that theirs is the best yet and will sell to the public at large, but they all leave pretty much empty handed as the market does not share their enthusiasm for their product. Is their judgement clouded as they see their idea through from concept to finished product? Are they chasing a pipe dream or could they just have done better market research and not wasted their time?

The other problem of course is that you also have to do the bits that you don't like in addition to the bits you do like. The inventor loves to invent but he also has to learn marketing, business finance, fill in tax returns, negotiate buying raw materials and pitch to potential buyers, none of which he may be good at, so the part he actually enjoys, inventing, becomes perhaps 20% of his day to day duties which doesn't sound like fun at all.

If you do decide to pursue a hobby as a career, you need to be very focused and dedicated to make it work, it is your future and nobody else is going to make it happen for you. Keep your ideas simple and focused as this will not only make it easier to achieve, but it will make your product easier for the public to understand. Keeping your product simple is not restricting yourself unnecessarily, it makes your goal easier and that brings other goals with it. You also need to be sure that you are backing a winner before sinking everything into it, if somebody gives you constructive criticism you need to listen to it as it will come from somebody who does not have a vested interest, somebody who isn't perhaps blinkered or blind to problems. Take a step back and look at the problem with fresh eyes.

It is widely thought that the likely reason you love your hobby so much is because there is no pressure associated with it, because it is done in free time there are no deadlines to meet, there is no quality control, so if the first time you make a dovetail joint you make a mess of it, you can just do it again. There is no pressure of where the next pay cheque is coming from, it's just for fun. However, that fun element can be lost when you monetize your hobby and when there is now some pressure attached to it. Not only might you be stuck in a job that you are disengaged from, you've also taken the fun out of your hobby as well which is your means of escapism.

It might be fun to create something in your free time but can you create thousands of them to meet an order? Will you still enjoy making them a decade from now? Can somebody else make them more cheaply or more quickly? Perhaps even market them more effectively. Even if you have a hobby that you love a great deal, you might not have what it takes to make it as a viable business. There's a big difference between playing video games in your home arcade and manufacturing and selling video games for profit five days a week, fifty two weeks a year.

2: Going Once, Going Twice

Chase the Chuckwagon

The name *Chase the Chuckwagon* comes from a 1983 promotional video game for the Atari VCS. The game was only available via mail order and to receive a copy you had to send a proof of purchase to the dog food company Ralston Purina who produced a brand of dog food called "Chuckwagon", hence the rarity of the game. Hardly anybody actually did this to obtain a copy of the game, in what would have been a fairly limited production run in the first place and it is certainly not an easy game to find today.

The premise of hunting down a rare game and the play on words in the name gave Mike the idea for a new website which he launched on March 24th, 2008. Actually it wasn't an original idea as somebody had tried it before with a site that failed, called vidiots.com.

He had this to say about the name:

> *"Basically, the promotion failed and supposedly very few of these Atari cartridges made it out into consumers' hands. Thus is (sic) became known as extremely rare with Atari Collectors. This helped (it) become the original "Holy Grail" for video game collectors and soon the name Chase the Chuckwagon became synonymous with the hunt we are all on to find rare and unique items for our collections.*
>
> *So now, you know it's not just some crazy name, but has a true meaning for hunting down and finding collectible gaming items. Once I discovered this URL was available, I bought it and the ChaseTheChuckwagon.com Auction site was born."*

Chase the Chuckwagon was intended to be an online auction site with which Mike hoped to rival the online auction giant "eBay", but Mike's site would be selling exclusively video game related merchandise. Mike was the founder and sole owner of Chase the Chuckwagon which initially came about as a means of saving himself some money. One of Mike's hobbies was to go to his local Swap Meets every weekend and pick up cheap items ranging from loose game cartridges for assorted systems to boxed, complete consoles. Some of these he would keep for his own collection but most were bought to sell on and hopefully turn a profit. No harm in that of course, lots of people do it all over the world.

Mike would then get his purchases home, photograph them and post them on his web site for people to buy. He had been picking up games in this way for some time and had been listing them on eBay, a service he had been using since 1997, but he had been growing increasingly tired of paying eBay's rising fees on every item that he listed. With his own site, Mike could list as many items as he wanted to and not pay any selling fees, and it had the potential to bring him a slice of the gamer market and make him very wealthy and the head of a major corporation in the video game world. That was his goal and that was the spark of an idea that drove the creation of ChaseTheChuckWagon.com.

The problem that Mike faced of course was exposure. Everybody knew what eBay was but nobody had heard of Chase the Chuckwagon, so items listed for sale were certainly cheap to sell but the downside was that they had only a very limited potential audience to bid up the prices and make it worthwhile for other sellers to use it.

This was Mike's main problem with Chase the Chuckwagon, getting a foothold in the market place and driving traffic to his site, and really that is the problem for anybody trying to build a new website to rival any of the big players. As wide open and accessible as the Internet is, it doesn't really support this model of providing an alternative option for consumers.

For example, think of video streaming sites, particularly those based around user content. The main one is of course YouTube which totally dominates the field and leaves the rest such as Vimeo to fight over the scraps. The same is true of research sites with Wikipedia dominating the field and its competitors again are left fighting for survival. Netflix enjoys a similar dominance for studio produced content and of course eBay totally dominates the online auction market, leaving sites like Etsy and of course Chase the Chuckwagon to pick up the pieces.

As legitimate as Mike's motives were, to create a cheaper and more focused site, it was always going to be an uphill struggle, especially for a site with such an unusual name, a name not immediately associated with its core objective, selling second hand video games and video game merchandise. After some development on the site, any items listed there with a fixed "Buy Now" price would show up in a Google search but Mike was still struggling to drive traffic to his live auctions so some positive action was needed.

This is where Mike had an idea, one that he would repeat later, more than once. Mike decided to hit the airwaves and in order to increase his potential market, he started recording a podcast. Mike was an avid listener of the Shane R. Monroe show "Retro Gaming Radio" and when he was at the Riviera Hotel in Las Vegas for Classic Gaming Expo 2007 he bumped into Shane and pitched to him the idea of putting his new auction related audio segment into Shane's show where he would talk about going to the Southern California swap meets and grabbing bargains and classic gaming items that he could then make available to listeners. Shane liked the idea and Mike's segment "Chasing The Chuckwagon" began shortly afterwards.

Seeing that the domain name chasingthechuckwagon.com was also available he bought that as well, and redirected it to the existing chasethechuckwagon.com.

Retro Gaming Radio ran from August 1998 to August 2008 and had evolved over time from a short Real Media show, released whenever Shane had content to share, to a monthly mp3 file based show running around 3 hours long. Toward the end of its run, Retro Gaming Radio became less regular and there were only 3 shows released in its final year. This was a bit of a problem for Mike because he was trying to increase interest in the items he was selling, but by the time the show was released they may no longer be for sale, so he needed a more regular podcast that was released more reliably.

Another contributor to Retro Gaming Radio was Scott Schreiber who recorded a segment called "The Hardware Flashback" and, as the name would suggest, he would discuss technical aspects of a wide range of hardware, from repairing arcade games and pinball machines to reviewing new controllers and video games. As Mike pitched his idea for an audio segment to Shane, Scott was also in the Retro Gaming Radio booth and got to spend some time with them both and got to know them. They had met casually at events before but had never spent any extended time together and Scott enjoyed getting to know Mike in those early days.

Mike explored various avenues to try and popularize Chase the Chuckwagon and would post about it on various retro gaming forums, don't forget that this was before the days of Social Media as we know it today, and the quick and easy exposure that we take for granted these days simply wasn't there, though the early signs were promising:

On August 6, 2008 Mike had this to say:

"I feel we are approaching a momentous occasion on Chase the Chuckwagon"

In its first four months the site boasted 670 members and a growth of 160 new members each month. There had been over 6,000 items listed and there were currently almost 1,000 live auctions running. There were sales of over $19,000 and it had risen to the top 120,000 sites in the USA and the top 550,000 worldwide out of over 10,000,000 at that time.

Still, to take on the might of eBay a change was needed, and a change soon came.

Vendazzle

Mike felt that the scope of Chase the Chuckwagon might be a little too narrow and he wanted to increase the potential market for his site so he began to search for alternatives and he found one in Vendazzle. Vendazzle.com had started prior to Chase the Chuckwagon but its owner had lost interest in it so Mike decided to pick it up in late 2008 and launched on December 9, 2008, to run it alongside Chase the Chuckwagon.

Vendazzle would be an auction site that was not restricted to video games, it could be used for anything (except video games) and Mike began to promote it around various forums and websites, offering free seller accounts to early members in order to encourage more traffic.

"The first 20 members to register on http://www.Vendazzle.com and PM me back here will score a lifetime seller membership. Pay no listing or final value selling fees forever on Vendazzle."

"ChaseTheChuckwagon.com, a video gaming auction site, was launched back in March 08. Since then we've grown to over 1,500 members, hosted over 43,000 auctions and sold over $50,000 in merchandise.

Now, at the request of our members we have launched a "sister" site to facilitate auctions for everything else (but video games). One registration gets you into both sites!"

"The ease of use and the familiar format will keep you coming back again and again.

Please check us out and register today.

So Cal Mike, Owner
http://www.Vendazzle.com
http://www.ChaseTheChuckwagon.com"

He got Vendazzle some early exposure after launch and on December 10, 2008, the website gamesindustrybiz.com published his press announcement where he described the move to Vendazzle as being driven by his Chuckwagon members, craving more Mike Kennedy auction sites.

"ChaseTheChuckwagon.com is a successful startup auction site dedicated to video games. Since launching in March 08 it has grown to over 1,500 members, hosted over 43,000 auctions and sold over $50,000 in merchandise. Now at the request of its members, owner Mike Kennedy, has launched an auction site dedicated to everything else. Mike says, "It was evident early on that our members were looking for another venue to sell things other than Video Games". Originally a video gaming auction site, Mike soon started to get requests for other things like toys, music & movies, etc.
A single registration gets you access to both sites."

Those sentences "O*ne registration gets you into both sites!" and "A single registration gets you into both sites!"* would become a cause for concern for some in the future but Mike was on the campaign trail and registered a Twitter account for Vendazzle in April 2009 but he soon lost patience with the site as it failed to bring in the numbers that he was hoping for. In fact, he amassed just 395 Twitter followers, less than half the number of accounts he followed, 806, and tweeted just 9 times.

It wasn't long, in fact, the following August, before he was offering Vendazzle up for sale and people were seeing his sales posts and discussing them on other forums, quoting his sales pitches:

Vendazzle/Chuckwagon Rinky Dink to sell 3000 member's info:

> *"It's still in the back of my mind. My video gaming dedicated auction site – ChaseTheChuckwagon.com is still taking much of my time.*

> *My other site, Vendazzle.com is also struggling since I don't have time to do it justice either. So if anyone wants to own their own site, cheap, let me know. Vendazzle.com can be yours and you can keep it running as is, or turn it into a niche site of your choosing. The Auction software is great and the guy who wrote it is very good to work with. And I can train you fully. Any takers :) Oh, and it's preloaded with about 3,000 members too."*

> *"How would you feel if you registered on a site (Chuckwagon), and had your info (along with 3000 others) transferred to another site (Vendazzle) and sold for "cheap" to someone who wants to run their own site, when the admin decided he didn't want anything to do with it anymore?"*

Thinking nothing of simply migrating his Chuckwagon user database over to Vendazzle and then selling off his members' account details, it was another case of nothing ventured, nothing gained for Mike but he would not be put off that easily and shopped around for another auction alternative, this time keeping it strictly video games again.

Gamegavel

Mike's passion and enthusiasm had got the better of him, not for the first time and certainly not for the last time, and Chase the Chuckwagon is an early example of Mike's propensity to act first and think later. That can be good in certain situations where quick action is needed, where the first reaction is usually the correct one. This is not an example of that. This is an example of passion and romanticism taking the lead over common sense, a trait that will haunt Mike several more times in the future as we'll see.

Chase the Chuckwagon was a great name for a video game auction site in a wistful and romantic way but not in a practical, business sense, and that is demonstrated by a similar site which launched around the same time, GameGavel.com.

Mike felt that the name wasn't really that important when compared to what the site has to offer in content and features, almost an "If you build it, they will come." type attitude and he compares it to eBay:

> *"eBay means nothing (well, maybe East Bay as that is where eBay is located – East of the bay). I had people say I should have named the site GameBay. I still laugh at that one."*

GameGavel was launched on February 1, 2008, just over 7 weeks before Chase the Chuckwagon, but had enjoyed slightly more success and, more importantly, had a better name, a name more suited to a video game related auction site. It had the words "Game" and "Gavel" in it for one thing.

However, its owners no longer wanted to keep the site going, presumably having failed to take on the mighty eBay, and Mike snapped up the name in the fall of 2009, and on October 24, 2009, he completed his switchover and rebranded himself as GameGavel.com.

At this stage GameGavel was solely owned by Mike and he wanted to promote it, improve it, add functionality to it and base his "empire" around it, his problem was that he lacked the funds to do it himself and so began a long and winding road of bringing funding into the company. The easiest way to do this was to crowdfund it and he tried that with a flexible funding Indiegogo campaign in June 2012, though it failed to reach anywhere near his $100,000 goal, so the path he chose was to bring in family and friends as investors and he "sold" parts of his company to raise the funds that he would invest in the GameGavel site. The shares were sold almost exclusively to family members, some to Tricia's family and some to the only non-family member on board at this stage, Scott Schreiber. Mike called Scott one day and said he was looking for investors for his company and told Scott that he wanted to offer a *"Friend's, Family, and Fools"* purchase of shares before he went public with any funding efforts. Mike was certain that with enough capital he could fund an advertising blitz to put GameGavel on the map. Scott asked him how much he needed, and Mike came back with a figure. Scott's response was simply; sell me as many shares as it takes to add up to that amount. Scott only saw it as helping a close friend with his venture which didn't seem too unrealistic at that stage in the game.

Bear in mind that this was in the early days of Mike's journey and Mike was an enthusiastic gamer who was trying to build something that we could all utilize and that would drive traffic to the Internet forums and to build a community. There was no sign of the future shady deals, suspect business practices and myriad lies that were to follow further down the line.

It was around this time that Steve Sawyer arrived on the scene. In 2010, Steve was, in his own words, a *"bad video game journalist"* who had been doing some writing on various sites, and Mike approached him about writing for GameGavel. He explained that he had little to offer him other than a place to write and there was no offer of money, but there was a chance to try and build a community. They threw some ideas around and Steve started writing blog articles and trying to spread the word about the site and its forums. After Steve had found his feet he began to have some ideas about future projects that he and Mike could get involved in and he presented those ideas to Mike, one of which was a video game magazine, another was a video game trading service.

According to Scott, if there was ever a hindsight moment hiding in plain sight, it was during these early days and the treatment that Steve Sawyer was subjected to. At the time it didn't raise any red flags because nothing in prior history indicated a problem. Certainly, Steve Sawyer didn't do himself any favors in the credibility department with his L.A. millennial, living in a garage, lifestyle but he would talk the talk of a credible industry player. This lifestyle and personality coupled with the threats made later did not compare favorably to Mike Kennedy's prior history and credibility as a more stable and established figure but these were early days and Steve had every faith that Mike was being genuine and that their ideas were joint projects that they would build and grow together. Everything seemed to be going well and Mike just needed to raise the capital to pursue Steve's ideas as he had told Steve that if he could *"just get 10% of that eBay market, man, then I'm off to the races."*

Steve describes Mike by saying that he definitely does not put a glass ceiling on his dreams, if he's going to dream, he's going to dream big, and adds that Mike has an ability to inspire the same thing in other people:

> *"He is a very good salesman and he can definitely get you amped up for all kinds of things. Like, you spend an hour on the phone with him and you're just like, Yeah, I think you could take on GameStop. Yeah, sure why not?"*

Early investors in GameGavel were: Michael B. Kennedy, Patricia L. Kennedy, Ron & Jane Schroer (Tricia's parents), Ronald M. Kennedy (Mike's father), Phil Adam and Scott Schreiber. According to documentation, any new investor was supposed to be approved by all prior existing investors but at the time this was a seat of the pants type organization involving friends and family so the legalities took a back seat to driving the company forward, and it wasn't until later that people began to look deeper into the murky finances of Mike's empire which would be titled "Mikenomics" by the YouTuber "Stop, Drop and Retro" in his excellent analysis.

For now, though, Mike had the finances he needed to give his site an overhaul and to have a developer build a new auction site from the ground up. He also had a new logo designed by 99designs. This is a process by which you submit your job request to a service who distribute it to their clients and then you get back hundreds of design offers. You choose the one you like the most and pick a winner who gets paid $99.

The site saw some steady growth during this early period, reaching 400 members on June 6, 2008, and once the Retro Gaming Roundup podcast started and shared the GameGavel forums, it saw some more rapid growth. By late 2010 Mike was boasting 5,000 members, 50,000 unique visitors, over 300,000 auctions and total sales of over $200,000 in video game related merchandise.

In 2016 the "About" page of GameGavel boasted having hosted over a million auctions and having sold nearly half a million dollars' worth of merchandise, making it the most successful video game dedicated auction site ever. A bit like one listener analogously comparing the Retro Gaming Roundup podcast to the best Ice Hockey team in Nicaragua, but still, the growth in those early days was quite credible.

Whether those numbers are genuine or not, this period was certainly the most successful in the site's lifespan and unfortunately Mike's penchant for new ideas would take his eye off the ball and GameGavel would become less exciting to him than the next big thing, or actually, just the next thing, and we will look at some of those distracting schemes as Mike tries to *"corner the market on Retro."*

One of the ideas that Mike had to increase traffic was to have a game made which was called "Vidgrid." Vidgrid was a tile matching game where you had to turn over tiles and see what picture was on the other side. The pictures were all items that were currently for sale on GameGavel and obviously the more you played, the more auction items you would see, and as the difficulty increased there would be more tiles per screen. Once you had lost all of your lives, you would be given links to some of the auction items that had been included in your game.

In another effort to increase traffic and the number of active sellers on GameGavel, Mike would offer, from time to time, free lifetime seller accounts and would revamp the selling fee structure several times to try and make it more attractive for sellers, especially those sellers who were currently on eBay selling huge numbers of items. There were options for monthly selling subscriptions of $2 or $8 with each giving different amounts of free listings for that month, later switching to a model of no listing fees, taking only 5% of the final value fee if an item sells and no fees if it does not sell. There were also tools developed that made listing items easier by giving members the ability to import CSV files containing all of their items and listing them all in one go.

For a short time, there was a UK version at www.gamegavel.co.uk but this was an entirely separate site that used the same membership database so that accounts would work on both sites, but there was no cohesion between the two and the UK site ran separately and never really gained any traction. After all, only around 200 of the then 4,000 GameGavel members were based in the UK.

Mike began running ads on other podcasts to promote his sites and he had them professionally recorded by Jeff Radio, a voice over artist and jingle producer. He also made sponsorship deals with several others, including All Gen Gamers hosted by Pete Dorr, John "Gamester81" Lester and Jason Hynie. In fact, at the time of writing, Pete Dorr's name was still being used to endorse the GameGavel website on the about page at GameGavel.com.

Mike was a guest on some episodes of All Gen Gamers, as well as several other shows, and if there was a chance of promotion, in particular free promotion, Mike took it, and why wouldn't he? He was looking to build awareness of his product, and again, this was before people began to look at Mike with a more cynical eye.

Mike was becoming fairly well known among certain gaming circles, he was an active member of the SC3 group and it was through this connection, but mostly those made through the recording of interviews on Retro Gaming Roundup, that he was able to build up these relationships and attract certain rare auction items to GameGavel.

One of those auction items was Red Sea Crossing for the Atari VCS, a game not known for certain to exist until a physical copy was discovered. Red Sea Crossing was created by an independent programmer in 1983 and turned up at a garage sale some time in 2007. In order to prove that the game was genuine, a member of the AtariAge forums tracked down the developer who recalled making the game and advertising it in a local religious magazine from 1983. The ad was finally found in an issue of Christianity Today from October 7, 1983 and is the only known instance of any publicity or promotion for the game.

Now that the game was known to be the genuine article it was listed for sale on GameGavel and described by the seller as *"the Holy Grail of Atari games."* The listing ran from August 29, 2012 until September 9, 2012 and started at $100. It ended at an impressive $10,400 which made it *"the most expensive loose Atari 2600 cart ever sold at auction to date."*

Another high price auction that was hosted on GameGavel was for the NES (Nintendo Entertainment System) game "Family Fun Fitness: Stadium Events", released on July 1, 1987. This was also a lucky pick up for the owner who found it at a Goodwill store in North Carolina for $8. The unidentified woman recognized the rarity of the game when she bought it as she recalled an earlier eBay auction for the same game that had netted its owner around $10,000. She says that during her purchase, her *"heart raced the whole time."*

The auction started at $12,000 and ended at $13,105 with which she planned to pay off her student debt and put a down payment on a house.

Both of those auctions were eclipsed by a copy of Air Raid for the Atari VCS which became *"The most expensive 'consumer available' video game ever sold at auction."* It was also only the third boxed version of the game to surface and the first to include its original manual. The auction broke a previous record of $31,600 for the game and sold for $33,433 after starting at just $1 and attracting a total of 31 bids over 11 days.

These high-priced auctions earned GameGavel some coverage on news sites and increased its traffic a little but ultimately, as newer projects garnered Mike's interest, the auction site would never really make it to the next level and grow exponentially. It was also harmed somewhat by the free seller accounts that were given away. That move vastly reduced the income for the site and eventually the only active sellers on the site were those with free lifetime accounts who paid no listing fees for items, plus there were no fees for anybody on items that didn't sell, so they would just leave their overpriced items on the site permanently and not incur any charges in the hope that one day some unwitting customer would come along and pay their inflated asking price.

It didn't have to be that way though because Mike came very close to selling the site to a group of Korean investors who approached him about purchasing it. They had an I.M.O. (Independent Marketing Organization) and they liked the look of the site, the name of the site and the backend for running the auctions and sales.

They were going to use it to sell in-game items and physical game related merchandise and enquired about how much Mike was looking for to sell it. This was during the first year of Retro Magazine when Mike could have made use of the money and he made the decision that he would be interested in selling it for $1,000,000 but the Koreans were valuing it much more realistically at around $80,000 to $100,000 and would not go any higher.

Mike's problem was that he didn't really have anything to sell other than the domain name because he didn't actually own the software that ran the site, and in fact he licensed it from the owner at $50 per month. Obviously the deal did not happen and Mike continued to own just the domain name while continuing to license the auction software.

Losing faith in his own site, Mike reverted to selling his items on eBay which tells you pretty much all you need to know about the reach that GameGavel had at the time and also the level of confidence that Mike now had in his own product. A product that he had hoped would one day form the hub of his empire rather than be an expensive weight around his neck.

3: The Podcast Years – Part 1

Getting Started

We know that one of Mike's hobbies was to go to his local Swap Meets every weekend and pick up hopefully cheap video game items and either add them to his collection or sell them, initially on eBay and later on his own auction site. His problem was attracting buyers over to his sites Chase the Chuckwagon, Vendazzle and GameGavel.

To try and raise awareness among the retro gaming community, Mike hit the airwaves as the presenter of a segment on the Retro Gaming Radio podcast that was run by Shane R. Monroe and would talk about the swap meet items he had picked up recently, the items he had for sale on the auction site and of course the auction site itself. He would also run competitions where listeners could win some of his Swap Meet pickups.

As mentioned, Retro Gaming Radio became increasingly inconsistent towards the end of its run which was a problem for Mike who was trying to increase awareness of his site. Another problem with being on Retro Gaming Radio was that it was the property of Shane R Monroe who controlled the whole show, so Mike and Scott did not get a say in when it was released or what was in it, but that wasn't going to work out as a long term solution for Mike or Scott, particularly as the show began to fall apart. Shane had become convinced over the years that his personality was the draw rather than the content, and that being the case he believed the audience would be assured regardless of when, or even if, shows were released. Show releases became less regular and offers by Mike and Scott to increase their participation and help with show releases were never met with much regard.

There was also some artistic license being taken at times during the edits, particularly in the interview segments. In 2007 Scott had accompanied Shane to Classic Gaming Expo in Las Vegas where they recorded several interviews with Video Game Alumni. Shane did not have working mobile equipment at this point and Scott brought all of the gear (purchased at his own expense) that was used for recording the interviews and the commentary of the museum walkthrough. Once these interviews were released, Scott noticed that several of the questions he had asked the interviewees had been edited out but the answers usually left in. Shane was editing the interviews to remove any credit for Scott and to maintain the appearance of a one man show which was how he viewed Retro Gaming Radio. Scott had also caught sight of Al Alcorn walking around the expo and managed to get a quick interview with him, something that wasn't easily done around that time, and he handed the interview to Shane on an SD card. Sadly, the interview was never aired and nothing ever came of it.

While editing the interviews in this way was certainly disingenuous and part of a general pattern of disrespect to the people helping to carry the show, it was of course Shane's show and he made every attempt to keep it that way both inwardly and outwardly. Toward the end, as the schedule started to slip, and the gaps between shows grew in length and frequency, it was clear that the show was coming to an end. The community was waning, the forums were becoming quieter and people were moving away from the show and finding other, more regular, gaming content to fill the gap.

Inevitably Retro Gaming Radio came to an end, though it did make a brief comeback as a strange hybrid of audio and web-based video, claiming to be the first show to incorporate sound and video, but it didn't enjoy the earlier successes that it had in its prime, and again finally came to the end in April 2013, having run for 21 months.

The end was announced in the Monroeworld forums by Shane himself and despite being part of the show, both Scott and Mike heard the news along with everybody else by reading that forum post. One of their disappointments at the time was that they were not given the courtesy of being told beforehand that the show had gone away. Despite hosting segments on the show, they were seen as outsiders as Retro Gaming Radio was a one-man show and they read about the end of it along with everybody else.

This was September 2008 and Scott wanted to continue to produce his Hardware Flashback segment but he needed a vehicle to carry it and he decided that he wanted to make his own Podcast and began looking for recruits to join him. Among several choices for co-hosts was Mike Kennedy, who had already established his ability with his swap meet segments on Retro Gaming Radio, and he reached out to Mike who was naturally enthusiastic. Scott also knew of another prime candidate from the Monroeworld forums for a third host to bring on board and he invited Mike James, known on the forums as miner2049er, and hereafter referred to as UKMike.

Scott, Mike Kennedy and UKMike had interacted many times on the Monroeworld forums, which is where lots of Retro Gaming Radio listeners and retro enthusiasts who would attend Expos and meet-ups initially met. The Monroeworld forums, in their heyday, would carry some great discussions, not all gaming related, and the members, particularly Scott, Mike and UKMike had built up something of a rapport and "knew" each other for years before they ever "spoke" or met in person.

UKMike had never done any podcasting before and was initially reluctant for the usual reasons: He didn't like hearing his own voice on playback and he didn't think that he had anything interesting enough to say and that people would want to listen to. In fact, one of the oddest feelings, if you've ever experienced it, is to hear your own voice played back, whether it is on a family video, on the radio or on a podcast.

It's just a strange feeling that takes some getting used to, but without question the formula was apparent, three equal co-hosts that could present the content with a knowledgeable approach and do so with an entertaining banter and a style that combined morning shock jock radio and three guys sitting at the bar exchanging comments on a given topic.

The three of them started to meet on Skype and began to map out ideas for their new show and what format it would take, but more importantly, they planned on how they could make it a regular show with consistent releases that would help to maintain momentum for the listeners and bring in a consistent audience. The show was always going to have multiple presenters with lots of varied content provided by each host and of course the regular segments featuring all three hosts in group discussions. The idea behind the magazine style show was that at some point, real life was going to get in the way, for at least one of them, and mean that they might not be able to dedicate the time that the podcast needed. In those instances, there would still be two more hosts to pick up the pieces and make sure that a monthly show still got released.

Mike Kennedy registered the domain name for retrogamingroundup.com and built the first website using a C.M.S. (Content Management System) with the hosting provider Network Solutions and he registered the social media accounts for the show.

Retro Gaming Roundup began broadcasting in February 2009 and has been released every month, without fail, since then. There have even been extra shows thrown in occasionally, whether they were special interviews, announcements or bonus Christmas shows. The ideology with which the show was created and that the show was not owned by any one person, it was owned equally by all three hosts and was always a team effort, is central to its success and its consistent release schedule. Bear in mind that the show generally runs about six hours each month, sometimes more, sometimes less, and this causes a problem for some listeners who have been described as having *"yet to discover pause technology"* and some seem to get scared away by a podcast that is so long.

The Podcast is described as a magazine style show and it can be consumed in much the same way. If you buy a magazine you don't necessarily sit down and read the whole thing in one sitting. You would flick through it, find an article you want to read and read it. You might then put it down for days before picking it up again and reading another article. There might be articles that you don't read and there might be articles that you read multiple times.

The podcast is no different, there are listeners that have long commutes or who have jobs that allow them to listen to long podcasts during their work shift and they will often listen to the whole show in one sitting. There are also listeners who break the show up and listen to it in short bursts. They normally have a whole month before the next one after all. There are also listeners that don't listen to every segment but who love a particular segment and will listen to it multiple times.

It was late 2008 when the three hosts first began discussing the show and what the content would be each month. Obviously there would be a "Hardware Flashback" recorded by Scott and a "Tech Questions" segment where he would answer technical questions sent in by listeners. Mike Kennedy would record various segments over the course of the show but at the start he would record his usual "Chasing The Chuckwagon" auction segment. UKMike would record reviews, usually on British systems that perhaps the American audience were unfamiliar with, as well as Guinness Gaming Records and Trivia segments. Each episode would also include an interview with a video game alumni and some of the guests down the years were true pioneers in the computer and video game industry.

In the first episode each host recorded a brief introduction about who they were, why they were making a podcast and what they would be bringing to it over the coming years. It was decided right at the start that there would be a monthly Top Ten debate, where each host would choose four items on the selected topic, giving a total of twelve items which would then be discussed and compiled into a final list of ten, with two being rejected. This has proven to be one of the most popular segments on the whole show and all three hosts had a great time recording these debates, sometimes arguing, sometimes with two ganging up on the third host, but always enjoying the great banter and loving what they were doing.

There would be a monthly News segment where they would read emails and articles sent in by listeners and discuss any gaming news that was current. In early 2011 Mike Kennedy had an idea that the News segment should be streamed live so that listeners could interact with the hosts, and each other, in a chat room. Occasionally there would also be a guest brought in during the Live News to discuss something that they had particular knowledge of or something that they were working on or something that they wanted to bring to the public's attention. There were also competitions throughout Live News where listeners would have to listen out for a prize alarm and then be the first to type a "phrase that pays" into the chatroom and they could win some show merchandise or an interesting item that Mike had picked up at a swap meet. Some listeners would also contribute prizes for their fellow listeners to win, William Culver (Willie) and "Kip" being particularly generous prize donors.

During the Live News all three hosts would have a webcam running so that listeners could see as well as hear and chat to them. Sometimes they would kick back, relax and have a few beers while recording a segment, usually the Live News, and Mike Kennedy was no different in this, he would enjoy a drink as much as Scott and UKMike, and not to put too fine of a point on it, Mike was usually recording at about 11:00 PST, during his working day. On one occasion he was so drunk that he fell off his chair when he lost his balance and on another occasion he is clearly seen putting a joystick down the front of his pants on camera.

The common factor across the show's audience is that they loved the rapport that the three hosts had and the segments that were recorded together were always fun to do. UKMike and Scott cannot recall a single recording session that they didn't enjoy sitting down to do. Ever since that first recording on January 28, 2009 when the first top ten debate was recorded, they have enjoyed recording the podcast and sitting down with their friends and discussing the hobby that they love. UKMike also recalls that some recordings were easier than others, some were more fun than others, some were done while feeling under the weather or at odd times of the day or night and some were done within a strict timeframe but all of them were fun and enjoyable.

In January 2012 the three hosts interviewed Steve Ritchie, the pinball designer, who was about to unveil his brand new Stern ACDC machine and due to Steve's hearing problems, caused by Meniere's Disease, the interview was not easy to do. The hosts would have to email Steve their questions and he would answer them over audio. Occasionally they would have a further, follow up question raised by something Steve had said and they would email that to him as well.

The problem was that Steve would answer all of the questions in the first email and then move on to the second one and answer those. This meant that any questions raised would be answered out of sequence and the hosts would have to try and steer Steve to the different emails. Once the interview was finished and they had finished asking questions and Steve had finished answering them, they then recorded themselves asking the questions that had been emailed. They also recorded some extra fillers to insert and make the interview flow a little more naturally.

When it came to editing the interview UKMike (who edits every show) isolated every question and every answer and then spliced each question and answer pair together. He then organized them into an order that meant each question and answer pair had a logical flow and when listened to in sequence the interview had a more natural feel to it and made sense to the listener.

Even with all of the work involved in doing that, it was still a great interview to record because they were talking to the great Steve Ritchie after all, and Steve has a great sense of humor, not too dissimilar to that of the hosts.

The phrase that they always used about this era in the show is "The Three Musketeers" and that's how it was. They would get together at least twice a month to record their segments and they would often talk in between recordings, just chatting online as friends do. It wasn't just a "business" arrangement that they had, they were enjoying their hobby with friends and building a community of listeners in their forums based around it.

Mike Kennedy had some advertising material recorded to use as promo for the auction site and they would run those in the show between segments and he would regularly talk about his sites and auctions in the show, using it to help bring people in to the forums where they would interact with the rest of the community between shows as well as during the Live News. In that era, this wasn't a problem. It would be a problem later, but at this stage they were enjoying putting out the show and working on it together. Promoting Mike's various ventures was happily done as it was universally believed that what he was doing was an honest attempt to create something good for the hobby, with the understanding that there would be a reciprocal payoff to the show should any given venture succeed. There were no warning signs in the early years that Mike would go off the rails and that things would turn out the way they did but they had an absolute ball in those early years.

One annoyance from the early years was that they could not get Mike to travel to game expos with them. Scott would cross the Atlantic and attend UK Expos including Play Manchester in 2012, Play Blackpool in 2014 and 2015, Revival Expo in 2013 and Revival Summer Solstice in 2016. UKMike travelled to the US to attend Classic Gaming Expo in 2012 and 2014, Portland Retro Gaming Expo in 2013 and 2016 and one of Scott's Arcade parties in 2015.

Mike Kennedy, however, would not travel to any expo other than Classic Gaming Expo because he could drive there in around four hours and Portland 2013 which he also made a sixteen-hour drive to. They could not get him to commit to a foreign expo and that was one of the possible early signs that he had other priorities. Not that it was a problem necessarily but he wouldn't just come out and say it. He would say that he had no funds or no time off work to allow him to make a trip but would then go off the radar for a couple of weeks as he went touring Yellowstone or California's vineyards in his Airstream with Tricia.

Ironically he once called Scott's mobile phone as he and UKMike were sitting in the Blackpool Expo Hall recording a show commentary, completely forgetting that he should have been there with them. Over time they just got used to reading between the lines with Mike and dealing with not having him at expos with them for the most part. Having said all that though, it really was still looked at as The Three Musketeers and they were a team putting out their show each month and chatting in between shows either on Skype or in the forums and they still had some great times making the show and recording their content, particularly the segments that they did together.

4: Going Postal

Cornering the Market on Retro

In his own words Mike was trying to *"corner the market on retro"* and he was looking to make GameGavel the first product in a series of sites and services that would make up his empire and eventually provide his professional living. He had the auction site that was growing, he had the forums that were growing and he wanted to expand upon the services provided by his group of sites.

> *"GameGavel is our first foray into gaming commerce, launched in 2008, and it has taken off nicely here in the USA although has been slower to take off with Euro gamers. GameGavel is an auction site like eBay but dedicated to gaming. We offer much lower selling fees, in fact, there are no listing or selling fees the balance of 2011 for Euro gamers who want to try it out. PostalGamer is being added to what we are calling The GameGavel Network. The GG Network is a group of sites offering gamers what we feel are better alternatives to the large corporate sites like eBay and GameStop. We want to create sites that are focused squarely on gaming and gamers."*

In this chapter we will look at some of those sites and services that Mike tried to get off the ground and add to the GameGavel Network, some with more success than others. We may see a pattern begin to form, we may not, but the point of this exercise is to demonstrate what Mike was trying to do as this will be important later. It may even help you to decide whether Mike was later trying to scam people with the Coleco Chameleon or whether he was just out of his depth and failed to deliver on his goals.

Retro Arcade Radio

The first site that Mike picked up was a streaming online radio station which ran on the California based Live365 service. Live365 was founded in 1999 and was largely used by hobbyists looking to create their own online stations but it was also used by professional radio stations who would broadcast over the air waves and simultaneously stream shows over the Internet, as well as Live 365 stations provided by popular radio stations and well-known artists such as Johnny Cash and Frank Zappa.

Users could create an account and create their own station that streamed audio content of their choosing, and listeners would connect using a web browser, a streaming player like Winamp or a smart phone app.

The Webcaster Settlement Act of 2009 expired in January 2016, and this was an agreement that had allowed smaller online radio stations, Live365 among them, to pay reduced royalty fees for the music that they were streaming. When this happened, Live365 investors pulled out and they were forced to lay off most of their employees in late December 2015. They took down their website and vacated their offices, so the few employees that remained continued to work from home.

The Webcaster Settlement Act was replaced with the Copyright Royalty Board which was adopted by broadcasters on January 31, 2016 and required them to pay SoundExchange an annual, non-refundable minimum fee of $500 for each channel and station.

In July 2016, Live365 was acquired by Jon Stephenson, owner of the content delivery network EmpireStreaming, and in August 2016 the website returned and announced a relaunch of the service but at the time of writing it is not clear how the new product will look and how it will be able to compete with some of the more modern streaming services like Last.fm, TuneIn or Spotify. Empire Streaming do make the claim of being *"in the Internet radio industry since the late '90s and we have a vast amount of experience behind us"* but like the eBay and YouTube examples given earlier, it is unclear how well they can compete with the more established streaming services.

Mike's Live365 station was called Retro Arcade Radio and Mike did not start this himself but picked it up from the arcade collector Peter Hirschberg who had started the station a few years earlier. The station streamed video game related music and video game theme tunes interspersed with mini interviews and retro themed advertisements every three or four songs.

There was a basic schedule that played more party type songs on a Saturday night for those people having arcade parties to use as a backdrop for their party. This was a paid service that Mike used and he paid monthly to keep the station going but it eventually died when the service was taken down in 2016.

Retro Arcade Radio did have listeners but not in huge numbers, it was more of a novelty type service that didn't really do much to bring people into the community but it did entertain some of those that were already there. Towards the end of its run, the station was managed by UKMike who changed the playlists and rotated the adverts that would break up the music, and once the service died, UKMike transferred it to his own site, chiptune.rocks.

Autogab.tv

Along the same theme of providing media for people, Mike came up with an idea called AutoGab.TV. The idea hit him while he was sitting in LA traffic one day and he thought that he could use that time more effectively. Mike more than likely "borrowed" this idea from Shane R. Monroe's Passenger Seat Radio but wanted to expand on it.

The blurb for AutoGab.TV was that on average, people spend two and a half hours per day in their car, so how could they better utilize that time?

> *"In your car you can be a singer or musician, sports commentator, movie or video game reviewer, philanthropist or politician. Your car is now your studio. Broadcast live to your "Tailgaters" or fans. Grow your audience and broadcast live to them while you are sitting in traffic, commuting to work or school, driving cross country or tailgating at a concert or sporting event."*

This is a very interesting example of one of Mike's ideas and contains several portents to future events.

- It wasn't an original idea; Mike didn't invent the concept of using this time more effectively. People have blogged, vlogged and podcasted from their cars before.
- Mike had no concept of how the technology might work or how to go about it.
- He prepared promotional material to advertise the service before actually coming up with a service.
- His promo announced iPhone and Android apps for the service.
- The promo material talked about remaining anonymous by blurring your image, or having options to hide your location.
- "Viewers" could view live AutoGab streams from the website, AutoGab.tv
- "Viewers could follow, or "tailgate" as many AutoGabbers as they liked and would be notified when a broadcaster they follow began broadcasting.
- You could view saved streams for up to 24 hours.
- There were even controls to allow you to watch one stream while listening to another.

Don't forget that all of this was on a service that didn't exist yet, and despite this being nothing but a few random ideas, Mike had the promo ready to go and even announced app pricing and a launch period.

> *"Coming Soon!*
> *Get the AutoGab app for $.99 when it debuts for iOS and Android, this spring."*

This really shows the way that Mike's mind works on these projects. As far as Mike was concerned, this was done. He had the idea and that was ninety percent of getting the job done. He had no concept of just how much work there was in bringing a service like this to fruition, nor did he have the ability or the team around him to do it. He was a salesman though and he already had his sales pitch nailed down. It really was pie in the sky.

Gamerspots

In April 2011 along came GamerSpots, which was actually quite a good idea, it just wasn't Mike's.

The site would be a community supported hub where the public could post information about sites around the world that might be of interest to video gamers. Let's say that you visited an arcade, a used games store, a Goodwill that carried lots of retro items, a video game auction, anything really that was video game related would fit. You would submit the site to GamerSpots and could include a small write up on what was there and why it was worthy of a visit. Other site members would go to the site and be able to find interesting locations in their vicinity, and beyond, and pay them a visit if they wished. Like I said, it was a good idea, it just wasn't Mike's.

There were already similar services running for locations that had pinball machines, an increasingly rare phenomenon, but to give credit where it is due, this one did have a website and a Twitter account (that was used about seven times) and did see some activity with people submitting their locations and write ups on them.

To try and encourage people to keep populating the site, there was a High Score table that showed how many locations each member had added, and one of the most prolific posters on GamerSpots was William Culver. Willie travelled a lot as part of his job and would often find himself having to pass the time in different towns and cities so he would go exploring and looking out for ideal locations to put on the GamerSpots website. In fact, Willie was the top submitter on GamerSpots but unfortunately the site was left to die on the vine as the next idea came along and took precedence.

Again, this is something of a pattern developing. Each new idea is the best idea ever and takes all of Mike's attention and focus at the expense of neglecting the current or existing ideas. Perhaps the best example of this will come later but here is a good, early example of it.

The Gamer Spots site was written by a developer called Matt Casey who had done a lot of work on GameGavel for Mike. Matt would be replaced later but he did the bulk of the work in initially building both sites and would also design and build version three of the Retro Gaming Roundup site when he was contacted by UKMike who had been given his name by Mike Kennedy. Matt was also an avid listener of the podcast so was familiar with, and to, UKMike.

Postal Gamer / Parcel Gamer

The next big thing that took Mike's attention and spelled the end for GamerSpots was Postal Gamer. This was a company that would work with game developers and publishers and help them make money from used games sales. This is the first iteration of the idea which would take Mike's eye off both GameGavel and GamerSpots while Retro Arcade Radio pretty much looked after itself.

Mike found an investment group in California called Angel Investors and he was invited along to present his idea to them. He had a slot booked during one of their sessions where entrepreneurs would come along and demonstrate their business ideas to the investment panel, a bit like the UK TV show "Dragons' Den" or the US TV show "Shark Tank."

Mike wrote a presentation for them, perhaps it was the one he wrote during a Retro Gaming Roundup recording session when his co-hosts would hear thunderous typing followed by a few mouse clicks and a pause and then more thunderous typing.

After Mike had delivered his presentation, he took some questions from the panel, who seemed interested, but their concern was that Angel Investors had an upper limit on the amount of investment available. They felt that Mike needed more investment than they could provide and they politely declined but did advise him to seek Venture Capital funding as he had a nugget of an idea that they felt could work.

Postal Gamer would have a central processing plant that would receive the games that people traded in and they would arrive in special Postal Gamer envelopes that would either be included in the box with a brand new game, or could be obtained from some other, as yet undecided, location. As they were processed, the envelopes would be opened, the games would be checked and then resealed for resale and the credit for each game traded would be applied to a customer's account. This could then be spent on the Postal Gamer website while purchasing other new or used games. Every game that shipped from the processing plant would include a Postal Gamer envelope so that it could be easily traded again in the future.

It was hoped that brand new games sold outside of Postal Gamer would also include one of their envelopes as it would be in the best interest of the publisher to do so because they would then see a share of the 10% promised. In fact, Mike estimated that in the first four to five years of Postal Gamer it would be able to give back a whopping $500 million that would otherwise have gone into the coffers of GameStop for example. He also had estimates of the company being able to purchase its own private Gulf Stream Jet in its third year.

Mike also planned to share his data with publishers so that they could see useful statistics like how many times an individual title is traded, how long after release a game is traded, what prices traded-in games were fetching etc. At the time, publishers did not have any of those statistics, and again, this is a good kernel of an idea but the key to it succeeding is getting those developers and publishers on board and that was proving difficult.

Publishers around this time were looking at ways to hopefully eradicate the used video game market. They saw no benefit from that market and they felt that if they could stop consumers from being able to trade games and buy used games then this would force more people into buying only new games, from them.

That line of thinking gave rise to the "Online Pass" which meant that once a game was played online by its owner, it could not be played online by anybody else. It would be locked to the original owner's online account, making it a waste of time buying the game used. There were several games that included this feature but there were huge grumblings from the gaming community at large and Mike was quite vehement on the topic:

"The Online Pass is a scam and I am pretty sure it is illegal as well. Companies are only guaranteed the initial sale of their product, regardless if that product is associated with costs after it leaves the warehouse. They are not guaranteed any subsequent sales after the first. This is why we don't see MGM demanding your friend pay them $20 when you lend that friend a DVD. This is why Ford won't bang down your door demanding money when you buy a used car. This is why Apple does not demand money from you when you buy a used iPad off Ebay.

We are not leasing these games, we are BUYING them. They are ours to do with what we want without fear of video game companies getting in the way. EVERY company has costs associated with a product after it leaves the warehouse. Video game companies who used the "servers" excuse are lying through their teeth and they know it. This has nothing to do with servers costing them tons of money. They are just hoping you are stupid enough to not research their claims and see through their lies.

Used sales have been around as long as business itself. The second hand market exists for nearly every single product imaginable. The video game industry is the only industry to stand up and scream and cry that the used business is killing them, while offering absolutely no proof on the matter. They are LYING to you. Do not fall for it. It is all a bunch of lies and manipulation.

Do not fear used game sales. Buy as many as you want. Don't buy games with Online Pass scams. It is just a scam."

Mike really wanted to take on GameStop in the same way that he was taking on eBay and he wanted to save the industry from itself, an industry plagued with growing development teams, rising development costs, rising game prices and online passes, an industry selling games that people generally finished within a few short weeks after release and that didn't generate any income for them after that. You would think they would be on board with him and the companies that Mike met with, including Microsoft and Nintendo, showed some initial interest. It was a new and interesting idea that warranted further investigation. Obviously the publishers they were keen to see a share of the market but how would such a deal affect them elsewhere?

What it came down to was their new game market. They felt that if they were seen to be on board with selling used games then that could hurt their new game sales. Consumers would know that within a couple of weeks of a new game release, they would be able to pick it up from Postal Gamer at a reduced price but the game would be tested and resealed and the developer and publisher would still get paid as a result of the sale.

One of the better points of this idea is that publishers would have some idea of how many games were being traded and how soon. Let's say that Game Company ABC release a game called Shoot Me In The Face 3 and that there is a market of 100,000 people willing to buy it. Game Company ABC need to produce and distribute 100,000 copies of it to satisfy that market.

Let's say that completed copies of Shoot Me In The Face 3 are beginning to be traded in after two weeks and that perhaps 20,000 copies are traded within three weeks. Could Game Company ABC have saved money by only producing 80,000 copies initially? Who knows? They certainly don't because they don't have those figures, but there must be a large portion of the gaming market that would be happy to buy used games every time rather than only buying new ones on launch date. Having said that though, with the nature of production costs and production runs, the savings on producing 80,000 copies rather than 100,000 copies are not quite negligible but are not significant either. The difference between producing 500 and 5,000 copies would be bigger but once you reach an economy of scale, which let's face it, most new game releases do, the incremental costs of production are not that great. The long and short of it was that they all saw a drop in new game sales being the likely outcome, as well as upsetting their biggest retail customer, GameStop. They all felt that the status quo was a good idea at the time, particularly when the market was undergoing some big changes in practice anyway.

It was around this time that there was a change in the company name as it seemed that the word "Postal" was causing some concerns because of its affiliation with the violent video game called Postal. Postal is a 1997 isometric top-down shooter game developed by Running With Scissors and published by Ripcord Games. The game attracted negative press on release due to its violent nature and Mike needed to distance himself from that as the slang term *"going postal"* had come to mean having some kind of mental breakdown, usually associated with violence. The game companies wanted to avoid that obvious association and the negative connotations that it carried, so the name was changed to Parcel Gamer.

> September 12, 2011
> *"... GameGavel, LLC has elected to change the name of their new online retail arm from PostalGamer.com to ParcelGamer.com. According to GameGavel CEO Mike Kennedy, this new name doesn't have the negative connotations associated with the word "Postal" and it does not tie them to using the U.S. Post Office for their delivery service method."*

One interesting addendum on some of the press releases from this time is a stark warning to what would come later, and that is exactly what role Mike had in this. Different interviews describe the situation differently, presumably it depended on which hat Mike was wearing on the day he gave the interviews. The situation is described as:

> *"brainchild of CEO Mike Kennedy and his business partner, Steve Sawyer."*

This is later described as:

> *"... part-time employee, Sawyer, who encouraged him to look into what he saw as a vicious circle in the used games business: consumers think games are too expensive, so they buy them used. Publishers continue charging $60 for a game, because they're not seeing any returns on the secondary sales.*

It's like the publishers have been forced into a situation where they're almost penalizing gamers for using the secondary market, Sawyer says."

Game Life describe Mike as a Co-Founder while Thumb Culture and Wired describe him as CEO. Pixelitis quoted Parcel Gamer's own site when they said:

"Parcel Gamer's concept and business model was designed by two passionate gamers who are tired of seeing the industry being compromised because of the existing used game retail model which has been running rampant and breeding discord between gamers, retailers and the publishers."

The Video Game Writers had this description, making it one of the very few examples anywhere that you will see any hint of joint ownership.

"A couple of entrepreneurs think they may have cracked the code with their new business, Parcel Gamer."

Though that statement is somewhat recanted in their very next sentence:

"The main thing is the gamers and giving them a better place to trade in their games, where they're going to get around 30 percent more for their trade-ins, which I think everyone will like," said Mike Kennedy, CEO of the GameGavel network, which includes Parcel Gamer"

These may seem like trivial differences or misunderstandings but as you will come to see later, words really do matter, and when there is an "I" used in place of a "We" and vice versa, it is done for a reason. Did Mike steal an idea and make it his own? He certainly picked it up and ran with it whatever the case. The question of who owns what had started to percolate around this time, because if Parcel Gamer belonged to GameGavel, just how was Steve Sawyer (who owned no shares in GameGavel) a business partner? What did that even mean? Furthermore, this also gives us a glimpse of the future, where what parent company owned which venture could become very fluid depending on the situation.

Once off the ground, Parcel Gamer would use a company called Bastian Solutions who specialize in the type of processing center that Mike would need to process the incoming and outgoing games. They already ran fulfilment centers for companies in a similar business such as Netflix, Jack of All Games and of course GameStop.

Mike did run the numbers after speaking to Bastian Solutions and he worked out some estimated costs of running such a processing center and set about building a business structure as well. Typically, with a business of Mike's, there was a board of directors and, typically, it included Mike alongside Phil Adam, the former president of both Spectrum HoloByte and Interplay. Phil is a personal friend of Mike's and Mike wanted Phil on board so that he could use his name to help him to get his foot in the door of some of the larger companies who might otherwise not entertain him.

Parcel Gamer were also quoting numbers that would be paid to publishers by this stage, a quarterly cheque in the region of six to eight dollars per used game sold, increasing if the publisher *"worked with them"* and included return envelopes in their new game cases.

Of the companies that were spoken to and met with, only one was willing to try it out but they made it clear that they would not be the first, they would only go public with the scheme if another major publisher came on board but sadly none of them did. Their major concern was upsetting their third biggest retailer, GameStop. They were happy for their name to be circulated around other publishers in an effort to lend credence to the idea but they were never mentioned publicly, until now, and that publisher was THQ. Eventually though, THQ themselves had to drop out as they tried to recover the losses they had made on the development and promotion of their uDraw tablet. This was a graphics tablet that worked with the Nintendo Wii, PlayStation 3 and Xbox 360 and had a pressure-sensitive stylus which was used to draw on screen. Initially the Wii version in white was quite well received but the later black versions for PlayStation and Xbox 360 were described as a *"disaster"* and THQ were left with around 1.4 million unsold units which their Chief Financial Officer blamed for the company's $100 million shortfall. Desperate to turn their fortunes around, they dropped out of any further risky marketing ventures before their final demise, so Mike was back to square one.

One of the driving forces behind Mike and Steve's idea was to support the physical media that game companies appeared to be moving away from. Mike has an enormous passion for owning a physical copy of a game. Something that looks good on a shelf, something tangible, something collectible and something that seemed to be becoming increasingly rare.

> *"The culture is changing, and a lot of what was fun and cool about game ownership is all going away."*
>
> *"Imagine not being able to walk into a store and peruse games. We're not against retail. I would hate the day that I can't walk through Target and see game kiosks."*

There were of course early critics of the business idea who felt that once a developer or publisher got their teeth into a shared market, they would want an increasingly large slice of it, much like the movie and music industries do with services such as Netflix and Spotify. Perhaps Parcel Gamer would have had their margins squeezed until the business model became impossible to maintain, or they could just cease working with those publishers. We'll never know if that would have been the case but if companies continue down the road of digital distribution and eradicate physical media completely then the argument is moot anyway. An interesting portent to a future venture is this:

> *"We want to extend the life of physical game media for as long as possible and making used games a new revenue generator for publishers is one way to show them there is still money to be made."*

Slowly through the course of Summer 2011 and the series of interviews that Mike and Steve did, the launch date slipped from Q3 2011 and Fall of 2011 to Q1 2012. Mike had teased that he had one publisher on board but they would not commit publicly until they had at least one more major company, and that was the reason for the launch slip. They were *"hoping to have between six and eight more by the end of October"* but without another company on board they had nothing, particularly when THQ also backed out in an attempt to save themselves. Mike and Steve still intended to launch as a purely new game sales website anyway but this never materialized.

EK Gaming / Mail a Game

Mike then switched tack and instead of trying an online model, he would try to work with brick and mortar gaming stores. EK Gaming is an interesting idea that Mike pushed quite hard to the video game industry and he did manage to get his idea in front of the big hitters like Microsoft and Nintendo. I don't mean just exchanging email with them (as we'll see later) but it is a fact that Mike did get to sit down and discuss this idea with them in person.

The idea came about in mid-2012 and was an evolution of Parcel Gamer and there were lots of game sites like Gamasutra, IGN and Gamepro, among others, that carried the story and interviews with Mike as he went into publicity overload to push his idea to the public, long before it was ready for public consumption. Mike was already talking about percentages, numbers and online passes before he had spoken to a single game studio about it. It would be a familiar set of supplemental information attached to each new venture, the projected earnings in the millions, percentages and payouts to participants.

There is a phrase that follows Mike through most of these schemes, and that phrase is "Putting the cart before the horse." In the case of EK Gaming Mike has his cart ready to go, and it is a great cart. Pretty soon he would no doubt do some investigation into what a horse is.

EK Gaming is a great example of a badly named Mike Kennedy product because it gives you no idea what it is about, so let me tell you. EK Gaming would be a used video game service, like no other, that would buy used games from players who no longer wanted them and sell them to people who did. Nothing new there, but what made this different was that the part of the money that was made from sales would be shared between EK Gaming and video game publishers and developers.

In a statement from June 2012 Mike told Gamasutra:

> *"The decision has been made to share 10% of every pre-owned game sale with both the video game publishers and developers. [...]*
>
> *There are some gray (sic) areas concerning game development and publishing and all is not cut and dry (sic). The bottom line is 10% will be shared in some way between the publishers and developers."*

Quite amazing!

This is only the kernel of an idea, in some ways just thinking out loud. There is no idea of volume, no sign of any deals with brick and mortar stores, yet we already know what percentage of profit will be shared and with whom? Cart and horse again? Certainly, because there were press releases galore about this one and its predecessor.

The basic idea was that EK Gaming would sign a deal with an existing High Street brick and mortar store so that they could set up physical kiosks in each store and gamers could return their unwanted games to the EK Gaming processing center and pick up "new" used games using any credit that they had earned. Mike did do some research on the potential market and found that the used video game market in the USA alone is worth around $2 billion annually and he wanted a slice of that and was willing to share it with developers and publishers to get it.

The benefits would be that developers and publishers would not only make money on new game sales but now on used game sales as well, not only the first time the game is traded in, but every subsequent time as well. Most games that are traded, are traded within two to three weeks of release, as gamers buy them, complete them and return them in place of something else, and yes this is a potentially huge market. Quite why a brick and mortar game store would give or rent space to a competitor is not clear but Mike did meet several times with Play N Trade who looked to be interested in the idea. In fact, they even went so far as to show Mike which office would be his when the deal was signed.

Mike met with them several times in the Summer of 2012 and told his co-hosts about it in August of that year, explaining that Play N Trade wanted to be 50/50 owners of the company along with Mike and Tricia. They didn't want to dilute the additional stock holders that Mike had brought in, so they requested half of Mike and Tricia's 84%, giving them 42% and Mike and Tricia 21% each. Mike was to spend one day every week at their facility in San Clemente, California where he would still be running the show and would have their art department and other resources at his beck and call. Play N Trade would not be buying their 42%, it would be given to them in return for use of their resources, access to their 150 national stores and their planned international stores as well as leveraging of the reach that they had among their owned and franchised stores.

Mike was quoted as saying:

> *"The additional traffic EKG kiosks could bring into the partnering retailer's stores would be quite significant. It is all about giving gamers the options they deserve and streamlining the process of trading in their games and getting new ones. Having both an online and street presence is important for taking on the other brick and mortar competitors."*

Unfortunately, it all fell apart when a more senior person at Play N Trade pulled the plug on the deal. Having thought about it, they were no longer interested. Hardly surprising really, they already had their own used game market to look after. Mike briefly tried another renaming of the venture as M.A.G. (Mail A Game) and a retooling of the same idea in June 2013, but again it went nowhere and finally he parked the idea and tried something else.

The various peaks and troughs of this didn't raise a red flag as to the legitimacy of the venture but it certainly gave pause as to how competently the venture was run, and how carefully partners were chosen and vetted. During this whole exchange Mike seamlessly changed positions without missing a beat, which did raise concerns about how competently his venture was planned. When Play N Trade was introduced as a partner they were presented with great reverence as being a nationwide retailer and a huge coup. When Mike was shown his office at their corporate headquarters he began moving things in and crowing about the future. A few days later, when that more senior person returned and put the brakes on this association, Mike was instructed to come and remove his things from the office and was told there would be no association. Suddenly, according to Mike, Play N Trade was *"a small fry operation whose VP drove an old Hyundai, so how well could they be doing?"*

Mike's next big idea was of course Retro Magazine but we will look at that in more detail later as things start to take a turn for the worse, and what have thus far appeared to be mere slips of the tongue or innocent mistakes begin to look like much more calculated steps on the journey from auction site to podcast to magazine to video game console.

First though, let's take another look at the Podcast Years...

5: The Podcast Years – Part 2

Drunken Podcasters

I've already used the phrase "The Three Musketeers" and another description that fits well is camaraderie, that's what the three hosts had. The show was a joint adventure and they each had an equal stake in it. In this chapter we will look at some of the best times that they had during the show and this will perhaps show Mike Kennedy in a better light than any other chapter in this book.

If you haven't listened to Retro Gaming Roundup and have no prior knowledge of Mike from before the magazine and console debacle, I think you may be surprised to read this chapter and realize that it is the very same person that we are talking about. Perhaps you may even figure out just what actually went wrong and why the Mike Kennedy described in this chapter turned into the Mike Kennedy that became the pariah of the community.

One of the great parts of the podcast is that small things evolve into show lore. The introductions for the show's individual segments are recorded on the fly and just come to be. One small snippet of UKMike opening a can of Guinness before starting a Top Ten recording was heard by Mike Kennedy who asked *"Are you drinking a beer while we're doing this?"* and that has been included in every show since as part of the intro for "Guinness Gaming Records." It also made it acceptable for the hosts to enjoy a beer while recording the show. They were, after all, just three buddies sitting around having a chat and discussing their hobby, the fact that they are not in the same room is irrelevant. This was just three guys shooting the breeze about video games and that relaxed atmosphere, camaraderie and rapport came across in each recording. They were enjoying what they were doing and the listeners were enjoying listening to it.

In January 2010 the drinking while recording went a little too far, though to be fair it was intentional. Mike Kennedy had the idea that they should play a game online together while enjoying a few drinks. They would try and recapture those times from their youth when they had played games with their friends and enjoyed the banter that went along with it. It would also hopefully stir some happy memories for listeners who would be able to relate to it. Following Mike's idea, they recorded a session called Drunken Mule which was put out as a special show, Roundup 15 in February 2010, where the three of them played an online game of Planet Mule.

For those that don't know, M.U.L.E. is a multiplayer game by Ozark Softscape that was published in 1983 by Electronic Arts. It was written for the Atari 400/800 but was later ported to the Commodore 64 which is where it saw most of its success. The basic premise is that it is a turn-based strategy game where four players (human or computer controlled) are stranded on the planet Irata (Atari backwards) and have to make sure that the colony survives and amasses enough wealth before the rescue ship arrives. The game gets its name from the transport and work animals in the game, M.U.L.E.s (Multiple Use Labor Elements), which are purchased and used to mine or harvest resources from areas of the planet that the player has chosen to occupy. Each player also has to manage the supply and demand of certain elements and can trade with other human or computer players. Sometimes they may tactically choose not to trade with a particular player if it will help them win the game.

Dan Bunten, one of the original developers, was working on an online version until their death in 1998 and it is possible to play the original Atari version online with an emulator plugin but in the show, the hosts were playing the online remake called "Planet M.U.L.E." which is free and is described as a tribute to its original designers Dan Bunten & Ozark Softscape.

When they planned this segment, based on Mike's original idea, they planned on playing the game online while getting steadily more and more drunk. A mission that they all achieved successfully, some more so than others. In fact, Mike Kennedy was so drunk that Tricia came to the microphone and explained that Mike would return in a few moments as he had gone upstairs to the bathroom and she came out with the classic phrase, that was clipped and replayed in the show;

"His eyes were red, his face was red and he said he was ready to puke!"

Much of what was recorded was edited out but what remains is a quite seamless conversation about all sorts of topics, not all video game related, as they just chatted about what was on their minds as they played the game against each other and there are some great moments in the recording. A recording that they all had a great time doing.

Another incident that involved Mike's drunkenness was when the podcast had a real scoop and broke the story of Ted Dabney's involvement in the origins of Atari. The company was founded by Nolan Bushnell, Ted Dabney and Al Alcorn but Nolan was always the front man while Dabney and Alcorn were the real engineers. Ted had eventually grown disillusioned with the business and said that the money (which was plentiful) did not make him happy so he left and retired to the mountains for many years.

With Ted out of the way, Nolan was free to spin the story of Atari any way he liked, which was usually with him as the man behind everything, claiming responsibility for Ted's engineering work on Computer Space among other things. With rumors of a movie about Atari starring Leonardo DiCaprio and following the storyline as told by Nolan, Ted came out of the shadows and told his story in full and frank detail, including some of Nolan's dirty deeds. Ted went on to say that if the movie came out and was not truthful, he would sue, and to this day the movie remains unmade. Ted's interview was included in RoundUp 24 from October 2010 and the show was titled "Oh She's Doing Fine" which referred to a quote of Ted's as he dispelled one of Nolan's lies about him not having a daughter. The lie had come about during the development of Computer Space when Ted had shown his progress to Nolan in his daughter's bedroom. Nolan was claiming that he had engineered it and it couldn't have been Ted because he didn't even have a daughter.

As Ted was now back, the hosts wanted to keep their interview a closely guarded secret until the October show was ready for release so that nobody else would find Ted and release an interview before theirs was aired. Unfortunately, Mike got drunk one evening and posted about it on AtariAge which meant that they had to rush a show out, recording all the rest of it and releasing it on October 7, 2010, as soon as they could after Mike's drunken post.

> *Posted Sat Oct 2, 2010*
> *We are excited to announce that coming in our October Retro Gaming Roundup podcast, next week, we will present a 2+ hour interview with Mr. Ted Dabney, co-creator of Atari and also the first commercially produced arcade game, Computer Space. This is his first aired interview ever!*
>
> *This is an interview you don't want to miss. As many of you know the story Nolan Bushnell tells about how Computer Space and Atari came into existence isn't exactly the way it was. Ted tells all and answers many of the questions we have all had for years about the birth of CS (Computer Space) and Atari.*

They would later interview Al Alcorn who confirmed a lot of what Ted had said but their efforts to interview Nolan on the show have so far failed.

On August 1, 2010, Scott and Mike attended Classic Gaming Expo in Las Vegas and on the Sunday evening during tear down after the show they were interviewing the late Keith Robinson of Intellivision Productions. Keith loved to be interviewed at this time while his team tore down the booth for him and Keith loves to talk at the best of times but particularly during tear down. While the interview was being recorded somebody walked up to the booth and stole a spindle of the show's promo CDs. The CDs were normally laid out on the booth and passers-by were encouraged to take one away as it contained sample shows that they could listen to and hopefully become a fan and continue to follow the show. This character didn't take one, didn't even take two or three, he took a whole spindle of one hundred CDs.

The thief was later identified and was well-known among his local computer clubs. The best part of it though? He was deaf. He had stolen one hundred audio CDs and he was deaf. He would thereafter be referred to as the Deaf CD Thief.

Rather than get mad and chase him or prosecute him the show hosts decided to turn the incident into a video game which would make them the first podcast to have their own video game, CGE Adventures. The game was written for the Atari VCS by a team made up of writers, programmers, artists and of course the three hosts. The lead programmer was a Retro Gaming Roundup fan called Todd Holcombe, a doctor by day and a programmer by night. He was assisted by Shaun Stephenson, another fan of the show, Pac Man Red, RevEnge and of course the three hosts who chimed in with the design work, the manual, the artwork, the packaging and of course the testing.

In the game you play the part of the Deaf CD Thief and you have to make your way around the maze of the Expo floor and find several items before being able to find, and steal, the stack of CDs and make your way out of the show and on to the Las Vega strip. All the time you are pursued by the three angry podcasters who will try and stop you. The final boss is a huge character based on Keith Robinson who will also try and stop you from escaping once you have stolen the stack of CDs. The game has been ported to several platforms including an online web browser version, a Raspberry Pi version and a DOS style text adventure.

In the "Thanks" section of the manual, Mike Kennedy says:

> *"I want to thank my Retro Gaming Roundup Co-Hosts, UKMike and Scott – There are no two other people I would want to share an Atari 2600 game with!"*

Another fun idea on the show, and again it was Mike Kennedy's initial idea, was to call Nintendo support. It happened during the recording of a Live News segment as they were discussing the Nintendo Game Boy that Mike was holding. He noticed that it had a support number that you could call if you had problems. Bear in mind that this telephone number had been around for a long time, at least since the Game Boy was released in 1989 and they were recording this in 2012, so over twenty years later.

Mike had the idea to give them a call so they patched the phone into the recording and rang the number. Lo and behold, the call was answered and it was still a valid Nintendo Support number, so there ensued an interesting chat with the support person at the other end about what kind of calls he would generally receive and whether or not anybody still called about the Nintendo Game Boy.

They didn't.

Spontaneous calls like that have generally worked out well for the show and another occasion where it happened was during a Live News recording, and again, it was Mike Kennedy's idea. This time they called the Mayor of a town called Marshfield, Massachusetts in RoundUp 31 from May 2011. A listener had submitted a news story about the town Marshfield, Massachusetts where a 1982 bylaw stated that local businesses could not operate coin-operated arcade games and so effectively, arcade games were banned. The hosts chatted about this for a few minutes before Mike suggested that they call the town and get the story from a local.

Initially they called the Mayor's office but, just before they were put through, the Mayor suddenly became unavailable and wouldn't talk to them. Not put off by that, they decided to call the local bar and see if anybody there would talk to them. As luck would have it, they got to speak to the barman there who was a local man and knew just about everything on the story, even the history of it.

He told them all about how the bylaw had got passed initially and how attempts to overturn it had failed both in 1994 and 2011. He was a totally random person for them to speak to, but he gave such a great interview and insight into the news story, so much so that the episode of the show was named after it, The Missing Mayor Of Marshfield, Massachusetts.

As a follow up to the story, the bylaw was eventually overturned in 2014 but not by much, the vote was 203 to 175, with most of those against the games making a return citing their dislike of family friendly restaurants being inundated with noise.

One of the running jokes throughout the years of the podcast that Mike was involved was that he was gay.

He isn't.

However, it seemed that every time he opened his mouth he would come out with double entendre that made it sound like he was, and these clips were isolated and added to the show soundboard so they could be played any time during the show.

Some of the classic Mike Kennedy lines are:

- *"I just love the balls knocking together"*
- *"but I do have a beautiful box"*
- *"and you blasted his ass"*
- *"I've got a guy that I'm going to give it to later and when we're done I'm going to meet him and give it to him"*
- *"I begged my Mom to ask the guy behind the counter if I could take a look at the hot pink box"*
- *"I'm the packer. I'm always the packer"*
- *"I'm gonna jack you guys off"*
- *"Having that thing coming up between your legs like a snake"*
- *"She would sit there on the sofa and watch Mike and I go at it"*
- *"More balls is good. The more balls, the better"*
- *"If you each could go in and play simultaneously with two different guys"*
- *"I'm right now, pretty wide open"*
- *"Don't be put off by the length. Work your way up and you'll be able to handle it"*
- *"It plays this kick ass slow-mo of this guy ramming your ass and taking you down."*
- *"It was kind of fun to screw the guy you're playing with"*
- *"Let me tell you guys where I want it first"*
- *"Watching four guys go at it. Oh Jesus!"*

Mike was always happy to play along with these and would laugh when they were played or when he came up with another new one. He really was a funny and integral part of the show. There was also a time when the topic of Liberace came up and the hosts were talking about all of the different kinds of forums on the Internet and Mike said that there were probably even Liberace forums which of course his co-hosts jumped on.

Every once in a while during a break in recording or during the Live News they would play a Liberace riff on piano and Mike would dance to it on camera. During one visit to Las Vegas for Classic Gaming Expo 2010, Scott took pictures of Mike outside the Liberace Museum shortly before it closed to the public on October 17, 2010, having been open since April 15, 1979.

Later in the summer of 2011, there was a great example of what I outlined earlier, whether Mike was devious or just very, very absent minded, not really thinking too much about decisions and just breezing through life.

The podcast hosts are great fans of Classic Gaming Expo of course, and when there wasn't going to be one held in 2011 they decided that they were going to Las Vegas anyway and they were going to hang out and talk about and play some games. The event that was organized by Scott was called E.G.C. (Emergency Gaming Convention) and wasn't a convention as such, it was just a bunch of people (hosts and listeners) hanging out in Las Vegas for the weekend. Keith Robinson of Intellivision Productions (a good friend of the hosts) was invited and agreed to come along and hang out with them.

They visited the Pinball Hall Of Fame, Toy Shack, Insert Coins and a few other gaming hotspots over the course of the weekend and the barcade Insert Coins agreed to let them all use a section of their bar area to record a live Top Ten debate with the hosts and listeners getting involved. The topic was the Top Ten Retro Games and the recording came out well with everybody getting into the spirit of it and having a good time. At one point, Mike scolded Tricia for saying *"ass"* which made everybody laugh and the whole thing can be heard in the August 2011 episode of the show, RoundUp 38.

Once they had finished recording the live Top Ten at around 9pm they decided to go and eat and Keith Robinson suggested they eat at the nearby Tony Roma's on Fremont Street because he loved their "World Famous Onion Loaf" so they made their way over there. They got seated and started looking at the menus by about 9.30pm and Scott noticed that Mike Kennedy was not there. He had been with them as they left Insert Coins and started the short walk up Fremont Street but now he had gone missing, so they waited for him.

He hadn't told anybody where he was going and had said that he was going to go and eat with them. They waited and waited for about ninety minutes and at about 11pm they decided they had to order as the restaurant closed at midnight and all this time Scott had been calling and texting Mike but had got no response.

Just as they had finished eating and were taking a group photograph of everybody there, in strolls Mike and lands right in the photo "Hey everybody, it's SoCalMike!"

as though he had been there the whole time. Scott asked him where the hell he had been after saying he would be right there. *"Oh, I went to a Loverboy concert."*

Loverboy were a rock band who formed in 1979 in Calgary, Alberta, Canada and whose biggest hits were "Turn Me Loose" and "Working for the Weekend" that they recorded with Columbia/CBS Records, Canada. Their live debut came when they opened for Kiss at Pacific Coliseum in Vancouver, B.C. on November 19, 1979, and their first, self-titled, album sold over one million copies in Canada. When it crossed the border to the U.S.A. in 1980 it sold over two million copies. In 1984 they recorded a theme song for the Summer Olympic Games in Los Angeles and their 1986 song "Heaven in Your Eyes" featured in the Top Gun soundtrack.

In 2009 the band was inducted into the Canadian Music Hall of Fame and at the time that Mike saw them they were on tour with Journey and Pat Benatar. To bring this back to video games, their song "Working for the Weekend" was available on the rock music radio station V-Rock which featured in the 2002 video game Grand Theft Auto: Vice City.

Mike had literally been on his way to the restaurant with everybody when he saw a sign that Loverboy were playing and had gone to watch the concert without telling anybody and leaving them waiting hours for him to show up just in time for photographs.

Another episode where an impromptu phone call was made involved a trip to Las Vegas where Scott had collected some business cards from the "flick-flick" guys on the Las Vegas Strip. These are usually foreign workers who stroll up and down the strip flicking the deck of business cards in their hand which they give out to people walking past. The cards are numbers for call girls that will come and meet you in your hotel room.

The hosts would normally give these cards away by putting them in with prizes that were sent out to listeners that had won them during the Live News segment.

During one particular segment, again it was Mike's idea, they called one of the numbers and UKMike pretended to be an interested client so that they could find out how the system worked, how much it cost and how it avoided the legal loopholes for prostitution. It wasn't done in a salacious way but was a fine piece of investigative journalism conducted on the fly, and yes, it was Mike Kennedy's idea.

The next time Scott and Mike Kennedy were in Las Vegas together, they recorded some of the show live from the 5 o'clock Somewhere bar at Margaritaville which is in the Flamingo Hotel on the Las Vegas strip. Tricia was in the bar with them and UKMike was talking to them via Skype as he had been unable to make the trip.

Scott went to the bar and ordered drinks for them all, choosing a ridiculously large margarita. As Scott knows the bar staff they were generous with their measures and he made his way back to the table balancing three enormous souvenir glasses festooned with umbrellas, parrots and all manner of garnishes. Mike took one look at them and said *"I'm not drinking a girl's drink"* but Scott told him not to worry, he wouldn't require another drink that day and to enjoy it.

They started drinking and recording the audio for the podcast and pretty soon the wheels began to fall off as Scott and Mike were becoming more and more drunk as time went on. In fact, Mike was so drunk that he could barely get his words out by the end of the show, not the end of his drink, and as his face became more flushed by the minute, he slurred more and more and made less and less sense until he had to be escorted back to their room by Tricia.

One of the great pieces of show lore is the ways that Scott and UKMike have pranked Mike Kennedy, not that it is difficult to do, but they did have to be more and more inventive each time. The first time they pranked Mike was for Classic Gaming Expo 2012 in Las Vegas. Scott and Mike were committed to attending the show and Scott came up with a plan that UKMike would also attend but without telling anybody. UKMike would just randomly turn up somewhere in Las Vegas and they would capture Mike's reaction.

Mike was so oblivious to the plan that in the months preceding the show the other two would drop little hints into the podcast and the recording sessions, and Mike being Mike, he would not put two and two together and figure out what was going on. UKMike would say to Scott, for example: *"How many mics will you have at CGE?"* and he would reply:

"Two Mikes. I'll have both Mikes at CGE"

Mike Kennedy was of course oblivious, as were most people. There were a few people in on the plan, including Mike's wife Tricia and a few other listeners who were also attending the Expo and who were going to help to film Mike's reaction at the reveal.

There were a couple of different ideas of how to pull this off, one was to pretend that Mike had run UKMike over with his car. They would wait until he was reversing out of a parking bay and UKMike would "hit" the back of his car and lie down on the ground. The problem with this was that Mike might actually run him over or they might get some additional, unwanted, attention from the public or even the Police. The idea that was settled on was that UKMike would hide in the bathroom of Scott's Hotel room and they would get Mike to go in there on some fake premise.

Mike Kennedy arrived in Las Vegas first and was camping close to the Circus Circus hotel in his Airstream with Tricia and their dogs while Scott, who arrived in town next, was staying at the Plaza Hotel on Fremont Street which is where the Expo was being held that year. UKMike was scheduled to arrive in Las Vegas at 18:18 on Thursday August 12, after flying from Manchester, UK to Philadelphia and then on to Las Vegas, but there was a delay as the flight from Philadelphia was forced to wait on the ground while a new route was found to avoid a storm that was moving along the original flight path.

UKMike and Scott were in contact while he was stuck on the ground in Philadelphia and Scott was keeping an eye on his incoming flight so that he could collect him from the airport. Eventually the flight took off and headed for Las Vegas.

It seemed that events were conspiring against them constantly because when UKMike touched down, the aircraft taxied to a spot where it could be met by an ambulance as one of the passengers had suffered a heart attack during the flight. The passenger was fine but had to be removed from the aircraft before anybody else was allowed off.

Finally, the aircraft taxied to the gate and the passengers were allowed to disembark. All the time UKMike was in contact with Scott who was by now at the airport waiting to whisk him back to the Plaza and get set up for the prank.

Once through baggage reclaim pretty quickly, having already passed through US Customs in Philadelphia, UKMike made his way outside Las Vegas airport to meet Scott in person for the first time ever. There wasn't any time for niceties though as they raced, as much as one can race, in a rental Crown Victoria, from the airport to the Plaza Hotel on Fremont Street.

This wasn't exactly a nice tourist drive along the strip, taking in the sights and sounds of Las Vegas, this was a hurried journey along the back streets of Las Vegas with Scott driving, as he described it, *"keeping his right foot planted on the throttle while modulating speed with the brake pedal."* No Crown Vic has ever been driven like that before or since, and nor should it!

Along the way they set Mike Kennedy up and told him that he should meet them in Scott's room in a little while so he could help to carry some equipment down from the room to the Expo floor and set up the Retro Gaming Roundup booth.

Eventually, and in record time, they arrived in one piece at The Plaza and raced up to Scott's room where they were met by a few co-conspirators and they went about setting up a camera in the bathroom, the scene of their reveal. They rigged up a tripod and camera to capture the moment from inside and they had a couple of people filming from the bedroom, Nurmix (Paul Nurminen of The Intellivisionaries Podcast) and retroshaun (Shaun Stephenson, a listener, a friend and a video game artist).

Scott made a call to Mike Kennedy and asked him to come up to the room while UKMike made his way to the bathroom and sat on the toilet with his trousers down and waited. Scott then asked Mike to grab a bag of equipment out of the bathroom and he opened the door, saw somebody on the toilet and closed it immediately. He went back into the bedroom and said *"Hey! There's somebody in the bathroom and it looked like UKMike!"* He then did nothing with that information.

UKMike stayed where he was and he could hear people talking, trying to get Mike Kennedy to open the door again and see who it was. He eventually did and finally recognized his co-host sitting there on the can. After he had calmed down a little and they had filmed his reaction, he began the Post Mortem and tried to find out who had known about the prank and for how long. He couldn't believe that Tricia was in on it all along and it was a really great moment in the history of the podcast, and more than that, it was also a great example of three buddies throwing each other under the bus and just generally having a great time.

They went out for dinner that night at the Hofbrauhaus, a German themed restaurant, and Mike still could not believe what had happened and that all three of them were there. UKMike describes sitting opposite him at dinner and says that Mike kept looking at him throughout the meal.

> *"To see his face change each time he looked at me, it was as though he was recognizing me all over again. He simply could not believe that I was there and that "everybody" knew but him."*

Not content to sit on their laurels, Scott and UKMike plotted another prank and it wasn't too long in coming to fruition.

The hosts were making plans to attend the Portland Retro Gaming Expo in Portland, Oregon in 2013 and it was decided that all three of them would attend but again, they would not tell Mike Kennedy and they put on their thinking caps to come up with a plan to "unveil" UKMike and again capture the footage.

This time UKMike arrived in Portland first via Manchester, Heathrow and Vancouver, getting into Portland at 15:06 on Thursday October 3, 2013. Scott flew in on the Friday morning and went to pick up UKMike from his hotel, thankfully this time not in a Crown Victoria, but as he made his way to Mike's room in what would come to be known as "The Murder Hotel" he passed a shirtless man yelling *"I aint going back to no jail!"* The irony of it was that he probably did.

There were a few errands to run and some equipment to pick up for the Expo booth and they spent the morning driving around town looking for a good venue to prank their unwitting co-host. As they were exploring and trying to make sense of the navigation system Scott asked UKMike if he could take the next right and UKMike told him that he could. It was a one-way street and they were going the wrong way towards oncoming traffic. As they drove down the street another shirtless man (possibly the same one but he was likely already in jail) yelled at them *"WRONG WAY BABY!"*

Scott shouted at UKMike: *"I thought you said I could come down this street!"* to which UKMike replied

> *"You asked if you could, not if you should."*

Eventually they got their bearings and decided on a suitable venue which was the Widmer Brewery Pub at 943 N Russell St.

Portland has more micro-breweries per capita than any other city in the world and Widmer was a great choice. Not only do they make great beer but they also have a pub attached to the brewery that serves great food to accompany their range of beers. The staff were also incredibly helpful and accommodating.

Mike Kennedy was driving up to Portland from Southern California and was due to arrive in Portland in the early to mid-afternoon and the plan was put in place. Scott spoke to the manager of the pub and they came up with the idea that UKMike would dress up as a waiter in the pub and he would be Scott and Mike's server. The manager agreed to reserve them a table in the window so that there was good lighting for the secret filming and they bought a Widmer Brewery T-Shirt for the "waiter" to wear and the manager agreed to let UKMike borrow one of their server aprons. The outfit was topped off with a ridiculous looking long-haired wig from Fred Meyers and a pair of glasses.

They now eagerly awaited Mike's arrival in the back of the bar out of sight and eventually he walked in through the door and Scott met him before they were taken to their table. After a couple of minutes when they got settled down, and with UKMike's then girlfriend filming the action, the dubious looking waiter made his way over to their table, gave them the menus and went through his finest waiter's patter in his finest USMike accent, asking if he could start them off with some drinks.

Scott ordered his beer and Mike Kennedy was looking through the specials board at the list of beers, some of which he knew. He was taking sneaky sideways glances at the waiter but would not look at him directly. To be fair he did look slightly odd, but then a lot of men in Portland do, shirts being an option apparently, and the wig was certainly putting him off his stride a little. Mike chose a beer and the waiter started to talk to him about the beer, hoping he would look a little more closely at him, but he didn't. The waiter kept on going through his sales pitch, telling Mike that they brewed that particular beer on the premises and that it was one of their best. Mike said that he had the beer before and liked it.

By this time Scott was beginning to lose control and was clearly hiding behind his phone as the ridiculous situation continued, the waiter looking completely ridiculous, sounding even more ridiculous and trying to engage Mike in conversation.

The waiter asked them if they were in town for the Retro Gaming Expo and started to talk to them about Pac-Man. Scott was by now beyond conversation and flat out laughing. Mike was impressed with the waiter's Pac-Man knowledge and the two of them had a weird conversation where they were talking to each other while Mike was looking everywhere around the room except at their waiter.

Clearly, he was not going to realize who it was so UKMike removed the wig and carried on talking to Mike until it got to the point where he had to tell him who he was. Mike sat there completely dumbfounded for several moments and finally it dawned on him that it had happened again. The first thing he did was pick up his phone and dial Tricia's number. There was a pause before he said *"Yeah, they got me again. He was a waiter this time!"* (The videos for both of these pranks are available on the Retro Gaming Roundup website).

They thanked the ever helpful and appreciative Widmer team again and all sat down for a good meal before heading over to the Expo hall to get the booth set up.

One of Mike's craziest ideas during his time on the show came during a Live News segment when the hosts were discussing pinball. They had been sent a news item about a pinball machine and Mike suddenly blurted out that it would be a great idea to design a pinball game that used a magnetic ball. The ball could then be used to pick up staples as it made its way around the playfield.

The game would start with the playfield "full of trash" and the object of the game was to clean it up. What Mike failed to see was just what a terrible idea that was. I surely don't need to spell out why but I'm going to anyway. The ball would be attracted to anything on the playfield that was metal, including of course any playfield toys, bumpers, posts, screws that were holding the game together, solenoids beneath the playfield and any other balls that were used in the game.

It would also make a huge mess of the playfield having random bits of metal and staples lying on the playfield and being picked up by the ball, which would then drag them around the beautifully painted artwork and ruin it within seconds, not to mention that at some point the ball would not be able to roll anymore as the staples and trash stuck to it. Mike would very often speak before putting his brain into gear and this example was no exception.

As you can see, at this time, Mike was an integral part of the podcast and was often directly responsible for a lot of the "shenanigans" that the hosts got up to. He was a fun-loving host, as were all three of them, always looking to play pranks or to do something fun on the show to entertain their listeners. It was actually as though the hosts were doing it to amuse themselves and that the listeners had a window into their world rather than the show being done for entertainment purposes.

Up until this point there is no question of Mike's reputation being tarnished or of his dedication and commitment to the podcast. Things were about to change though and it is probably at around this point where we really see that begin to happen. None of his ideas for other ventures had thus far threatened his position on the podcast or the amount of time that he dedicated to it.

That was all about to change with the arrival of Retro Magazine.

Left to right: Mike Kennedy, Walter Day, Scott Schreiber, Steve Sawyer (E3, 2011)

The Bathroom Prank (CGE 2012) – The first time all three hosts met in person

The Three Musketeers (Flamingo Hotel, Las Vegas, 2012)

The Waiter Prank – (Widmer Brewery, Portland, 2013)

6: Publish or Perish

It was sometime in 2013 that Mike Kennedy first raised the topic of producing a retro themed magazine with his co-hosts, although it obviously stemmed from the original idea around 2011 that Steve Sawyer had brought to Mike. We have seen that Mike was trying to expand the range of sites under his GameGavel banner and his ideas had come and gone, some receiving more attention and gaining more traction than others, but none of them had thus far caused an issue where the podcast was concerned. Scott was an investor in GameGavel and so far Mike had tried to add value to the property which would benefit all concerned, especially the investors.

Retro Magazine was the first sign of real trouble and it created a rift that would never really close again and it also changed the way that Mike was handled by the other two hosts. It was during this era that Mike's lack of organization and preparation for the podcast became increasingly frustrating, but that lack of organization and preparation paled into insignificance when compared to some of his very dubious decisions and some outright lies.

During pre-recordings, the hosts had discussed many times how the magazine would look, what content would be in it and who would be responsible for it. It was clearly defined very early on that the magazine was not being produced under the guise of Retro Gaming Roundup, it was being done under the GameGavel banner. This wasn't a problem for the show, it just had to be defined to save confusion later.

Mike and Steve Sawyer had gone their separate ways for a couple of years while Steve *"did his own thing"*, which had included work for Hardcore Gamer and Retro Gamer, but he returned to GameGavel in 2013 and revived his initial idea for GameGavel Monthly. By his own admission he *"didn't know shit about shit"* so he just put something basic together and sent it to Mike, saying that they had something, it wasn't pretty, but it was something that they could work with.

Together they had been building the written content on GameGavel and growing the community, and Steve suggested that there was a void that they could fill. They had seen Retro Gamer from the UK and felt that they could also do a retro magazine but with less focus on the developers and interviews and focusing more on the games themselves and the people that played them. Everybody was writing about the developers and the development process but nobody was concentrating on games and gamers.

Steve's initial efforts were little more than a digital pamphlet created in Microsoft Word which they decided to sell on GameGavel for $2 for each monthly issue and they would look to increase the page numbers and the list of writers as time went on. Steve recruited David Giltinan who was at the time presenting a podcast called Ultra Mega Death Ray, a self-proclaimed Geek Show, and David began writing articles on GameGavel and Steve outlined the magazine to him as they put the first primitive issue together. By Steve's own admission, the first issue was horrible, having taken them only a couple of weeks to complete, but it was enough to sow the idea in Mike's mind and for them to sell a few via GameGavel. This grew into the bigger idea for a fully-fledged, glossy print magazine that would eventually become Retro Magazine which Mike had always talked about as being his own idea, when in fact it was the brainchild of Steve Sawyer.

In September of 2013 one of the buyers of the initial digital pamphlet was a man called Mark Kaminski who saw that there was a kernel of an idea here and he offered his services to work on the magazine. His initial thoughts were:

> *"OMG! Great content, bad execution.*
>
> *Pull it down or make it free for now, don't charge for this yet. Once bitten twice shy! No offense but this NEEDS my help. Let me lay it out and send it back to you this weekend. Please send me the word doc so I can easily grab text. Also need the best quality of the original photos."*

There was still no definite name for the magazine yet and Mike was throwing names out such as Attract Mode, The GameGavel Digital Mag, Video Game Invader(s) or VGI for short and he estimated that they had sold around forty copies.

Mark told him that he would like to make some layouts or a cover and was offering his services free of charge as he was a listener to the podcast and was grateful for the show turning him on to buying a Neo Geo arcade cab. He felt like he owed Mike something at least and he began working on layouts. Mark was useful to Mike as he had worked in, and had contacts in, the print industry who could provide printing, publishing and distribution. While Mark worked on that side of things Mike was putting together a pitch to recruit some writers for the as yet unnamed magazine:

> *"Video Game Invader*
> *The Independent Digital Video Gaming Magazine*
>
> *We want to enlist the best, most famous and influential gaming journalists from the past two decades and reunite them to create a monthly digital video gaming magazine (with quarterly print, option) like no other. Created independently and without boundaries, Video Game Invader Magazine will be the most unbiased and truthful video gaming magazine on the planet offering only the most intelligent, thought provoking and entertaining video game reviews, interviews, insights and editorials spanning the entire history of gaming. [...]*

This is a great model because we create one magazine each month and can sell it to thousands of gamers with no incremental costs and it's transmitted digitally. And, we believe reuniting a team of this stature will get considerable trade and consumer press and would be the talk around gaming forums and communities high-and-low. This will add to the momentum of this Kickstarter campaign!

Depending on the success of the campaign this could become a more "full-time" position vs. freelance/under contract; if that is a direction that would interest you."

Mike went back to Steve and told him about Mark's message and how he thought that Mark could help the magazine become something bigger and better than their skills seemed to be able to produce. Steve had no reason to doubt Mike's motives and felt that if they were *"able to make this idea something better than what my limited skill set is, then sure."* Steve just wanted to produce a magazine that was an alternative to Retro Gamer and to produce something in a way that *"makes everybody happy and returns some of the spirit of why we're even into this to begin with you know, it's the games."*

Now that they had an idea for content and somebody who could do a proper magazine layout, Mike was always happy to listen to ways he could monetize the magazine, even in those early days:

"Hold your breath – it's a male demographic – all you need to do is land some medical ad for cholesterol and you'd be in the money. Right now I'd say focus on getting readership up and monetize it down the road."

Music to his ears, you might say:

"I like where you are going with this."

Mike's e-mail signature had grown in size and stature and now included links to his various social media pages as well as describing him as;

"Mike Kennedy, Founder & President
GameGavel, LLC dba GameGavel.com"

Mike was also now trying to recruit some big name writers like Andy Eddy, Ed Semrad, Seanbaby Riley, Pat Contri and Patrick Scott Patterson and it is well known that they were later well paid for their articles, initially there was talk of perhaps $1,000 for Seanbaby's column and $800 for other writers though Pat Contri was only paid $100 for his, as well as a profit share as the magazine grew and generated more income. Mike was also dropping names into the e-mails that he sent out, some of whom withdrew their commitments or outright declined from the start. The list he was quoting at this time was:

> *"Jeremy Parish, SeanbabyReily, Chris Kohler, David Siller (Sushi-X from EGM), Martin Alessi, Kevin Steele, Keith Robinson and a few other lessor known contributors. And we have other well-known folks still being called upon that could join the team in the next few days."*

Cart before the horse again? Mike seemed to be taking sending an e-mail to somebody as having them on board and later had to delete their names from promotional material and the Kickstarter campaign, Dan "Shoe" Hsu, for example.

The name for the magazine was decided on in September of 2013 but drew questions from writers such as Martin Alessi who knew of the British spin off magazine from Retro Gamer which was also called "Retro." Mike gave it one more attempt at calling it GameGavel Magazine but was advised against it and Retro was finally decided upon once again, and in late September it had also now slipped to being a bi-monthly issue rather than a monthly issue. The domain readretro.com was registered by Mike on October 12, 2013.

Scott and UKMike, among others of course, were asked to be writers and there was a lot of discussion about how the magazine and the show would have a synergy, the first part of that (the show helping the magazine get funded) was a daily utilization of the Retro Gaming Roundup social media and lots of talk on the show about the project as it went through the promotion and Kickstarter phases. The payback was supposed to comprise of several things, among them were a rundown of show highlights, possibly including, though not restricted to, funniest lines, interesting items, a full page advert and transcripts of interviews that were recorded for the show.

In the run up to the Kickstarter project going live, the magazine was discussed a lot, probably more than any other single subject in fact as Mike was throwing around lots of ideas and writer names, some of which would change from conversation to conversation as they either committed to coming on board or declined and were discounted. It was a constantly evolving situation as Mike seemed to announce new writers as though they were committed, simply on the back of contacting them. Some of them did indeed come on board but many others declined and Mike was forced to recant their names.

It had been a couple of years earlier, in June 2011, that Steve Sawyer and Mike Kennedy had attended E3 and were accompanied by Scott, who recalls very clearly the time spent with Mike and Steve driving around L.A. and walking around the show floor for three days as Steve and Mike threw ideas at each other and planned out their magazine. There was a moment of hindsight too as it became clear that Mike was there to further the cause of GameGavel and what would later become RETRO magazine, so Scott found himself alone in promoting their podcast at this one of a kind opportunity on the biggest stage there was in the video game industry.

Each day generally began with Scott and Mike picking up Steve from his garage apartment and heading to the convention center. The day concluded with dropping Steve off and then heading back to Mike's Trabuco Canyon condo for some food, quite a few drinks, and some great laughter.

"The bulk of the time in the car was spent listening to Steve and Mike banter back and forth with their ideas on the magazine, the business operations, structure, and the content of the venture. I just didn't give it the attention it deserved at the time, but you have to remember a few things. Firstly, Mike hadn't done anything to raise any concerns yet, and secondly, Mike had not discussed the magazine much with his podcast co-hosts, so much of the banter sounded like pie-in-the-sky (like a young start-up company that had just been funded, only it wasn't) and it certainly didn't seem like it was immediately part of the GameGavel company.

In fact, this point about RETRO's relationship to GameGavel was brought up later and had a great deal of importance about how the Retro VGS and its relationship to GameGavel was handled. However, at the time, if there was a take away, it was that Steve and Mike were without a doubt co-creators of whatever this publishing venture was to become, and Steve was every much a part of this as Mike was, and seemingly the greater contributor as he was punching up Mike's ideas into something greater than Mike had originally imagined."

There was a great deal of talk about the magazine's content on Retro Gaming Roundup too and Mike really did sell his co-hosts an idyllic situation here. Mike assured them that the magazine was under GameGavel in name only, it was essentially the magazine of the podcast and they would use it to promote themselves and enjoy cross pollination of their audiences where podcast listeners would buy the magazine and people reading the magazine would listen to the podcast. In fact, the Kickstarter campaign mentioned them specifically:

"Do you long for the great video gaming magazines from back in the day? Magazines with some heart and soul without all the big media fluff? We sure do, and that is why video game auction site GameGavel.com and the RetroGamingRoundup.com podcast decided to team up with some of the most popular and influential gaming journalists and personalities from the past three decades to introduce an independent print, digital and online publication dedicated to the past, present and future of the video gaming pastime that will hearken back to the amazing magazines from the 80's, 90's and early 2000's."

The campaign also featured Steve, and the Kickstarter video even included the artwork from the cover of their first GameGavel Monthly that Steve had put together. Mike would run the magazine and he assured them all not to worry, they would be included in it and they could run ads in it as well as write articles on a paid for basis. Scott and UKMike took him at his word and as questions arose, they were answered, and they continued with the podcast as normal. As for Steve, Mike was telling him:

"Dude, you're still going to have a stake, this is still our thing. It's just going to be better. That's all. It's going to be better but now we're going to take it to Kickstarter, we're going to actually get some money into this thing. I'm going

to be able to take care of you guys. I want to be able to pay you money, like a regular human being type money if this thing gets funded."

Deciding to take Mike at his word and not to worry Steve felt:

"You know what? It sounds like you got a handle on this my friend. Take my idea, breathe more life into it than I can with my limited resources and capability. That's what a good business partner and a friend should do."

Having put in the lion's share of the work on the new project so far, designing the brand, doing the layouts, co-designing the Kickstarter campaign, producing the sizzle video and designing the website, Mark Kaminski was now keen to have his arrangement formalized so that he would begin to see some reward for his labors thus far and moving forwards. This happened on October 1, 2013.

"This is an agreement between Mark Kaminski and GameGavel, LLC a California Corporation, on October 1, 2013.

GameGavel, LLC agrees to give Mark Kaminski 5% ownership in GameGavel, LLC in trade for early conceptual and developmental work on a new digital and print magazine, titled RETRO. Mark has agreed to offer his services free of charge until which time the magazine is generating enough revenue, in which, GameGavel, LLC agrees to then compensate Mark for his work at an agreed upon contractual price.

It should be noted the 5% ownership will only be extended in the event the magazine launch Kickstarter campaign reaches the goal set forth in the campaign and publishing continues forward.

In the likely event the publishing continues, Mark will assume the role of Creative Director and will preside over the magazine's layout, design and appearance.

Should the magazine be sold at some point in time, GameGavel, LLC will agree to give Mark 30% of the selling price as Mark was an integral part to bringing this magazine into existence.

Mike Kennedy, GameGavel, LLC"

The agreement was signed and returned and the Kickstarter campaign went live on October 5, 2013 (notably a week before the domain name had been registered) and ran until November 4, 2013 (30 days), with 2,345 backers exceeding the $50,000 goal, with a total of $75,759. Mark Kaminski was actually the first backer as soon as it went live with his $1 pledge and he was able to get in so quickly as it was actually him that made the campaign go live, having spoken to Mike who was supposed to do it, but who was, at the time, getting drunk at Portland Retro Gaming Expo with Scott and UKMike as they drank UKMike's Scotch.

Scott had taken to Twitter to try and promote the Kickstarter and reached out to Debbie Gibson who kindly retweeted it, the exact relationship between Scott and Debbie is still shrouded in mystery:

@Acro2pilot
@DebbieGibson Not as worthy as many causes you retweet, but can you help a fan with a dream? Just need a small push http://t.co/SGSpKs3yzn
06:05 AM – 29 Oct 13

Debbie Gibson @DebbieGibson
@Acro2pilot: @DebbieGibson Not as worthy as many causes you retweet...
All the best with this!!! http://t.co/SGSpKs3yzn
08:20 AM – 29 Oct 13

Prior to the Kickstarter campaign, and during the early part of it, Mike had penned himself as the Editor In Chief, but after Mark had outlined the list of tasks that Mike would need to perform in that role, Mike decided to recruit Brandon Justice instead after finding him on LinkedIn about two thirds of the way through the Kickstarter campaign.

As the Kickstarter continued to move forward, Scott noticed that Steve Sawyer was no longer involved and he asked Mike Kennedy about it. Scott describes it as not really being an *"ah ha moment but rather one of mild curiosity"* and Mike told him that Steve wasn't really involved other than writing some stuff and wasn't really a part of it. However, Scott recalled the situation differently and describes;

"the two of them co-creating the project right in front of me during the week of E3, they were bantering back and forth developing the idea but it didn't put up a red flag because there was no history of dishonesty and people leave projects all the time, teams change, and it didn't stand out."

Clearly Steve agreed with Scott and saw the situation very differently to Mike, he had felt that he could trust Mike as they had been friends for a while and worked on projects together. They'd been to E3 together with Scott of course and spent hours in the car with him but he did begin to worry a little when Mike brought Brandon Justice on board and asked Mike if he was really sure about his appointment. This was the first sign for Steve that something might be amiss and it also changed the dynamic among himself, Mike and David Giltinan. Prior to Brandon's arrival, David had been very friendly towards Steve, to the point of it being a little odd, but now that Brandon had arrived, David was less and less receptive to Steve and was communicating almost exclusively with Brandon. Steve called him on it and came to the conclusion that David was just a *"suck up"* and was ingratiating himself with the new Editor In Chief, and as Steve sensed himself being pushed out by the new arrivals, he turned to David for help in furthering his cause and asked him to stand up for him, but his pleas fell on deaf ears.

Mike was also becoming more elusive and would not answer Steve's telephone calls and emails, having redirected communications through Brandon, but having dealt with Mike over the years, Steve knew that Mike did not know how to handle direct confrontation and was trying desperately to avoid it. Steve questioned the wisdom of Issue 1 featuring the game Mighty No. 9 on the cover when 2013 was the

20th anniversary of the game "Doom", a much more influential title, and he felt it was a much more sensible idea to use that on the front cover and to have that as the magazine's main article, but again, he was ignored as Brandon was calling the shots.

Seeing that he was now well and truly being pushed out, Steve reached out to Mike:

> *"I worked my ass off for you for years and kept loyal hoping that one day you would see an opportunity fitted for me and remember all the stuff I did for you.*
>
> *I made that magazine because I thought you could breathe better life into an idea that I had than I could. And you did. I just didn't expect you to yank everything away from me like you did. And you know you did. You gave it to one of the most mistrusted names in this industry, and along every step of the way you tried to make me like it. [...]*
>
> *You betrayed me, betrayed Revue Labs and you betrayed my trust, and now you won't even give me the courtesy of an email or a phone call before you try and send the hounds after me? [...]*
>
> *"I don't have the resources to hire an attorney, and I don't think you have the amount they wanted to sue you for. [...]*
>
> *Unless you want to settle out of court. But I'm not doing ANYTHING with you without documentation and a notary public nearby. I've learned that lesson. [...]*
>
> *So what do you want to do? Should we duke it out online and in LA municipal or do you want to avoid all that drama? I need an answer by the end of the day. [...]*
>
> *I'm sorry dude, but you're not my friend. As such I no longer feel bad about pursuing this as far as I can and as loudly as I can. Or maybe instead of avoiding this thing you should just tell people I made the fucking magazine.*
>
> *Steve Tom Sawyer"*

In hindsight this was the template for things to come, friendly pep talks, partners that do most of the work and are suddenly dropped for new partners while being described as only having been minor players, if even that, isolation of team members so that all communication went through Mike Kennedy and the ever shifting sands of ownership. In reality Steve was soft fired from the magazine by virtue of just no longer being involved as somebody new was brought on board, and certainly his "replacements" were not told the whole truth about his involvement, so it isn't fair to blame them as active participants in harming their predecessors. Of course the new "team" were presented with the magazine as an original Mike Kennedy idea rather than the co-creation that it was involving Steve Sawyer.

Steve watched as his project went through Kickstarter and got funded with him excluded and it pushed him over the edge, so much so that he made death threats against Mike Kennedy. Steve was down on his luck at the time and was living in little more than a rooming house for $300 a month, $300 that he didn't have, and he saw post after post on Facebook from Mike all about the magazine and the Kickstarter, as well as seeing pictures of Mike and Tricia on vacation. As he sat there getting angrier and angrier, he flipped, seeing Mike as the reason for his current situation and misfortune, and he called him, threatening to choke his eyeballs out of his head.

This was presented by Mike as the ravings of a mad man, and that Steve had had some sort of a breakdown and was making threats, which the police took seriously enough to visit Steve's home and to consider attending E3, which is where Steve had threatened to find Mike. At this point Scott and UKMike still believed this characterization of the Steve Sawyer situation, however, with hindsight, Steve was a big talker but he was not a liar. He was an honest man who had been wronged and stolen from.

The police visited Steve and he showed the detective the Kickstarter page, the Retro website, communications between himself and Mike and also the magazine that he had produced, which had given Mike the idea to take it further. The detective could see it from Steve's point of view and agreed that it seemed as though Mike had stolen the idea from him, but he advised him that he could not call people and make threats, that was crossing the line. If he wanted to pursue Mike, there were legal ways to do that and he should pursue those but must desist from calling Mike and threatening him.

Let off with a warning, Steve did reach out to Mike again and was much calmer this time, outlining his position, that Mike had stolen his idea and had excluded him from its success, to which Mike replied, *"Well, none of us are making any money, I'm losing money if anything."* This didn't help of course, and they agreed that Steve would be paid for the article he had written and would walk away. He was never going to be allowed back in and he was wasting his time trying, so he came to the conclusion that Mike had walked over him to get what he wanted, describing the situation as: *"Your legs are a ladder, your head is the step."*

There were also some financial questions from Mark about the arrangement of the LLC, the GameGavel network and the relationship between the different entities and obviously this would not be the last time that a similar question arose.

> *"Hope everything is well and you enjoyed your bubbly last night. Let me know when you are free to talk. We have to hash out a few minor legal details.*
>
> *Per my attorney, I can't really "own" 30% of a magazine if it's owned by GameGavel, and I have 5% of gamegavel. RETRO would need to be set up as its own LLC for me to own 30% of it, but I can own 30% of the equity and profits of that property if it's owned by GameGavel. That is the difference.*
>
> *As readretro.com is part of the RETRO property, it needs its own Adsense account to keep it separate from GameGavel as well for auditing purposes."*

Mike responded:

> *"What we agreed was that IF the magazine is sold I would pay you 30% of the proceeds from the sale (and Brandon now 20% of the sale) and the remaining balance would go to GameGavel, LLC. That is what we discussed*

in the beginning. Proceeds from subscription sales, advertising and what not would all be part of GameGavel, LLC and profits there would get distributed to GameGavel, LLC owners of which you own 5% of the parent company. We can talk about it today."

Mark tried a different tack:

"I was unclear on the agreement. How do you feel about us just setting RETRO up as its own company?"

Mike didn't like that idea at all:

"It has to run under GG as that was my intention all along to bring revenue into and promote GameGavel. Makes no sense to do this. You will get 30% of the mag if we well (sic) it and you have 5% of the entire parent company. I think that is as good as it gets ?? [...]

Intergi is who we are using for ad placement, not adsense. ReadRetro will be set up as a separate domain, but still reside under the GameGavel main account. I can get stats and earnings reported separately for each domain."

Things now ramped up a notch as Mark aired his frustrations:

"Mike, I want to be level headed and explain the situation. Here is my concern. Basically I believed I was getting 5% of Gamegavel and 30% of RETRO as a property. I created the look, feel, name, branding etc. and worked hard to make this a property. I never understood the agreement that I had no stake in the Retro property as its Co-creator. If GameGavel just IS Retro. I'm still only getting 5% of Retro which is not reasonable considering what I've done to create this property. Owning 5% of GameGavel means that I have no control over anything GameGavel does. I have no say in anything over the property of RETRO. The only thing I have is the value of GameGavel. The problem, is that you can spin off Retro into its own company, and I would have nothing really. And I have no legal power to do anything about that. It's just an asset. It's like if you sold an old oven to someone. I can't stop you from selling the oven. You would need to get money for the oven, but could claim a bunch of losses on it, and say it's only worth $50. And then I'd get 5% of $50. But not really, because that money wouldn't be mine anyway, it'd be GameGavel's and you would profit/loss it until it's gone. Retro doesn't technically exist yet. You haven't filed anything with the IRS. Maybe got an EIN for it. But it sounds like you just using your legal entity of GameGavel for everything. So... I request that you separate Retro now, before you start filing taxes. Just get an EIN for the magazine (Can apply online, it's free, takes a few weeks to get it.) and then we register it as a corporation (Couple hundred bucks, some paperwork but also no big deal, no lawyers, whatever. Easy) and then divide shares and assign officers. Now we have a separate company. If you want GameGavel to own part of that company, you can give GameGavel your shares of stock. Understand in the event of your death or retirement, the magazine becomes property of who, Gamegavel shareholders? I would be

completely screwed. It should be its own company. I'll handle the accounting and registration if you would like.

I feel it's totally reasonable since I'm not being paid for all of my work and connections and the future value is questionable. It's early days for pay in this venture. I don't' need a salary out of this. I want a partnership to create a real brand here."

"Here's the way I look at it. I wasn't in this for GameGavel and I really didn't understand the agreement. I believed I was getting 30% of the magazine. Then you said you also were giving me 5% of gamegavel (which I wasn't asking for). I think GameGavel stands to gain from associated advertising in the magazine and links to auctions and such. If you want to make GameGavel a partial owner of Retro, that's fine, you can give your shares to GameGavel. However, I would like to see Retro split out into its own company so that I'm a 30% partner, and that in the event anything happens (Such as you dying or getting amnesia) that my interest and work in this thing is protected.

Mike, I'm the guy that came up with putting this Kickstarter thing together with you, I am the Co-Creator. The name, look, feel, marketing, doing the layout, video, ads, the printing, the shipping, digital dist research, that was all me. I'm the designer sweating over it. The writers get paid a bunch of money for doing their part. I'm getting basically nothing for the most important piece, which is actually creating a brand and making the magazine and site. Without me, the Brand doesn't really happen. I'm not trying to be threatening about it. However, I know what value I bring to the table, and my intention is to make this RETRO magazine #1 and website a serious property. I have a history of creating successful brands. I can't do this if I know that if RETRO sells for a million bucks that my take on it is going to be $50,000. That wouldn't even be a year's pay at a normal job doing design work for a magazine. More importantly I want to have some say in the direction of this property.

Mike, my lawyer said forget the 30% of Retro if it sells. That doesn't exist. Retro isn't its own company, so it means nothing really. You could claim a bunch of losses on it, and say it's only worth $50. As for agreement you have, there really is nothing preventing you from just canning me and hiring a different creative person and leaving me with the 5% of GameGavel today. So I'd get 5% of Retro's profits and maybe a full time job in the future at an unspecified pay? That is simply not worth my time. I don't see how you think that is fair either considering what I've done here.

I'm trying to have you look at it, from my side. RETRO can help GameGavel, GameGavel can own the other 70% if that is how you want it. I don't need shares of GameGavel (1% would be nice :)), and I hope GameGavel grows into a huge thing and you make millions and you live on your own personal island drinking out of a coconut. I am in this for Retro. I want to make a great magazine and web property and I think we can definitely do that. However, I want it to be fair so that if anything happens, I'm protected. Isn't that reasonable? Clearly you think there is future value in RETRO as well. If RETRO does well so does GameGavel.

We can discuss it, but I'm pretty firm on this Mike. Getting 5% of Retro and no pay is not reasonable considering what I've done to create this property. I don't want to be the next Ronald Wayne from Apple who was an original partner with 10% and got $800 on the sale of the company. Let's do what's right now, before it gets complicated by tax history and more and more people getting involved.

Let's talk about it this evening, I'm very reasonable and willing to work it out, but I don't see how 5% of the magazine is worth it for me to the kind of work needed here. I think this is all very reasonable, and if you don't see it that way, well I dunno."

"So basically, if I understand your conversation. I don't get paid until GameGavel makes enough money to pay me for my time, as a worker. And then if the company makes money, I get whatever 5% gets me? Ha! That's fucking retarded. Sorry man, I thought I was getting 30% of the Brand I developed, not this crazy deal! I guess I bring nothing to this in your eyes. I'm just some dude who works for free for GG essentially?

The thing with start-ups... I'm taking losses now and being a "starving artist" to get it somewhere. If it gets to the top you'd only leave me a small percentage? Ridiculous. I'd think you'd want me to be inspired by all this and work to make it something incredible. The reality is the magazine isn't worth anything right now. So why are you being tight fisted? I don't get it. RETRO will be built, primarily, on my labor. Yeah, the writers play an important part but they get paid regardless of how well the magazine does. The only guys that are doing real work are Brandon and myself. Trust me I bring a skill and the experience to this that nobody else has or I would take a lot of money to hire in.

I was never interested in GG and I don't see it ever making anything. It's a small site without a lot of users."

While avoiding these present and future money issues, Mike was also shirking some other responsibilities, aside from bringing in Brandon as Editor In Chief once he knew how many things he would have to do.

Just as Issue 1 was ready to be given the final sign off for printing, Mike went AWOL. He and Tricia took off camping and nobody could get hold of him. Although the team were happy that the magazine was in its final state and could be printed they needed the sign off from Mike but were unable to reach him. So, confident in their work, they sent it to print and left Mike to his wine tasting and camping.

Ironically, Mike had also gone AWOL when Chase the Chuckwagon went live, though only he was on staff at that time, and he went on a week-long camping trip meaning that he had to set up the game categories using the Internet via his phone.

More trouble was not far away as it wasn't long until Issue 1 hit the virtual shelves and it became clear that all was not well, but before that, Scott and UKMike had called Mike Kennedy out in early December of 2013 with regards to their various social media feeds.

The Retro Gaming Roundup social media feeds were full of posts for GameGavel and Retro Magazine and a few for Retro Gaming Roundup of course, but the GameGavel and Retro Magazine feeds did not have a single one for Retro Gaming Roundup. They needed that fixing and called for a meeting with Mike. Don't forget that in every episode of the podcast for months prior to this, Mike Kennedy had also talked about the magazine and promoted it on the show, again, not reciprocated obviously.

This meeting marked a sea change in the way that they would deal with Mike. In the past it had always been on an even basis as they each had equal standing within Retro Gaming Roundup and in the case of disagreement, two would out vote the one and they had operated like that successfully for almost five years. However, now they were to approach things differently and had to deal with Mike in a more business-like way and separate out their differing interests.

The deal that they offered Mike was to either:

1. Cease posting about GameGavel and Retro Magazine on the Retro Gaming Roundup Social Media feeds.

2. Post on a one for one basis on both feeds, so for every GameGavel post on Retro Gaming Roundup, there had to be a post about the podcast on GameGavel or Retro.

Not wanting to lose out on the promotional possibilities, Mike chose option 2. Unfortunately, he didn't stick to it, so Scott and UKMike then began deleting any posts that did not have a corresponding one for one post on either GameGavel or Retro Magazine. Being a kind of "fire and forget" type of person, Mike didn't notice and continued oblivious until the topic came up again over Christmas 2013 when Mike finally addressed the subject, saying that he had;

> *"been a bit consumed with the magazine lately, even neglecting GameGavel a bit."*

UKMike told him that he hoped there was still a Retro Gaming Roundup advert in the first issue of Retro and that was when Mike Kennedy dropped the bombshell that forever changed the relationship between them all. Mike said:

> *"As far as premier issue, RGRU is in the Sites We Love section and mentioned with each of your bios. There is no direct advert for it. The GameGavel 1/4 advert was added last minute as there was a space to fill."*

Wait a minute! So Mike had promised them advertising all along, for months, he had talked about how it could help the podcast out and carry adverts for it as well as their articles, and now here we are, before Issue 1 is even out. Mike had clearly used and abused the podcast's social media feeds and the podcast itself by continually promoting GameGavel and Retro and now none of that reciprocal advertising was going to happen. He had sold them down the river. Another meeting was needed, and the tone of this meeting was to be one of incredible frustration as Mike had to continually be brought back to the problem statement, that the arrangement of reciprocity had not been honored.

By now it was early January 2014 and Mike Kennedy was travelling around Phoenix, Arizona with his boss and was unable to Skype with them until the end of the week and maybe early the next week. I don't doubt the validity of that situation as he did indeed frequently travel to Phoenix with his job for Creform Corporation but it did also seem that he didn't think it was that important and that he could use his sales patter with his co-hosts and brush it over again. A pattern of behavior was starting to become obvious, and while the prior events only became red flags in hindsight, this one was huge and was waving right in the faces of Scott and UKMike. It would not be the last red flag, nor would it be the last attempt at a "Have a Coke and a Smile" dismissal of a dirty deed. That clearly wasn't going to be allowed to happen again. Not this time. Mike continued to stall for time as he travelled but he did find time to drop this bombshell on hi co-hosts:

> *"First off, I won't be using the magazine to self-promote any podcasts. It's just not something that is normally done in magazines. GameGavel will be featured as it is a revenue generator for the company and it makes sense to tie it together but will be done so with a page on GameGavel news, cool listings and a featured seller. It won't be an advertisement per say (sic) and limited to a page."*

What!!? A complete about turn! Absolutely no advertising for the podcast in Retro Magazine! On top of that, Mike was still planning to use show content in the form of transcriptions of their interviews.

> *"[...] maybe some payment."*

> *"If we agree and decide to use any RGRU material, like transcribed interviews either online OR in print, RGRU will get credit for the interview and maybe some payment. Of course, RGRU will continue to be mentioned in your bios as in the premier issue."*

He had also made similar promises to his other writers when recruiting them, again before the Kickstarter began:

> *"We have no problem with our contributors promoting themselves and other ventures they may have."*

Worst of all though, he was now asking to make some changes to the podcast so that there would be no association between any of his drunken online antics like falling off his chair or sticking a joystick down his pants on camera and the clean-cut image that he wanted to build for the magazine. He didn't want to be known as a *"drunken podcaster."*

> *"On another note, it would be my preference to keep RGRU "our" independent podcast. Once we formerly associate it with GameGavel, the business" .... "I think we could come under fire for our less than PC take on things and it could negatively affect the business side of things."*

The Mike Kennedy that they knew had gone, within two forum posts, from "Bro" to, as he would later yell into the phone, *"I'm a CEO Goddammit!."* It was then made very clear to Mike just how the situation would now be handled as UKMike told him:

> *"That means that Retro and GameGavel won't be used as a vehicle for RGR.*
> *That leaves a real bitter taste in my mouth as RGR has continually been used as a vehicle for all GameGavel related projects. Now all of a sudden the favor is not returned with a polite #### you.*
> *What this means is that the relationship between RGR and all GameGavel projects has to be a business one. So if Retro or GameGavel use any RGR material it is on a paid fee basis. That has to work the other way too with any mentions of GameGavel and Retro on RGR being in the guise of paid ads."*

Scott's response was much more brief and would only include two words.

The machinations behind the show were clearly shifting, while at the same time, and in the background, with all of this is going on, they also had the issue of Mike wanting to close down the GameGavel forums so he could switch them to Retro Magazine, which meant migrating the Retro Gaming Roundup content away from there and also the possibility of the three of them organizing Classic Gaming Expo 2014 together.

Scott and UKMike had to make their feelings clear but an all-out war was never really on the cards at that point as they still believed that Mike was their friend and partner in the podcast, they just had to formalize the arrangements between all of the different existing and future projects, some of which were bound to conflict with each other. Mike was beginning to see the seriousness of the situation but he was still on the road with his boss and couldn't talk freely.

> *"Just know I have a nasty old knot in my stomach about this and hope we can move it all forward positively :)"*

What concerned Scott and UKMike was the complete about-face that had happened, almost overnight:

> *"I am thinking of ways to integrate the podcast better. I think RGRU should sponsor the Icon Interview section. Then we can use that as a permanent plug for the podcast. I will work on that."*

had now changed to:

> *"First off, I won't be using the magazine to self-promote any podcasts. It's just not something that is normally done in magazines."*

This heralded the arrival of one of Mike's biggest early mistakes as far as the podcast was concerned: Brandon Justice.

Who is Brandon Justice you might ask? A valid question that was certainly asked of Mike as he tried to have his co-hosts "report to Brandon" as though they were somehow subordinate to him. Brandon Justice was the guy that Mike brought in to be his Editor In Chief for Retro Magazine and he had previously worked for EGM as their Executive Editor until they fired him in mid-2001.

Justice had angered readers with some of his game reviews, in particular his review of the Sega and Gearbox game "Aliens: Colonial Marines" which read like a hit piece but gave a score of 9/10. Some felt that it was an ironic score while others felt that Justice was just not a good writer who could not express his views properly. His employer, Publisher Steve Harris, stated that Brandon Justice was not fired over Colonial Marines, but that it:

> *"[...] is actually related to actions that took place prior to last week."*

The 9/10 score followed a scathing review of the game itself which prompted accusations that EGM had been paid for a favorable review. EGM denied this with the following statement:

> *"This post will hopefully let me set the record straight on how EGM handles reviews in general—and this particular piece specifically.*
>
> *Let me begin by stating that I find it more than slightly ironic that many (if not most) of the critics who have questioned the veracity of Brandon's opinions are doing so by passing erroneous speculation off as fact themselves. EGM wasn't paid off. EGM didn't sell advertisements to Sega or Gearbox or receive any compensation from anyone associated with Aliens: Colonial Marines. EGM didn't attempt to change or influence Brandon's opinions. And EGM has always, and will always, stand behind our reviewers regardless of criticism."*

Some suggested that Justice himself had been paid off rather than EGM or that he had not actually played the game at all before reviewing it. Either way his review and score did not help to endear him to EGM readers or his employers as they did not indeed, as promised;

> *"stand behind our reviewers regardless of criticism."*

Perhaps he wasn't fired because of his review or the scandal surrounding it, perhaps it was because he was not popular among EGM readers and had caused Internet flame wars with his views on pretty much anything other than Xbox. He had angered fans of EA and called anybody who disagreed with him *"retarded"* or *"trolls"* but the final straw perhaps came when he compared Nintendo GameCube fans to Nazis at a skinhead rally. Readers were so angered that they started a petition to get him fired. Whether he was fired, moved or left of his own volition is up for debate but he certainly left EGM. An article on IGN ends with:

> *"[...] we wish our friend and former co-worker the best of luck at his new job and we look forward to the day we can bash his products."*

Well, they didn't have to wait very long as he was now Editor In Chief at Retro Magazine.

Mike had found Brandon and made him an offer to work on the magazine which Brandon jumped at because he was currently working in a Denny's. Throughout his tenure at Retro, Brandon would be paid around $2,000 per month, which was more than even the best paid writers, but he was notoriously unavailable during the morning and would be found in a bar most evenings. Perhaps this is why some questioned his dedication and why the magazine release schedule began to slip.

Steve had earlier questioned Brandon's appointment and again asked Mike if he was sure about what he was doing and Mike was confident, telling Steve not to worry but Steve did worry and did not hit it off with Brandon meaning they did not have a good working relationship or chemistry of any kind. What made it worse was when Steve saw the first issue of the magazine and noticed that Brandon had listed him as merely a "contributor" which Mike explained as:

> *"Well, yeah, you know he is the one making these decisions and these calls right now."*

Steve felt that he deserved at least a creative credit as the magazine had been his idea in the first place and he was not pleased, to say the least, and told Mike that:

> *"if anything, this is my mag I created this. I came up with this idea. You took this idea. Just because you raised all this money and you did this and that, doesn't mean that I'm not entitled to some kind of credit."*

Just like Steve, Mark Kaminski had some initial reservations about Brandon's recruitment but as he wasn't going to be writing any game reviews he felt that they could move forward but;

> *"tread lightly and proceed with caution. We don't want to start off with integrity issues. I'm anxious to hear from you."*

Having earlier caused some resentment with Mark over financial arrangements, Mike now chose to start bringing in new names in highly placed roles, however imaginary, and now both Mark and Brandon were feeling the pinch as Mike tried to make his vision clear.

> *"Hey Guys,*
>
> *My mistake, I thought we had all agreed to make Coin-Op Story four pages, but Brandon has said that was not the case and that we had agreed it stayed at six as it was conceded from being the cover story. Ultimately, I will agree with Brandon's decision as ED.*
>
> *Next, since we started this, I have been pulled back and forth between you guys. I've tried to establish some responsibilities for each of us but for some reason this all gets tossed out the window many times in the creation of each issue. Moving forward we have to all agree to let each of us do the jobs we are here to do and respect that all of us are doing what we do for good reason and to help produce the best magazine we can produce. Anything having to do with*

the layout/design and "branding and manufacturing" of the magazine is Mark's domain. Anything having to do with the editorial side of things is Brandon's domain. I, as Publisher have the ability to make decisions over each of your domains and can override anything I feel needs overriding. To date, I have been very happy with everything both of you are doing and have tried to stay out of each of your ways and give you both the freedom to do what each of you does best. [...]

We are half way through and coming off what will probably be a record month for subscription sales. With everything I have on my plates, I have to stay focused on driving promotions, retailers and advertising and can't keep getting side tracked over the little things we often are complaining about. Seriously, let's all just do what we are best at and great things will come!"

Mark was sticking to his guns though:

"I'm not backing down. I didn't start this magazine to give up my voice to Brandon. Good luck to you, please send me my shares. You agreed with me! Today was the deadline for everything to be in final – it doesn't look like it will happen."

In the midst of trying to define roles, Mike was keen to have Tricia's name included in the magazine, despite her not having worked on it, and he tried to find her a place in the credits and the masthead which clearly put Brandon's nose out of joint as Mike put her in a role that Brandon was actually responsible for.

Eager to keep her name in the credits Mike tried to shoehorn her in again:

"I just want to get her in there as she will be part of this if it gets big enough. Mark didn't want her as Photo Director as there were no photos to "direct" this issue.

Let's just add her back in as Photography Director as she will come into play in future issues."

A Photo Director with no photos to direct? The issue would crop up again in March of 2014 when she was yet again removed, having not worked on the magazine and this caused yet another issue between Mike and Mark, aside from the financial ones. Tricia had been boasting to friends that she had her name in a magazine that was on the shelves in Barnes And Noble, but when they looked inside, her name was absent. This sent Tricia into a rage, a rage that she took out on Mike and which Mike took out on Mark.

Mike now had something of a problem. Had he been calling the shots himself where the magazine was concerned, he could have honored the promises that he made to the show and his co-hosts but now that he had "employed" an Editor In Chief, they were calling the shots and running the magazine how they felt it should be run. Again, Mike found himself with a decision to be made. As the owner of the magazine he could have overruled his Editor In Chief but then what would be the point of employing somebody with publishing experience and then not letting them do their job as they saw fit? There was no point in having a dog and barking yourself, so to speak. Either way, he found himself between a rock and a hard place as far as his editorial staff and his co-hosts were concerned.

As the first issue was being planned Scott had an arrangement already made with Mike that his first piece for the magazine would be a deep dive into the technical aspects of the first coin operated arcade game, Computer Space, and Scott recalls that;

> *"Out of the blue this guy named Brandon calls me up and starts telling me what would or would not happen and I didn't even know he was part of the mag. So I filled him in that as part owner of the company that was producing the mag and having a pre-existing agreement on what my contribution would be that this conversation was over."*

Brandon obviously reported this to Mike who then called Scott to start smoothing things over and it was immediately clear that he had been telling a different story to different people but again, without a history, Scott chalked it up to the chaos and the pace of trying to take on such a big project as a first timer, but of course this put Mike in a tricky position and it was one of his own making. He had made promises that he could now no longer keep. He could either back his Editor In Chief or his podcast co-hosts, and as the two had very differing opinions there was no common ground. As Mike likes to do in these situations, he backed his own project, the magazine, and tried to use his sales patter to smooth things over with his co-hosts, *"telling them it was raining while pissing up their backs."* Finally, they began to see that they could no longer take him at his word.

UKMike had this to say with regard to Mike's sudden U-turn on including the podcast in the magazine:

> *"That seems to me like you took those ideas to the retro team and they said no.*
> *[...] If you don't want RGR prevalent in the mag that's up to you, and you've explained why, and we have to respect that.*
> *[...] I agree we should move forward in a positive way if we can and I love our podcast and the relationship we have, but I never did like being the poor relation."*

Scott was in agreement on the matter of the relationship between the podcast and the magazine:

> *"UK (Mike) summed up my thoughts as well, RGR was there backing these (projects) all along and is now the poor cousin. I too surmise that a decision has been made. Discussions about RGR integration have very specifically excluded two thirds of RGR and are in stark contrast to the hype prior to launch. This isn't a matter of diplomacy or explaining it the right way, the shabby treatment of RGR after years of it backing these ventures is just wrong. Its SoCal's domain to run Retro as he sees fit, but on a personal note I would have no enthusiasm for RGR supporting any other ventures from that group."*

We can now begin to see evidence in black and white of what would be the future business-like relationship between Mike's projects and Retro Gaming Roundup, and again he was trying to outline his distancing of himself from it for reasons of imagined respectability:

> *"I am not trying to treat RGRU as the step child here. But (the) fact is it's not under the company umbrella and more importantly our free-wheeling say what we want model could get my business in trouble (IF it is formerly tied to it) and I just can't take the chance at this stage in the game. I am courting outside investors, adding retail partners, etc. and as shitty as it is I think we can all agree we have said things over the years that could be an issue in this respect."*

The new relationship was very clear for all to see and set the tone for another SoCalMike trademark business practice, putting somebody or something at "arm's length" to protect someone else, usually claiming it was them that he was protecting, this would lead to a pivotal moment that hardened the resolve to take down the Retro VGS/Coleco Chameleon venture later.

UKMike sent a powerful response.:

> *"Understood, but that should have been made much clearer and much earlier [...] rather than promising things which you cannot deliver, both offline to us in Skype and online in the podcast. That is our bone of contention, or mine at least, that what was billed before launch is not what has been delivered, and will not be delivered in the future.*
>
> *Moving forwards we now have no misunderstanding. The GG network is how you want to make your living and more power to you for getting off your ass and doing it. Scott and I now realize that in a bind you will side that way and we can move forward with that knowledge.*
>
> *If your involvement with the Podcast causes a problem for yourself or your company, then you have a decision to make, and I think we all know which way you would go. I want to make it very clear that I categorically do not want that to happen as I think the 3 of us do a bang up job together, but it is ultimately your decision. [...]*
>
> *As for changing the show I am dead against making a conscious effort to bow to any peer pressure whether imagined or real. [...]*
>
> *I think it is obvious that we are not going to be the biggest podcast in the world with multi-million dollar advertisers, but at the expense of being able to say what we want rather than tow a company line to keep an advertisers buck, I say we stick with what we have as it works.*
>
> *I would rather be free to enjoy my hobby my way than pay lip service to an advertiser. This is not going to be my job so the money is irrelevant to me at this stage."*

Predictably, Mike Kennedy's response ignored the main issue at hand:

> *"As long as RGRU remains independent and no formal relationship with GG then I have no issue continuing on like normal. We just need to decide on how to*

handle the promotional aspects in either direction. RGRU was kind of always meant to be a personal/hobby venture for me/us and that's how I would like to keep it for the same reasons UK (Mike) mentions.

But, GG has always been the potential money earner and I thought that is why we all agreed to promote it so that one day the potential was there to work full time there, at least for UK and me and grow the company for the stockholders, of which Scott is one.

Let's discuss all this, but cruise business as usual, relocate the forums, look into the EXPO and continue on."

Scott tried to press the point again:

"How about addressing directly and specifically the total absence of these concerns during the rah-rah promo phase. Must be a half dozen times UK or I have pointed to this as the problem and it keeps getting talked around. [...]

Hobby venture or not there was a lot of pom-pom waving and exploitation of RGR with platitudes of it benefiting as a family member and it is not the case after the fact. That matter of trust is far more valuable to me than a stock certificate in anything."

Mike's response was:

"Guys,

We still plan on running "house" adverts for the podcast on the ReadRetro.com website when it goes live, and we still have adverts on GG that anyone who is in their members area sees with a banner – those have been running non-stop for over a year (login to GG and you will see it).

We just aren't saying anything anywhere that would officially tie RGRU with GG/RETRO, and we've never done that anyway. But I will still give it good billing on the website and magazine when it makes sense, just like I used to do on GG. Literally, nothing much has changed. We will have tons of traffic over there so we can expect a good dose of solid promotion for the show."

Which again failed to assuage any argument and skirted around the issues so Scott gave up:

"Whatever. This is pointless.

You're either not seeing it or you're not acknowledging you're seeing it.

Either way I can't be ####ing bothered going around again. Just read back and repeat."

He was quite clear on the way forward though:

Promotion is 1 to 1 in terms of show releases. Retro magazine releases can be published on RGR outlets if the Podcast releases are similarly published.

No mention of GG or Retro on RGR.

RGR funds not to be used for GG or Retro purposes.

Expo Booths won't be shared with GG.

Move the forums.
Move the domain.
Move the site.
Move the e-mail.

Mike Kennedy would later look back on this and blame Mark Kaminski for the U-turn in an audio clip that UKMike called "The Sinking Of The BusMark" when he said:

"I had my hands tied with Mark as he wanted to distance the show from the magazine."

UKMike would sarcastically reply:

"I just didn't tell you that and continued to blither blather so I could continue to use the show for promo."

It became evident that Mike was very clearly communicating that his co-hosts were way down the organizational chart and not dealing with him directly. At this point UKMike and Scott stepped down as writers for Retro and Mark Kaminski tried to mend the rift and bring them back in, not knowing any of the details as to why they had left, he made a very kind and heartfelt request that they return to writing while Mike Kennedy resisted, accusing them of being hotheads.

Having no beef with Mark, they returned for another issue which only served to re-open old wounds as it was again devoid of show content and Scott's article was heavily edited and had important aspects removed.

At this point Scott, UKMike and Willie Culver all bowed out for the final time and did not write for the magazine again. Mike seemed to have no problem with Willie's departure though and *"couldn't axe William fast enough even though Willie was doing work for us."*

Mike was quite clear:

"Just use my name. Also, we need to make sure William is not mentioned in magazine masthead contributor credits.

Thanks :)"

Mark questioned this decision but ultimately, Willie was out. Scott looks back on writing for the magazine quite whimsically when he says that:

"Trying to see it from Brandon's side he calls this guy up to give an assignment and gets told to go #### himself!"

While not exactly telling Brandon to do the same, Steve Sawyer had by now turned his back on his hijacked creation and walked. Meanwhile, Brandon had some opinions on the deal that Mike had done with Play N Trade in that they were quite non-committal and promised everything without really promising anything. Their e-mail conversations went back and forth and there was no guarantee of anything at the end of it and Brandon wanted to move away from them and do a deal with somebody more willing to commit such as Geek Box.

In fact, Mike did a deal on Issue 1 with Play N Trade in that they would distribute the magazine to their stores around the U.S.A. but Mike was dealing with their head office, not the stores directly, many of which were franchises, so when Mike shipped the magazines to them and sent them invoices, they had no knowledge of what they were or why they had received them and a lot of the stores simply threw them away. He had also given Play N Trade exclusivity so that no other store within a fifty-mile radius of a Play N Trade carrying the magazine were allowed to sell it. Apparently, it no longer mattered that they were *"a small fry operation whose VP drove an old Hyundai."*

Mark Kaminski's opinion on the matter was: *"We took a bath on Issue 1 and maybe a thousand issues went unpaid for."*

Mike contacted some of the stores and some of them agreed to carry, and pay for, the magazine and some did not, so he continued to deal with the stores that were on board and forgot about the others. Again, the problem with this was that they had a sixty-day retention, so they didn't pay for the magazine for two months which meant that Mike had to find the money to print the next issue before he had been paid for the previous one and that was a problem.

From around Issue 4, Mike did not have the funds to continue printing the magazine and he had to turn to his uncle, Lloyd Fritzmeier. Fritzmeier is the CEO of Franchise Operations for Arby's and to allow his nephew to be able to print his magazine he would loan Mike $17,000, then after sixty days once Mike had the money in from the stores he would repay the loan but with an interest rate of $2,000. Yes, that's $2,000 interest on a $17,000 loan over a couple of months. No wonder Lloyd was rich. Mark Kaminski spoke to Mike about this and advised him that he would be able to get a much lower interest rate with a business loan from a bank, or maybe even a loan shark, but Mike would not look for alternate sources and told Mark *"No, that's what it would cost."*

Maybe the $2,000 was a way for Mike to take money out of the company or maybe it was a genuine deal he had made with his uncle, but either way, it was bleeding money from the coffers of the magazine, money the magazine did not have and could not afford to lose.

One of the frustrations that Brandon had was that Mike was paying people to write for the website and this didn't bring in any value to the property or increase subscriptions or ad revenue as the world did not need another Kotaku, but one of these writers was David Giltinan. Mike described David to Mark as a kid who was down on his luck and Mike wanted to help him out but it may have been David who introduced Mike to Daniel Kayser with whom Mike replaced Brandon Justice as Editor In Chief.

With Brandon gone and replaced by Daniel Kayser, who was also offered shares in lieu of payment, Mark Kaminski's days were also numbered as he still had an ongoing financial discussion with Mike and of course had greatly upset Tricia by removing her name from the magazine credits. He was now surplus to requirements. Not only could Mike remove the headache he was getting from Mark via Tricia, he believed he could also avoid having to pay Mark the large sums that he was due if he fired him.

Mark had now seen the writing on the wall and on February 20, 2015, would try to negotiate his financial package with Mike again:

> *"With Year One officially behind us, we need to finalize what the compensation package will look like moving forward before I can continue any more work for GameGavel LLC effective immediately. Once we have some signed paperwork I will resume work. Thanks for your considerations. [...]*
>
> *I'd like to get something ironed out before Monday so I can get some work in this weekend. Are you open at all tomorrow to discuss? Thanks!"*

Mike responded later that day with:

> *"Sure. Were you happy with the $1K/Month in lieu of any commissions? If it turns out we hit it big sometime throughout the year and can afford to increase this than we can discuss if and when that time comes. This would be a minimum beginning this month."*

Mark again pointed Mike back to their earlier agreement, though why he expected to get paid at all when Mike had lost his Social Security Number twice already is unclear:

> *"I'm looking to be tied to the success of the company. I would propose my compensation is $1,000 minimum per month or I would be guaranteed 20% of all company Ad sales + $0.25 per subscription to RETRO whichever is the greater number. I will create Ads, Marketing, social media maintenance, web seo and layout and design of RETRO magazine. After the completion of 3 issues I will be granted +1% of the overall company and after 6 issues I would be granted an additional +1% stake, so after issue 12 I will have a total of 10% stake in the company. This contract will be effective for the term of 12 months or until issue 12 has been completed. Either party can walk away with a 60 day notice. [...]*
>
> *What are your concerns with the option for the 20% + $0.25 per issue if the sales shoot up to exceed the $1000 per month min? [...]*
>
> *Mike I can respect what you said, but at the end of the day, I don't have nearly as much skin in the game as you do. I could drop down to the $1000 or 10% of Ad sales + $0.25 per magazine (whichever is greater) for a 12 month term with payment on the 20th each month* with a 30 day window for either party to cancel the contract with the +1% after 3 issues and +1% after 3 more issues.*
>
> *Under this model, you'd have to sell more than $10k in ads to exceed the $1000 min.*
>
> *While I'd like to continue working on this project, I've put in a lot of time and effort for little pay, taken time from my family and passed on other projects that would have been more beneficial financially. I conceived the brand, I've paved*

the groundwork and put in an incredible amount of work for 18 months. I think it's only fair to be tied to any potential success.

Since there was some cross-over we can skip the Feb commission check and start with payments on the 20th each month. First payment would start March 20th.

It sounds like if we don't hit some numbers in the next month, there won't be an issue 8 or April commission check to worry about :)

Let me know.
Thanks
Mark

**If the 20th of the month falls on a weekend, the payment will be issued on the Friday prior to the weekend."*

Not giving up easily, Mike countered:

"I would like to stick you at $1,000/month and no commissions AND if we tie into something big that significantly increases our revenue during this 12 month period we will renegotiate the $1K/month and increase it as that revenue will allow to be more in line with what you should be making. I would also follow your 2% ownership earning but will have to say that will be the max I can extend moving forward (10% Total). And I would need your design services potentially on the GG and console side of things to be included as well."

Either not recognizing or choosing to ignore the strength of Mark's feelings on the matter, Mike returned to his sales patter and blither blather to try and smooth things over until he could replace Mark.

"Just that Daniel's main income in the beginning, when he and I decide to activate it, is 30% of the ad sales up to $5,000 and 50% of ad sales $5,001 and over. So far, though he is like me, letting what income we have stay in to pay the writers first. The company will need at least 50% of ad sales to help cover its costs and expenses. Like I said, should this thing all take a turn upward we can renegotiate. For now you and I as owners, not workers, have to be as conservative as possible because we are running out of $ fast. In fact, I transferred $7,000 from my 401K into our account today to offset printing/mailing costs for #6. That is about all I have left to personally put into this at the moment so something big needs to happen soon. Still waiting on the $2K from Zenith, hopefully coming this week and just sold another $1K full pager to Paradox for Pillars release in March. Let's stay positive and keep working this best we can until something big happens."

If that didn't work, there were always threats to fall back on and Mark could always *"just forfeit all the work I've done for free."*

"Mark,

Please call me as soon as you can this morning. We have to resolve this, this afternoon so I know what I need to do to move forward and potentially find a new layout and design person of (sic) you choose to break our contract and walk out of the situation.

I spoke with an attorney friend of mine before talking about this with my corporate attorney (which I am really trying to avoid) and according to him, since we have a signed contract it is binding and I have no obligation to give you anything more than what we agreed upon and signed.

Secondly, he said since the Kickstarter campaign and campaign goal/budget was designed around this signed contract and successfully funded that we have an obligation to fulfill the rewards to subscribers who have already paid for the subscription and that by you walking out and breaking the contract you leave me with a liability of possibly having to hire a layout and design person for the going rate, and this was something that wasn't built into the budget of the Kickstarter campaign and I could seek legal action against you for those payments if you break the contract.

So after laying awake all night thinking of our options I really only see two:

1) We agree to commit to create the six issues sold through the Kickstarter campaign based on our original contract and you earn that 5% and 30% share and have an opportunity to be paid for your services at the going rate once GameGavel, LLC is able to pay it.

OR

2) You walk away from the signed contract and forfeit the 5% equity in GameGavel, LLC AND the 30% proceeds from the sale of the magazine should it ever happen. I will agree to not seek any damages from you regarding the layout and design work and will pick up the pieces and negotiate with someone else to takeover that work. I will also rename the magazine and utilize a different logo style.

Either way, I need an answer by noon today so I can get on with the process of getting this magazine out the door and fulfilling the contract I have with the 2,345 backers who have paid to get their magazine(s)."

Discussions and ill-feeling continued but they did indeed keep working, if not staying positive, until it was time to find funds for the magazine's second year. Some were surprised when a Year 2 Kickstarter was announced as Mike had been quoting healthy sales numbers and subscriptions and had also exceeded his funding goal in Year 1 yet still he was going back to crowd funding for Year 2. That wasn't a huge surprise to those close to him who knew what a financial disaster the magazine had become and whom he had told that he had bought himself a new pinball machine with some of the Kickstarter funds.

It came as a surprise to Mark though as he questioned the wisdom of raising magazine prices for the coming year but Mike justified it by saying that he intended to increase the page count and only raise the price for Year 2 backers, not existing backers. He was also once again on the promotion trail and trying to build enthusiasm for Year 2 which was fast approaching and he sent out a promotional blast on September 29, 2014:

"It's hard to believe that nearly one year ago, the team here at RETRO hit the crowdfunding trail on Kickstarter towards our eventual launch. And thanks to the help of backers like you, we're now in the home stretch of year one, with only two issues remaining for most early adopters.

We've learned a lot in the last year, and are prepping a shiny new Kickstarter campaign for RETRO year two, where we plan to deliver a bigger, better RETRO for you, our fans and loyal supporters. We can't say enough about how important each and every one of you has been to the success of RETRO Magazine, as you all account for our single biggest group of subscribers.

Year two is nearly upon us, and we've got big plans that will require a higher subscription price going forward, but as an added "thank you" to those of you who've supported us out of the gate, we're happy to announce we've put together a limited-time early-bird offer to all original backers for a year-two subscription at the same price you paid last year ($30 delivered in the USA or $36 internationally)!

If you're interested in taking advantage of the promotion, all we ask is that you resubscribe in the next two weeks (this offer ends 10/7/14) as we prep for our year two Kickstarter launching mid-October. By resubscribing now, it will help us determine our minimum goals for the campaign in year two, as well as help us set the lowest bar possible for a host of planned improvements, such as a larger page count, occasional poster inserts, the addition of adding more of your favorite gaming journalists/personalities and increased trade show presence and advertising throughout 2014 and 2015.

The more year-one backers who commit now, the more of these and many more ideas have to come to fruition, so we hope you guys take advantage and sign up today!"

A price increase was in the offing and it wasn't very clear where all of the money had gone because there were constant complaints, largely ignored by Mike, about magazines not being delivered and writers not getting paid. There were more who were keen to contribute to the magazine and also the website, whether Mike could afford to pay them or not:

"Hey Guys,
Just a reminder, I am not really looking to add any more writers at this point unless they are big names and will be a big draw. Web can't support any new writers at this point. And wouldn't be fair to pay the others and not this guy. We can field these and file away for later, but don't lead anyone on at this point."

Mike largely blamed Brandon for the fact that magazine issues were running late and not being shipped on time. In fact, the schedule had slipped pretty badly, and Mike had by now grown tired of working with Brandon, hence his replacement by Daniel Kayser. It would also fit the growing pattern of getting any ideas and work out of people for little or no recompense and bringing in new, more enthusiastic staff who would accept shares in the worthless GameGavel LLC.

Mike would describe it as anything but worthless and actually claimed that it was worth more than Retro at this point but it is a fact that it was losing money. He had also talked many times to Scott and UKMike about his *"web guru"* that had built the site and code for him when in actual fact he was just licensing it and didn't even own that.

The GameGavel site had been running for a few years and should have continued to grow as it had in the early days but Mike had completely mismanaged it and had given away so many free seller accounts that it generated no income other than through ads. In fact, out of approximately 120 completed auctions during February/March of 2014, 90 of them had been Mike selling issues of Retro Magazine. Of the remaining 30 or so completed auctions, 80% of them were run by sellers with free accounts so it generated no income at all for that period at least and had cost money to run once he had paid the monthly license fee.

In fact, Mike's other sites all needed some work on them and they also had to find a way to distribute the digital copies of the magazine without them being easily pirated but allowing genuine purchasers to access them in multiple ways. Initially this had been set up by Mark Kaminski but had been almost cobbled together with GameGavel requiring one login, Retro requiring a second login and the digital magazines requiring a third login via Digital Genius. This was largely done to save having to pay Apple thirty cents per digital copy for users on iOS, so Mark began looking for a programmer to do the work as Matt Casey was no longer on the scene.

The first person to respond to the ad was called Mike Fuqua who Mark found initially to be a little odd to work with but it turned out that Fuqua had some health issues and was agoraphobic, but he did some great programming work. He wrote a system that could distribute the digital issues with a single login and which would embed the user's name into each page to protect them. He also did some fixing work on GameGavel and GamerSpots as well, but the problem that Mike Kennedy had with Mike Fuqua was that he wanted to be paid up front for a lot of his work and would not work for worthless GameGavel shares or promises of wealth in the future, he wanted money and Mike didn't have it to give him so Mark again found a programmer by the name of George Pople from Pittsburgh.

George Pople was working as a freelancer at the time and was, according to Mark, a real smart cookie who reverse engineered what Fuqua had done and they were able to use their own existing databases to help distribute the magazine digitally. Again, George wanted paying for his work but the work was crucial and it went ahead.

Soon after, Mike introduced his new *"Tech Guru"* a man by the name of Sean Robinson. Even when Sean was on the scene they still used George for some work that Sean was unable to do, or said he had done but hadn't.

Sean spoke to Mark a lot as they worked together and he would tell Mark some weird and wonderful stories about how he was one of the first fifteen employees at Earthlink and that he was the early voice talent on Homestar Runner which was an early Internet flash show with a cult following and would do impressions for Mark over the phone. Mark saw this as an opportunity for publicity and urged Sean to do something with the voice but Sean would never do anything in public. Mark looks back on it and says *"I should have known but I was a dumbass and I believed him."*

Sean was given the remit of maintaining and improving all of the GameGavel properties and was given access to the backend of Mike's websites and systems. It is doubtful whether he actually did improve anything and when questioned would say that he was *"doing a bunch of database work"* which later would allegedly include *"installing backdoor access"* and *"a free plugin to prevent black-hat, fake Chinese traffic"* which had been driven to the site on purpose, and with Mike's knowledge, to boost traffic numbers and to get more web advertising. Sean was unaware of this at the time and was blocking it.

Sean was also given access to the GameGavel forums and this is one of the issues that had haunted the Retro Gaming Roundup hosts as there were continual issues with the level of access that people had. There was a private forum area that the three show hosts would use to plan episodes and top ten lists for future shows but these began to show up for other forum members who were not supposed to be able to see it. This was reported to them several times and passed on to Mike who presumably had Sean "fix" the issue only for it to recur and be reported again.

It was also around this time that Mike began to have some problems with his laptop and Sean told him that he would be able to fix it so Mike gave it to him. Sean did indeed fix it but it is possible that he took a complete image of Mike's hard drive. Everything that Mike had on his laptop, his whole empire, his current workings, his future plans, everything, Sean could have access to and could later use the material to embarrass Mike during the Coleco Chameleon fiasco if he needed to.

Even if Sean had managed to get the GameGavel site to work as Mike wanted and even if it had started to generate some income, what Mike did not make public knowledge was that he had a $60,000 rider for *"management services"* and this would have been taken out of the LLC and paid to Mike before anybody else got a penny. Perhaps this was why he was so keen that Retro not be a separate entity and that his staff got shares in GameGavel rather than Retro, and this is the deal that Daniel Kayser was brought on board with, so who was Daniel Kayser?

Kayser is a writer and presenter and is perhaps best known for his work on GameTrailers TV and GameTrailers.com. He is also the Founder and Editor-In-Chief of industry blog EpicBattleAxe.com as well as having written for GameDaily.com, IGN and Hardcore Gamer. Having been around and covering the games industry for quite a while he is quoted as saying:

> *"My passion for gaming is only surpassed by my desire to take the industry forward through the entertaining and informative content I seek to create."*

Once on board Daniel sent out an email to the Retro staff and it included further evidence that Sean Robinson was still on the scene but not always getting things done.

"Good morning, gang! CONGRATS on crossing the $40K mark and thanks again for all of the effort in getting the AreYouRETRO page live! Sean, are you still experiencing issues with the Survey Monkey poll? If so, is there anything I can help with?"

Mark was also still promoting the magazine and trying to garner further interest by occasionally logging into Mike's email account and sending out emails on his behalf as he had not followed up on several leads that Mark had sent to him, including one at Nerd Block.

"Here is a quick high level breakdown of what I believe our strategy for the next 4 weeks should be: [...]

Focus on getting into a box at some capacity: Loot crate, Nerd Block, Booty Bin, Geek Fuel."

He sent a reminder to Mike before taking action himself:

"Subject: Reach out to these folks – they do a specific Game themed box www.nerdblock.com"

Nerd Block did reply to the email Mark sent on Mike's behalf and he urged Mike to jump on it and set up a requested chat with them:

"I think you should attack it today. Like I mentioned Friday they are at least at 30k subs.

Might get us a nice little bump and buy us time to get into Loot crate deal. Let me know if you hear anything."

He didn't hear anything because Mike never followed up on it and these are the same *"Management Services"* that were going to cost GameGavel $60,000 but were getting it nowhere.

Mark also became Mike's personal assistant in that when logged in to Mike's e-mail account he would set up podcast appearances for Mike to help publicize Retro, and not surprisingly, these are the ones that Mike followed up on. These were easy pickings, he loved to talk and go through his sales pitch and would take any opportunity he could to wax lyrical about his wonderful magazine. He made quite a few podcast appearances through 2013 and appeared on several shows including Arcade Outsiders, DJ Grandpa, Second Opinions, Game Stitch, I Heart Podcasts, The Intellivisionaries and All Games. He still had to be prompted to set up these interviews though from time to time:

"Date: Tue, Oct 22, 2013 at 11:24 AM
Subject: Email this guy right now please
To: Mike Kennedy <socalmike@gamegavel.com>"

Mark pursued the Nerd Block deal on Mike's behalf because they could potentially sell 30,000 copies of the magazine to Nerd Block, a subscription service similar to Geek Box or Loot Crate where you can subscribe to a monthly box full of goodies related to your chosen interests and they would typically contain T-Shirts and other merchandise.

Mike had an interesting take on this particular deal though as he felt that those 30,000 one-off copies of Retro that would go to Nerd block were separate to the regular issues of the magazine and therefore he did not owe Mark anything for securing them or as a percentage on the deal.

All this time that Mike was in podcast promotion mode and Mark was managing his e-mails there were also messages about subscribers not receiving copies of the magazine that they paid for and several video game stores that wanted to carry the magazine on their shelves but never received any inventory that they could sell. Scott and UKMike would occasionally receive these emails as a last resort when people who had unsuccessfully tried to contact Mike through the magazine site resorted to using the podcast site instead. These were passed on to Mike but still there were more coming through all the time as Mike seemed to not really be doing very much at all to improve the reputation and distribution of the magazine. Bear in mind that he already had people's money from Kickstarter and perhaps he felt that he didn't really need to look after his customers.

> *"On another front, I hate to bring this up, as I really do feel like I'm pestering you guys, but I never received a print copy of the magazine. I personally bought a subscription as a gift to someone for Christmas, but never received my comp issues to my house.*
>
> *Also, (again, hate to be an annoyance here), but I only received payment for my very first article that I wrote back in November. I'm attaching two invoices; one for the two unpaid articles and a new one for my most recent submission for issue 8 I sent to Daniel March 3."*

Writers and customers like this, often sent via the Retro Gaming Roundup site, were either completely ignored or became the victim of Mike's sales pitches and urged not to worry, everything was OK while behind the scenes it was rather different.

Other writers were also experiencing similar issues and even from the outside, Steve Sawyer was also aware of money problems surrounding the magazine and he began to find out details that Mike was being accused of not paying people which he found hard to believe, bearing in mind the funding that the magazine had received for its Year 1 Kickstarter campaign, $75,859.

> *"Really, $70,000 plus where he's saying he only needed 50 to really do it, to do it like full-scale grand opening Super Bowl style and we aced that and we have 20K over and he's saying, he doesn't have money to pay people. To date for that magazine, I made I think less than 700 bucks when I'm the dude who like handed him the idea for the thing and then I find out he's stiffing Pat Contri."*

Pat Contri (Pat The NES Punk) was indeed being "stiffed" by Mike who had contacted him to see if he would be interested in writing for the magazine when it was Kickstarted and Pat said that he would as Mike told him that he would be able to write about pretty much *"whatever I wanted."* That turned out to be somewhat true, but after some drama. Pat was offered $100 per article, which he was happy with until he discovered that other writers were being paid a lot more, especially as Pat's name was one of those that had been used heavily during the promotional phase for the magazine.

Organization behind the scenes seemed to be haphazard at best as Mike had promised one thing but Pat was mainly dealing with Brandon who was not easy to work with and was promising something else. In fact, in addition to Pat's name being used heavily by the Retro team during promotion, Pat had also been using his own social media feeds to help raise awareness among his own fans whom he felt had been done a disservice when he was not offered an article for the first issue. Pat felt that if any of his fans had signed up and backed the Kickstarter, they would be disappointed not to see him included in Issue 1. In fact, he even had a fight on his hands to be included in Issue 2. That would have been unacceptable to him because it would have meant him being absent from at least a third of the Year 1 issues when at least some of his fans were backing it to see his work in print.

Pat's experiences with Brandon echoed those of others involved as he found him overall to be a poor communicator and somewhat dismissive. He also gave poor direction and was asking Pat to write articles about things like "exploding barrels in video games" which Pat felt did not play to his strengths and his area of expertise, the Nintendo Entertainment System, and he appealed to the team to let him do what he did best. That was, after all, why he had been brought into the writing team.

Brandon would also give very short notice to Pat when he needed an article, sometimes he was only given a week to write a featured article and Brandon would either be late with communications or would not communicate at all, disappearing for weeks at a time and not responding to emails or messages on Skype.

Finally, though, Pat got his articles into the magazine but unfortunately, after his first article, his by-line was not included so readers did not know who it had been written by and he found that odd at best but also quite unprofessional. Even when he pointed out the omissions to Brandon his by-line was never included again after that first article. What's more, the quality of the editing of his articles was poor, as some of the edits were *"totally incorrect"* and even contained grammatical and spelling errors that were not present in the originals that he had submitted.

Once Brandon had moved on, Pat dealt with Daniel Kayser which really didn't help as there were no suggested solutions to the problems that Pat had, other than a wish for *"starting out fresh"* which did nothing to convince him that things would improve and in fact, re-affirmed his feelings that he had no wish to continue writing for Retro.

Ignorant or dismissive of Pat's feelings, the team used his name in promotion for the Year 2 Kickstarter campaign but without his permission and he could only see things going one way, down. Not confident in the magazine's ability to fund itself, a feeling he shared with many others, he took stock of the situation. The magazine could not fund itself, there was a lack of professionalism, he did not have a good working relationship with anybody at the top and some of the payments for his articles came in months late, sometimes two issues behind.

Even from the outside looking in, he could see that the issues were at the very top, and with no changes at the helm, things would not improve. If they were going to get better, they would have done so in Year 1, yet the same problems kept arising and all he was offered was a chance to start out fresh.

Though he felt that the magazine looked good in its layout and had some good content in it, he felt that the content was becoming something different to what was sold to backers during the Kickstarter campaigns, again a feeling he shared with many others. The magazine had been crowdfunded twice based on its content covering retro games, yet now, with the arrival of Daniel, it was covering new titles with a retro twist and many felt that It had lost its roots and should have remained purely retro. Pat's time as a writer was *"mostly frustrating and a waste of time"* and he won't be putting *"Former writer for Retro"* on his resume any time soon.

It was during this phase of not paying writers and shipping Kickstarter perks that Mike came out with the phrase *"The dog who barks the loudest gets fed first"* which left his team bemused because they were obviously keen to send out the merchandise that had been promised as stretch goals on Kickstarter but which were not yet materializing.

> *"(It) was promised on the KS – so we have to order them today and I need shirt sizes. You need to ship both posters together with stickers and buttons to save on shipping Mike."*

Behind the scenes, things were not getting any better, there had been changes of staff and still there were problems. Presumably because Mike was still making a lot of decisions and "running" things. Mark was still bashing his head against a wall over the finances and his recompense for all of the work he was doing with the magazine, including work that Mike should have been doing but was clearly not. Mike was too busy coming up with hair-brained schemes and ideas for new ventures and getting tied up in thinking about those instead of fixing the issues with the magazine, so Mark was beginning to seriously doubt his ability to stick to the task.

> *"Brilliant thought process. Seriously, I was trying to run a magazine, get strategic partnerships, wrangle our EIC that was always MIA, and handle customer service while he was busy thinking about the "next big thing." Keep in mind, Mike was unavailable or not allowed to talk business after 5pm PST weekdays and generally unavailable on weekends because it was wine tasting time or dog grooming day. Mike liked to position himself as a serial entrepreneur. I've never known an entrepreneur that put in so little time and resources. He was very smart in that aspect of getting a team of other people to create his brand*

and business. The best businesses are the ones that can operate without you, but this was not the case with RETRO. I'm almost certain half of his ideas were birthed like Athena from the head of Zeus, but from Mike hitting his head falling off a toilet drunk on wine while reading one of his wife's women's lifestyle magazines."

Distractions like this were driving the magazine nowhere and by now Daniel had been in situ long enough to realize that the situation was pretty bad and attempted to rally the ever changing troops with a group-wide e-mail.

"Hey guys, after the Loot Crate call I've been doing a lot of thinking. We need to discuss RETRO, it's goals, and our game plan ASAP.

The fact is that we're all over the place. I've come on board to steer this thing in the right direction and am proud of what we've been able to do to get organized and that we have a clear creative vision thus far, but as a business, this thing is a flat out mess.

We all know that it's make or break time as we're running out of funds to produce the magazine. In order to do that, we need to decide what RETRO is, what it does better than anyone else, and how everything we do focuses on accomplishing a single goal THAT WE KNOCK OUT OF THE PARK before we move on to additional projects and biting off more than we can chew.

What separates a GOOD IDEA from a SUCCESSFUL BUSINESS is having the ability to execute. There's a reason why the Loot Crates of the world take time to make decisions – because they have to focus on the one thing they do better than anyone else and make sure everything they do compliments that goal/ image. Shotgunning ideas out into the world and hoping one of them sticks isn't the way to go.

The reality is that RETRO isn't even an organized business at this point. It's still a fan product forged from a Kickstarter campaign that, while a good idea, woefully miscalculated its cost in ensuring it had the ability to deliver what was promised. [...]

You know I believe in RETRO as I've put my name behind it and dedicated the last three months or so to working on this project for free, but the reality is that I've got about another month before I'll simply have to find a job to pay the bills and do this on the side until it can do the same. That said, I do believe we can fix this ASAP if we focus on our strengths and ASK THE TOUGH QUESTIONS that need leadership and answers ASAP!"

Daniel also had a haunting message about what was to become another major headache for the organization, and I use the term "organization" loosely.

"We've got WAY TOO many things going on, including pushing a console that has the potential to alienate a large section of our audience and the people we work with – which is an entire other project that needs to be done RIGHT. We've got too many people involved in RETRO right now for its own good. We need to FOCUS on a single goal – getting the magazine to be profitable in both digital and print forms – and then grow from there. Things are really a mess right now IMO."

More on the console later, but Daniel had spookily predicted trouble down the road.

> *"We currently have a backlog of inventory just sitting there. This is an investor's DREAM – to have inventory that costs nothing to maintain and has current value at anywhere from $1-$3 per copy! If we focused our efforts, we can drive traffic to the site via advertising, sponsored newsletters, and with the new theme fan-targeted outreach. Folks should arrive at the site, see nothing but the available issues, preview an issue, see how awesome it is, and pay to download the whole thing. Digital back issues for $3 each or buy a full year digital subscription for $10. We up-sell them to the subscription at checkout ("Thanks for your interest in this issue of RETRO! Pay $7 more now and get a full year's subscription!") That's what would make us unique. We have no business having daily news, features, forums, THREE DIFFERENT logins and God knows whatever else until we can do THAT and totally kick its ass. [...]*
>
> *The world doesn't need another Joystiq, Kotaku, Polygon, etc. Hell, those places are closing up shop. Why are we copying them with our website? LET'S SIMPLY SELL THE BEST LOOKING MAGAZINE WITH THE BEST CONTENT AT AN INCREDIBLY VALUABLE COST TO THE CONSUMER!!!"*
>
> *"Apologies if this comes off harsh, but I'm sick as a dog right now (I caught what my kids had) and we all know that if we don't do something NOW, we won't have the opportunity to work on this project much longer."*

Clearly this is aimed every bit at Mike who was making some terrible business decisions. He clearly had a staff around him that were willing the magazine to succeed, had ideas about how to make it do so and were attempting to steer him towards doing that, if not outright doing it for him, none more so than Mark of course.

> *"I'm on board. I realize we need a Hail Mary pass. I agree the website with ads only makes us 300 or so a month and 90% isn't relevant to what we are seeking to do. I can personally scrap the site but I have a big project this week that takes me thru Thursday. Most of this lies in ad buys via Google, podcasts, social media as I see it.*
>
> *Obviously we need to catch a whale in the next 2 months -and I don't know how we spear one. Is it a partnership with destructoid in the interim? Maybe a play with arcade block gets us another month or two of financing? Can we make a push with mighty number nine to give away our issue 1 digital and hope to convert a % of their base? Do we give issue #6 to everyone at PAX? I don't know.*
>
> *Think big and I'll back you Daniel!*
>
> *What is the follow up with loot crate? Can we put a postcard in their next Box asap to judge engagement? We have the funds to cover that."*

Daniel was in agreement:

> *"All great thoughts and necessary ones as well. We just need to think about what we can focus on and how we can push everything towards that singular goal.*
>
> *Revamping the site, focusing on digital back issue sales (which costs us nothing but advertising), and a Nerd Block partnership or some other partnership to keep us afloat for the next few months? That can work.*

I feel that focus is what is needed most right now and we need to have a plan on paper to execute. If we can't execute on that, we have to re-asses all of RETRO's goals. You've gotta walk before you can run."

Mike was again under pressure from Mark for not paying writers and for not fulfilling the Kickstarter stretch goals such as the shirts which were by now over a year late, having been shipped to Mike some eight months previously.

"Mike, it's time to give the books a hard look and understand what's been promised to subscribers so that we can account for it. We also need to have a plan in place to ensure our contributors and core members are being paid on time. We can't have overdue bills with these folks so goals at least need to be set to accomplish that."

While Daniel and Mark were trying to steer the rudderless ship, others were busy behind the scenes duplicating each other's work, treading on each other's toes and confusing their roles a little as they tried to save money on printing costs by having them *"cut our paper quality in half and instead of putting mags in bags, to sticker label them and mail bundles to stores not in boxes but with a plastic zip tie around them... I totally lost it."*

Caught in the headlights, Mike reacted to a situation created by Paul Wylie:

"Hey Paul,

I need to make it clear Mark Kaminski is our point man for the printer. His twelve year relationship with QUAD and Ali is why we are getting rates 35% lower than what we should be getting in the first place. He is also our Creative Director and should remain the person responsible for putting out the magazine we committed to making in our Kickstarter. And that is a premier quality magazine. Let's just all be sure of our costs and make sure they are factored in to our overall revenue model/selling/subscription prices. If you need printing pricing, quotes or have any questions or concerns regarding the printing feel free to email or call Mark directly to get the information and he will continue talking with Ali."

Mark chimed in:

"Please direct any questions you have for the printer to me and I will have them answered for you. I am the sole contact for Quad."

However, if there was a song sheet at all, not everybody was singing from the same one:

"Mike please call me ASAP. I just got off (the phone) with Ali.

Paul again just called her and told her different instructions.

I'm not sure what his issue is here Mike, and I still have not so much as had a phone call from this guy.

It's completely embarrassing and unprofessional to have Paul calling Ali giving her different instructions than what I've requested AGAIN.

I don't care if Paul wants to ask the printer what color the sky is, ALL communications need to run through me, period. It goes for the entire organization. I'll get him answers to whatever we would like. If it's financial, I'll get you CC'ed on it.

If Paul wants to add value right now, have him do one of these 3 things:

1. *Grow our subscription numbers*
2. *Sell advertising*
3. *Get us investor money*

Thanks
Mark"

Hassles like this, the situation with the lack of money and of course the strength of feeling from Tricia about her name continually being removed from the credits came to a head and, after further discussion on the matters, Mike and Mark had reached an impasse, so Mike decided the easiest course of action was to let Mark go *"because I got him a deal with nerd block and he didn't want to pay me anymore, and I stressed him out, and the shit with removing his wife's name from the masthead."*

Still, even after his dismissal, Mark was trying to help out people that were owed money, himself included of course, and would reply to people still chasing payments from Mike.

"Mike and I had creative differences so I'm no longer at RETRO. I can't talk about the situation per my lawyer until the end of the month. Keep me posted on the 30th if you aren't paid by then. Seriously sorry about this."

What Mike did not realize in firing Mark is that he did not have any of the files that Mark had used to create the magazine and he tried to strong arm Mark into turning them over to him on Saturday April 11, 2015.

While his e-mail signature cited him as "Mike Kennedy, Founder & President, RETRO Media Network" his notice to Mark cited him differently:

"TO: Mark Kaminski
FR: Mike Kennedy, President GameGavel, LLC
RE: Release of Services

Dear Mark,

As of today, April 11, 2015, your services are no longer required as RETRO Videogame Magazine Creative Director with GameGavel, LLC DBA RETRO Media Network.

You have until 12:00PM (PST) Monday, April 13, 2015 to turn over all digital assets involved with the creation of RETRO Videogame Magazine including page design templates and logo artwork. This property can be submitted digitally or if that is not possible due to file sizes, we will agree on another form of media to contain and send this property. If this property needs to be sent by other means we will extend the due date accordingly by a few days.

After this property is received by GameGavel, LLC DBA RETRO Media Network, I will send you the certificate indicating the 8% minority ownership of GameGavel, LLC DBA RETRO Media Network. Until you have turned over this property of GameGavel, LLC DBA RETRO Media Network you will not receive the certificate and the offer will become null and void.

Mike Kennedy,
President, GameGavel, LLC DBA RETRO Media Network"

Mark was now gone from the project and Mike had nothing. He didn't have the templates that Mark created, he did not even have access to the readretro.com website any longer and there could be no further updates to the site. In fact, Mike had no option but to turn his attention to the sister site shopreadretro.com which he had recently registered on March 20, 2015.

His disgruntled former staff were also now beginning to talk to each other, in spite of Mike's efforts to the contrary, and they soon found out that they all had a lot of shared experiences in common so it wasn't long before somebody reached out to Steve Sawyer:

"I think this was right around the time he was starting to talk about the (Retro) VGS and I got a message from one of those two people, Mark or Brandon. I'm not going to say which, but I will say that it was really funny because when I was raising such a stink about like, "Dude, I've helped bring this thing into life and all that" neither of those two dudes wanted to stick up for me at all, because I'm sure like at that point in time they're like, "If I can kind of put this guy lower in the totem pole, forget about it." but now, they're coming to me crying like poor mouth, "Mike really screwed us over." and I'm like, "Yeah, I know. I told you so."

Not only had Mike lost control of his site but he also had no money to carry on paying for the magazine, its staff and its upkeep and he also had to try and take back control of the empire as he had given so much of it away in lieu of payments. Most of the owners were his friends and family who had no interest in helping to run things and had been silent partners but some of them were disgruntled "employees" who were in no mood to help him out of the hole that he had dug himself into.

His other problem was that he was using the shares that they had to his advantage by saying that they were of value, or soon would be, but in fact he had made a huge blunder right from the outset when he had initially registered the LLC. He had registered it as member controlled instead of manager controlled which meant that he did not have any control of the runaway mine cart and he needed to change things within the LLC.

As usual with Mike, this was not made clear and he attempted to do it surreptitiously as he tried his sales patter to explain it away as a clerical error and asked all of them to sign a release document allowing him to regain control and to change the entity to manager controlled.

The situation was as follows:

Entity Name: GAMEGAVEL LLC
Entity Number: 201029410278
Date Filed: 10/20/2010
Status: ACTIVE
Jurisdiction: CALIFORNIA
Entity Address: [WITHHELD]
*Entity City, State, Zip: *withheld by the author*
Agent for Service of Process: LEGALZOOM.COM, INC. (C2967349)

The list of shareholders and their stakes were as follows:

34% $7,500 Michael B. Kennedy
34% $7,500 Patricia L. Kennedy
7% $0,000 Mark Kaminski
5% $0,000 Brandon Justice
5% $0,000 Phil Adam
5% $0,000 Paul Wylie
5% $8,330 Lloyd Frtizmeier
2% $3,332 Scott Schreiber
1% $1,666 Ron & Jane Schroer
1% $1,666 Dave Wakefield
1% $1,666 Ronald M. Kennedy

One of the names that stands out on the list is Paul Wylie who had caused the printing issues with Quad, the printer for the magazine and he had been given a 5% share in the company?

"First off, let's welcome Paul Wylie to the GameGavel/RETRO team. Paul has become a tremendous asset to the business side of things and has been working on and off with me in some capacity the past few years. He is a veteran in the gaming industry, having served Activision as Vice President of Global Operations and has held other high-level executive level positions at a variety of larger companies. [...]

Looking at the Game Informer media kit, and understanding they got to those impressive circ(ulation) #'s because of their relationship with GameStop really got me thinking.

I think we need to start really selling the entire network we have created, the marketplace and the content sites. I think utilizing the auction site as a vehicle to sell subscriptions and vice versa needs to become priority. I am thinking about raising our auction selling fees from 5% to 8% and then offering a Loyalty program where members pay a fixed price to include a reduction from the 8% to 5% selling fees + they get a subscription to the magazine. And, all magazine subscribers automatically get entered into the GameGavel marketplace at this reduced fee level as well. That way both are feeding each other and both are benefiting from the other. Both grow.

I think this combination of C2C commerce/retail + the magazine/website content could exponentially elevate RETRO's circ(ulation) #'s AND also increase GameGavel's user base so both become giant revenue earners.

Start thinking about this business model along the lines of GameStop and Game Informer. How can we tie our two properties together to benefit gamers and give them real value. I think GameGavel if we sell it properly and grow its user base could become a real player in the used game market by allowing our readers/members to "cut out the middle-man (GameStop)" and sell their own games directly for selling fees less than eBay. That is what we need to sell.

Start thinking."

Ignoring Daniel's earlier good advice to focus on doing one thing well and not getting sidetracked into shotgunning ideas, the legal tangle that Mike was in came down to whether or not any of these shareholders actually legally owned anything, the reason being that as any new shareholder was brought in they were meant to be approved by all existing shareholders. This had not been done from day one. On the one hand Mike was saying that their shares held value, yet technically they did not actually own them. Where friends and family were concerned this wasn't a problem, but not everybody was feeling so charitable and refused to sign and return the agreement allowing him to gain control of his company.

Mike had two options:

1) Leave things as they were and hide under a rock.
2) Buy back the shares from the disgruntled members who were causing him a problem.

Of course he wanted to do this as cheaply as he could.

"The other option is to make you an offer for the stock before I send it to you. We did have a $38,000 loss in 2014 so based on that most would say the stock has no value. I will make you a one-time offer to purchase what would have been your 8% for $500/share = $4,000. I can add this to your final compensation payment by months end.

That is my max offer, however, and you can take it or leave it. If you aren't interested we will continue to proceed with getting you admitted into the company as an 8% owner per our plan.

This wouldn't have any effect on your agreement to receive 30% from the future sale of RETRO if and when it might occur.

Let me know on this by Monday. Thanks,"

Confused by the low valuation, Mark queried Mike's thinking and discussed the matter with Scott and UKMike before replying:

"I find it odd your valuation is nearly half of what you said it was worth before I created RETRO and the company purchased the jag cases. I have another potential buyer interested at a higher valuation, so I'll probably just sell to them instead. I'll keep you posted."

Not bluffing as he did have a potential buyer, Mark couldn't resist a little dig at his former employer:

> *"P.S.*
> *Looking forward to that next issue, it's been ages since I've seen one."*

Mike attempted to call his bluff and tried again to make him sign the operating agreement, claiming that it was necessary in order for him to have his ownership become official:

> *"The current situation is that you have nothing to sell as the "ownership" has not been formally issued to you. To formally issue you the agreed upon 8% "ownership" you would need to sign the operating agreement. There was an amendment to the original GG, LLC op agreement that changed it from a "member run" company to a "manager run" company. That is all that has been changed due to the fact that none of the other members are running the day-to-day operations of the business, they are passive investors.*

When that didn't work, Mike was forced to plead poverty instead.

> *In addition, there is still a commitment to publish two issues to satisfy the majority of the outstanding subscriptions and that is a debt/liability to the tune of about $40,000 of which, there is little to no company income coming in to produce those magazines. To that extent, I have continued to personally subsidize the creation of the magazines whenever required (sic)."*

Eventually, on January 28, 2016, they came to an agreement that Mike would pay Mark $7,000 for his 7% stake in GameGavel and he would spread the payments as below unless he was able to pay any sooner.

> *March 1, 2016 – $1,500*
> *April 1, 2016 – $1,500*
> *May 1, 2016 – $1,500*
> *June 1, 2016 – $1,500*
> *July 1, 2016 – $1,000*

Meanwhile, Mike was trying everything he could to get the other members to sign and return the operational agreement. He would call each one and tell them that they were the only one holding out. He told Scott that everybody else had signed and he said the same thing to Mark but what he failed to realize is that the two of them knew each other and were in contact about the whole situation. This had only one real effect on Scott, it pissed him off.

Mike would try a similar trick later on where the console was concerned and different teams were working on it. He did not realize that each person he threw under the bus was added to the list of people that began talking to each other. Even at this stage Sean Robinson was in the loop and outlined his own position.

"See attached. This is the original operational agreement Mike gave me when he had offered me stock in his company to do work for him. I scanned the paperwork including exhibits into PDF files. [...]

To confirm once again I never signed any stock agreements or ownership agreements with Mike and have never had any ownership in any of his companies... he tried to get me to do it, but never happened...

I also have the updated agreement you forwarded to me from Mike showing Daniel Kayser being an owner in the company. If you don't have those documents anymore, let me know and I'll forward those as well.

Speaking of Daniel or anyone else getting stock in Mike's GameGavel LLC, one of the documents is a "New Member's Consent" form. Basically anyone having stock in the company should have signed this document. Page 4 of the operational agreement under section 7.2 says for the company to give/sell stock to anyone, all other members must give written consent, so this is yet another "uh oh" for Mike with him selling, giving away, etc stock in his company. I'm sure your attorney can use this for good on your case, but it also seems like it would make it so you and Scott couldn't gift me your stock if that was something you really did want to do as you mentioned... but either way, I don't want it ;-)

-Sean"

The above passage is extremely interesting as it confirms one point and raises another. It confirms that indeed any new members should have been considered and approved by existing shareholders and it raises a point that Scott and UKMike had discussed several times. The two of them had joked to each other that Mike had got so lost in raising capital by "selling" shares that he may have given away more than 100% of GameGavel LLC.

This was a fact that was raised by Sean Robinson who informed Mike that he had actually sold 101% of GameGavel by giving Mark Kaminski 8%. The document above shows Mark as owning 7%, yet Mark has documentation to prove that he owns 8% which would indeed raise the number of shares to 101%. Mike was arranging to buy back 7% of GameGavel from Mark and to leave Mark with 1%. While Mark is fine with that, it still leaves Mike with a problem, he has unwittingly over sold his shares.

You can see that Sean mentions in his email that Daniel Kayser was also a shareholder and it is believed that he took over the shares owned by Brandon Justice which Mike had bought back when parting company with Brandon. If he didn't do that then at some point he had recalibrated the decimal system and issued 106% of GameGavel LLC.

Mark looks back on the situation somewhat cynically, and not surprisingly, as he was still owed money by Mike and likely would be for a long time to come.

"Mike got an injection of cash and decided he could pay another designer less than the $0.25 per issue deal we had. Oddly enough I made less than Seanbaby on 5 of 7 issues for designing the books cover to cover. Sean was our highest paid writer, $800 a spread and he did very little promotion, provided no images or very shitty google search images when he did supply anything along with his article."

At its height, the magazine had around 2,500 subscribers but Mike was quoting much larger numbers to game stores, advertisers and potential investors, numbers of over 10,000 were quoted based on *"people passing around the magazine or multiple people in the home reading it."*

With time running out, if it had not already run out, and the release schedule a dim and distant memory, Mike still owed his Year 2 backers Issues 11 and 12 but he had no funds to produce them. Luckily Issue 11 was mostly in the bag and he just needed to lay it out and print it. Issue 12 was another matter though, he did not have the funds, or indeed a writing team, to produce the content to fill it so he had to be inventive to raise the funds to meet his commitment to his backers. He needed a cheap and easy way to do that and he found it.

Following Issue 11 he produced a 200-page compendium made up of the best bits of the previous eleven issues called Retro Replay Volume 2 (Retro Replay Volume 1 had been produced after Issue 5 and was a special edition that was distributed via Geekbox). Magazines do this from time to time but you would have expected it to come after the first twelve issues rather than partway through the run, but Mike could not afford that luxury, and it was an issue that was largely already produced of course, again he just had to lay it out and get it printed because he didn't need to pay any writers for it. Unfortunately, it didn't exactly fly off the shelves in the way he had hoped.

Issue 12 was another story though as his writing team had already deserted him and his editors were now no longer on good terms with him, so he had to make it an interview special. Interesting though these are, it wasn't by choice, it was the only way that he could fill the magazine himself without needing his non-existent writing and editing team.

With his Kickstarter commitments now met, he was off the hook, and one might think that he would disappear into the ether and become a footnote in history, but that is not Mike's style and would not be in keeping with his desire to *"corner the market on retro."*

With GameGavel the auction site in tatters and costing money to run, not to mention Mike's $60,000 rider, the magazine was also out of funds and readership numbers so could not sustain itself, even issue to issue, yet it was unthinkable that Mike could return to Kickstarter or Indiegogo to fund it further. Mike was almost out of options but he did have one avenue left to explore, he wasn't going to fund the magazine himself, after all, he claimed to be being "courted" by Patreon as he tried in vain to raise the crowdfunding revenue to continue to produce it. This was in spite of previously saying publicly that he did not need to resort to crowd funding for Year 3 at all. His first statement on his last bastion of hope, Patreon, was certainly accurate:

> *"After crowd-funding our first (12) issues, RETRO Videogame Magazine has gained notoriety within the landscape of interactive entertainment."*

Notorious indeed, but the tagline for the magazine was now to "Celebrate Gaming's Past, Present, and Future" though quite how the present and future qualify as retro is not clear. What is also not clear is quite how this new Patreon funding scheme would work with no clear commitments as to the number of pages per issue, paper quality, binding method or the intended release schedule, but God loves a trier, and Mike was indeed trying everything to salvage his reputation and his source of income.

By that I mean your income.

7: Classic Gaming Expo 2014

Classic Gaming Expo is the brainchild of John Hardie, Keita Iida and Sean Kelly and is now the property of Jon Hardie, Joe Santulli and Sean Kelly who also own the Video Game History Museum which was, until 2014, a travelling museum of rare and one of a kind items from the world of classic video games. The three owners would normally store the museum exhibits, for the most part, and would then take them out on the road to shows like E3, (Electronic Entertainment Expo), GDC (Game Developers Conference) and of course their own CGE (Classic Gaming Expo).

The long term plan that the owners had was rather than be a mobile museum, they would have a permanent home and that they could also use this permanent home to host Classic Gaming Expo which has been held at several locations across several states through the years. At CGE 2014 John Hardie announced that they had been successful in finding a permanent home in Frisco, Texas, so it is unlikely that they will organize another Classic Gaming Expo in its traditional location of Las Vegas.

CGE focuses on the classic era of video games and most often features alumni from the good old days of Atari, Intellivision and Activision and in its first year was held as a part of the World of Atari show, hence the focus on Atari, though it has recently expanded to cover other companies, guests and speakers.

CGE generally consisted of a vendor floor, a panels room, an arcade and of course the Video Game History Museum. The vendor floor was where retro themed vendors could sell merchandise, consoles and games etc. The Panels room was where the alumni talks were held and people like Howard Scott Warshaw, David Crane and Rob Zdybel would host panel discussions about their time in the industry and tell stories about how they got into writing games and working for Atari, among other things. The Video Game History Museum is a separate room where the three owners displayed their museum exhibits including things like the only color Vectrex in the world, Atari shop displays, prototype Atari consoles and other rare and valuable items, some of them very valuable indeed.

The great thing about a show like this is that you could literally arrive at CGE, buy a game from a vendor, listen to the developer talk about how he conceived and wrote the game and then have it signed by them.

In 1999, CGE made its debut as Classic Gaming Expo in Las Vegas at the Plaza Hotel where it would stay for 2000, 2001, 2002 and 2003 before switching to the McEnery Convention Centre, San Jose, California for 2004. It was again held in California in 2005 at the San Francisco Airport Hilton in Burlingame and then in 2006 it skipped a year before returning to Las Vegas, its spiritual home, in 2007 at the Riviera Hotel. There was then a gap before the next show in 2010 at the Las Vegas Tropicana and 2011 was another gap year before it returned to its first home, the Plaza Hotel, Las Vegas in 2012 (the first time that the Retro Gaming Roundup hosts all met in person) and there was another gap year in 2013.

As 2013 rolled on and there was no announcement of a show for 2014, Scott decided that another year without a CGE was not going to happen as it was bad for the show that he loved to attend. Other expos that had started up at around the same time, or even since, in particular the Portland Retro Gaming Expo and the Mid-West Classic, had grown year upon year and had enjoyed a loyal following that would return each year and who could plan it into their schedule, safe in the knowledge that it would happen. This was not true of CGE as it skipped several years and would often be announced at short notice meaning that it stayed around the same size with visitor numbers of a few hundred people.

There are no accurate attendance figures for any of the shows as the team did not keep records of them, but ask them and you get figures ranging from 800 to 1,800, I would say that those are conservatively high estimates, but compare that to the visitor numbers for the Portland Retro Gaming Expo for the year 2012 which were around 3,000, doubling their previous year's attendance, and by 2016 they had tripled that with figures of over 9,000, and the Mid-West Classic which had similarly grown its audience to 10,000 by 2015.

Once the momentum was lost with CGE not being a guaranteed annual event, and with little or no talk among fans between shows, it did not enjoy the same exponential growth enjoyed by its contemporaries. For example, the owners also had the unusual strategy of closing down their forums in between shows so that people could not discuss it and keep the interest in the show alive. They felt that it would be confusing to be discussing the show if it was not going to be held, and the missed years of 2006, 2008, 2009 and 2011 meant that it was almost like starting a new show all over again each time.

Classic Gaming Expo is also an important event for podcasters and YouTube channels as they can guarantee that there will be video game alumni present for them to speak to, get autographs, and more importantly, get interviews for their shows. At one event alone you might get a dozen or more interviews which will last a year of monthly podcasts and hopefully until the next CGE.

Scott wanted the show to continue to grow and decided to take action, plus he also liked to visit Las Vegas, and it was during one of his frequent trips, during December 2013, that he was attending a cat show called Catsino Royale which was hosted by the Catalina Cats Cat Club at the Riviera Hotel on the Las Vegas strip. He asked if he could meet the show organizer and they started chatting about the logistics of organizing such an event and if they had any feedback about their working relationship with the Riviera Hotel. Having his interest peaked, he asked for the name of the person representing the hotel and went to make an enquiry. Within minutes he was told that they would be right down to speak to him.

They had a brief chat and arranged a more formal meeting for the next day. This meeting was with a lady called Darla Scheile and Scott outlined his plans for organizing an expo the following year, 2014. The Riviera had of course hosted Classic Gaming Expo previously and was experiencing something of a downturn and were eager for the business and to attract more locals to the Hotel as well as run more family friendly events. CGE seemed to fit the bill rather well and they began to look at the previous shows held there as Darla could access the number of hotel room sales as well sales figures for food and beverage over those weekends. Those figures pointed towards a number much lower than John, Joe and Sean's estimates, but even so, it made running the show there a worthwhile endeavor for the hotel.

Scott had already had extensive discussions with John Hardie about the potential opportunity of running CGE for them and he showed Darla some pictures of previous CGEs with the number of consoles on display and the number of games in the arcade and explained how many he was going to bring this time around. His photos suggested that previous shows had anywhere between 300 and 800 attendees, around 30 to 35 arcade machines and little over a dozen consoles. He had also spoken to the Mundo brothers who produced and sold the event T-Shirts about their estimates on attendee numbers and, based on guesswork and the number of badges they had left out of a print run of 800, their figures also seemed to suggest something around 500.

One of Scott's main concerns during these negotiations was that he wanted to minimize his financial risk as he was funding the event himself. He could potentially end up vastly out of pocket and wanted some reassurances from the Hotel that should there be a problem, for example a natural disaster, he wouldn't take the full financial hit for that. He just didn't know what would happen if the week of the expo a tornado blew through Nevada and nobody travelled and used their hotel rooms. These were all unknowns that needed to be ironed out.

With some sterling use of the dry-wipe board and some Venn diagrams, he put forward his proposal and tried to minimize his own risk, asking the hotel to share some of that risk on attendance figures that were simply an unknown at that point. The presentation was based on reverse engineering the available media from past CGEs and interviews with CGE staff and volunteers, and Scott demonstrated that he could increase the expo floor space and therefore the number of vendors, triple the number of arcade and pinball machines, increase the number of consoles and TVs by a factor of ten, add new features such as movies and expanded panels and add an extra day to the event. He also intended to advertise locally which had not been done in the past. In fact, CGE 2014 would be advertised on the screens right outside Caesar's Palace on the Las Vegas strip and ticket deals would be made available for local families. Scott also made frequent trips to Las Vegas during the year to meet with local vendors and gaming stores to hand out flyers and recruit vendors to display at the event. There were also frequent meetings and interviews with local TV, radio, and print media, several of which attended the show and broadcast live from the hall before opening. As a consequence, a local hair stylist also found an additional booking that morning.

Armed with an agreement from the hotel and his new-found knowledge, Scott again reached out to John Hardie with a view to organizing the show later in 2014. The three owners had been guests on Retro Gaming Roundup and they had obviously met at the show before so this wasn't a case of a stranger approaching them, they knew Scott and were familiar with him. The premise of the discussion with John Hardie was that the show would remain under the original ownership, but as they did not have the time or inclination to run it in 2014, Scott would lead a team that would run it for them with total autonomy and hopefully maintain the momentum of the show for 2015 when they could perhaps go back to running it again themselves.

John discussed the proposal with his co-owners and Scott discussed it with his podcast co-hosts and slowly but surely an agreement was reached. Classic Gaming Expo 2014 would go ahead, John, Joe and Sean would retain ownership but it would be organized and run by the hosts of Retro Gaming Roundup along with a few assistants who would also be brought in. As Scott was the main man behind the idea and was funding the show, he would take the lead and he went about building a team of people that would help him bring the show to life.

Scott got to work quickly and registered Vegas Retro Expo LLC as the company to run the show and set about writing a "Show Operations Manual" that would be referred to as the "SOMbitch." There was an initial meeting with the team that Scott put together on March 8, 2014, and those present were: Scott Schreiber, Mike James, Mike Kennedy, Mark Kaminski, Lonnie Johnson, Pat Dardeko, Shaun Stephenson and Willie Culver. Invited, but not in attendance, were John, Jo and Sean but it was not unusual for there to be long periods of no communication with them. The outline of the show was that it would increase from a two-day event to a three-day event beginning on a Friday and running until the Sunday evening and that people would be allocated a department to oversee and manage, with Scott having the overall management role and making any financial decisions.
The structure for the team was:

Directors: Scott Schreiber, Mike James, Mike Kennedy
Con Ops: Scott Schreiber
Con Ops Assistant: Mike James
Web Presence: Mike James
Arcade Dept.: Pat Dardeko, Lonnie Johnson
Console Dept.: Willie Culver
Vendor Hall: Mike Kennedy

Panels/Movies: Shaun Stephenson
Media And Promo: Mark Kaminski
Video Game History Museum: John, Joe, Sean

There were some great volunteers, some of whom were Las Vegas locals, so not only were they a great help, they could easily loan equipment and would even accept deliveries of show equipment months prior and store it until it was needed. TJ Birmingham was one such Las Vegas local and a huge help to the show, as were Darrell and Salvador. Retro Gaming Roundup listener Joshua Witt was also a huge help and manned the registration desk. A rough time schedule was also laid out for the longer show.

- Wednesday 9am Scott Schreiber, Mike James and Mike Kennedy meet at Riviera expo office to get keys and arrange for table and linen delivery
- 1pm layout of tables begins followed by tablecloths for expo, panels, and meeting hall
- Follow on tasks; electrical, console and arcade begin
- Thursday 7am all dept. heads meet at expo hall and begin vendor setup
- Friday 8am open for vendor setup
- Vendor area closed and secured at 5pm
- Arcade to stay open until midnight
- Saturday morning, show opens
- Vendor area closed and secured at 5pm
- Alumni Dinner
- Arcade to stay open until midnight
- Sunday morning show opens
- Show closes at 5pm

Several ideas and goals were set, some of which would be met and some of which would not, though some of those not met failed for reasons beyond the organizers' control while others required a little additional management.

- Panels run as close to show floor as possible but separated for audio reasons
- Geoff Edwards to host an episode of "Starcade"
- Increase size of arcade area
- Increase size of pinball area
- Increase size of console area
- Run game competitions
- Have a separate music room for bands etc.
- Increase number and scope of vendors

There was also a plan for the show program and how Retro Magazine would be able to tie in with the show. Obviously, Mike Kennedy was on the organizing team, and would also need to spend time in the Retro booth, a tricky balancing act for somebody with a lot of commitments and distractions, but his free booth would be payment for his help in organizing the show. He would also broker a deal with Scott over how Retro would produce the show program and some show specific content in the magazine. This was a welcome move in the right direction and Mike made a deal and lived up to it, so there was new hope that the previous problems had been attributable to Mike simply being overextended and overwhelmed and that he was getting back to his old self. Sadly, the notion didn't last long.

Mike was put in charge of recruiting vendors for the show and would be their main point of contact. He was also, by now of course, running Retro Magazine and trying to promote it where he could but Scott and UKMike were now dealing with him and his projects with a more business-like arrangement. Potential costs and content were discussed and a deal was reached where Retro would produce an A5 sized program with show info, sponsor information, vendor promotion, panel timetables, adverts for Retro Magazine, GameGavel and Retro Gaming Roundup (among others) and also a planned blank page at the back for people to collect Alumni signatures.

In return for producing the program, Retro would be given a prominent booth near the entrance and Mike would be free of show responsibilities once Saturday arrived. On the Friday Mike was required to staff the registration desk and deal with vendors arriving as well as guests who could access the arcade after opening.

Meanwhile Scott and UKMike were pre-empting some predictable problems that may arise:

> *"SoCal in particular has to be very careful not to spread himself too thin representing too many projects. If Retro are present at an expo there will certainly need to be staff representing it as SoCal will have expo duties ahead of other things that weekend including GameGavel. It may be wise to have people there representing the auction site as well, particularly if GameGavel are running a booth there. My understanding is that RGR will not have a booth.*
>
> *It's all well and good doing an expo as the 3 musketeers and I look forward to it but we have so much to think about up front outside of actually organizing the thing."*

There had also been some earlier discussion between the two:

> *"If we should do an expo (and it is not yet certain that we will) then it will be under a brand new LLC or similar as we discussed and therefore will not be owned or run by the podcast or any of our other ventures. We established that very early on.*
>
> *All 3 of us need to be absolutely certain whether we want to be involved with an expo LLC or not*
>
> *If any of our ventures are involved in any way then it will not be as owners/ organizers and we will need to discuss that all further."*

Outwardly though, the show was going ahead and a press announcement was made. This was one of the two things that the original CGE crew had wanted to retain control of, the press release and the alumni invites. When it was clear that the show was going to be bigger and better than ever before they seemed to view that as a slight on them and took it personally. It was clear that they wanted Scott to color within the lines, but he was never going to do that, and they didn't seem to grasp that making the expo the best it could be was the only possible outcome, still they did their best to put the brakes on.

The press release was delayed by a month despite numerous requests being answered with something along the lines of *"it would be done in the next few days"* but they did find the time to make a few angry calls asking how various alumni had found out that there was going to be a CGE 2014. Apparently they were more concerned with the word NOT getting out. The delaying tactics would reach asinine levels with their attempts to delay the release of the alumni guest list until it was of little to no promotional use and apparently attempting to harm the outward appearance of the organization by not having that available. The press release was a formality anyway as Mark Kaminski was already primed to unleash a fully fleshed out and ready to fire campaign of print, broadcast, and online releases and, within moments of it being issued, the real media blitz began.

> *"The Classic Gaming Expo (CGE) is coming back September 12-14, 2014 and teaming up with the Riviera Hotel and Casino Convention Center to give gaming fanatics an unforgettable Vegas experience. The original retro gaming expo, 15 years in the running, promises to deliver a gamer's dream from the 60's classics to today's hottest products. CGE will showcase an expanded collection of over 40 arcade and console video games, including an impressive Pinball Hall of Fame coin-op collection of over 40 classic pinballs and video games located in the hotel lobby. The Video Game History Museum will be exhibiting nearly 7,000 square feet of rare items like prototypes, limited-release items, accessories, and memorabilia.*
>
> *Delivering a true Sin City party, CGE is packing in the action with contests, tournaments, prizes; exhibitors and vendors featuring must-have products, and musical acts performing retro- and tech-themed favorites.*
>
> *The original CGE team has paired up with sharp new management to deliver an incredible event. Join the largest attendance of alumni to hear exciting panel discussions and special keynote speeches. If our extended expo hours have you exhausted from late-night gaming, sit in on exclusive documentaries and movies with Q&A sessions by the creators, and make sure to stop by the charity auction of rare video game items."*

News of who was running the show was beginning to leak out and Rick from Portland Retro Gaming Expo soon got in touch:

From: Mike Kennedy
To: Scott Schreiber, UKMike
Subject: CGE

I've not said anything about this to anyone, but it seems word is sneaking out somewhere??? I've not responded to Rick yet.

---------- Forwarded message ----------
From: Rick Weis
Subject: CGE
To: Mike Kennedy

Hey Mike,

Is it true that you three are looking to start running CGE now?
I hope it's true I think you would do a great job running it.
Rick

Once the publicity machine was rolling there was a series of discussions between Scott and John, usually where the owners weren't happy about something, and it was usually the press releases:

"Sean, Joe and I agreed we would like to be involved in the press release process. That's one thing we've always been really anal about."

Up until now Scott had been dealing with John Hardie who was passing messages back and forth between the two groups but it wasn't long before Sean Kelly began to speak out directly, a move that was not unpredicted and had been planned for. With so much on the line there had to be a contingency plan for the owners pulling the plug altogether, so all communications were kept within the new team's infrastructure so that nothing relied on John, Jo and Sean passing messages on, still, after seeing the press release, Sean Kelly came out of the blue wanting to delay its release at the 11th hour:

"As much as I anticipated Sean Kelly would be a hot headed ass I didn't think it would come on the eve of our most important and already delayed press release. If you have distributed the release as planned then no problem, you did as you were asked. If you have not, then please do the following:

1. *Contact me.*
2. *If you cannot reach me change any reference to www.cgexpo.com to www.vegasretroexpo.com*
3. *Release it as planned through every source possible.*
4. *No hesitation, strike hard and strike fast.*
   Scott

Scott had received a text message from Sean who felt that his nose had been put out of joint somewhat and he had reached out to Scott to say that:

> *"Just remember that the three of us run CGE"*

Which conflicted with John Hardie's earlier public statement:

> *"We (CGE Services, i.e. myself, Joe Santulli and Sean Kelly) will NOT be running a CGE this year. [...]*
>
> *I can tell you that we have the utmost confidence in their ability to run CGE as good as we can. [...]*
>
> *After several discussions we came to an agreement where he and his team would run the show this year since we were not able to do so. We have agreed to be involved in an advisory role and will still be participating in the show."*

One of the things that upset Sean was that Scott had issued press releases and that he had made contact with the Alumni to invite them to the show. It seemed as though Sean thought that only the three owners could communicate with the alumni but as Scott said, *"It's all over the internet and we do know these people independently of CGE."*

Sean was also concerned that the upgrades to the website, the increased traffic via the social media outlets and every announcement of a "new feature of CGE," "never before seen at CGE" or "bigger and better than before" were in some way shaming him and his past work. Scott assured him that this was not intentional and was simply happening as a result of them having ten people, each one dedicated to doing one thing well rather than just three people who were also trying to run a museum project. As Scott said at a press conference; *"They were running the entire expo with 3 old fat guys, we have 10 old fat guys!"* They were bound to get more done and they would be *"fools to stay within the boundaries of past performance."* Scott also clarified that his team had long term independent relationships of their own with these people and that it was inevitable that the alumni would talk to them about CGE first but he would honor his agreement with John Hardie to forward them on to John, Jo and Sean for alumni relations.

After further discussions, the alumni email eventually went out:

> *Dear ( ),*
>
> *We'd like to take a moment to invite you to Classic Gaming Expo 2014, the premier classic video-game event of the year. This year's show is being held at the Riviera Hotel & Casino located on the world-famous "Las Vegas Strip". The dates for this year's show are Fri. September 12th through Sun. September 14th. We have a ton of activities planned for CGE 2014, and we would love to have you take part in the festivities.*

We'll be updating the web-site with more information in the coming weeks but we have some announcements currently on-line at: www.cgexpo.com.

As in previous years, we will again be hosting a special alumni reception dinner on Fri. night September 12th which is only open to distinguished guests such as yourself. This is a great opportunity to rekindle old friendships and make new ones with many of the people who, like yourself, helped to create this industry. Obviously any family members or friends who accompany you would welcome at the dinner as well as the show itself.

If you decide to attend, please let us know their names at your earliest convenience so that we can make arrangements for their admission to the dinner and the show.

This year, we are celebrating the 15th anniversary of Classic Gaming Expo which we started way back in 1999. We've made several changes to the show based on feedback from our attendees, most notably that the show will run for 3 days this year, starting on Friday with a lighter schedule that will include movie and documentary screenings related to videogames and their culture. Expect to see more arcade and console games set up to play as well as more vendors. Many of our most popular events are returning including the Saturday Night Charity Auction, Alumni keynote sessions and the Videogame History Museum will have 7,000 sq. ft. of historical artefacts at your fingertips.

We love to have our alumni friends talk about their careers and we're confident that our attendees would be thrilled to hear you speak about your work in the industry. If you would be interested in presenting a keynote speech or taking part in a panel discussion, please let us know.

On the other hand, many of our alumni guests just prefer to mingle with their counterparts and meet the fans of their work. The choice is up to you.

If there's anything we can do for you or if you have any questions regarding the show and its activities, just drop us a line.

Thanks for your time and we hope that you can join us at CGE 2014!

Best Wishes,
John Hardie, Sean Kelly, & Joe Santulli
Organizers, Classic Gaming Expo 2014

Scott warned his team that *"Sean may continue to some extent to be sand in our shoes but I don't see any major threat from him"* and he pressed ahead with confirming alumni attendees. As he said, his team had to be able to publicize the show that they were running and that he was funding, so the press releases continued as department heads began promoting their attractions and competitions.

From: William Culver
To: Mike James
Subject: Console webpage content

Hey Mr Mike!

Do you have a link to the console page I can look at?

I have my first contest set up and would like to add it. It is with Gamester81 with the grand prize being a signed copy of his game. It will be a high score contest playing his game on the ColecoVision with the winner playing against Gamester81 himself and getting a signed copy of the game.
[...]
Thanks!
Willie

As the arcade staff, Pat and Lonnie, were trying to source arcade cabs for the show, Scott had posted an update on the number of machines that people could expect to see there, which included those from local collectors in Las Vegas and also the 35 or so machines that CGE owned. This also seemed to upset the show owners as around this time Scott noticed a social media post from John Hardie showing a truck unloading arcade machines in Texas. In the background were the show banners and signs that were staples of CGE and Scott quizzed John about it. Those machines, owned by CGE, were part of the agreement that he had with John and they were supposed to be in Las Vegas until after the expo. John informed Scott that he had shipped them as he no longer had any storage facility in Las Vegas to which Scott retorted *"Well did you ask me if I had any?"*

This meant that the show could no longer count on those machines as they were not going to be shipped back from Texas, but luckily, others came to the aid of the show and machines were sourced from places like Flipper Wonderspiel on Fremont Street, who were a retailer and an arcade, and most of the pinball machines at the show were provided by them. The Pinball Hall Of Fame did not provide any machines as they didn't want to drive them across town, but they did put on a free shuttle bus for show attendees to get to and from the Pinball Hall Of Fame.

Promotion for the show was going well and thanks to Mark Kaminski the social media interaction was ramping up as well as he reported:

"Just a heads up – Crazy Taxi on iPad is free today.
And our twitter feed should go over 1k today, not too shabby! Considering it was 400 a week ago."

Scott had an interesting, if non-committal, dialog when he contacted the Wounded Warrior Project. He wanted to give a discount on entry to CGE for all veterans who were a part of the Wounded Warrior project.

From: Scott Schreiber
Sent: Saturday, March 15, 2014 1:15 AM
To: WWP Info
Subject: WWP General Information Email

Please contact me via email or phone at [NUMBER WITHHELD]. I am an Army vet and now operate a video game expo (www.cgexpo.com) operating in Las

Vegas and want to get any WW into my show for free. I have worked with WW before for a car show, and willing to be vetted.
Scott Schreiber

The reply he got was somewhat formulaic:

Hi Scott,

First and foremost, thank you for your service to our country! Second, thank you for your interest in supporting Wounded Warrior Project(r) (WWP). WWP is grateful for the overwhelming support we receive from the American public and supporters like you. With the mission to honor and empower Wounded Warriors, WWP is the hand of friendship extended to warriors encouraging them as they successfully transition to civilian life. WWP provides 19 free programs and services to Wounded Warriors and their families specifically structured to engage warriors, nurture their minds and bodies, and encourage their economic empowerment.

Cause related marketing campaigns are strictly regulated and must comply with Internal Revenue Service regulations, state commercial co-venture laws, Better Business Bureau Standard 19, and federal and state consumer protection and advertising laws. Accordingly, WWP does not authorize use of its trade names, trademarks, service marks, logos, domain names, and other distinctive brand features without prior approval.

We want you to know WWP reviews every corporate sponsorship request received and a WWP teammate will contact you if there is an opportunity to collaborate.

For other unique and meaningful opportunities for your company to get involved, please visit the "Give Back" tab of www.woundedwarriorproject.org.

Thank you and have a great day!
Kind Regards,
Strategic Partnerships

Scott was unable to resist a reply:

From: Scott Schreiber
Sent: Saturday, March 15, 2014 1:15 AM
To: WWP Info
Subject: WWP General Information Email

Thank you for the lovely form letter, I am certain it is an effective solution to further provide an opportunity to develop this for our vets.

From the very header title of "Strategic Partnerships Generic" right down to the enthusiastic commitment to maybe get back to me, I feel that your group is certainly the way to go.

Rather than making a simple phone call to the local VA events coordinator and getting an invite out in 10 min of effort I think I will wait for future communications regarding cause marketing and other boilerplate information.

Scott

There was also some concern that the team was not being given all of the information that John had agreed would be passed on to them. John, Joe and Sean operated the info@cgexpo.com email address and were supposed to forward on any emails about the show (other than alumni ones meant for them) to Scott for processing but this was not being done, or it was being done selectively. It seemed that while outwardly everything seemed rosy, somebody still felt that their nose had been put out of joint and they were trying to put the brakes on all of the improvements that were coming to CGE. Fortunately, with the infrastructure that the team had built, and by eradicating the old contact information from the newly designed website, the only people likely to use the old CGE email address were past participants, alumni and perhaps prior press, but still it was a concern worth looking into.

To test the theory, the team sent emails to the legacy info@cgexpo.com address, from fake accounts relating to show participation and activities, and not one of them were forwarded to Scott, however, he had some bigger concerns that he wanted to iron out first rather than throw a spanner in the works and call them out at this stage.

"I also sent a few test emails from fake accounts and none made it to me. So, until I get most other things with them moving along productively I want to let the email issue drop, sort of. What I do want to know is:

1. *What they are doing? What are they saying to potential vendors, speakers, etc. that impacts our ability to operate the show?*
2. *What they are not forwarding? We want to know what they are not passing along to us such as press, vendors, speakers etc. so that we can (if desired) reach those folks and make deals.*
3. *Eliminate them from the site totally, the one spot that the info@cgexpo.com email is present on the alumni page (as far as I know) let's just remove that totally. If alumni contact us to that I will forward it and if it ever comes up I will tell them we have a Hero1 robot auto forwarding from that email to theirs before we ever see it.*

What we do have is written permission from Joe to access that email and the username and PW to do it."

There was also potentially a leak of information going the other way as Sean Kelly had seen a document that had not been made public. Whether this was via a leak or had been sent to him innocently by a member of the team is not known but he was questioning the show layout.

"Hey Scott?

I was looking at your tentative layout and wanted to point something out to you. You have us setting up the museum in section 5 which is not where we had the museum in 2007 and is also not the 7000 sq ft you have been advertising. When we were at The Riviera, we had the museum in sections 3 & 4 which was the 7000 sq ft section. From what I can tell, it probably shouldn't matter if the arcade/console room were swapped with the museum as you have it in your layout now. We already know the museum can easily fill that room and the console/arcade section would probably be just as happy with a little less space in section 5.
Let us know what you think as we're kind of trying to get some item placement ideas going for the museum now.

Sean Kelly
Organizer, Classic Gaming Expo"

Scott responded:

"Hi Sean,

Can I ask what layout you are referring to, we haven't posted anything yet and I have drawn up several cases, none of which are final. That said, the Riviera's documentation on rooms sizes and ceilings do not all say the same thing, the documentation online, the handout, and the fire marshal plan are each different.
Their math doesn't even match up, on one case they have a 109x60 room = 6322 (OK) and next they have a 46x58 room = 2500 but the math says 2668. The Riviera handout specs room 5 at 6322sq ft and room 3 & 4 at 6096sq ft making room 5 larger, on another sheet they are both the same size and the CC fire marshal plan has both areas at just a hair over 7k. A primary concern is traffic flow and security after hours, the layout we settle on will make sure we address everything.
Scott"

Mark meanwhile was looking for ways to improve the web reach that the show had.

"From: Mark Kaminski
To: UKMike

Hey Mike,
I had a quick question / suggestion. I know you did a lot to the site and it looks a million times better than it previously did. Was wondering if you would be open to a WordPress theme to kick the SEO into the next level?"

UKMike replied:

"Mark,

It was Scott's idea to mimic the old site and keep it similar this first year so I did just that.

Also, we've only got FTP access and not the server itself so I doubt they have WordPress installed.

If you wanna do that in the future I've no objection but I guess it would be Scott's call."

As they did not have access to the site's controls they were not able to install WordPress and stuck with the existing site that UKMike had written, beyond that they were never able to get the login credentials for the site as the owners said they had lost the account details and never found them over the seven months leading up to the show.

A note by Scott about UKMike and his work:

UKMike had the frustrating task of building a ship in a bottle, putting together a modern full(er) featured website and a parallel infrastructure using nothing but FTP access. He employed his professional skills and always ensured that updates (which were numerous and daily) were always posted and that our access was protected.

UKMike kept the digital heartbeat of the show safe and functioning and much of it had to be done rapidly and confidentially since not everyone was onboard for our success. We had a fairly tight and secure infrastructure with reasonable visibility into the legacy CGE crew's communication.

There was still the issue of another unreleased press announcement to resolve though, and Mark contacted Scott to say:

"I don't think Mike (Kennedy) sent the press release out to games press because of Brandon. Brandon did have some decent comments to add to it. I think Brandon is going to draft something and send to me shortly. I actually signed up my own games press account and was given access today. As soon as Brandon makes the tweaks I can upload on Monday am. You don't want it posted at this point because it won't get coverage over the weekend and then will be considered old news."

So Scott took up the issue with Mike.

"I got in touch with Mark and what we need to know is did our press release that was approved for release get distributed on your end? Or did Brandon somehow become involved and it not get released. If it did not it will be released Monday morning and Mark has an account for that now as well.

My hope is that the press release was not delayed due to any feedback from Brandon."

Scott then clarified the issue for future reference.

"Prevention; Brandon Justice is not, in any capacity, a member of this organization and no internal CGE business is to be shown to him ever."

This should have made it very clear to Mike that Brandon Justice was not involved and this was not Retro's expo and he had duties to fulfil in the expo's interests as he had agreed. It had got back to Scott and UKMike that Brandon was keen to help out with organizing the show and they had heard anecdotally that it had been put very differently to Mike by Brandon, that this could be *"our show"* and could be used as a vehicle to heavily promote Retro Magazine. Of course Mike was all on board with that but it was not going to happen at any cost. At one of the early staff meeting conference calls Mike kept talking up Brandon and how valuable he would be. He was told that *"Brandon ####ing Justice"* was not welcome on the calls and is not a staff member but Mike made at least three attempts to add Brandon to the skype session and he was disconnected each time. Clearly Brandon was sitting by his computer with Skype running waiting to swoop in, but as Scott stated:

"I don't need ideas I've got plenty of my own. I knew if we let that camel's nose under the tent we were going to have the camel in the tent and it was never going to go well. It was never going to stop. No, not gonna happen."

Scott was at the helm and the show was run via Vegas Retro Expo LLC under the umbrella of Retro Gaming Roundup, with Retro Magazine helping out with the program. In fact, as it turned out, by the time of the Expo, Brandon was nowhere to be seen and did not attend. These rules had been clearly defined and outlined to Mike, in their now usual business-like way, and from there on in were largely adhered to.

However, after an initial rush of vendors registering via the site and via email there was something of a lull, perhaps to be expected but then there was some anecdotal evidence that perhaps vendor emails were not being replied to and new vendors were not being sought. Mike Kennedy definitely knew how to access the vendor email account as he had earlier asked UKMike about it:

"Hey Mike,
What's my email for the expo? And how do I access it?
Thanks!"

UKMike had identified a few gaps where known vendors had not yet been added to the website because he had not been given the information to add and he and Scott began to look into it.

"We have some gaps that we could fill.
Our Podcast partners (Intellivisionaries, ColecoVisions, STR) and other known attendees (GameGavel, Retro) are attending but have maybe not confirmed yet.

I assume that they are going through the same processes as other exhibitors but have they done that yet and been missed or do they need to complete that process at this point?
Do we need to reach out to them and remind them?"

Scott followed up:

"[...] these are separate issues that UK(Mike) has correctly identified as outstanding.
SoCal was supposed to send me a banner and link to retro subscriptions for the website (that will credit CGE for subscriptions), that has not yet happened. Nor have we confirmed that we have an Ad and press release in Retro 3, I hope to get those confirmed when SoCal returns Sunday night from camping."

Yes, Mike had gone off camping again, not to say that he shouldn't be allowed time off on the run up to the show, but it was becoming clear that maybe his priorities were once again becoming skewed toward his own projects to the detriment of everything else:

"From: Mike Kennedy
Sent: 29 March 2014 23:00
To: UKMike

Hey Mike,
Sorry. Didn't get anything recorded before we left. I am going to record some stuff in advance when I get back so it's ready for the next few shows.
Mike"

Of course, this was passed on to Scott, mainly concerning the upcoming podcast episode as much as the expo:

"From: Mike James
To: Scott Schreiber
Sent: Sunday, March 30, 2014 01:30 PM

That's our boy!!"

Scott decided to do a little digging and the words that he brought to mind were those of one of his favorite professors, Dr. Lester Field, as he levelled some well-earned criticism at a student: *"An honest man never lies, a pragmatic man never lies about something that is easily verified."*

"That got me curious so I checked on the vendors email account and it is pretty barren, unless he is using other accounts or is using a mail client like Outlook he isn't doing much, and maybe because those emails are not recorded in the outgoing mail folder etc. But as far as webmail goes there is no sign of any emails to vendors, only a few replies to vendors that contacted him. I fear that it

is possible he did not compile a list of past CGE vendors and reach out to them, if he did he didn't do it with webmail using the vendors account. And of course he isn't taking calls or answering emails this weekend, so I will hit him up when he gets back and quiz him on the details.
-Scott"

UKMike had a pretty good idea of what progress had been made with vendors and commented *"I think it's almost certain he didn't do any of that."* Hoping to resolve the issue soon and pre-empt any further problems, Scott posed the question:

"And given the no segments before taking off for vacation, if he also dropped the ball on CGE, what then do we do with the bigger problem?"
Scott"

UKMike had the following observation:

"Do we have a list of vendors and can we pick up the slack or will somebody else do it?

He is almost halfway through the 6 issue run for Retro and I can't see it surviving beyond that as by his own admission he has no advertisers.

He is gonna have tons of free time soon enough."

The conversation continued:

"Give me a day and I can run down nearly every potential vendor from recent CGE and other shows and get a message to them. After that another few days for the fine details of checking past CGE and expo pictures for other vendors not as easily found and then expand the search from there.

The bulk of them would be in that first day. I would do that myself to get the train moving. I know some discussion has been had with a few vendors that are not reflected in the emails so I am going to ask and listen before I bring down the axe just in case. I am suspicious though.

Yep, when Retro crashes and GG is back to mediocrity does he go back to being as valuable/reliable as he was in the past (back when it was amusing and not detrimental) or does he roll over for the next whiff of success?

Scott"

UKMike checked: *"Are you picking up that mail in the meantime?"* and Scott assured him that:

"3 days is not life or death, and it will give me a spot check to see if emails are coming in and out. If he isn't doing anything other than chatting with the few vendors I know of (INTV, Good Deal games, Portland, and Hyperkin) there isn't much to pick up until I create it. I will tell him we had an IT issue we are fixing due to reticulated frammiss folder permissions and while checking the email database I saw the many unopened emails and no outgoing and then quiz

him. He would likely just resign without trouble but I wouldn't want him having access past that moment."

Scott also took some interim action and asked UKMike to make a change: *"Might want to make the standby email go to me, you know....."* It's a good job he did because there were several confused vendors being ignored.

"Couple of questions I have emailed you but no response yet:"

"Hi... I don't see [withheld] on the exhibitors list. Do we need to supply you a banner or something?"

So Mike was neglecting vendor duties, unless you count using them to peddle his magazine and adding a note about the expo as an afterthought that is.

From: Mike Kennedy
Sent: Thursday, June 19, 2014 2:07 PM
*Subject: * RETRO Magazine*

Hey [NAME WITHHELD]

Great catching up with you at E3. Let me know if we could still get our hands on a couple of those LED Atari controllers. Also, we do have some ad space left in our next issue that I am trying to fill at the last minute.

Any chance I could persuade you to buy a ¼ page for $250 or ½ page for $400?

Also, please let me know soon if Innex wants to secure some space at Classic Gaming Expo in Sept. Only about 5 spots left.
Thanks again,
Mike Kennedy

Having had enough by now, Scott took decisive action.

"I locked him out of the vendors email via a password change (I doubt he is checking it, it would be an interesting indicator if he did contact us saying he could not log on) until I can contact him and find out what he has been up to and take action accordingly."

Scott picked up the slack and began contacting and recruiting vendors while checking the email account for activity:

"From: Scott Schreiber
To: Mike James
Subject: Vendor updates

Check out the nice vendor updates that the vendor manager is sending! No wait, he doesn't even have a written list of vendors,... Kind of like the kid who shows up to class with no paper or pencil.

About a month went by before the next meeting to discuss the expo and Mike attempted to sign in to the vendor email account unsuccessfully. He told Scott that he couldn't log in and unknown to him, he hadn't been able to do so for the last month, nor had he even tried to. Mike was not pulling his weight again and Retro Magazine had taken his attention away from the job in hand. Mike promised to get back on track but they would have to keep a watchful eye on vendor registration to make sure that it ran smoothly.

The problem was eventually resolved and there was a great line up of vendors at the show including Intellivision Productions, Toy Shack, Hyperkin, Brett Weiss, Gamer's Paradise, Portland Retro Expo, Game Repair, Anime Revolution, Too Many Games, Intellivisionaries Podcast, Steve Lin, Game King, Good Deal Games, Rawk Threads, Retro Magazine, Adam Cohen, Songbird Productions, Christa Carpenter, Evan Burman, Shark Robot, and more.

There was also another team that did their best to derail the expo, and that was the unions. Hotels are forced into using union labor which is intended to protect the jobs of the people working there. You can't simply walk into a hotel and start moving tables around, the union are supposed to do that and employ somebody to do it. The problem with this is that they have something of a stranglehold on the costs for doing so. Scott had constant run ins with them as they tried to do jobs that they simply were not required to do, just so they could invoice for it.

> *"The biggest headache at running a show like that was that the union was constantly trying to pad their bill and they would happily do so, to the level of bankrupting the expo, and that was not happening. They were shameless and asking for money for jobs that they weren't even doing or weren't needed."*
> *[...]*
> *"I had one call with a union rep and it ended very badly. I hung up on them, so I called the hotel rep back and said look, the union is trying to kill the expo. They're coming back with astronomical prices for things that we don't need and it can't happen. To the hotel's credit they got the Union off our back but I knew that those mother####ers were gonna be lurking and looking to pad out that bill any way they could*
> *[...]"*

There was another fly in the ointment during the planning phase, and that was somebody who felt that they were worthy of an invite but did not receive one. This was the legend in his own mind, well-known misogynist and self-proclaimed console player of the century, the late Rudy Ferretti. Having previously attended CGE, Rudy felt that not only should he be on the invite list, but he felt that Patrick Scott Patterson should not be on the list, and he was pretty angry about it. At first he took to Twitter to vent his anger:

> *"Well if a BUM like psp can be Alumni How could Nevada's best gamer and one of the best in the world not be????? I can prove my work"*

Scott's reaction was plain and simple:

> *"The twitter DM bombs and emails are as expected for a psycho trying to self-promote. Just block and ignore, if he makes any over the top efforts I will refund his registration and let him know he is out."*

Rudy is well known for his abrasive attitude and very high opinion of himself, so when his rants did not gain the desired attention he took to different methods.

> *"From: Scott Schreiber*
> *To: Mike James, Mark Kaminski*
> *Subject: Disgruntled former attendee*
>
> *He actually set up a website to fight against Scott Patterson being at CGE. http://patrickscottpattersonexposed.blogspot.com/2014/03/why-patrick-should-not-be-allowed-to.html*
> *Wonder if he knows how fast I can click REFUND in PayPal and inform him he is not attending?*
> *-Scott"*

NOTE: I leave the URL in the book only so that people can visit, if they so wish, and see that (at the time of writing) there was not one comment, like or share from anybody other than the original poster.

> *"I assume PSP knows?*
> *[...]*
> *We don't want PSP to kill the guy at the show but as a former wrestler he may be up for making a film about it."*

Was a play-off really an option?

> *"Yeah, PSP actually considered signing the petition himself as a goof. He should have because it is meaningless, only three people control who is admitted to the show and he isn't one of them.*
> *[...]*
> *The game has to be something absurd, something like Strawberry Shortcake's Musical Matchup on the Coleco, or Superman N64, or maybe something with insanely long gameplay like Ultima 7."*

When Rudy's communications and petition failed, he tried again.

> *"Been a major contributor over the years it's sad and pathetic you allow a fraudulent piece of trash like PSP Patrick Scott Patterson to speak to make OUR community any dumber than they may have been before.....*
> *Especially over a real personality and gamer like myself and Las Vegas local*
> *Second one of you clowns from the Twitter account sent me BS about a doc but never followed up and un followed me after*

You have me blocked on your CGE page FB it's really pathetic and sad that is how you treat someone who has been coming to the show since 2002 and this Loser PSP first time ever because he puts false info out there for your retro mag you allow HIM.......

Anyways I'm insulted you did not make me a speaker I came into competitive gaming in 2003 proven not 2008 and lie and say I was around in 81"

Scott did not rise to the bait however.

"I have NOT replied to this yet, and may not, ignoring him might be the best way. But thought you all might have a chuckle. If I do reply it will pretty much be to say his next outburst will result in his being banned from CGE 2014.
Scott"

The situation would soon resolve itself however when Shaun passed on an email.

"Out of the blue I just got an email from PSP saying he is unable to attend CGE. No explanation, just cannot take part. I would love to know the background to this but after quite a lot of work to make it happen in the first place, this is kinda surprising."

Mark mused about what might have happened.

"Ugh, I'm guessing he (Rudy) sent him death threats"

Scott announced the news to the rest of the team.

"The other bit we need to be aware of as staff is that we have a banned individual now. Rudy Ferretti was banned for ongoing harassment and threats to CGE staff, guests, and speakers. We will show his pic at the all hands meeting on Wed at the expo, the hotel has banned him from their property so if we see him we call hotel security and they toss him. Ok, sorry to hit you with two negatives but they come with the territory.

After he began contacting people regarding his banning from CGE2K14 (if he directly found out or assumed this is to be determined, and will be) we had to make a decision on when to act. Our goals are first to protect the CGE guests, and secondly to protect the CGE name. Nobody but himself is to blame for this and we are but one moment on his very long time line of belligerence. I will give further information at the all hands meeting on Wed before show setup but the short story is that he has been banned for harassing and threatening communications and the hotel has taken this very seriously and banned him all together for the duration of the expo. As of this evening I have refunded his ticket and sent the following message with the refund. Keep in mind it is a balance of attempting to tamp down communications from him to everyone while leaving the ultimate prerogative for future years up to CGE Services although from speaking to Sean they seem to be on the same page.

"At the unanimous decision of the board of directors you are banned from Classic Gaming Expo 2014 for harassing and threatening communications to CGE staff, guests, and speakers. The hotel has also banned you from their property for the event. Further communications could make the ban permanent."

Now while we keep our wits about us, let's not dwell on this. We have an epic CGE ahead of us and I for one am ready to GO!
Scott"

Some people don't give up easily though and Rudy contacted the hotel directly.

"Hello CGExpo Team,
An attendee is claiming to need to assistance and had not received any response from your team. Could you help him out? He is trying to confirm that his order for attending the expo was received. He has indicated to me that he has already paid via PayPal but he still had some other questions about attending including confirmation of receipt of payment and black badge readiness. If you could help him out that would be nice."

To this day, nobody connected to the expo knows what a black badge is.

Rudy's threats were taken seriously and dealt with accordingly, as the team were well aware of his reputation for endless barrages and relentless hounding of individuals. Luckily Rudy did not attend the show as he later claimed, though the team could not be too careful and Hotel Security were on the lookout for him as his picture was passed around.

Showing just what he was capable of, in August 2020, Rudy was to die in a suspected murder suicide where he is believed to have shot his ex-girlfriend, Amy Molter, and then himself in his Dover, New Hampshire home.

There were some light hearted communiques among the more serious ones, generally when somebody was unable to navigate the website.

"From: Scott Schreiber
To: UKMike
Subject: Can you fix this for the stupid

Can you make this flash:
All passes can be collected from the registration desk at the expo. on the http://cgexpo.com/register.php page?
Some people are still emailing me that they don't know how to pick up their tickets.
Scott"

The replay came shortly after:

> *"From: Mike James*
> *To: Scott Schreiber*
> *Subject: Can you fix this for the stupid*
>
> *No flashy. Scrolly."*

So the show started and Mike Kennedy was spending the Friday on the registration desk with volunteer Joshua Witt, but it seemed like every time Scott or UKMike went by the desk, Mike was gone. Josh would say that he had gone to his booth or he was being interviewed about the magazine. There was always an excuse and it was a constant job to keep him at the desk. Josh was a trooper, as were the Mundo family members who had worked the desk in years past, despite Mike leaving them short-handed they did an amazing job at keeping the line moving and were very accurate in their work while doing it!

Friday afternoon saw the largest intake of people picking up their badges so Mike's job was to be there. Right after the Opening Ceremonies where the organizers addressed the show attendees, Scott handed Mike a package of materials including Alumni badges and a camera and told him to hot foot it to the registration desk as it was getting busy. Mike took off and Scott went off to speak to the departments before also heading to the registration desk. As he was making his way there he bumped into Sean Robinson who said hello and asked him how the show was going. Scott opened the Expo door, looked inside and said *"Pretty good!"* and as he did so, he saw Mike sitting in the Retro magazine booth being interviewed and promoting the magazine. Scott went over and interrupted and told him *"What the ####? It's an hour into the show and that is not your job. Your job is the front desk, go do your job."* So he reluctantly headed back to the front desk, completely forgetting the package that Scott had given him, so Scott had to follow him with the package.

> *"Every time I went by the front desk he was nowhere to be found and he was right back in his booth. He had no level of commitment whatsoever."*

The front desk was indeed very busy, and while there is no definitive number of attendees for the expo, an accurate guess can be arrived at because the number of badges that were ordered (1,000) sold out completely and once they were gone, wristbands were used instead, approximately 600 of them, giving a total of around 1600 people through the door over the weekend.

One of the great things about CGE 2014 is that there were some world premieres over the course of the weekend and the team took great pride in that. Good Deal Games launched seven new games on the Atari VCS and four ColecoVision games, Elektronite launched a new game, the Intellivision flashback cartridge, the LTO Flash, made its first appearance, Howard Scott Warshaw debuted the new film "Atari: Game Over" with a special screening and the show's main sponsor, Intellivision Productions, launched their brand new Intellivision Flashback console, even though AtGames who manufactured the unit had told them that they could not launch it there, so they were very clever in how they managed to do it.

The consoles that would be available for sale at the show were all covered in a limited edition cardboard sleeve which was signed by the Blue Sky Rangers. This sleeve was only available at the show and nowhere else. The cost of the special sleeve was $100 but it came with a free Intellivision Flashback console inside.

The console was a massive hit at the show and Intellivision enjoyed a great showing at the expo. Intellivision Productions, staffed by Emily Rosenthal and the late Keith Robinson, were dear friends and a joy to work with. They were given show sponsor status, with the majority of the cost waived, and most of Saturday was structured around their launch, TV crews were brought by their booth, and many of the best laughs of the expo were shared with them. Scott and UKMike wanted to show a gesture of thanks to the department staff so they purchased a few cases of the new INTV console and distributed them as gifts. Intellivision Productions, being who they were, gave a reciprocal discount and there was a wonderfully funny moment where Emily approached Scott during the expo and told him:

> *"This is absolutely awesome for us, a perfect event for the launch, you know you're getting your pick of the numbered consoles other than #1, that is for Keith, what number do you want?"*

Scott grinned back at Emily and Keith: *"You know…."* After a long pause Emily burst into a suitable mixture of amusement and disgust: *"No way, how old are you, 14?"*

Signed, sleeved, special CGE edition #69 resides on the shelf in Scott's Retro Gaming Roundup studio to this day.

It was arranged that at 5am on the Saturday morning the TV film crew would be there to shoot a series of live segments to air on the morning show. Naturally Keith and Emily were told about this so that they could conveniently just happen to be at their booth "setting up" and could get the promotional coverage. Emily left to get her hair done right away and stayed up all night so as not to mess up her new "do" and arrived at 5am looking fantastic before nailing the TV appearance.

One of the most memorable events of the whole expo for Scott was during vendor setup. As he and the hotel rep, Darla, who was accompanied by her intern, were doing a walkthrough of the halls, they were chatting about how well the setup was going and how excited many of the staff were to see the show. One of the rules that had been put in place was that no vehicles were to be driven into the expo hall, the reason being that such a thing called for a union to put down protective plastic over the carpet, for a fee almost as large as the entire expo budget. As Scott and the hotel staff were conversing, a minivan loaded with cases of the new Intellivision consoles burst through the door and headed toward the Intellivision booth at an impressive pace, half sticking out the window was the white hair and beard of none other than Keith Robinson with a big grin on his face. Scott looked at the hotel reps and told them he would handle this immediately. Darla was very gracious and assured him that it was not an issue.

On the Friday night there was also a swap meet where anybody could book a table for $20 per hour and swap or trade with the public from 6pm until midnight and it was a great success with a steady stream of would-be buyers. Another thing that was new to the expo was Cosplay and the organizers teamed up with the biggest Cosplay group in Las Vegas, Anime Revolution.

On Saturday they organized an Anime Cosplay Contest and on Sunday a Gamer Cosplay Contest, both with a cash prize of $250. Entrants could register via the Vegas Retro Expo website, with the emails going straight to Anime Revolution.

One of the high points of the weekend was of course the Alumni Dinner where the show pays for drinks and a meal for the organizers and alumni and it is also one of the most expensive parts of the weekend. Hopefully though, the names of the alumni attending the show are used in media and promotions to raise attendance and therefore increase revenue in order to pay for it.

That's all well and good if you get the names of the alumni with sufficient notice. After months of contacting John, Joe and Sean for the names of attending alumni (something updated on a near daily basis on the CGE website in prior years) and getting nothing but assurances that the invite would be sent about one month before the expo, they had just 18 names, and the legacy CGE staff were upset that they had those. Just days before the expo they were handed a huge list of names, however, it was now too late to use them very effectively for promotion. This was not an accident.

> *"CRITICAL UPDATE TO ALUMNI NAMES*
>
> *Sorry for the cluster#### but we were handed a real shit sandwich.*
> *Good and horrible news, actions needed.*
>
> *Guys, those mother####ers have dropped yet another bomb on us and we need to deal with it. After releasing only 18 alumni names to us they threw a shit fit over a that extra "S" on Garry Kitchen's name (yes that is still going on) and demanded to handle alumni scheduling, as they promised to do and then did not do.*
>
> *They managed to piss off Shaun Stephenson I fear we may have lost him for the expo and now they drop the master list of alumni attending the expo which is the biggest year yet but it means two things, less than two weeks prior to the expo they are of little to no value for promo and draw but are going to cost thousands (read 7~10k) to feed at the alumni dinner.*
>
> *I will be sending you a list of those alumni in the form of a forwarded email, so please ASAP scrub and update the website and tweet the shit out of it, maybe one per hour.*
> *Scott"*

During the show there were of course lots of announcements made over the PA system such as upcoming panels, requests for contestants for competitions, special offers taking place at certain vendors and of course the obligatory lost children. In reference to Mike Kennedy's "catchphrase" that he used at the start of all his audio segments, each member of the team that made the announcement would begin it by saying "Hey everybody! It's SoCalMike!"

Mike would be sat just yards away in his Retro magazine booth and didn't catch on straight away. In fact, the team had to make several fake and humorous announcements before he realized what was going on. They then began to dedicate songs to him and play them in between live performances by 8bit Weapon, ComputeHer, Evil Weezil and The British IBM. In fact, Aidy (Adrian Killens) of The British IBM would be witness to a key event in the future of the podcast as CGE 2014 was drawing to a close.

The whole team was looking at spending most of Sunday evening completing tear down and clearing out the vendor booth area. Monday was spent with a hire truck taking the arcade games back to their rightful owners, returning the pipe and drape to the rental company and storing all of the televisions that they had amassed.

Mike Kennedy was leaving on the Sunday evening for his four-hour drive home, and as he was leaving he went over to talk to UKMike who was helping to tidy away the vendor tables and miles and miles of pipe and drape. UKMike was talking to Aidy at the time, and they paused their chat to speak to Mike. They said the usual farewells and planned a date and time when they would do their next recording for the podcast and settled on a couple of dates as options then said they would be in touch and Mike left.

Aidy looked at UKMike and said, *"Mike didn't seem very enthusiastic about that. Is he still enjoying the podcast?"* UKMike remembers that thought sticking with him and replaying the conversation over and over in his head. Indeed, just a year later, Mike Kennedy would be gone from the show.

Once everything was taken care of, the pipe and drape returned, the hire truck offloaded, the expo hall closed down, the keys handed back to the Hotel and nobody was in hock to the Mafia for thousands of dollars, there were some discussions with John, Jo and Sean about the future of the expo.

Scott wanted the show to continue year upon year, and though he had just run the most successful CGE to date, the show did not belong to him. He made several proposals to John who again would relay the discussions to his co-owners and pass their thoughts back to Scott. The proposals and possible outcomes for the future of the show were, as Scott saw them:

- The show would be run by its owners in Frisco, Texas
- Scott would take over CGE completely and hold it in its spiritual home, Las Vegas
- Scott could run a version of CGE in Las Vegas, either;
- CGE Las Vegas alongside CGE Texas
- CGE presented by Vegas Retro Expo LLC
- Scott would use Vegas Retro Expo LLC to run a new annual Las Vegas Retro Expo

John came back with the news that they had no interest in relinquishing CGE or running it in tandem in any way, so if there was to be a future for a retro gaming expo to be held annually in Las Vegas, it would be up to Scott to do it with his own company and in his own name. Whether or not this will happen has yet to be decided but one thing is for sure, it couldn't be in the hands of a better team.

> *"I'm sure they're going to read this and say: "Hey you know that's ####ed up that you're calling us out." Well what you did was ####ed up. I'm sorry, it is, but I wouldn't say that's the sum total of everything that we think about them. Certainly they created the expo that we know and love, they did a good job of running it. Yeah, we did a better job but deal with it. It was out of respect and out of fondness for what they did that we asked to take it over and continue their work, so yeah, they're gonna be pissed off that we publicly outed some of that behavior but it happened. That doesn't mean all the other good things didn't happen, they certainly did, and one day if they would ever address that and maybe apologize for it, that would be a pretty well-received thing. Not gonna happen but you know it would be well-received."*

8: The Back in Time Console

On December 10, 2012, a thread was started on the Retro Gaming Roundup forums. The thread was titled: *"Is there a market for a new 8Bit Console?"* and the opening post went like this:

> *"I was just thinking about this the other day.*
>
> *Does anyone reckon there'd be a market for a brand new 8 Bit console? i.e. not a hacked together computer or a clone but a completely new dedicated 8 Bit console."*

Having got this far into this book you might think that you know who started the thread already, but you would be wrong. It was not Mike Kennedy. It was in fact Adrian Killens of the band "The British IBM."

The responses were not positive, and SID Kidd64 would say:

> *"To put it in the words of a famous female pinball service technician: No,no,no,no...NO!"*

It's not clear exactly where Mike first got the idea for producing a new console but his old partner Steve Sawyer thinks he knows when he says *"I might have to apologize to a couple of people. I think this in some way might be my fault."*

Steve and Mike had been talking way back in September of 2013 and Steve had thought it would be neat if *"Retro became this culture thing."* He put an idea to Mike when he said: *"What if we had the Retro Channel on Twitch and it's nothing but classic game shows, and there's Retro Radio and we're just going to play nothing but songs from 1979 to 1989."*

Steve continued; *"We could even do games." "We could be like a game publisher."* Mike rallied *"We could do the Retro video game system."* To which Steve was enthusiastic when he said *"#### yeah we could!"*

> *"Oh, I'll be damned. He actually went and did it. I never thought you're going to take that conversation seriously, but there you go. He's like actually going and*

doing it and I felt this pang of recognition because I was like, oh crap! I know the conversation that we had that might be responsible for planting that seed in his head."

Wherever the idea came from, Mike discussed it with Scott over the telephone and Scott felt that there was no real market to justify the investment needed, and while he might be personally interested in such a venture coming to fruition, he didn't think the market and general interest would support it. As he recalls:

"I remember the call very clearly, SoCal called me one day and said he had two questions. The first question was how hard would it be to design and build a new console similar to the 1st – 3rd generation systems. The second question was; Did I think there was a market for such a console. To answer the first question, I told him it wasn't necessarily a complicated thing, it is a simple single board computer and it wouldn't be hard but WHY is the question. There are already many existing consoles from that era, each with an existing library of titles, and in many cases well understood development tools, if you want to make new games of the Atari VCS or NES era why not make games for those existing systems and their modern day clones? In regard to the second question, I told SoCal that I did not think there was a market large enough to support it. The example I gave him was that if there was a new system with NES like performance, along with a selection of new games for it, that I would buy one for the novelty, but I don't think there are enough of "me" out there. My thought at the time was that it was a solution looking for an opportunity, but who in the mass market was looking for $20 games on $50 carts, just for the sake of carts?"

Mike posted in the thread:

"I think there would be enough people interested in buying one as well as people ponying up to write some killer new games that would be only available via cartridge. Let's do a KICKSTARTER!"

That had become a bit of a catchphrase on the podcast where Scott or UKMike would blurt the phrase out every time Mike had a dumb idea, which was quite frequently.

"Let's do a KICKSTARTER!"

Scott would post his thoughts in the thread too, which were pretty accurate:

"I don't see a viable market in that there are already many original 8-bit systems with large libraries of software developed by top developers that are widely available. If you want an 8-bit console you already have your pick, and at a lower price than you could do as a new production. You can buy an original production 8-bit cart for less than the cost of making just a new empty cart shell, you can't put a new cart out for anywhere near as low as you can buy originals for. Do I want one to be made? Sure I do. I wish the new Wii had been cart based

and it could have been, flash is so cheap that they could have put games in a cart and been able to expand way beyond the disk based storage.

But I think Aidy nailed it, using a Pi or a Droid board (as was already done) with a USB or SD device acting as a cart is far more economical and easy to create for a marketable price."

Whatever the thoughts on the forum, behind the scenes the hosts were discussing viable options for such a system with the working title "The Back In Time Console" with a group of industry veterans on Skype. There were multiple meetings involving Scott, UKMike, Mike Kennedy, Steve Woita, Bob Polaro, Phil Adam and for one call at least, Ed Fries. A critical part of this whole story was that Mike lacked the skills and the means to turn an idea into a reality, he had gained a great deal of experience in manipulating and leveraging the experience and talents of others, and up until now he had got away with it. What happened during these conference calls (and the attendance varied from call to call) was nothing less than a product development roadmap. This group of people took Mike's one-line concept and began fleshing out the details of how it could end up as a product on the shelf.

Steve Woita is a video game designer, programmer, and hardware engineer who has worked at such companies as Apple, Atari, Sega and 3DO and has worked on lots of hardware projects such as fixing an issue on the Apple 2 motherboard, which was later approved by Steve Wozniak, and working with Keithen Hayenga he developed a prototype interface that would allow four game paddles and two joysticks to be connected to the Apple 2. This interface was approved by Steve Jobs and went into production as the Joyport. Steve has also written early games for the Atari VCS such as Asterix, Garfield, Quadrun and Taz as well as working on Kid Chameleon, Sonic Spinball and Sonic the Hedgehog 2 for Sega and he was eager to get back to working on some games again.

Bob Polaro had written accounting packages for Adam Systems and had worked at Atari with Steve Woita where he wrote several games including Desert Falcon and the arcade ports of Rampage and Defender. Bob too was keen to get writing games again.

Phil Adam is a friend of Mike Kennedy's who had worked at Interplay Entertainment where he was head of sales, marketing and business development before becoming President. Earlier he had been President of Spectrum Holobyte and was responsible for bringing Tetris to the western world. He had also worked for Konami and Electronic Arts.

Ed Fries had worked for Microsoft on their Office packages before requesting a move to the newly formed games division to become Vice President of game publishing during the era of their first Xbox console. Some within Microsoft thought him crazy for making such a move but Ed built and led the game division and turned it into the powerhouse that it is today. After leaving Microsoft in 2004 Ed has worked with several start-ups and he has used some of his free time to program homebrew games for the Atari VCS including Halo 2600 and Rally (a port of the arcade game Rally-X).

All of the Skype call participants had appeared on Retro Gaming Roundup before, some of them multiple times, and Phil Adam had appeared on the very first episode, so they were all known to each other and most had met face to face at various expos around the world.

The person who was not on the call but who had previously been consulted was the late Curt Vendel who was also a friend of the show and a personal friend of Scott's. Curt was tasked by Atari to design and build the Atari Flashback, and he had been given just ten weeks to do it so that it could be released for the 2004 Christmas market. The first Atari Flashback systems were marketed by Atari and produced by AtGames who would later take over their marketing from 2011 onwards.

As with all of these type of flashback units it would come with a series of games built in that would run without the need for additional hardware such as cartridges. They would come with two joysticks in the box and they plugged directly into a television, hence the generic name for this style of unit, "Plug n Play". The original Atari Flashback would, along with its joysticks, resemble a miniature Atari 7800 and it would run its games via emulation using an existing processing chip called a N.O.A.C (Nintendo On A Chip). This chip meant that it had to use emulation to run the original 20 Atari ROMs that were burned into it which had the knock on effect of some of the games not having the correct colors or sound, and the games that were originally played with paddles had to be adapted to use the bundled joysticks.

Curt agreed to do the work but he made it clear that he also wanted to make a second unit that would be much more in tune with the original Atari hardware and would not require emulation but would run the games natively, making it much more appealing to Atari purists. This second unit, the Atari Flashback 2 would also allow him to add a cartridge slot so that it could be used with original Atari cartridges. Sadly, the slot itself was not included but the solder points on the circuit board were, meaning that owners could quite easily solder their own to the board if they so wished.

Curt got his wish with the release of the Atari Flashback 2 in 2005 which was a much smaller unit and resembled the system it imitated, the original Atari VCS, and included twice as many games as its predecessor. Not all of its games were official releases, such as the excellent but unreleased Save Mary, and not all of them were original Atari games as it contained Activison's Pitfall and River Raid.

The joysticks that came with the system also resembled the original Atari CX40 joysticks and not only that, they were cross compatible with the original Atari VCS, so you could use your original controllers with the Flashback system and vice versa, including the Atari paddle controllers, though these did not come with the unit of course. The paddle games were also hidden from the menu and could only be accessed by entering a code with the joystick. The player had to press up once, down nine times, up seven times and down twice which represented the year 1972, the year that the paddle game Pong was released.

The other interesting thing about the Flashback 2 was that it ran on an original chip which cleverly contained all of the circuitry from the Atari VCS unit, so the games ran as they were meant to and the controllers worked as they were meant to. In fact, it modelled the original hardware so accurately that small bugs that were present in the original system were also present in the Flashback 2 chip.

Curt seemed like an ideal fit for the Back In Time Console but unfortunately he was having some health issues and could not commit to the project, whether he wanted to or not.

The conversation among the remaining participants centered around the viability of creating a new cartridge based console and all aspects of a system, such as what the hardware would look like, what software it would run, if any, what the cartridge interface would look like and whether it would emulate old systems and be able to play the cartridges that people already owned. There was also a lot of discussion about software and writing games to play on it.

Some of the conversations basically consisted of all the participants throwing out ideas and then discussing them further. This all took place after the release of the Ouya console which had been funded on Kickstarter and had already hit the shelves, so they discussed the Ouya's good and bad points so as not to repeat their mistakes. It was also after the release of the Retron 5 which ran games via emulation and played only original cartridges from classic systems rather than having its own software library.

What the assembled group wanted was a neat looking system that was not made up of multiple slots as that would mean they were just remaking the existing Retron 5 and they discussed the possibilities for adding additional functions via after-market connectors. Out of the box, the Back In Time Console would be able to play original games using its only slot, probably on top of the unit, though it could also be an SD Card style slot on the front, but it would also be fitted with an interface similar to USB so that users could connect add-on cartridge interfaces via a cable that would be sold separately.

These after-market cables would plug into the USB slot on the unit, and on the other end of the cable would be a cartridge slot so there would be a cable for each retro system that the unit would support. Customers could buy the Atari 2600 cartridge cable, the Sega Master System cable or the Super Nintendo cable for example and then be able to play the original cartridges that they already owned.

The controllers would be able to play each system and the unit would switch modes depending on which cartridge cable was connected. It would ship with a wired controller, though wireless controllers would also be available, again as after-market purchases. It was undecided at this stage whether or not it would be compatible with original retro controllers as well as original retro cartridges but it was certainly discussed. What was also discussed was the type of games that would be original to the system and written specifically for it and it was unanimously decided that they would be retro inspired games but written especially for the system rather than ports of games already available via Steam for example.

Games were discussed a lot, as well as who would write them, and whether or not there would be third party support and how those third party games might be released. Would they have a Nintendo type Seal of Approval where they would have to be approved before release or would they have to be approved at all, for example could anybody write and release a game for the system?

During the first call, Ed Fries told the group that there were certainly a lot of ideas being thrown around, and while that was good, it was all a bit of a mess and from the sound of it they were almost certainly talking about two companies rather than one, a hardware company and a software company. He also advised that one should be started before the other or he doubted that it would be financially feasible.

Having had more experience than perhaps the rest of the team put together in building and managing a games console launch, as well as running a software house, he outlined some very important points that the team should bear in mind for the organization before it moved ahead any further.

Ed advised them that everybody who was involved should have their role defined. It should be laid out in black and white what each member of the team brought to the table and what they would be expected to do moving forward. He also felt it was critical to define who was a part of this venture because it could lead to a number of problems regarding compensation and ownership. What Ed clearly meant was that each of the stakeholders participating should have an official standing for their protection, because at the moment they were just a bunch of people throwing around ideas like they were going out of fashion.

Ed also told the group that he could not be a part of it and he would have to bow out. This was because he was actually an advisor to the group behind the Ouya and if he were to continue discussions it would create a conflict of interest and he did not want to put himself, or the team, in that position. Everybody thanked Ed for his input and he disconnected. He had in fact helped far more than he could have known, unfortunately only some of his advice was taken on board and certainly not all of it.

What was apparent, from the moment any real talk of emulation began, was that the notion of an 8-bit or 16-bit CPU executing native code was a dead end, because to emulate consoles of the 8-bit to 16-bit era a much more powerful processor, more memory, and a totally different architecture was called for. This shift in design and everything that it dictated seemed totally lost on Mike who just didn't grasp what it meant and he would mix and match the buzzwords incorrectly. Throughout the meetings it was very clear that Steve Woita wanted to get to work on software and make some games but he would likely have to write the Operating System first.

The final call that UKMike recalls being a part of, which is also the last call that Scott was involved in, took place late on a Friday night (in the UK) and it was agreed that Mike Kennedy and Steve Woita would look into starting up the software company and Scott would continue along with the hardware side so there would be some parallel development and they agreed to reconvene the next Monday. This meeting either did not take place or took place without Scott and UKMike, as would all meetings after that point, though they would only discover this fact later.

Meanwhile it turned out that Mike thought he had gleaned all that he needed from the assembled team and, as he had done with Retro Magazine, he cut out those that he did not consider necessary and continued without them. He had in fact discussed it again with Ed Fries via email and Ed told him that he didn't think it was a very good idea at the time.

> *"The idea pretty much stalled out at that moment as no one thought it was a good idea. That was until E3 2013 where I started to see all these retro indie titles come to life on the main stream consoles. Then I brought it back to life with Steve Woita and he and I went to find an engineering partner.*
>
> *I had Scott hook me up with Curt Vendel, however, and Curt was too busy and fighting his cancer to come on board the team. Then I reached out to a couple other contacts of mine that I knew had the time and ability to work with me on this, and went with them until one got pulled out of the deal due to a "real" opportunity at the time."*

Mike was in contact with Ed again around that time and Ed was now of the thinking that if this idea was going to succeed, then maybe the time was now right for it. Retro Magazine was still struggling, was not being run properly and was being somewhat neglected by Mike as he relied on his team over there to turn it around as he further distracted them with side projects and bounced ideas off Mark Kaminski, who at that time knew nothing of Mike's earlier planning meetings for the Back In Time Console, and who seemed to be Mike's go-to man where logos were concerned, and Mark was asked to design a logo for a new company that would be making;

> *"RETRO style games for mobile devices and possibly consoles. They will be addicting, easy to learn but hard to master games. Studio will be led by Ex Interplay and Spectrum Holobyte President Phil Adam. Joining Phil will be a veteran team of game developers/enginners.(sic)*
>
> *The name Zenergy is taken from the words Zen, Energy AND Synergy so think about that when creating the logo.*
>
> *Any other questions?"*

Any other questions? Just a few I imagine, like how could he design a logo for a software company whose name kept changing from day to day as he came up with alternate names like BIGgameIDEA, gameQbator and of course Zenergy.

In fact, on the site www.angel.co Mike is listed as:

> *Mike Kennedy*
> *Entrepreneur and founder of GameGavel.com,*
> *ReadRETRO.com, Zenergy Games.*

Mark humored him though, and enquired:

"I would need to know more about it before I start blindly stabbing at logos..."

Mike tried again:

"Ok, can you do a couple logos for BIGgameIDEA.com? Thinking something with a pixelated lightbulb. Or whatever you can think of. Let me know if you can whip up an idea or two."

By now his patience had worn thin and Mark tried a different tack:

"OMG do you need some ADHD medicine or are you puffin on a meth pipe over there? I had a pretty awesome logo for gameQbator earlier you said to scrap. Lol! Anyways I'm knocking out pages and Martin has been totally boss helping out. Still have missing articles and what not. Obviously we won't make tomorrow, but if Alex and Brandon can bust it this weekend I don't see why we can't be wrapped by Sunday evening.

If this logo is for the NDA idea have you looked at anything like gamepitch.com?"

NDA idea? Mike was already talking of NDAs and who or what was the topic of those NDAs? What was he hiding from whom? Not put off, Mike replied:

"Already tried gamepitch it's taken lol
[...]

Send me the gameqbator one if you still have it.
[...]

I think we might get snickered at with bator in the name so thought I would change it to something else and that was BIGgameIDEA.com. I think I will stick with the second one if you want to work on something there."

Mark asked him where he was supposed to find the time to do the logo and how he would be paid for it.

"Hey Mark
Scratch the logo I can have Tricia do it."

With Tricia designing a logo and Mike setting up social media feeds for the software company he inadvertently sent a tweet to Retro Magazine's followers which caught Mark's attention:

"Can you give me a call today?
I'm interested in Retro Action Entertainment and why they are tweeting to our twitter followers how to subscribe to our magazine? Am I missing some information here?"

Mike had apparently been logged into the wrong account when he had sent the tweet:

> *"I was accidentally logged into that twitter accunt (sic) when I replied to that guy. That's all."*

Mark was curious about Retro Action Entertainment and followed up with:

> *"Well in general, I would like to hear more about Retro Action Entertainment. We've really not had much of a conversation about it, which seems bizarre to me.*
> *Is it part of GameGavel network?"*

Ironically this is a question that Scott had previously asked about Retro Magazine of course, and would later ask about the Retro VGS console. No wonder Mike was being evasive about the twitter account and the company because he had registered it in September 2014 using his home address, where buzzfile.com shows 3 companies to be registered.

> Retroaction Entertainment, Inc.
> Contact: Phil Adam
> Title: President
> Category: Custom Computer Programming Services
> Industry: Computer Software Development and Applications
> Entity Number: C3715468
> Founded: September 29th 2014
> State of Inc: California
> Website: www.retroactionent.com
>
> Retro Action Entertainment was formed by a team of passionate gamers and industry veterans who believe a great game starts with great gameplay. Their game development team consists of legendary game developers whose games were the building blocks of this great videogame industry.

(Don't bother visiting that URL, like many of Mike's projects it has been left to die on the vine). Earlier that month Mike had already registered a slightly different company. Was this intended to be the hardware company that would run alongside the above software company?

> Entity Name: Retro Entertainment Technology Inc
> Entity Number: C3823713
> Date Filed: 09/08/2015
> Status: ACTIVE
> Jurisdiction: California
> Entity Address: [WITHHELD BY AUTHOR]
> Entity City, State, Zip: Trabuco Canyon CA 92679
> Agent for Service of Process: LEGALZOOM.COM, INC.

Once again Mike had taken an idea created with others and cut them out of it. The penny dropped for UKMike at Classic Gaming Expo 2014 when he was standing by the registration desk before the show opened on the Friday afternoon. He was talking to Bob Polaro who was showing him a game that he had written for iOS called Chicken Shift where you had to move ramps so that eggs being laid by chickens at the top of the screen would roll down them to safety at the bottom of the screen. UKMike recognized it as a port of the 1984 arcade game Chicken Shift: Back to the Coop.

Bob then showed him a second game in which you played a bug who had to run around a single screen avoiding larger bugs and enemies while eating smaller bugs and treats. Again Mike recognized it as a port an arcade game. This time it was the 1982 Williams game "Bubbles" where you play the part of a soap bubble in a kitchen sink and you have to clean the sink by wiping away ants, crumbs and dirt while avoiding brushes, sponges, cockroaches and razor blades until you grow large enough to be able to defeat all but the razor blades.

In fact, if you search the Apple or Android store you will find Chicken Shift for sale by the developer Retro Action Entertainment and the following information:

> Developer
> Email mkennedy@retroactionent.com
>
> TRIVIA: Chicken Shift: Back to the Coop was programmed by Bob Polaro. Bob was also the lead programmer on the arcade ports of Defender, Rampage and Road Runner on the Atari 2600.

Ironically, at Portland Retro Gaming Expo in 2016, Scott and UKMike were talking to Rebecca Heineman about the whole debacle and she informed them that Mike Kennedy had originally asked her to port Chicken Shift. She had asked him for payment to do it and Mike was elusive and told her that he would pay her once it was done but she declined. Over the following weeks Mike continued to ask her to do it but each time she told him that she wanted paying for doing it and Mike obviously wasn't keen on doing that so he had got Bob Polaro to do it instead.

Retro Action Entertainment also went to Kickstarter with a project to bring a bundle of Intellivision games to PC and Mac in 2014. As we know, Keith Robinson was a friend of the podcast hosts and Mike had set this up via Keith and former Blue Sky Ranger Dave Warhol, again a previous guest on the podcast. Dave would be the one who would rewrite the games for the new platforms and they would include Astrosmash, Shark! Shark! and Night Stalker. Mike also sent out an e-mail to GameGavel members about it.

> *Hello GameGavel Members!*
>
> *It's been a long time since my last communication with all of you, mainly due to our launching of RETRO Video Game Magazine a couple years back. RETRO is now well into its second year and has a current circulation of over 35,000*

people, has subscribers in over 30 countries and is on the streets at both Barnes and Noble and Hastings Entertainment stores across the U.S.A. Needless to say, this has been a huge undertaking but one that is now reaching its stride.

With that being said, I strongly believe GameGavel needs a relaunch and rebranding to tie in more closely with the success of the magazine and will soon be renamed to simply, RETROVideoGameAuctions.com. RVGA will then be advertised in side (sic) every issue of RETRO magazine to drive traffic to the site. It is all finally coming together as planned. Media and Marketplace unified to bring RETRO gamers a gaming network like no other.

[...]

Another venture that may interest you is our tie in with Retroaction Entertainment, Inc. and their Kickstarter campaign to bring back some of Intellivision's best games in updated and modernized form, beginning with three of Intellivision's most iconic games, Astrosmash, Shark! Shark! and Night Stalker. You can support this Kickstarter here and we recommend the $25 Pledge as that will get you ALL THREE games (Windows or MAC) + a digital subscription (or extension of an existing subscription) to RETRO Video Game Magazine.

If any of you have questions about any of this feel free to email me directly at socalmike@gamegavel.com. Thanks again to all of you for sticking with GameGavel over the years and know we are still working diligently to grow this into the leading auction site and marketplace for RETRO gamers.

Mike Kennedy, RETRO Media Network

Mike was again being very clever here with his wording of the statement:

"Another venture that may interest you is our tie in with Retroaction Entertainment, Inc. and their Kickstarter campaign..."

The Kickstarter was a dismal failure which went live on May 20, 2015 and ended on July 4, 2015, after being backed by just 164 backers to the sum of $6,890 out of a $100,000 goal. The fact that it received no updates over this 45-day period did not help and was another Mike Kennedy project that was left to die, and die it did. It should be noted that the target for the funding wasn't down to either Mike or Keith Robinson, the games were actually made by Realtime Associates who vastly overpriced it and Mike's role in this project was to assist them with the Kickstarter, presumably explaining why it didn't receive any updates over the 45 days. In fact, the company only has one game available for sale, that being Chicken Shift, and did not produce any others to completion. The pace with which Mike's ventures were coming and going had caught the attention of Scott and UKMike and it seemed that every month there was a new idea as Mike sought to put himself on the entrepreneurial map.

So Mike had clearly taken on board the advice of Ed Fries, that the console team had been talking about two companies, a hardware company and a software company, and that one should be started before the other. He had not, however, taken Ed's advice on clearly defining everybody's roles, he had just cut out those that he felt he did not need any more. He hadn't told anybody about this, other than his friend Phil Adam of course, he had just simply stopped calling them and dropped them from the project.

There was a stark warning of this during a recording session for Retro Gaming Roundup on February 23, 2015, when the three hosts were debating the Top Ten Worst Atari 2600 games and Mike Kennedy said that he had a deadline that he had to be finished by as he had another Skype call scheduled with Steve Woita and Bob Polaro. As they had both been Atari developers, the three hosts decided to bring them into the call and have them give their feelings on each of the picks in the top ten list.

When they were finished recording, Scott and UKMike dropped off the call and Mike, Steve and Bob continued their call, presumably about either the hardware or software company that Scott and UKMike had been cut out of.

With the penny dropping on the software company for UKMike at CGE, the penny would drop on the hardware company for Scott during another recording session for Retro Gaming Roundup on March 22, 2015, where Mike was talking about the console and what progress he had made when he let slip a mention of his *"hardware team."*

Scott immediately questioned Mike about it and described that the last time he had heard anything there was a software side and a hardware side and that he was a part of the hardware side of things. He talked of hearing a rumor that Clay Cowgill was involved with it at one stage and then wasn't, so he asked Mike what the deal was and Mike said that he didn't know and seemed confused. Shortly after Mike had dropped the *"hardware guys"* comment, Scott got to thinking;

> *"I wonder who the "hardware guys" are, there is a really small pool of people that it could be, and I could eliminate a few names it was not. About that time I recalled seeing a few Facebook posts by Sean and Clay about some hardware development that seemed suspicious so I hit them up. It was a very, very cordial thing."*

He hadn't yet put the whole picture together but it was clear that something was afoot, he had been soft-fired and was no longer considered to be a part of the project by Mike, and he had a very cordial discussion with Sean and Clay regarding the console venture. There was a lot of mutual *"Oh OK, that makes sense"* and *"Haha that's funny"* sort of talk.

> *"They were not surprised to find out where the early work came from, and I was not surprised to find out they had been tapped for the project. There were no hard feelings, especially since they were leaving the project in a week or two anyway due to Clay's employment by SONY"*

They concluded the calls in good spirits and would talk again many times in the future. As Mike tried to explain the situation to Scott he fumbled for words and came out with the fact that he had been talking with Scott about:

"doing some sort of a controller with an SD Card slot, coming up with a new console"

Mike explained (incorrectly) that they had gone to Curt who had bowed out and then moving on to Clay Cowgill who also bowed out and then bringing in;

"this other guy who is a video game hardware guy, but I don't know, Scott."

Mike then dropped the line that told Scott everything he needed to know to dissect what was going on behind the scenes. Mike, who knew Scott's extensive background, uttered *"Huh, umm, what, Scott, do you know hardware?"* with the word hardware having an upward swoon like a teenager asking a parent for an advance on their allowance. This prompted Scott to dig further into situation and find out exactly what was going on as Mike got very cagey and seemed to be choosing his words wisely as he describes having some loose conversations about it and then:

"somehow Steve Woita got involved and Steve and I have been kind of continuing on that conversation since we talked about it."

Scott then reminded him of Ed Fries' suggestion about defining everybody's role and outlining who is and who isn't a part of it and what they are doing. He then advised Mike that he should do that for his own good as well as anybody else's, as anybody who was once a part of it could later come back and say *"Well, I was a part of that and can claim portions of it."* Which of course they already had done in the guise of Steve Sawyer with Retro Magazine.

Mike tried to explain this away by saying that they had only had a couple of conversations, but Scott reminded him that;

"That is the foundation and formation of the idea, right? That would be like Steve Wozniak and Steve Jobs in the garage and all of a sudden he's across town building something. You've got to define that stuff, right?"

Again, Mike never did define the roles clearly, he just cut the people out that he felt he didn't need. He had got what he needed from them and thrown them under the bus.

Scott and UKMike were due to attend Play Blackpool, a retro expo in the UK, and told Mike that they would be sitting in front of people like the retailer Funstock who could distribute his magazine and the console and they would be interviewing developers like Jeff Minter, whose games Mike wanted to port to his future console. As annoyed as Scott and UKMike were, Scott was a part owner of the company and with the magazine and the auction site circling the drain it was in his interest for this console to succeeded, UKMike had been repeatedly told he would be brought in as part of the GameGavel/RETRO empire as a position became available, so they both maintained some level of focus on helping the company succeed. They told Mike to send them anything that he wanted them to address with the British distributors and developers and they would do that for him. Mike agreed and promised to send them a clear case for an Atari Jaguar so that they could show it off at the expo, but of course he never did send either of them anything. In fact, far from involving them and defining their roles, he would again cut them out of any involvement and spoke to Funstock himself about them being a distributor for his console, a fact that UKMike discovered later.

By this time, Mike had bought the injection molds for the original Atari Jaguar console which at the time were sitting dormant in a warehouse. The Jaguar had sold very poorly in its two-year life span and Atari were looking to recoup some of their losses when a company called Imagin Systems from San Carlos, California came knocking. They bought the injection molds that the Jaguar case was manufactured in sometime around 1998 and they repurposed it to house one of their own products, a dental camera, even using the cartridge slot in the top as a memory expansion port for their HotRod camera. More importantly they also had all of the legal releases signed by Atari, relinquishing any interest that Atari held in the Jaguar and its design.

The molds are made of steel, though some can be made of aluminum with steel registration pins that hold them aligned together, and are exceptionally heavy, and during the production process they are injected with polycarbonate and they press the parts individually. The molds had originally cost Atari around $250,000 to manufacture and were sold to Imagin Systems before they showed up on eBay and failed to sell for $4,500.

In 2014 Mike had called Steve at Imagin and arranged to travel up to see them in the warehouse, and he ended up buying them for $6,000 with GameGavel funds, meaning they became GameGavel property. This was not the complete set of molds but it did include the molds for the Jaguar shell and the Jaguar cartridge. The controller had not been needed by Imagin Systems and presumably either they or Atari had destroyed it. Mike intended to use the molds to produce the shells for his console rather than go the familiar, and simpler, route of companies like Intellivision and Atari who had used AtGames to produce their Flashback units in newly designed and fabricated shells. Mike would repeatedly claim that the shortcut of having these molds would save the company an incredible amount of money, an amount that escalated with each telling of the tale, when in fact it only added to their complications. Not only did they now have to design their motherboard around fitting in the shell, they also had to ship a larger package to customers than was necessary for a purpose designed console case.

Steve Sawyer, a friend of Tyler Bushnell, Nolan's son, had told Tyler about Mike's plan and he knew it would give his dad a good laugh. When Nolan found out, he said *"Why would you put it in that thing?"*

While the dental company had handed Mike an amazing stroke of luck by already modifying the molds to remove the back panel (allowing for a much broader range of back panel connections) it was far from the huge head start that Mike believe it to be. As far as he was concerned he just had to stuff a circuit board inside and he was done.

Now needing something to put inside the Jaguar shell, Mike reached out to *"a couple other contacts of mine."* The *"couple other contacts"* he refers to are Sean Robinson who in turn reached out to Clay Cowgill.

Sean Lee Robinson is an interesting character throughout the story and has mainly lurked in the shadows, only rearing his head occasionally. Sean is well known to the gaming community of the American west coast and is the topic of many discussions online with some message boards carrying messages warning members not to do business with him. Whether Mike knew about Sean's dubious past or not is unclear but that dubious past was to come in useful in the future.

Sean's criminal past is not hard to find and ranges from 1997 motoring offences such as speeding tickets and knowingly driving while his license was suspended to more serious crimes in 1999 such as fraud, when he was passing bad checks, and is described in court documents as a fugitive.

The Google Group rec.games.video.arcade.collecting contains lots of chat about Sean and some of his dealings with game collectors and their tales of doing business with him. Members talk of sending him money and not receiving goods;

> *"he sent the tracking number something like 10 days ago, and that seems a bit long for a package to make its way cross country.*
>
> *I have heard excuses from Sean (perhaps they are true) ranging from "My laptop is in the shop" to dental work.*
>
> *I want my money back, or I want a valid tracking # so I can start looking into an insurance recovery on the item.*
>
> *If anyone wants to add to this thread, its fine by me – and if any of the people who sent me emails see fit to do so, this would be a good time to enlarge this thread and pool our resources to recover what we may be owed."*

Sean's reputation was beginning to get the better of him, and in the same way that people who had been burned by Mike were talking to each other and comparing notes, they were also doing the same with his *"hardware guy"*;

> *"Hi, saw your post on the newsgroup.*
>
> *I will gladly give you a reference.*
>
> *I have had a few transactions with him.*
>
> *He likes to make promises that he doesn't keep.*
>
> *He 'bought' a pinball from me and then cancelled his $1800 PayPal echeck.*
>
> *He said he was going to go to the bank and get the money and bring it with him when he picked it up. Yeh, right.*
>
> *Included in that purchase was some other arcade stuff that I let him take home- he came to my house to pick up an inexpensive item that he bought off eBay, and while here he browsed around and we made a package deal for the other stuff and the pinball. Meanwhile, he is now selling those items that he didn't pay for.*
>
> *I called him several times and emailed several times regarding the money he owes, not only for the pinball which he didn't get, but also for the stuff he does*

have. Now he says I am harassing him.... He said that his POS asteroids game which doesn't work would cover all the stuff that he took. The wire harness is messed up, power supply messed up, artwork on sides are half peeled off and the pcb doesn't work- he said it was just the power supply that didn't work. Yeh, right. He took home a working Star Trek color x-y game in a tempest cabinet, bootleg Galaga board, several marquees, Galaga wire harness with the transformer and isolation transformer, a nice smoked plexiglass for a Pac-Man, etc....

Do I feel raped?? Yes!! But that's what you get when you are a trusting sort of a guy- or is that 'stupid idiot'?!!"

This was not an isolated case either:

"Is this the same guy that goes by the eBay userid: allmightyarcade ?"

"Yep, that's the conniving son of a bitch.

And you can quote me..."

Others were now chiming in to warn those potentially dealing with Sean:

"I have read many of the posts by people complaining about Sean Robinson. I can no longer sit silent. I feel obligated to warn future victims of his scam.

Sean Robinson is running what is commonly known as a "Ponzi" type scam.

What is this you might ask? Here is how it works. The scam artist tells you he has something you want to buy. He waves the "you can trust me" flag and points out his legitimate deals that he has done in the past. An example of this might be positive feedback on E bay.

Now keep in mind that not all his dealings are a scam. He will honor the smaller deals. When the scam artist gets you to send a lot of money, based on past dealings, that is when he gets you. He never had what he said he was going to sell you and most of the time you get ripped off.

When you get nothing in return the scam artist just tries to smooth talk you and gives you a sob story.

The scam artists' real intention is using your money to pay other debts. Basically he is "floating" his debts with your money. He might pay you back, but only when he hooks someone else for money. That's how it works."

Slowly but surely, the net began to close:

"Finally, I would like to add that it has recently come to my attention that Sean Robinson is under investigation by local law enforcement.

Not a surprise.

Yes, this is true. If anyone has any information regarding a scam with Sean Robinson or one of his aliases (Kendall Robinson), please contact the Hemet Police Department at 909-765-2400"

"A friend of mine got ripped off by Sean Robinson. My friend is working with the Hemet Police in their investigation to stop this criminal. I hope anyone else that

has information that might lead to the arrest and conviction of Sean Robinson provide whatever assistance they can to the Hemet Police to get a conviction of this crook."

"I recommended everybody he owes money to contact the Hemet Police Department so we can get this scum bag locked up for a long time.

I've given him over 8months for him to sort the problem out, and he failed to prove me wrong, so I have no words to describe what kind of guy he is..."

"Sean Robinson is now driving a truck for Markline Vending. He's doing collections on his route :)"

As people began to come forward, we get a report of a strange telephone call. This won't be the last strange phone call in this book:

"I received a phone call from someone claiming to be a detective from California, asking about the negative feedback I left him some time ago. The feedback I left was due to the runaround I got concerning a payment on a manual. Without going into detail, I never received it and lost the eBay credit on the deal when I gave him the benefit of the doubt.

Well, this 'detective' asked me a few questions about the deal, and obviously I didn't have any info that I could help him with. But what I wonder is if this guy was really a detective, or someone from this group.

The guy didn't speak very professionally, and mispronounced words like 'expedite' and 'investigation.'"

Perhaps this call was genuinely from the Police Department as they were indeed conducting an investigation into Sean, but it is also possible that it was Sean himself as he does often call people and try to fish for information, including calls to the author and to people that the author has recently spoken to.

"I received a followup call from a Hemet, CA, police department detective today asking for more information regarding a cocktail table arcade machine a friend of mine bought from Sean Robinson (AKA Ken Robinson, AKA Kendall Robinson) which Sean never delivered. Sean also promised a refund and never followed through always trying to smooth talk why the refund was being delayed.

If you have information and evidence to add to this investigation (such as copies of cashier's checks, email correspondence, etc. that might lead to the arrest and conviction of Sean Robinson please provide whatever assistance you can to the Hemet Police department."

"I first ran across him somewhere around the late-1999 / early-2000 timeframe, when he was using the handle 'Seanrox' on IRC and forums. He had started hanging out at a couple of technology-related meetings in the L.A. area that I had been going to on a regular basis, and after talking over the course of a few weeks it became apparent that we were both interested in classic computer

systems and arcade games. Over time, other people with similar interests also got to know him.

For about a year or so, everything was cool; he'd even go to parties that people in these same groups held at their homes. Then things started – gradually at first – going South.

Some of us (myself included) started not receiving items that we'd paid him for. No big deal at first, they were just delays... But then he'd drop off of the face of the planet for weeks at a time, only to show back up again out of nowhere. Every time he showed back up, there was a new reason for him going incommunicado: a sick or dying grandparent, major car problems, trouble with his marriage, issues at work. OK, shit happens. Just sort it out when you can; we'll hang on for you, dude. Keep the cash, we know you're good for it.

I'd like to make one thing very clear just in case it isn't: Sean Robinson was offering these excuses in person. Remember: we're talking late-2000 / early-2001 here by this time. Sure, there was also email and IRC involved, but the world of social media as we know it now simply didn't exist then. People actually met and talked and interacted directly. A radical and unsettling concept for many readers, I'm sure, but that's just how it was back in the day.

As we were to later learn, Sean Robinson was running a much larger Ponzi scheme in that he was using money received from one arcade collector to cover debts to another, and that Ponzi scheme was happening with a much wider circle of people who we didn't know. But, as it typically goes with most Ponzi schemes, they can never bring in enough cash flow to both cover the outstanding debts and provide working capital. He was out of financial runway, and we were going to learn how far the extent of his swindle actually went.

At various times, he had also told different people that he was in a band with Kip Winger. Or someone from Kix. Or... <Insert Hair Band Name Here>. Either way, he and them were gonna be partying down in Japan for the next twelve months, so he wouldn't be able to get in contact with anyone in L.A. in that time. You know, with the rocking hard and sake and geishas and all that.

Ignoring the fact that a year-long tour of Japan would mean playing the same venues three or four times over, we smelled a giant pile of bullshit. Calls started being made – and received.

One of the calls that was received was from a detective investigating many complaints of grand theft against Sean Robinson. I got one, as did a few other people I know. The questions were pretty much the same across the board: how do you know him, how long have you known him, have you had any financial dealings with him, and how did those work out?

This was when we knew he was totally, utterly, and completely full of shit. He was facing charges in California that were going to send him to prison for at least a year, and the band tour of Japan was a cover story for the time he was about to spend in the clink. From speaking with the detective, we ascertained that his dealings were much larger than the flakiness we'd suspected of him."

Sean was finally arrested, charged and convicted on several Felony counts and not surprisingly, there wasn't much sympathy among the gaming community as he served his prison sentence:

> *"Oh, & 1 last note... he sure was STUPID!! I mean if you're gonna rip off people dont give em your name, phone numbers, address, personal info, thats what threw me about him. His info checked out so I figured he was legit... dumb, I tracked him in a seconds.. just like everyone else."*
>
> *"They do have him in the lock up there because I asked the officer on the phone!! I said do me a favor and put him in the cell with BUBBA who needs a new boyfriend"*
>
> *"I hope he is rotting away, he certainly deserves all he gets inside."*

There is no doubt that Sean Lee Robinson is a convicted criminal and, having paid his debt to society, he was a free man once again so he returned to the gaming community in the Pacific North West, in particular, the Commodore Computer Club.

Sean and Mike Kennedy were both active members in various arcade groups around California and of course Sean had done, or claimed to have done, some web development work for Mike's various sites. Perhaps Mike was drawn in by Sean's tag line from his website SeanHQ.com which was founded in the early 1990s:

> *"If you can dream it, I can build it."*

He also paraphrases John F. Kennedy:

> *"When it comes to creative design some people see things and ask 'why?' I dream things that never were; and say 'why not?'"*

Sean's site also offers an eerie warning of what was to come:

> *"...with my technical expertise services I strive to prevent and solve any technology crisis."*

Whether Mike's motives were entirely genuine when he reached out to Sean to help him with the hardware side of the console is not clear but if anything were to go wrong and especially if money was lost, Mike could point to Sean's criminal history and claim that he had been yet another victim of fraud and claim plausible deniability.

Clay Cowgill however, is a very different story. Clay was known to Scott and they share a passion for cars as well as engineering and Clay is certainly an accomplished engineer. He is well known in the field and his site www.multigame.com has been selling his own arcade replacement and upgrade kits since 1996. He is one of the owners of the barcade "Ground Kontrol" in Portland, Oregon and also runs his own company "Embedded Engineering LLC. Sean sent an email to both Clay and Scott, officially introducing them to each other:

"...At this point Scott is aware that we were both involved with hardware and software specs for the project from mid-November 2014 until we both bowed out February 26/27 2015.

So without any further delay, Clay meet Scott, and Scott meet Clay... and there was much rejoicing... YAY! Now we can have an email chain to keep things going and see where Mike's Crazy Train ends up... probably off the rails... queue Ozzy Osborne's Crazy Train....

Sean"

Nicknamed "The Mad Scientist" by his wife, Clay has worked on many of his own projects including programming the homebrew game "Vectrex Moonlander" and his company is able to design, produce and distribute consumer electronics, industrial applications and multimedia systems. He has worked with companies like Big Electronic Games, Chicago Gaming Co., Disney and Sony. One of the products he worked on, the Rio Riot portable audio player, won a "Best of CES" award in 2002.

Clay breaks the process down to three key words; design, develop, deploy, and he was asked to get involved on the Back In Time Console when he had been contacted by Sean Robinson (whom he had met a couple of times before) in early November of 2014 to see if he would be interested in speaking to Mike about designing a new console. This kind of thing was bread and butter to Clay who agreed to speak to Mike about it and see if it would go anywhere. He gave Sean his number to pass to Mike who called him on November 17, 2014. From this conversation Clay gleaned that Sean and Mike were friends and had been working together on the idea for some time but had not really got anywhere.

There was nothing *"defined"* and they did not have a starting point from which to begin designing the hardware such as design documents, hardware requirements, hardware specifications or product ecosystem. Scott had never transferred his work to Mike and he had no intention of doing so with all the dirty deeds going on, so all that Mike had for Sean and Clay was a cloud of buzzwords that he didn't really understand. What was made clear though was that Mike wanted hardware as quickly as possible, he was very keen.

On December 1, 2014, Clay sent Mike some sample designs based on work that he had done previously on other projects and that he could have up and running in a relatively short space of time and was looking for direction from Mike but none was forthcoming.

Clay worked on ideas until December 19, 2014, when he felt that he had done all he could until some things were finalized such as what features the programmers would need and what performance options were financially viable. He was also doing this work without payment of course but would be paid further down the line with a royalty payment if the unit ever came to market.

With Clay taking an intended back seat, Sean continued where he had left off and worked on several different off the shelf hardware architectures and running existing emulators to see what their most likely candidate would be to run the unit. Based on Sean's work it was decided that they would use the AM3354 processor from Texas Instruments, an ARM processor that had been tested using the cheaply available BeagleBone Black development board. This would enable them to run an operating system such as Android or Linux very easily. It also had built in USB support and booted very quickly.

Clay watched as things ticked over slowly until around February of 2015 but still without any defined system specs or desired video modes and output options. He did notice that it was being talked about and hyped publicly by Mike before there was even a design on paper and he saw this as an *"excellent sign that it was time to officially part company at the end of February and pursue other opportunities."*

Clay handed Mike two pieces of advice:

1. Finalize the hardware specs once and for all.
2. Use the newly acquired Jaguar molds for a production run of empty cases to sell.

The money raised from selling the Jaguar cases could be used to initially recoup the investment in them and also to build up the capital needed to develop the hardware properly. Once the hardware was developed and running, he could then use crowdfunding to meet the costs for fulfilment and shipping of the developed unit. Clay notes that:

> *"Almost immediately the emphasis of the project shifted to 'how soon can we get this on Kickstarter' with a 'smoke & mirrors' demo system for a video (well before a complete system architecture had even been settled on) and that 'cart before the horse' mentality combined with my past experiences in the toy/gaming industry set off my 'this isn't going to end well' alarms and accelerated my urge to exit"*

Before he left the project for good, Clay outlined the required budget and the process for Mike to reach the fulfilment stage and he broke the development process into four phases:

1. Initial prototypes
2. Second prototypes
3. Production pilot
4. Final Production

The first two phases were necessary to make sure that there was a working system that they were confident would make a sellable product, and the figure that Clay estimated Mike would need to reach the final phase was around $70,000, just for the hardware portion (including design time, schematic capture, PCB layout engineer time, bill of materials management, FCC scans, debug and bring-up, prototype fabrication and components and about 14 weeks of full time equivalent effort). That did not include software, mechanical design, tooling, supply chain/component engineering, manufacturing engineering, packaging or marketing.

What left Clay befuddled was that he could not understand how Mike was taking this information in, that he would need around $70,000 and 14 weeks, and then turning that it into needing just $7,000 and 30 days. One of the phone calls that Scott and Clay had centered around these figures. Clay told Scott about the final feedback he gave Mike and it sounded familiar, the figure had almost doubled from what Scott had given to Mike but the design had evolved greatly since then and the cost increase seemed reasonable to him. Scott and Clay agreed that Mike wanted to hear none of that and didn't have either $70,000 to build it right and that his plan was something, anything, in a shell to look the part. Faced with the choice between doing it right and opting for "Smoke and Mirrors," Mike chose smoke and mirrors, and with Clay gone he had the perfect partner in Sean to provide just that, unfortunately Sean too was out at this point.

Back at square one, Mike had to start again but at least he had learned some new buzz words and had some more technical information that he could quote to the next engineer in the line. One of the phrases that Mike would use however, showed exactly the extent of his knowledge and just how out of his depth he was.

His *"hardware team"* had been using terms like *"running close to the metal"* which means the games would run much like they did on the original Atari VCS which had no operating system built in. The only code that ran was contained on its cartridges and the games were written in Assembler Language which is a language that talks directly to the hardware. It has no operating system like Windows or Linux running, no drivers, no DLL libraries, the code literally talks directly to the processer and opens and closes gates and switches logic values. This makes it hard to write but extremely efficient, which it had to be to run full games on Atari cartridges that were 2kb, 4kb or 8kb. A modern text file on a computer is bigger than that these days.

His "software team" were quoting terms like *"running Unity"* which is a game development platform but which is not as efficient as Assembler as it does not talk directly to the hardware. This makes games much easier to write on different platforms and port to other systems as they run on top of a standard software layer, common across all platforms but it means that they are much larger in file size and nowhere near as efficient.

Mike was mistakenly going around telling people that his new console would *"run Unity close to the metal."*

What?

"Run Unity close to the metal?"

That is one of the most ridiculous statements he has ever come out with, and he has come out with quite a few.

New Editor in Chief Daniel Kayser and Mike Kennedy

CGE 2014 Opening Ceremony (left to right: Willie Culver, Shaun Stephenson, Mike James, Scott Schreiber, John Hardie, Mike Kennedy)

Mike Kennedy finds Retro Magazine

Mike Kennedy's Twin Galaxies Card

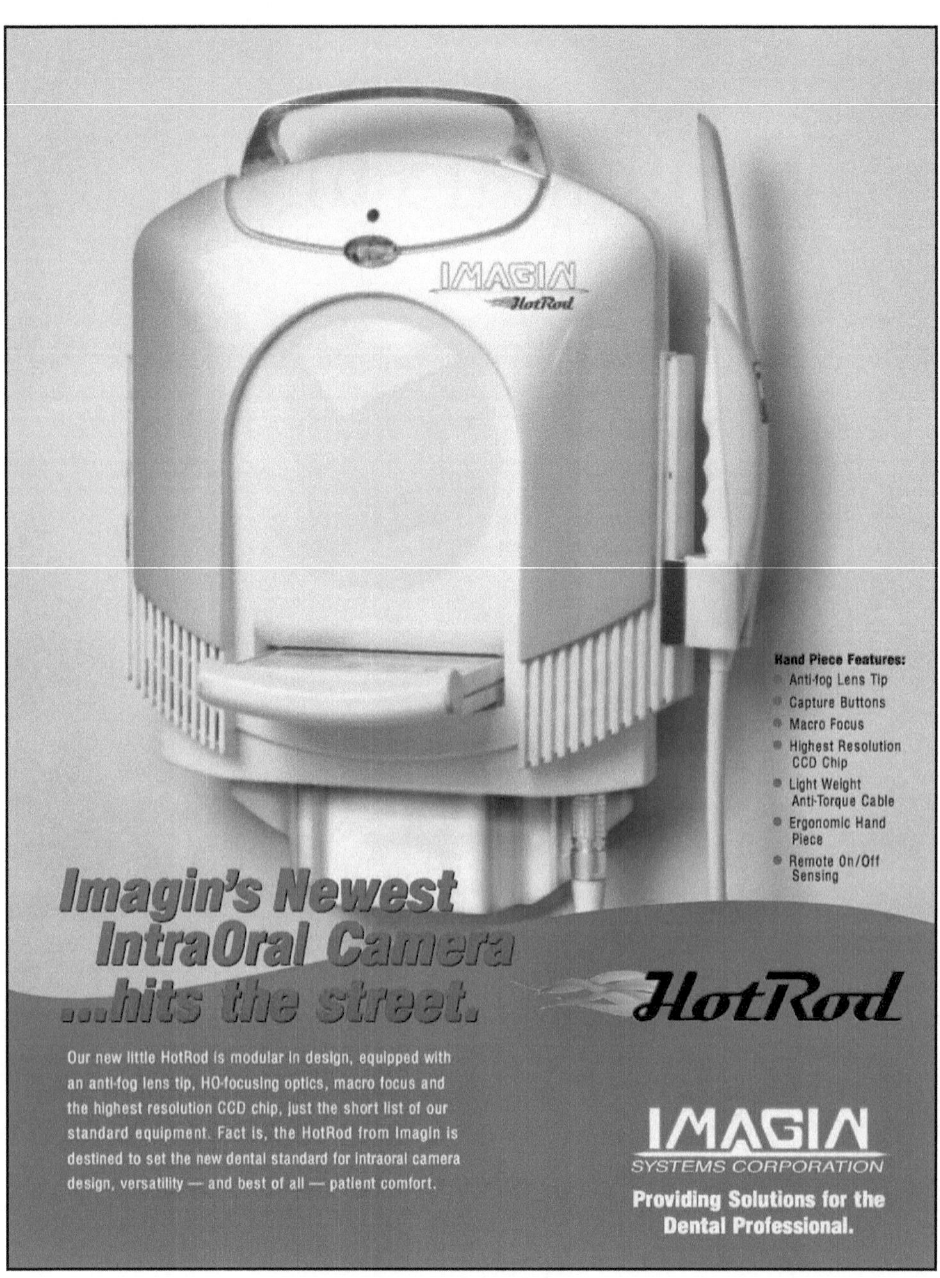

HotRod Dental Camera

Atari Jaguar molds ready for delivery to GameGavel LLC

Sean Lee Robinson

9: Cool Without a Fan

Following the departures of Clay and Sean, one permanent and one temporary, Mike went back to his original vision for the console that he wanted to build. He wanted a new console that played new games and, as usual, he had a new name for it, the Retro VGS (Retro Video Game System). There were already systems available that played your old, original cartridges, but Mike wanted to be able to play new games as well as those old classics.

> *"A cartridge-based system, just like the Atari. You can still find Ataris at the swap meet, cartridges, 30 years later, plug them in and it all works. To me that's the coolest technology out there, with that longevity. A lot of us grew up with it. The kids these days are going to miss out on that."*

Following another visit to E3, Mike had noticed how Microsoft and Sony were dedicating large parts of their booths to new games made by independent developers, the indie scene, most of which had retro roots and he saw that these games were being taken very seriously and being embraced by the industry. His concern was that if they were a digital download, how could you play a game that you bought today in twenty years-time? Even if your Xbox or PlayStation were still working at that point, the servers that held the games would be long gone and Mike did not want to face a future like that. He wanted to treat the games of today as he treated the games of yesterday, he wanted to be able to pick up his cartridge in twenty or thirty years' time, plug it in and be able to play his game.

> *"The point is, there have been some great digital mobile games, retro mobile games, and they're just lost in time. Some of these deserve to be preserved. ... at least for these types of games, if you enjoy them, you can buy them on these cartridges and play them for most of your life."*

It wasn't only for game preservation reasons that Mike wanted to return to cartridges though, he also wanted to build a system with no moving parts to increase its lifespan. Sony's PlayStation 1 and PlayStation 2 had notoriously poor lasers in them for reading the game discs and these parts would often fail over time, rendering the console useless and unable to read games. That wouldn't be an issue with his own cartridge-based system, though that format would bring its own problems. The cartridge slot for example would need to be robust and have resilient pins to continue to make a good electronic connection with the pins in the cartridges. Again, some retro systems have notoriously weak or troublesome cartridge slot pins such as the NES which would develop a red flashing light issue when the game is not properly seated. Replacement pins are available for the NES if this happens and many have been sold and fitted over the years.

The reason that cartridges were replaced with moving parts and optical discs was simply down to storage requirements as optical discs could hold much more information at a fraction of the cost of a cartridge, but as the types of games that Mike envisioned on his console would not require huge amounts of storage, that wasn't an issue. Largely because retro style games may not require as much storage in the first instance, but also, memory is much cheaper these days and is available in many different forms that can hold much more data than an optical disc can. In fact, some modern day systems have gone back to a solid state format for games, such as the Sony PlayStation Vita which supports flash storage up to 2TB (Terabytes). Compare that to a Blu-Ray disc which can store 25GB (Gigabytes) on a single layer disc and 50GB on a dual layer disc.

Though Mike's intentions were clear, there are some flaws with his argument. He wanted a console that would support the current generation of retro inspired games from independent developers that they could sell on cartridge. The Retro VGS would not have any kind of network connection and would not be updated (officially) once it was released. That meant that consumers had a choice when a new game came out. They could buy it digitally through an online store such as the PlayStation Network, Microsoft Game Store or Steam and play it on their PC or they could buy a physical copy on cartridge for the Retro VGS.

Games on Steam are generally much cheaper because the costs of sale to the publishers are minimal, whereas to produce a game on a physical cartridge and ship it to the buyer the costs are much higher. That cost is, of course, passed on to the consumer and reflected in the price of the game. Typically, the style of game that Mike was talking about would be anywhere from $2.99 to $9.99 on a marketplace like Steam but the prices being talked about for games on the Retro VGS were between $30 and $60, with most being in the $30 to $50 range. That is a huge difference. Yes, the buyers of the Retro VGS were getting a game that they could hold in their hand, that they would own and could put on their shelf with the rest of their collection, but how many people are there out there who would be willing to pay that premium price for the pleasure of owning a cartridge? Unfortunately, there was no kind of market research done so nobody knows but I would suspect that it is a small and ever decreasing number.

The whole concept was a huge risk, but to minimize that risk they would add the ability of the Retro VGS to play existing games on existing cartridges for systems like the Atari VCS, Intellivision, Nintendo Entertainment System, Super Nintendo, Sega Master System and Sega Genesis. Mike's latest hardware engineer had wanted to hold back that information but Mike had leaked it and talked incessantly about it, so the information was out there. They would sell add-on connectors that would allow you to connect your existing cartridges to the Retro VGS and you could play your existing games using emulation as the touted FPGA chip would be told by the cartridge to behave in a certain way.

What is emulation and what is an FPGA? Emulation is a method of recreating hardware in software. Take for example a classic video game console that contains a series of chips with each providing a certain function, some control sound, some interpret inputs from the controller and some control the video output to the television. Of course these can be combined so that a single chip can perform multiple functions but for the sake of simplicity, each chip performs a single function. These chips can be off the shelf, common components or they can be specifically designed for that job in that console. Where possible it is cheaper and easier for manufacturers to use existing off the shelf chips but not all did.

Contained on those chips, and in fact burned permanently into those chips, are instruction sets which programmers configure and send instructions to, i.e. if the player presses button A, the chip controlling the inputs reads that and acts accordingly, registering the input with the necessary components and the game ROM to tell them that the player pressed button A.

Those components exist in hardware, you can see them, you can touch them, they're tangible. Emulation seeks to recreate that hardware environment within a software environment. On your modern-day computer, you can install an emulation program which mimics that set of chips, so when you load a game ROM into the emulator, the game sees what it thinks is a set of chips but is in actual fact your software program behaving like a set of chips. The problem with this is that software doesn't always portray hardware with complete accuracy, and when trying to emulate some of the more recent video game consoles, performance can be an issue as it takes more time and more processing power for your computer software to behave like other chips.

An FPGA (Field Programmable Gate Array) is a way for hardware to emulate other hardware. If you have a chip controlling the sound output, once that chip is created, that's all it does. It is after all just a series of transistors, of logic gates and it has inputs and outputs which it cannot change. An FPGA on the other hand is much more intelligent, more expensive but more intelligent, and it has the ability to reconfigure itself and change the way in which its gates work and change the way in which it operates. FPGAs also have the benefit of being able to perform many logical operations simultaneously through their parallel structure, whereas microprocessors perform their logic operations sequentially (though modern processors do add some parallelism through something called pipelining). This can mean that routing signals through an FPGA can be slower than through custom-designed microprocessors, but the parallel structure of an FPGA can allow faster total throughput.

The FPGA at the heart of the Retro VGS would recognize when a Super Nintendo cartridge was inserted and would reconfigure itself to mimic a Super Nintendo. Likewise, if a Sega Master System cartridge was inserted it would reconfigure itself to mimic a Sega Master System.

To the uninitiated that may sound incredibly complex but there are systems available which do exactly that, despite Mike's claims of the Retro VGS being the first consumer device to run on an FPGA. What's more is some of these other devices do it without the need for the additional components that Mike was hoping to sell at a later date, for example, the Retron 5 and the Retro Freak which have multiple cartridge slots built into them and recognize what type of cartridge you insert in the relevant slot. After learning a loose definition of what an FPGA is Mike thought he knew all he needed to know but the lack of comprehension was stunning and came through loud and clear when he spoke.

FPGAs are a very broad family of products. Some are simple devices that can handle signal switching, for example determining that a cartridge is present in a slot and routing the lines from that slot to the processor so that the cartridge in that slot can be read, but it would lack any audio/video functionality and not have a use in emulation. Still other FPGAs are very purpose specific, highly specific and extremely costly, for example the FPGAs used in modems on satellites are chosen so that new "hardware features" could be implemented in orbit when the hardware is permanently deployed and no longer physically accessible. Neither of these two FPGAs, varying from a few dollars to tens of thousands of dollars, would be of any use in running video games, but to Mike, an FPGA was a single thing, rather like saying that he had a vehicle without regard to the type of the vehicle. Is it a vehicle that you use for commuting or is it a mobile crane that is capable of building skyscrapers?

Mike repeatedly claimed that this console would see the first implementation of an FPGA in a consumer device, which was an idiotic claim and it was clearly known by Mike to be a false one. The MCC216 is a retro gaming device that is sold online and which debuted at CGE 2010. It's designer, Dirk Dudenbostle, was interviewed on Retro Gaming Roundup by Mike and Scott, who bought one for review on the show. The MCC216 is an FPGA based device that boots up as one of several possible retro computers/consoles by selecting the hardware configuration at boot from a menu. Not only did Mike know that FPGA based consoles existed, he had interviewed the designer of one and had held it in his hands. Was this the inspiration for his console? Not likely as he didn't really comprehend what he was looking at, it would need to be explained in simple terms that he could more easily misinterpret. This was part of the world of an overwhelming lack of facts that Mike operated in as he added, deleted, and mixed various terms together. He had no concept that the addition of a claimed feature or console capability might dictate a totally different architecture.

In addition to the MCC216, Mike was also going to have to compete with the much cheaper series of "Flashback" style consoles that were coming out in newer versions from Atari and from other companies like Intellivision and ColecoVision. These consoles were also much cheaper than the Retro VGS was going to be, even if it managed to make its intended $150 price range. The option for hardware emulation was provided by the FPGA and the FPGA was driving the price up, but without it, was there even a market for this console?

Mike was trying to encourage enthusiasm and collectability for his system by selling the console in different color options and with matching controllers. The game cartridges would be available in plain black but Mike was talking about having the first five hundred copies of each game in gold or silver, hopefully making them more collectible. He would also try the same thing with Retro magazine, making Issue 12 available with three different covers, hoping that people would go out and buy all three versions.

With a vision in mind, Mike set about finding a new hardware engineer to help him to make it happen. Enter stage left, John Carlsen. John was born to parents who had met while working at IBM and he grew up in Silicon Valley, about half way between Atari and Apple, and that got him thinking about technology and he decided that he wanted to build his own computer and a company in the same way that Steve Jobs and Steve Wozniak had done with Apple. Around age 10, he began tinkering with electronics using scrapped circuits that his father brought home from his work at Control Data Corporation, which had been co-founded by Seymour Cray. He learned to maintain a disk drive made from salvaged parts so that he could continue to play games and learn to write code on his Atari 800.

He also started running a repair service out of his parents' house and while still at junior high school he bought the Atari field service inventory from a national chain store called Video Concepts when it closed down. He also got a summer job at Atari where he worked in technical support. After getting to know the Tramiels, he also worked through his first semester as an engineering student at San Jose State University, this time it was at the new IBM Almaden Research Center.

Through the brother of a BBS (Bulletin Board System) friend, Carlsen heard that Nolan Bushnell was starting a robotics business and he got hired and worked there for a year or so. He would later give Bushnell his coin-operated Atari Pong game as he knew that Nolan had given his last one away and Carlsen's parents wanted it out of the house. In the bottom of the cabinet was the original documentation which Nolan flicked through with a huge smile on his face as he read off some of the names within and recalled those early Atari days.

Later, Carlsen worked for Activision (then Mediagenic) and Media Vision, and co-founded Iguana Entertainment in Sunnyvale, California on August 14, 1991, along with Jeff Spangenberg, Mary Beth Campbell, James Moon, Darrin Stubbington and Matt Stubbington. After moving with the company to Austin, Texas he reversed engineered the Sony PlayStation and created dev kits for the game developers to use while they wrote games for the system. He also built similar dev kits for other systems such as the Super Nintendo, Sega Saturn and, ironically, the Atari Jaguar. The dev kit he built for the Super Nintendo cost around $500 each compared to the early official Nintendo ones which cost around $60,000. Ironically, the first dev kits that John remembered seeing had been at Mediagenic and they were on the desk of none other than Steve Woita.

After Iguana Entertainment, he spent the late 1990s designing integrated circuits at one of the two large FPGA makers, Altera, and following his reverse engineering of the Sony PlayStation, which took about six months, he got a call from Sony in 2010 about going to work on a new project for them. They wanted to build a low cost PlayStation for their emerging foreign markets and he built a battery powered, handheld plug and play console that could be bundled with a selection of games, all of which were compatible with his unit.

As the project gained traction, Sony executives felt that the device might adversely affect their sales of products with higher margins, so the project was killed.

In March of 2015, while living in Palm Springs, John found Mike Kennedy online after seeing news about the console project and, thinking it would be interesting to work on the Jaguar design again, and also to reunite with Steve Woita, he decided to get in touch. Mike was happy to recruit John with his varied game industry experience and thus began the next phase of the console development process.

Mike had been posting several 3D renders among his promotion for the console, way too early of course as he had nothing to really show other than the Jaguar molds but he did put them to good use by having a run of shells made in clear plastic and selling them online to Jaguar collectors. In fact, by his own admission, he made enough profit from the sale of these clear shells that he recouped the $6,000 that GameGavel had paid for the molds.

He had also been very public about the controller that would be shipped with the console, though the plan at this stage was to bundle two with each console. Mike had covered a third party Wii controller made by Interworks Unlimited in an early issue of Retro Magazine and he reached out to them about providing the controller for the Retro VGS. Their controller had a d-pad, shoulder buttons, four buttons in a SNES style layout, Start and Select buttons and dual analog sticks. It connected wirelessly to the Wii but Mike wanted them to make it connect to the Retro VGS via a USB cable and hopefully address one of the main criticisms of the controller, the fact that it wasn't very reliable. Lots of people owned the Wii version and complained that it would randomly lose connection with the console and some complained of dead buttons that no longer worked.

Mike had tested some controllers and found them to be reliable and said that they felt great but if anybody was worried about it, the Retro VGS would also have 9-pin connectors on the front so that people could use their existing Genesis controllers or Atari joysticks, and John Carlsen assured people that if they had a 9-pin controller of any kind, it would work with the Retro VGS. He would also put in support for multi tap connectors, even if it meant including a menu where each player would press the buttons on their controller to configure the console so that it knew who was pressing what and when. There would also be support built in for other USB controllers such as joysticks, trackballs and mice.

John set to work, unpaid of course, and got a set of requirements from Mike and Steve who had just two each. Obviously the primary consideration for Mike was that it would have to fit inside the Jaguar shell and that it would play the retro style games that were already being developed independently for old consoles. Steve wanted a console and games that would work instantly after lying unused for 50 years. He also wanted to include an FPGA that could be used to emulate the classic systems, although he refused to use the "E" word. John was the new recruit, Mike and Steve were in charge, and they made it clear that their four conditions were not negotiable.

John began the hunt for components and set about designing a system that would meet the requirements outlined to him, but when he went back to Mike with an estimated cost for producing the unit and an estimated retail price, Mike couldn't believe how expensive it was. John explained that the non-negotiable requirements of FPGA for emulation and 50-year data retention, as well as using the confinements of the Jaguar shell had driven the cost up. John showed Mike some comparisons of similar hardware devices that were in the same price bracket but Mike wasn't happy. He had been posting everywhere and talking to all and sundry about a price point of $150, but now it seemed that their design brief had doubled that to the $300 range. Finally, John designed a low cost unit without the FPGA that was viable to market at around $150 but that price did not include any profit margin. Mike had been way off with his figures and, as Mike is prone to do, he had been talking about it all over the place, on podcasts, on YouTube videos and of course on Social Media and Internet Forums.

Pretty much in promotion overdrive, Mike took every opportunity to talk about the console and it definitely generated a huge interest but unfortunately not all of it was good. One of the forums that Mike would visit to promote his ventures was AtariAge, and there was a huge discussion thread developing there as people discussed potential specs, compatibility, pricing, likelihood of success and asking questions about all the above. Of course, the main question was about the lack of a prototype and Mike was asking people to be patient but would then do an interview where he would talk about all the things that the console would do, before it even existed. Over time this hype and marketing spiel that Mike was coming out with could not be backed up and people began to question everything that he was saying.

Over at AtariAge *"The villagers are growing restless"* and were clamoring for the team to release specs and hardware information but instead all they seemed to get were announcements of new colors and limited edition games.

One of the biggest issues that people had was Mike's constant name-dropping, something he had previously done while recruiting a writing team for Retro magazine. He would talk at length about all of the people and developers who were going to write games for the system and would name-drop them everywhere. He talked about being contacted by over 150 developers who wanted to have their games on cartridge and would talk about all of their games. Some of the names he frequently quoted were Capcom, Konami, Namco and Sega and he gleefully told everybody that their games would be coming to the Retro VGS.

Whether he was *"in talks"* with these companies or had emailed them a couple of times (certainly the definition of *"in talks"* was pretty flexible) he was definitely in touch with a developer called Eli (Eleazar Galindo Navarro) from Piko Interactive, a company who produce and publish games on retro systems. Piko Interactive were behind the Super Nintendo game "Super Noah's Ark" which grew in popularity after being mentioned by the Angry Video Game Nerd and was the only unlicensed Super Nintendo game to be available during the console's commercial lifetime. Piko Interactive also acquire a lot of unreleased games that were cancelled during development and remain unfinished so that they can finish and release them, again on cartridge for the original retro systems, though some are also available for download on Steam.

Eli had first come across Mike with regard to Retro magazine because he had an idea about making guides to be printed in the magazine but it never worked out. Mike contacted Eli later and asked him to start selling his games on GameGavel, giving him a free seller account, but again it didn't work out because Eli felt there was not enough traffic on the site. They also talked later about Piko Interactive placing an advert in Retro Magazine and they agreed on a quarter page ad for $60. However, about an hour after they agreed, Eli cancelled due to another commitment and some at Retro thought that Eli was trying to wrangle some free ad space and that the negotiations were a waste of time.

Sometime in early 2014 their paths crossed again when Eli heard about the Retro VGS and Mike asked him if he had any popular games. Eli told him that he had lots of games that sounded like they would be a good fit and he told Mike that he would be interested if Mike actually had something. Mike told him that he had the Jaguar molds and that they would use cartridges to which Eli replied *"Okay, that's my thing, cartridges."* Mike explained that he didn't have the details right then but would be in touch later, and would Eli please not mention anything about it in the meantime.

They met each other briefly in June 2015 at the 21st E3 and Mike told him *"The price is going to be 300 bucks."* Eli couldn't believe it and he told Mike he wouldn't sell any consoles at that price but *"Oh, well it's your project. You can charge a thousand bucks if you like, but I'm just telling you."*

A few months later Eli spotted a forum post by Mike on NintendoAge where he was promoting the console and talking about getting homebrew games for it from the NES and the SNES platforms. Eli found this confusing because Mike still did not know what hardware the console was going to use let alone how it would play these games?

Mike got back in touch on the run up to the launch of the Indiegogo campaign and told Eli that they were ready and were about to "Kickstart" it so what games did he have? Eli sent Mike a list and mentioned some of the more popular titles like

Super Noah's Ark, Dorke and Ymp and Jim Power but he noticed that every time Mike promoted the list of games he was hoping to bring, it seemed to create a backlash with people asking why this game and not that game.

Still there was no word about the specs of the machine but Eli had discovered that it was claimed to include an FPGA which would run all the NES, SNES and Genesis games that Mike was talking about by burning the games to the new style cartridge, and on boot up the FPGA would configure itself to that system and run the game. The game code itself would be the same as the SNES code that Piko Interactive were using already so the only difference would be the cartridge pin layouts but that would be handled by the FPGA, so all of Piko Interactive's games would be compatible. What's more, they wouldn't have to do anything themselves, they would just submit the game ROM and Mike's team would produce the cartridge.

Another developer frequently mentioned was CollectorVision who had heard about the Retro VGS in early 2015 when Mike had told them about it. Mike already knew John Lester of course as they did the ColecoVisions podcast together and John is also a co-owner of CollectorVision Games. CollectorVision was made up of:

Jean-Francois Dupuis: Founder, Game & Graphic Designer
Toby St-Aubin: Manufacturing, Shipping & Customer Service
John Lester: P.R, Marketing & Community Manager
Russ Kumro: Lead Programmer
Marc Hall: Lead Programmer
Benjamin Marcus Allen: Music & Sound Composer
Oskar Alvarado: Game & Graphic Designer
Jean Michel Girard: Programmer
Brian Burney: Hardware Design
Jérémie Marsin: Webmaster
Vincent Godefroy: Package & Manual Designer

Mike told John Lester that he was interested in bringing their game "Tiny Knight" to the system and he wanted it to be the console's pack-in game (which included a 1-year platform exclusive). In return for this, CollectorVision Games would receive a royalty payment for every Retro VGS console that was sold.

In August 2015 some of the CollectorVision staff met Mike and John Carlsen at the Game On Expo where Mike informed them that everything was set for a Kickstarter campaign in the Fall and they were aiming for a target price of $150. That's half of what Mike had told Piko Interactive just two months earlier at E3.

Scott and UKMike were partially perplexed at the rapidly changing and never-ending alteration of the prices and claimed capabilities, to call it specifications would be a bridge too far. I say partially perplexed because, being experienced in hardware and software development and deployment, they knew that the actual development of hardware could not possibly be keeping pace with the claims. They knew there was no hardware to match these ever changing specs so they knew there was nothing but a cloud of talk, but what was perplexing was how the world didn't seem to notice! There were a few comments here and there citing these facts on the AtariAge thread but they quickly got buried as new speculation over game lists and claimed capabilities continued to be discussed.

Things rolled along until October 2015 and in the run up to the Indiegogo campaign being launched, Mike recanted his earlier royalty offer on each unit sold and halved it (recanted and altered agreements being an integral part of the Mike Kennedy business empire). Obviously CollectorVision were angry, but that was nothing compared to how angry they were when they saw how much money was being asked for in the crowd funding campaign.

Mike was still in heavy promotion mode and was addressing the pricing of cartridges and games, despite not knowing what was going to be in them, and in April 2015 he wrote:

> *"I just wanted to address the cartridge pricing. We will be doing all manufacturing of both the consoles and cartridges here in the USA (PCB's however, will be contract manufactured and arrive to our facility as a sub assembly), under our own roof, in Southern California.*
>
> *Carts will be priced based on the games that are on them. For example, a new game from a fledgling indie or homebrew developer might be priced $19.99 while a popular franchise sequel might be $40-$50 depending on licensing costs mainly! And everything between. So the short answer are (sic) carts will be priced from $19.99 to $49.99.*
>
> *We are targeting the console to be $149.99. The retail box will include the console with four controller ports (2 x USB for the 2 pack-in controllers and 2 x 9-Pin ports for classic controllers), a pack-in game (possibly up to three pack-in games only for Kickstarter buyers), HDMI cable (and possibly composite and/or S-Video too) and AC Adapter. There is a small chance this might have to price out at $179.99 based on system hardware which will be a gamers and developers delight ... but doing all we can to try and stay at that $150 price point.*
>
> *More details will be revealed about system hardware and development criteria soon."*

By *"soon"* he meant the next day:

> *"To answer the question will the RETRO VGS be PC/Linux based or Android based. The answer is neither as we are going the FPGA route. My partner Steve Woita puts it best:*
>
> *- Steve Woita, "If a developer wants to make a Neo Geo game, they would include an HDL file that configures the FPGA to operate like a Neo Geo. The developer would code their game to run against the Neo Geo platform. This HDL code along with the actual Neo Geo game will be on the cartridge. Once that cartridge is placed in the RETRO VGS, it will become a Neo Geo and play that game. So in this case, the language is: 68000 and Z80 code."*

Note, we aren't doing this so much for hardware emulation of older software, but more importantly, giving developers of various levels the ability to program their new games using what they are already familiar with (Atari, SNES, NES, GENESIS, etc.). In a sense we might also be able to replicate an Android system and open this up to Unity developers as well. So basically, low level, Unity, etc. could all be possible. Also, it's important to note that cartridges are the real brains behind our console.

We are working on board layout, bill of materials, etc. so should have more info on this in the next few weeks.

- Mike"

Not to overstate the obvious, but cost estimations follow, they do not lead. The cost of the bill of materials for example is also impacted by volume, yet, cart before the horse again, Mike knew the retail price for his console and had not got a clue as to how he came up with that number. The villagers were still restless and Mike addressed them:

"Hey All,
I am "still" enjoying reading everyone's comments and criticism. We are really trying to be transparent about this entire process

The hardware team consists of professional hardware guru's and they are all retro gamers at heart so this is all in great and very capable hands. So sit tight, speculate or criticize, whatever you want, but be patient as we continue to solidify details and make future announcements."

Even according to Mike's own staff accounting, there was, at that time, only John Carlson working on hardware, surprising for an organization that would use pluralization of singular people, such as public posts, press releases, and other correspondence all coming from one source and containing the same catch phrases and writing style. From the outset, John was against the use of the FPGA and he asked Steve Woita to justify its use as it drove the costs up so much, but Mike was in agreement and he wanted the FPGA to emulate everything up to and including a Neo Geo. What John tried to explain to them was that adding something as "simple" as that drove costs up quite a bit because it meant that they had to add more infrastructure and auxiliary components as well as changing the routing on the PCB, which in the case of an FPGA, or even changing from one model of FPGA to another, required a massive re-design.

John was keen to use a larger processor and smaller, cheaper FPGA but was having trouble convincing Mike and Steve that this was the way to go, particularly at the relatively small volumes they would be purchasing. John couldn't simply call a major semiconductor vendor and ask for their best prices, a far cry from his days at Sony and dealing with orders in the millions.

Mike would later lay all of the blame and the responsibility for the price increases at John's door when in fact, John was simply "designing" what he had been asked to design. In fact, in interviews, Mike would often give out inflated costs that were higher than those that John had given to him.

They did manage to relax some of the non-negotiables but using the Jaguar shell, and shipping something of that size when complete, still meant the price could not be reduced to where Mike wanted it to be. That didn't put Mike off going on the promo trail though, and during that summer he and John would appear on a panel at the Game On Expo on August 29, 2015, in Phoenix, Arizona.

Prior to them hosting this panel, John had specifically asked Mike not to mention the console price point as it was a particularly touchy subject and a bone of contention with potential customers. Unfortunately, Mike is not that easy to control, and once he is in sales mode he runs off at the mouth and disengages the filter between brain and mouth. Predictably it was only a few minutes before the subject of price came up and Mike blabbed that they were currently way over their intended $150 price point.

The video of the panel shows John looking decidedly uncomfortable and he persistently interrupts Mike throughout. Scott sat in his studio with a cigar as he watched the video of the Game On panel on YouTube, it wasn't totally shocking to him but it did again confirm that no hardware could actually follow such a chaotic plan. The team continued on the interview trail though, including Retro Gaming Roundup of course, just two weeks later on September 13, 2015.

This interview was the first time that all three members of the current console team had been interviewed together and it served a dual purpose for both the two hosts (Scott and UKMike) and for their guests. The hosts were a little incredulous that the team had agreed to appear, after all, was Mike so confident that he did not fear the repercussions or did he even understand the risks? As Scott recalled; *"In what world was SoCal going to come on my podcast and have me fawn over him and the new team that replaced us?"* The guests, Mike, Steve and John, wanted to build anticipation for their upcoming crowd funding campaign as well as clear up a few questions that had been asked and not answered thus far about their technical specs and the existence of a prototype. The two hosts wanted to get the journalistic side of the story out to their audience, but more importantly, they wanted to document their involvement and they wanted to document the true history of the console, because a lot of it was being reinvented by Mike to erase prior participation and events as he tried to clean up the timeline of the console's history.

When the interview began, UKMike and Scott had an agenda of topics they wanted to get the team's comments on and have recorded, largely this centered around the prior contributors to the project and who had been involved and when. Before they even got to the first few items Steve Woita went on a totally unexpected stream of consciousness as he rattled through the list of topics almost as if it had been placed in front of him. His answers were honest and affirmed what the two hosts knew, and Mike followed along with a string of "umm yeah" type affirmations. Once they had what they needed and had pretty much finished the interview, Scott texted UKMike to say that they could end any time and the interview drew to a close, although they did stick around for a few extra minutes.

Perhaps the most serious telling moment was when Scott asked John what FPGA they had settled on and John replied that they were not ready to reveal their vendor relationships. Scott muted his mic and began yelling, then texting to UKMike that they had nothing, NOTHING! Suppliers of off the shelf components in modest quantities is no secret to anyone. As Scott explained;

> *"At the low production numbers they were looking at there are only a few vendors and the discount structure for volume purchases (which they would have been on a low tier of) is built right into the website and catalogue. You don't call up Digikey or Mouser and set up a golf outing with their VP of purchasing to discuss purchasing 1,500 of their finest Cyclone V FPGA ICs. You go to the website and see what the pricing at that quantity is."*

This deflection was so laughable that it was apparent they had nothing, something the hosts already knew instinctively, but another confirmation only served to help. Something else that the Retro VGS team had no idea about was that by now Scott had been tipped off about a second company being formed, the tip off coming from Sean Robinson of all people, and that the molds and intellectual property that had belonged to GameGavel had been transferred to that new company.

The Retro VGS Facebook page was awash with promotion and talk of pending games and lots and lots of 3D rendered images of how the console would look, close ups of the controller and cartridges, even pictures of a controller being held in front a TV running a game to give the illusion that it was being played, but still there were no details, nothing concrete on hardware specs. There were lots of options for different colored consoles though. One commenter put it:

> *"Who in the year 2015 has $300+ to spend on such a console and only has a TV with RF input? This whole thing is beginning to seem like someone is having a manic episode and documenting it online...along with some 3D renders."*

Facebook was where a lot of the activity was taking place but as people began criticizing the idea or the lack of hardware specs, their comments would be deleted. In fact, lots of questions were also being deleted and only positive comments were left alone. Many AtariAge members not only had comments deleted but were also banned from the page. It was fast becoming a full time job over at Retro VGS Towers just to manage the Facebook page in a fever pitch attempt to control the narrative where they could.

> *"Hello Everyone! I wanted to address our decision to remove some posts from our Facebook page. As you all know, for better or worse, we have been very transparent on our progress and this is something we will continue to do as we move forward. Things have been changing very fast as we add/remove and*

finalize our design. We have learned from everything we've posted and read all your comments. Moving forward we will be launching our campaign soon that will address and fill in all the final information (and reveal a few more nice surprises) and there is no sense confusing new folks that discover this page with all the information that has lead up to our final working design. In the end, we will be offering a very compelling product for a very competitive price. And we hope to give you all enough information so you can make a wise decision to back our campaign or not. Thanks again to all of you who have been following along with our progress and know we won't let you down!"

As the crowd funding campaign approached Scott received an e-mail from Sean Robinson:

> *From: Sean R.*
> *To: Scott Schreiber*
> *Date: Thu, September 17, 2015 11:09 pm*
> *Subject: The latest with RETRO VGS*
>
> *Hey Scott,*
> *Check this out:*
>
> > *"uh oh. I hear rumors of indiegogo... that's where kickstarter's rejects go to take people's money and not deliver a product (pretty much every single time actually) ... that's definitely not a good sign guys :(my heart just broke."*
>
> *Only so hard you can push 'work for free' (especially in California where it can turn around and bite you on the ass when the state wants their tax cut on people that *should* have been payed (sic) as employees ...)*

Indeed, there was a huge amount of discussion on Facebook and forums about whether the console would be crowd funded on Kickstarter or Indiegogo and there was a lot of discussion behind the scenes too because the team seemed to have stopped mentioning Kickstarter and had changed the button on their Facebook page which had originally said "Kickstarter campaign."

The way that Kickstarter works is that somebody with an idea, but no funds to make it a reality, start a crowd funding campaign with a specified target amount that they will need to make their project happen. They create a campaign page explaining their project and the different support levels that people can pledge, usually starting at $1 and rising to different levels with different perks for the higher support levels. People can then pledge funds over the course of the campaign, usually around a month or so, and if the desired total is reached, the pledgers are charged and the money is sent to the project to allow it to happen. If the target is not reached, the project is unsuccessful and nobody is charged anything. For a successful campaign, Kickstarter take a 5% fee on the total funds raised and a handling fee.

Indiegogo is considered the less strict of the two platforms and they offer two different fund raising options, fixed funding and flexible funding. With fixed funding, a campaign has to reach its set target for it to be funded and for any money to be sent to the campaign which has to run for thirty days or less. With flexible funding it does not matter if the campaign reaches its target amount or not, any money raised is kept and the project will be rolled out, usually with lesser goals or fewer features to match that lower budget.

The other main difference between the two is that Kickstarter will only charge pledges when the campaign is successful, whereas Indiegogo will take the money straight away and refund it if a fixed funding campaign is not successful. With both fixed and flexible funding, Indiegogo charge a fee of 4% of contributions for successful campaigns, but for unsuccessful flexibly funded campaigns they charge 9%.

John Carlsen reported that the decision to use Indiegogo rather than Kickstarter had been made some time earlier, and Mike had said several times that Indiegogo *"have been courting us"* but thus far all of the promotional talk had been about using Kickstarter. Mike Kennedy made the final decision to use Indiegogo and he made it at the last minute. He also used the term *"Why did we switch, kind of, at the last minute?"* during the interview that the team did with Retro Gaming Magazine so it may be that he had been holding out as long as possible to use Kickstarter but when it became clear that they couldn't, he accepted the change.

He had emailed UKMike following the interview that the team did with Retro Gaming Roundup on September 13, 2015 and asked him if he would be able to edit out any mention of Indiegogo as there was a chance that they may still use Kickstarter. UKMike was moving house that week and told him that if he sent the timestamps where the edits were needed then he could possibly do it before releasing the interview on the day that the crowdfunding campaign launched. Mike never sent the timestamps and they did not switch to Kickstarter so no edits were needed.

The main difference between the two sites, that affected the Retro VGS, was the issue of the working prototype that had thus far been absent. Everybody was asking for hardware specs and proof of a working prototype but none had been forthcoming and this meant that they could not officially use Kickstarter. Mike Kennedy only spotted this issue about three weeks before the campaign was due to go live when he was reading the forum thread about the console at the NeoGAF forums. Clearly Mike hadn't done his due diligence and it was brought to his attention when a NeoGAF member posted that in the Kickstarter rules it states that:

> *"Technical drawings, CAD models, and sketches are awesome and encouraged, but photorealistic renderings that someone might mistake for a finished product are prohibited."*
>
> *"If your project will involve manufacturing gadgets or other products, we ask that you show as much as you can about how you're going to do that, including*

> *things like a production plan, an estimated schedule, and any other details you can provide for backers.*
>
> *Projects that involve the development of physical products must feature explicit demos of working prototypes. While you can run a project focused on the creation of a prototype, you can't offer the product that is under development as a reward."*

The team, by their own admission, were *"not ready to show an explicit demonstration of a working prototype."* but there had been some discussion with Luke Crane at Kickstarter about this policy and Luke was willing to give the Retro VGS team a pass on the issue but John Carlsen felt that it was dishonest to not follow their publicly posted rules, and also, Mike had lied to them on September 9th when he told them that he had a working PCB.

> *"We have our console and cartridge shell injection mold tooling and real samples, real controller prototype (Ouya showed a block of wood) and a working prototype PCB."*

Of course John knew that they did not have a working PCB and called Mike out on it so Mike shared an e-mail from Luke that read:

> *"Ouya came through during a very different time on Kickstarter. We're constantly updating our rules and procedures. Under our current rules, you can show illustrations and wireframes and animations, but no photorealistic renderings. Sounds like you'll have no trouble meeting those requirements."*

John stood his ground and told Mike that Luke's pass was not valid because it was based on the lie from Mike about having a *"working prototype PCB."* The team had also spoken about keeping production of the Retro VGS local, and within California if possible, which is where Indiegogo are based as opposed to Kickstarter who are based in New York. Mike had this to say:

> *"In the end, you know, behind the scenes, Indiegogo had been courting us for the last few months. They called me and said they were very proactive about it. Kickstarter could care less, right? They were fat, dumb and happy with all of these things. You have got Indiegogo over there who is a still a very large credible, viable, crowdfunding source that has been around longer than Kickstarter. They are not as prevalent in the game world, which is true, and that was always a concern of ours to this day."*

Indiegogo had shown Mike some figures on their past campaigns and an article written by TechCrunch showed that the median average for hardware campaigns was higher on Indiegogo than it was on Kickstarter.

While Mike was the public face of the console and was out there posting in forums, being interviewed on podcasts and deleting all of the negative Facebook comments, he was much less public about something that he did 11 days prior to the Indiegogo campaign going live. He had started a new company that would see the console assets owned by GameGavel transferred to it without telling any of the investors and partners in GameGavel LLC. All along, the console was supposed to be a part of the existing LLC, in fact he had confirmed as much to Scott Schreiber who is of course one of the investors and owners of GameGavel LLC and who had asked a similar question when Retro Magazine was launching of course.

"No, no, no, it's part of Retro. It's got the name stamped right on the front."

However, this was now not the case as Mike had registered Retro Entertainment Technology Inc (entity number C3823713) on September 8, 2015.

Later, Mike would insist that the console was always a separate venture and that the assets always belonged to the console company(s), a story belied by that fact that the company didn't even exist until days before the crowd funding launch. Something was not right here. Since April of 2015 there had been an ongoing issue among the members and owners of GameGavel LLC and of course Retro Magazine with regard to the finances of the companies. Of course we have seen that writers and in-house staff were not being paid on time, if at all, and Paul Wylie had tried to reduce the quality of the paper used to print the magazine on but Mike was also being cagey about the shareholders as well. Some had come and gone, some had been given 5% of the company and had left within months, others had been there from the start and did not have either their share certificates or the cash equivalents. Mike was also trying to change the company registration from member run to manager run but he needed the members' approvals to do so.

He had to request the consent of all GameGavel LLC owners (Michael B. Kennedy, Patricia L. Kennedy, Brandon Justice, Mark Kaminski, Ron & Jane Schroer, Scott Schreiber, Dave Wakefield, Ronald M. Kennedy, Lloyd Fritzmeier, Phil Adam, Daniel Kayser and Paul Wylie) and each one was requested to sign and date it to show their consent to Mike changing the company registration. Of course some were blissfully unaware of any wrongdoing thus far and signed it, others however were much less willing to do so.

Mark and Scott, for example, had seen the complete mismanagement of the Retro Magazine project and faced with the pending launch of the biggest Mike Kennedy project to date, would they completely relinquish full control of the company to Mike or would they want things to remain as they were? Clearly the latter as they had seen GameGavel become a forgotten site as the magazine took precedence and now the console loomed to take Mike's attention away from managing their investment. Of course, the company under which the magazine and auction site lived had already been gutted to support the console, and both Mark and Scott were told that they were the only ones who hadn't signed the document. This version of events only worked in a world where Mike's isolation tactics worked, but Mark and Scott were talking to each other thus invalidating Mike's narrative.

Scott was preparing to file a lawsuit against Mike and his new companies and consulted an attorney on the matter of signing the letter. The attorney advised him to go ahead and sign it under duress.

"It won't matter in the end because he is getting nailed to the wall."

Scott had this to say:

"Then about the time of the Indiegogo, I find out that he had formed a second company and that the molds and intellectual property and proprietary material now belong to that company. I was never told of this. I was never told the company existed and I'm a shareholder in GameGavel/Retro. So our company was devalued. Obviously, the time and effort and focus on this distracted him from the magazine. The quality has declined, his editor just resigned, GameGavel is totally neglected. There's nothing going on there. So even if he claims that the company was made financially whole and that the purchase of the molds wasn't a factor, it still devastated the company that we all were shareholders in, and beyond that, even if it's somehow legal, it's horribly unethical to do that."

Mike tried to explain himself:

"First off, I personally loaned the $6K (via a bank transfer from my personal account to GG, LLC account) to GameGavel, LLC to purchase the Jaguar tooling and will recoup that "loan" and transfer the tooling assets (to the console company) from GameGavel, LLC once the console company is able to pay it back. So to break it down, the console company will pay the $6K to GameGavel, LLC which will then in turn, pay off my loan made to GameGavel, LLC. The tooling will be paid for ultimately by the console company and the tooling assets transferred from GameGavel, LLC to the console company. And I get the $6K back I personally I loaned to GG, to buy the tooling in the first place.

Next, GameGavel, LLC and its owners are still of utmost importance to me. I have other family that bought in and obviously I still want them and you to have an upside in that investment. It is always top priority!

But in order to compensate Steve Woita with shares and other future potential investors/partners on the console side, it had to be set up a separate entity as I have no more "shares" available to give out in GameGavel, LLC.

The two companies will still play off one another in arm's length transactions that will benefit both companies. Example, all buyers of the console will get a one year digital and/or print subscription to the magazine and pay GameGavel, LLC for those subscriptions. Once those consumer subscriptions run out the subscription renewals will go straight through to GameGavel,LLC and the magazine. And we will be advertising GameGavel.com in the magazine to a growing subscriber base (from console sales) that will allow for it to start growing again.

Also, the console company will be paying the magazine the going page rate for 10-12 pages of content in each issue dedicated to the console.

Game previews, developer interviews, etc. That is another way the console company will aid in the growth and sustainability of the magazine."

This wasn't the only, or the last, questionable explanation attempt by Mike, who at one point opined that he had moved the console under a separate company to *"protect"* GameGavel shareholders and partners in case the console project failed. Some glaring questions arise from that explanation. Firstly, if Mike had intended to use GameGavel LLC to legitimately produce the console, why did he need to change the way that the business was managed? Or if Mike had always secretly intended to use a separate company to produce the console, why involve GameGavel at all? Why not register the company earlier and then use that company, or a loan to it, to buy the molds? Instead, he claimed to have loaned the money to GameGavel which bought the molds but had then given the molds to a new company which was not owned by all of the original investors who now had seen the company that they owned shares in, be asset stripped and devalued.

His second explanation was that he had given away all of the GameGavel LLC shares that he was able to and so he needed to start a new company that he could then give away, namely to Steve Woita.

"I started a new company for the console as I don't have any stock available on the GG/Magazine side to give Steve or any other hardware person meat in the game so I had no choice."

Had no choice? The whole Indiegogo campaign was based around them funding not only a new console but also paying for offices, for building a prototype and in fact to start a whole business, so why did he need to give Steve Woita anything? Steve would be more than compensated if the crowd funding was successful and he would have a full time job, paid for by the campaign backers. As Scott put it:

"If that is the case, why take the loan and give it to GG, why not just make a personal purchase, no need to involve GG unless you originally planned to use them under GG and then decided not to.

GameGavel LLC is so important that he rebranded their forums with the Retro artwork. The only sellers are those with free accounts who likely never visit other than to relist items that haven't sold."

UKMike posed the rhetorical question:

"How many businesses start by stealing from another business, against the traditional method of the founders putting their own hard-earned cash in and taking a risk."

There was another big problem with Mike's explanation as well, he was going to include with every console sale a one-year subscription to Retro magazine and then the console company would pay Retro/GameGavel for that subscription. The problem with that idea is that the console company would only have money that came from crowd funding, so each backer is inadvertently paying for the magazine subscriptions when Mike and the team were saying that they were doing everything they could to bring the cost down. In fact, they were increasing the cost to prop up the console company and now the magazine and GameGavel as well. The house of cards was swaying.

Finally, the console company would be paying for coverage in Retro magazine, with 10 to 12 pages in every issue being dedicated to the console, its games and future developments. Is that not a huge conflict of interest? Paid coverage for his own console in his own magazine? How is that objective journalism? All 10 to 12 of those pages are essentially worthless as far as honest, ethical journalism goes.

Mike ended his explanation with:

> *"I am in no way abandoning GameGavel, LLC and its owners. The bottom line is that the auction site and magazine are barely sustainable on their own and this other company will help with its overall future growth."*

Scott wistfully mused:

> *"But I committed corporate fraud cos I love you guys so much!*

That's not how business works. It might be how the government works, when we ran out of money, we printed more, but the IRS gets to do that and the Treasury Department, not us. We go to jail for that stuff."

On September 19, 2015, the Indiegogo campaign went live with the slogan **"Remember When? Play Again!"** a slogan that would return to haunt Mike later, but for now he had more immediate concerns as the campaign caused the Internet to go nuts. The target for the fixed funding campaign was $1,950,000.00 and it was set to run for 45 days. Yes, that is $1,950,000.00 and the tag line for the campaign was:

> *Play new video games without frustration. Insert a cartridge, turn on the power, and have fun!*

Backers had a choice of pledge levels and rewards of course:

> *$10 USD*
> *Make It Happen*
> *Easiest way to show your support for our project and say no to patches and scratches! Get full credit toward a future purchase for the amount you pledge.*

$25 USD + Shipping
Take Control
Get a genuine RETRO VGS USB controller that can be used on any USB enabled device! Plus, get full credit toward a future purchase for any amount you pledge over the reward tier amount.

$299 USD + Shipping
Early Bird Black RETRO VGS
Get a black RETRO VGS with power adapter, RETRO VGS USB controller, HDMI cable, and full credit toward a future purchase for any amount you pledge over the reward tier amount, plus: – Bottom label printed with BACKER EDITION – Digital subscription to RETRO Video Game Magazine ($18 Value)

$349 USD + Shipping
Personalized RETRO VGS
Personalized Backer Edition RETRO VGS in Legend Series or Jewel Series or Black Everything included with the Early Bird Black RETRO VGS Backer Edition and full credit toward a future purchase for any amount you pledge over the reward tier amount, plus: – choice of any Legend, Jewel Series colors or black – Lower serial numbers and ships before lower-priced rewards – Digital subscription to RETRO Video Game Magazine ($18 Value)

$399 USD + Shipping
Bronze RETRO VGS
Treasure Series Bronze Personalized Backer Edition RETRO VGS Everything included with the Jewel Series Personalized Backer Edition RETRO VGS and full credit toward a future purchase for any amount you pledge over the reward tier amount, plus: – Bronze color – Lower serial numbers and ships before lower-priced rewards – Digital subscription to RETRO Video Game Magazine ($18 Value)

$424 USD + Shipping
Silver RETRO VGS
Treasure Series Silver Personalized Backer Edition RETRO VGS Everything included with the Bronze Personalized Backer Edition RETRO VGS and full credit toward a future purchase for any amount you pledge over the reward tier amount, plus: – Silver color – Lower serial numbers and ships before lower-priced rewards – Digital subscription to RETRO Video Game Magazine ($18 Value)

$449 USD + Shipping
Gold RETRO VGS
Treasure Series Gold Personalized Backer Edition RETRO VGS Everything included with the Silver Personalized Backer Edition RETRO VGS and full credit toward a future purchase for any amount you pledge over the reward tier amount, plus: – Gold color – Lower serial numbers and ships before lower-priced rewards – Digital subscription to RETRO Video Game Magazine ($18 Value)

$499 USD + Shipping
Elite Backer Edition RETRO VGS

Lowest Serial Numbers and Earliest Shipping Highest contributor gets serial #1. Serial numbers start at #1 and ship in order of contribution amount, from highest to lowest, with any tied amounts ordered by earliest contribution first. Plus a RETRO Video Game Magazine print subscription ($33 Value)

Delivery for the controller level pledges was estimated to be February 2016 and the consoles were expected to be delivered in November 2016. So where was all of that money going?

Two thirds of it would be used to "manufacture contributor's rewards" which leaves $650,000, of which 37%, or $240,000, is for *"stipends (about half our normal wages) so we can afford to do this full time."* This equated to $80,000 for each of the three team members, which, if as they claimed, is *"half our normal wages"* they must each be earning a small fortune in their day jobs. Perhaps you might think that with those salaries they would be able to rustle up the $70,000 that Clay Cowgill had estimated for a working prototype.

As I mentioned, the Internet went nuts when the campaign went live, the huge funding target of course was top of the agenda and the fact that it wasn't just a console that was being backed but a new business with offices, salaries and of course the prototype. Yes, still, there was no prototype, but there were lots of publicity shots and lots of 3D renders of the console and how it might look. There were also some misleading pictures being posted on the Retro VGS Facebook page, one in particular showed somebody holding the controller in front of a television that was showing the game The Adventures of Tiny Knight. How was this possible? There was no prototype and the controller was still not finalized in its design but here was somebody apparently playing a game on the system with it. At best this was misleading and at worst was outright fraudulent.

Supporters and detractors were asking questions on Facebook and were summarily having their comments and questions deleted, lots of them were banned from posting on the page as Mike immediately went into damage limitation mode. The PR side of things was handled terribly and Mike reacted very badly to any criticism, usually lashing out at negative comments and community members who did not tow the party line. He would later apologize for the way he reacted but it did massive damage to his legitimacy and highlighted his lack of ability to manage a project of this scale and scope.

One of the features of the Retro VGS was that it would be able to play existing cartridges from retro systems like the Super Nintendo, and in order to do this it would use the FPGA in hardware and a "core" in software. The FPGA would reconfigure itself to be a Super Nintendo when it detected the cartridge and the core would act as the software layer to make the game run properly. As this was relatively new technology in this arena, there was not a supply of cores freely available that the Retro VGS could use, although there were some either fully developed or partially developed at the time. These were the work of an engineer and AtariAge member, Kevin Horton, with whom Mike had discussed the project and the two of them had initially come to an agreement to use Kevin's cores with the Retro VGS, however, things were about to change.

> *"They were all happy to talk with me at first, and the 3rd skype call is when I was discussing licensing my FPGA cores to them.*
>
> *I didn't get any more calls after that, except the one two weeks ago that he cancelled at the last minute.*
>
> *It was at least 2 months between the last skype call and the blown off meeting.*
>
> *I was just floored when he said 'they weren't sure' if it would have the FPGA on it ... days before the IGG launch.*
>
> *I knew from day one that it was going to be a gilded turd of a project and it would never, ever make funding.*
>
> *Back when I talked to him, it was around a $1M project.*
>
> *Guess it ballooned after that, adding on $80K/year per person "wages" and money for frigging office rent and other crap.*
>
> *Might as well make everyone foot the bill for your dream, eh?"*

Once Kevin saw the amount that the team were asking for, that the FPGA was now gone from the base system, cutting him out of any deal arranged, and the costs that Mike was quoting as necessary to build a prototype, he spoke out and posted some of the work he had been doing on his own console idea.

> *"Well, after seeing their IGG page, and how the FPGA is gone? or significantly reduced from their system, I can't stay silent any longer. As many know, there was talk of various "cores" on the RVGS, and that I was going to be the dork supplying them. Anyways, I thought I would inject a little bit of sanity into the whole "FPGA videogame system" realm and show off what I have been able to do alone, and without any kind of outside funding."*
>
> *I started working on FPGA videogame cores and systems back in 2004, when I made my first prototype "FPGA videogame" board.*
>
> *This system worked and is what I developed the FPGA NES and FPGA (Atari) 2600 on.*
>
> *Then in 2010, I decided to update my project and designed and built a second prototype system. Since plastic enclosure design was expensive, I made it fit inside an NES cartridge shell, and the connectors would stick out the back, where the cartridge would otherwise normally fit into the NES system. This prototype was used to design the rest of my systems (17 to date).*
>
> *With this board, I finished up A LOT of systems. All of these systems are DONE and 100% finished and tested, ready to be targeted ("ported") to nearly anything with an FPGA inside it:*

- *Nintendo Entertainment System*
- *Sega Master System*
- *Sega Game Gear*

- *ColecoVision*
- *Atari 2600*
- *Atari 7800*
- *Nintendo Gameboy*
- *Nintendo Gameboy Color (has 1 or 2 tiny bugs left, but 99.9% of the games run)*
- *Intellivision (with Intellivoice, computer add-on, etc)*
- *Odyssey 2 (with The Voice add-on)*
- *Creativision (with tape drive support)*
- *Arcadia 2001*
- *Adventure Vision*
- *Videobrain*
- *RCA Studio 2*
- *Fairchild Channel F*
- *Supervision*

Then in 2014, I decided to make my third FPGA Videogame board, the "possibly sellable" version. This board was a huge step up from the last, and is on par with what the RVGS has and can do IMO. The interesting part is this board exists and I have designed it and wrote code for it.

The goals for this board were these:

- *Make something I can sell!*
- *Include ALL the outputs possible for video and audio, but only if people paid extra to keep costs down if you were only interested in HDMI*
- *4 USB controller ports*
- *High speed SD card interface (4-bit mode, 50MHz)*
- *Menu buttons for the user so he does not need to dork with the controller*
- *RGB status LED*
- *Expansion port for cartridge adapters (the right side connector)*
- *Be able to run all the current cores + SNES, Genesis, Neo Geo, and possibly PS1 (PlayStation 1) era systems*
- *1080p 60fps video output*
- *Ethernet port*

  The board is 6 layers, and was my first board in Altium after I switched over in 2014. It was a lot of fun to design and it helped me to learn Altium. I got the boards made which cost around $600 (for 10 of them), and bought parts (another 400-500 bucks). There's no less than TWO Cyclone V FPGAs on here- Itchy is designed to be the "user interface" and video scaler/processor, and Scratchy is the "engine" that does all the core running and nothing else.

  I noticed in the IGG that they are allocating around $100K(!) for prototype development. This is an insane amount of money, considering I am in for *around $1000-1200 on my latest "advanced" prototypes- around 1% of what they are seeking. No, I am not going to start asking for money, just thought it was interesting to point out. Total development time from concept to prototype PCBs+parts was around 2-3 months. This included the design time in Altium, learning Altium, and getting the boards manufactured.*

Just thought I'd drop the bomb in here about how I have basically created what they are trying to create, but actually have gotten it manufactured and did it all on a shoestringish budget.

There's also video of each system running on my YouTube channel "kevtris".

So Kevin was able to do all of the work that the Retro VGS team had thus far been unable to do, i.e. build and prove a working prototype. Their campaign could have worked out completely differently if they had just been able to do that. Of course Mike did not react well to Kevin's revelations.

"Wow. Kevin ?!?!
First off, we were going to pay Kevin his asking price for the licensing of the cores and this was built into our funding goal ($10K/core) and had another $50K +/- in our funding budget to pay him for the 16 bit cores he has yet to develop.

And these could have been shared with the community or whatever, not exclusive to us. And I could care less if Kevin used these cores to sell his board in addition to ours, he could have had both opportunities. We are selling two entirely different kinds of products. It really is amazing how everything gets turned around in these forums.

We are just three legitimate guys who want to bring a cool product to market. It's as simple as that. And set up it up as a real sustainable business that can continue to support the platform for a long time.

As of this post, I am going to chime out here as there is nothing that even remotely comes in the form of meaningful constructive criticism. And Kevin, I guess we will look elsewhere for our core development."

Mike continued on Facebook:

"When he actually does some homework on what it would take to "consumerize" his product and put his bare board into a console shell, add a controller and pack-in game, and incorporate the ARM and both the digital and analog output, go through the regulatory process, etc. he will find out he can't do it for any for any less than we can. I guarantee you all that!"

As I said, Mike would later apologize for his outbursts, but his actions are clearly not those of somebody who should be running this project and he had attacked Kevin, thrown him off the project and not addressed the elephant in the room, the lack of a Retro VGS prototype. If Kevin could do it on a shoestring budget on his own, why could the three of them not do the same? It goes without saying that none of Kevin's work would be paid for unless the crowd funding campaign was successful and people joked about Mike just throwing Kevin under the bus as if he could just pop down to the *"core store"* to get what he needed. Without Kevin, he had pretty much nothing.

Kevin responded on the AtariAge forums as he does not use Facebook and his *"comments would be deleted anyway."* He explained that Mike was misrepresenting things slightly as the $10,000 figure mentioned for each core was actually $10,000 for systems like the RCA Studio 2 and Fairchild Channel F and more popular and technical systems like the NES and Atari VCS would have been closer to $50,000.

The $200-250 price that Kevin had quoted did in fact represent a complete system and not just a bare board as Mike had said.

> *"This is a board, case, and power supply. Pack-in games are not required (though I could throw in a homebrew NES title maybe). Controllers would probably be extra, but since I accept USB controllers, you can plug literally any HID and use it. This means controllers, keyboards, and mice. Obviously it'd be kinda hard to play a 2600 game with a mouse, but I'm more thinking for FPGA computer projects and not just games."*

Kevin outlined that he had no plans to launch his console as he did not think that people would pay for it, or that there was a big enough market, but he may consider it in the future if there was sufficient demand. In fact, the demand was there and on February 7, 2018, Analogue, Inc. launched their Analogue Super NT. The system was based on an Altera Cyclone V FPGA chip and it supported 8BitDo wireless controllers, original Super Nintendo and Super Famicom controllers and cartridges from all regions with an output resolution of 480p, 720p and 1080p at 60Hz over an HDMI connection. Priced at $189.99 it achieved critical acclaim pretty much across the board with Forbes calling it *"The new benchmark for all retro consoles".*

It was designed and manufactured by Seattle-based company Analogue Inc. and engineered, of course, by Kevin Horton. The system fulfilled its promise of not using emulation and running games with no lag and 100% accuracy, delivering the tagline:

> *"Explore and re-live one of the greatest video game systems of all time with no compromises."*
>
> *"The core functionality of the system is engineered directly into an Altera Cyclone V, a sophisticated FPGA. We spent thousands of hours engineering the system via FPGA for absolute accuracy. Unlike the knock off and emulation systems that riddle the market today, you'll be experiencing the 16-bit era free of compromises. The Super Nt is designed to preserve video game history, with the respect it deserves."*

Perhaps Kevin's success proved that Mike had at least some of the right people in place to bring his console to life, but he either didn't know it or didn't want to pay them until he had his $1.950,000.00 in place. Either way, Kevin was cut out of Mike's project and his interactions with the team had stopped some time earlier, with their last scheduled meeting on September 8 being cancelled at the last minute, as Mike was still not sure if the FPGA would be included in the system, meaning that they would not need Kevin's cores. In general, Kevin found them very unprofessional and the constantly changing hardware specs and rising costs were a bad sign as they seemed to be building the system they wanted, rather than the system the market wanted or would support at the cost that was quoted. He did have some advice for them though:

1. *DO NOT think about patenting the cartridge bus. Patents are stupid. I should know, I own a patent. It's expensive to get, and takes YEARS to get it. I doubt something as simple as a cartridge bus would be worthwhile to patent anyways; there's going to be so much prior art involved it's not funny. A patent isn't some kind of magical shield- all a patent does is literally give you a license to sue. That's it. Without money, you cannot defend your patent, rendering it worthless. Don Lancaster has some great tips on why you should avoid patents.*
2. *You vastly underestimate how much time and money it will take to get this thing through certifications (i.e. CE, UL, CSA, whatever). I am a veteran of the certification racket. It took about 3-4 months and cost a lot of money. I don't think it needs to be certified anyways. Only the power supply has to; this is the reason you see lots of things that have an external power brick these days and not so many things have internal supplies any more. Some company makes these things and gets them through all the certifications for you. If your thing runs on low voltage, you can self-certify it.*
3. *Get the boards manufactured and assembled in China. Made in USA is nice, but it will literally cost 30-50% MORE money to get it made here, and the quality tends not to be as high as China. This is highly ironic to me. I wished getting stuff made in the USA was viable but for lots of things, sadly it isn't. One of my YouTube vids I explained how I tried to get PC boards made in the USA and the misery I ran into.*

Even after all of this, Kevin was still willing to work with them and license his cores.

> *"Moving along ... contrary to popular belief, I'd still license my cores to them. Their money is just as green as anyone else's. They asked me if I would make the prototypes for them, but I politely declined because I didn't think I was going to get paid to do it (unless the crowdfunding went through). After that, their interest in me kinda waned and I didn't hear anything for a couple months until the blown-off meeting. I can't afford to work on someone else's project free with the possibility of getting paid. If I'm going to work on a project that doesn't pay it is going to be my own stuff."*

In the meantime, the IndieGoGo campaign was running and the money started to roll in quite quickly at first. After just one hour they had raised $26,000 which rose to $37,000 over the second hour, then it predictably began to slow down, rising to $49,000 after eight hours, $53,000 after thirteen hours and $58,700 after thirty-two hours.

The funding seemed to be fluctuating as well, with some backers dropping out as people either saw negative comments on Facebook, or found the by now huge thread at AtariAge, where it was being discussed ad nauseum. A notable backer was Garry Kitchen who pledged $1,000 but later withdrew his pledge. Mike posted a note to say that this was due to PayPal seeing the transaction as fraudulent, but whatever the case, Garry pledged again at $1,000, but this was negated as others withdrew their pledges and the campaign started to lose money and backers.

Mike was posting lots of updates and dropping names again including Apple, Atari and Sega but nothing about the actual hardware that people were expected to fund, and the terms "snake oil" and "vaporware" were posted and deleted. It was fast becoming a game of cat and mouse to see if Mike could keep up with posting positive promo and deleting comments from detractors. Eventually, they would remove the comments section from the Facebook page completely, presumably so that Mike could get some sleep, assuming he could sleep, as things were not going in the right direction despite some very ambitious reminders about the various funding goals:

> *"At $3,100,000 – about 60% more than our minimum goal – we increase the size of our FPGA, making RETRO VGS the first video game system capable of recreating classic systems through reshaping its own hardware!*
>
> *At $3,800,000 – less than twice our minimum goal – we increase the size of our FPGA again, nearly doubling its size from the previous goal."*

It was right around this time that Scott spoke to Mike for the penultimate time. He had confronted him about the second company and the transfer of GameGavel assets, reminded him of the promise that the console fell under the GameGavel/Retro banner and that he did not accept the scheme to cut out the GameGavel partners and strip the company, only to transfer the assets to the new company. Mike kept talking around the issue and Scott kept bringing it back to that one point. Scott offered Mike a way out of this mess and a way out of any potential legal proceedings and his two requirements were simple, were made public, and were the only satisfactory resolution:

- Return all assets to the original company.
- Acknowledge all contributors.

Of course Mike flatly rejected this, saying that he couldn't do that because he needed the second company to be able to offer a new round of stock. Mike was then told, in no uncertain terms, that if he chose to reject this offer then action would be taken. Scott wasn't about to show the cards in his hand but he very succinctly told Mike:

> *"Then I'm going to kill your ####ing console."*

This was one warning that Mike should have not ignored. It was made in good faith from a business partner and former friend and he should have listened. As Scott puts it:

> *"Some dogs you don't stare in the eye and challenge, and by the time you hear that low growl the best you can hope for is to turtle up and not expose your vitals. Mike stood there grinning, saying 'nice doggy.'"*

However, it was quite clear that Mike was so far out of touch with what he had done, with the market and with public enthusiasm for the system that was never going to get anywhere near to being funded. He had also alienated Piko Interactive by excluding them from the campaign and Eli had this to say on September 20th:

> *"They have deleted their announcement on Facebook for Super Noah's Ark 3D and obviously not included it on the Indiegogo. They haven't notified me in writing but I take it as a strong sign we are out of this."*

Seeing this comment Mike contacted Eli to smooth things over and Eli passed on the new information:

> *"Actually last night I got an email from Mike saying he was going to add some other of our games tomorrow but I politely declined and told him we will not move forward with this project*
> *So we are officially out.*
> *We will concentrate on known retro platforms and digital distribution."*

Ironically, people were contacting Eli to tell him that he was lucky and that he may well have dodged a bullet by being excluded as things were not improving on Indiegogo.

> *September 21, Day 3: 172 backers, $60,041 total pledged*
> *September 22, Day 4: 186 backers, $66,188 total pledged*
> *September 23, Day 5: 187 backers, $65,956 total pledged*
> *September 24, Day 6: 193 backers, $67,580 total pledged*

September 25th was a busy day for the Retro VGS team and things took a turn for the worse in more ways than one. Whatever had preceded this day, there was going to be no coming back from this. Firstly, John Carlsen released a video claiming to show the Retro VGS Lab and a working prototype and secondly, John "Gamester81" Lester released a video interview with Mike Kennedy to promote the console.

The John Carlsen video was the only video that John ever made for his YouTube channel (which he subsequently deleted) and was shot on his kitchen table. Mike would later deny any knowledge of this video before it was uploaded, but in fact he was lying, John had shown it to both him and Steve Woita before publishing it, and they had actually discussed it before it was shot and Steve had encouraged John to use the term "Retro VGS Lab" in the script.

John did not want to make the video as he did not want to show any hardware because he was planning on submitting patents for a lot of his work but Mike was getting a lot of flak and insisted that they needed to demonstrate at least something. John finally relented and shot a video of "something" running underneath a clear Jaguar shell and hooked up to a monitor. The hardware that was on show was partly the result of a recent change by Mike which John had been re-engineering and so, to say that the lab was a mess of parts and tools is an understatement.

To the untrained eye, not familiar with electronics, it may have been convincing, like the random bits on the set of a sci-fi movie. However, to anyone knowledgeable in electronics it was apparent that somebody had run around the house collecting anything that had something to do with electronics and piled their findings on the table, it was a mass of such unrelated items. The team had stated that they only had HDMI working, yet it was running on an analog only monitor on the table, the soldering iron was more useful for large wire sizes and useless for fine soldering on modern circuit boards. The list goes on, and John commented later:

> *"At that point in development, there were lots of parts on evaluation boards that were loosely wired together. Still, it worked, and gave us lots of computing power at the right price."*

As it turned out, the video was quite damaging to the project and raised a lot more questions than it answered. Kevin Horton had this to say about it:

> *"I found it highly amusing he covered the dev boards with a plastic shell to obscure it.*
>
> *We figured out what the green board was, it's a 256 macrocell CPLD, so not much of an FPGA.*
>
> *The red board is obviously some kind of ARM SOC, maybe an Allwinner one since those are real cheap."*

The video also brought Sean Robinson out of the woodwork:

> *From: Sean Robinson*
> *To: Mike Kennedy*
> *Sent: Sep 25, 2015*
> *Subject: Video*
>
> *Hey Mike,*
>
> *This video that John Carlsen just posted should not be up IMHO... not sure if you've seen it or signed off on it... but wow... you think people are freaking out now, this video just added a few tanker trucks of gas to the fire...*
>
> *"Welcome to the RETRO VGS Lab".... basically his kitchen table with a pile of things not important...*
>
> *[LINK REMOVED]*
>
> *I'm really trying to watch out for you and throw you a life line here...*
>
> *but this is video is bad...*
>
> *-Sean*

Mike was blissfully ignorant though:

> *From: Mike Kennedy*
> *To: Sean Robinson*
> *Sent: Sep 26, 2015*
> *Subject: Video*
>
> *Actually getting some of the most favorable responses yet on our FB page. I could really care less what others are saying about it in the forums.*
>
> *Mike*

Sean was also feeding Mike's responses to Scott, whether out of journalistic integrity or to try and stay in the loop of what was going on behind the scenes is not clear, but he was keen to keep the lines of communication with Scott open, even hinting at a military background to ingratiate himself.

> *"Hi Scott... and you called Mike to try and help him ... he still doesn't care... the Mike you knew is gone, and by your own admissions to me and others as well as your AtariAge comment you've known this for years... pending how the conversation goes with Mike and I on Monday, I'll most likely be moving forward on what I need to do...*
>
> *... like you, I have a military background... 4 years active duty in the Marines... yes, you don't throw your own people under the bus, Mike continues to do this... the things he's said about me are legally defamation and slander... which I have documented proof off (sic)... I also understand that you keep things within your unit, but Mike was out of your unit years ago... lets call what Mike has done basically treason IMHO... I do not see Mike pulling the plug on this train wreck... looking forward to your reply on my comments..."*

Sean was also discussing his part in the early life of Mike's idea and his lack of reimbursement for it:

> *"Let us not forget all the time and money that Clay and I put into this project over 3 months before bowing out... if/when they fund or get some money, you bet your butt I'll be asking Mike for payment on my invoices for that work... even if it didn't get used in the final design, we put in the hours, time, research, prototyping, etc.... boo hoo John Carlsen... get in line buddy :)*
>
> *As for his video... "working with a couple great patent attorney's" ... well those can be $250-$350+ an hour... but did you notice he didn't even mention names? Probably because no attorney is on payroll... and if a name was out, we could call and ask questions... and they would say "well I did give them a 30 minute free consult, but they have not hired me"*

Whether Mike cared about forums or not, the fund raising was stalling and the team were in a mess as they deleted Facebook posts and went into damage control trying to justify their huge funding target and how the money would be spent. It was time to hit the campaign trail again and Mike was in dire need of a friendly face and an easy interview. He got it when John Lester interviewed him for his YouTube channel in a video that, like John Carlsen's Retro VGS Lab video, would do more damage than good in the long run, not just to the Retro VGS but to the community as a whole.

Mike was in verbal diarrhea mode and fell back into his sales pitches, dropping names and companies like they were going out of fashion and talking about how he couldn't understand the criticisms levelled at him, his team and his console. Most of it went unchallenged, don't forget John and Mike were friends from doing the ColecoVisions podcast together with Willie Culver.

Mike easily fielded the questions from John, who also had a vested interest in the console succeeding and being funded as CollectorVision were hoping to port their games to it very easily if it was able to run Super Nintendo cores as they already had games, either already released or close to release, for that system. They also had the pack-in game deal of course now that Eli had been excluded.

The problem of "bug free" games had arisen and Mike passed this off by saying:

> *Mike Kennedy: "... if they're done right, we'll have a game on there that works straight from the box. No glitches or major catastrophic bugs. Yeah, there were bugs that got out back in the day and people loved them. They loved to find them and a lot of them were Easter Eggs that had come to be in there and so there are little things that kind of escaped and what happens when you burn these to ROM, you're pretty much screwed, right John?"*
>
> *Gamester81: "Right, sure."*
>
> *Gamester81: "Okay, so Mike earlier you mentioned in our discussion that the price of the system initially was going to be around 150 to 180 and then you go to the campaign now, and the systems start at $300 each.*
>
> *So, can you go through the process of the pricing and why the increase of price and what exactly people are getting in the bundle?"*
>
> *Mike Kennedy: "Yeah, sure. So yeah, like I said. Originally, we're in the 150, 180, 200 hot price range and this is when we were originally architecting this to be more of a BeagleBone Black type board and this wasn't something that we were going to buy and expand here. We were going to rearchitect and re-engineer something very similar to what BeagleBone has done. [...]*
>
> *It's hard to boil hundreds and hundreds and hundreds of hours of conversations that we've had down to a short few minutes but the bottom line is, the parts that we're putting into this for even a smaller FPGA and processor, and all the other things that are going into it to, converting the digital to analog and all that stuff and we have to have a big board in there because we're using the Atari Jaguar so John has had to kind of engineer a board into this existing shell versus engineering a board that's going to go into something brand new that we can form around it."*

Despite Kevin Horton showing how prototypes can be built and made to work cheaply, Mike chose to ignore his words and the evidence that he had posted.

> *Gamester81: "Yeah that seems to be another concern that people have is the fact that there is no working prototype. Can you elaborate on why there isn't one?"*
>
> *Mike Kennedy: "For sure, yeah. Well, there is no working prototype because we can't afford to bring a working prototype to market. I mean to bring a prototype to market for a consumer product is much more in-depth and much more expensive than creating a prototype for something that is not going to be a consumer product. We can go through three or four or five iterations of a board. The first one never works, that's what I'm being told. I don't have any reason to doubt that. These guys have done it before. It's like the first one, when you get it as close as you can. There is a science to this and it takes a while to get it to work. It's very expensive and then you got the regulatory. I mean I was just told by a guy at your expo John, at the Game On Expo that they had just come out with a handheld system and he said they spent 90 grand ($90,000) on FCC and another international (audio drop) That's all part of bringing this to market and it's just expensive. I mean if Sony prototyped a unit, do you think they'd spend a few thousand or a few hundred thousand? They'd spend a few hundred thousand because it's a consumer product."*
>
> *Gamester81: "I hear you, for sure. Now, I want to kind of address, you've gotten some heat on some websites. I'm going to name AtariAge as just one example.*
> *A lot of people were, basically, one guy is saying that he can make an FPGA board for much less and people were saying that, "It's too expensive" or blah, blah, how do you react to that? What's your response when you hear stuff like that?"*
>
> *Mike Kennedy: "Yeah. Well, I'm not going to stoop down to the level of everybody over there of course you know, trying to keep this all positive."*
>
> *"The facts are you cannot, nobody can make an FPGA system any cheaper than we can. We've spent hundreds and hundreds of hours trying to get it as low as possible and you know we've done it. I mean his board was, again, when I first started talking to you guys about this, we were talking about an FPGA that will play up to Neo Geo sized games. Well, to do that, not only do you need a bigger, more expensive chip, you need some accompanying circuitry and parts to fold around that to make it do that. That all adds up."*
>
> *Gamester81: "Sure, fair enough, fair enough. So your goal is raise at least close to $2 million for this thing?"*
>
> *"Can you elaborate on where the money is being spent because that's a big goal, a very ambitious goal."*
>
> *Mike Kennedy: "Yeah. Well, $2 million, two-thirds of that is going to go towards making the system and after costs of goods and so that left over money after*

we assemble it, after we buy the parts and assemble it and package it and fulfil it and all of that, you know it's yielding us somewhere around 70 bucks each. So we're figuring we gotta sell about 6,000 of these, times, it's actually we're around that."

Gamester81: "It's pretty close."

Mike Kennedy: "If there's money left over after we build it then that money has got to go to starting a business. We're not an existing business. A lot of these companies that start Kickstarters or Indiegogo or whatever, they're an existing business. They're launching a new product and so they can go out there and set a really low goal for it because they've already got the business side of things. They're already an ongoing business. We're founding a company based on this and, "Hey! Why don't we go out to venture capitalists or the angel investors?" I said, "Well, guys seriously I mean this is a project that's got to come from us," from the gaming crowd and community to believe in us because if this is anything other than a cloud gaming project, it's not going to get funded at to the VC level at least at the beginning.

I mean it was my hope that we go out and raise $2 to $3 million here and then we can say, "Hey, there's really something here. There's a market here. There's people that want this. We can take it and expand upon it." Then you go out and get the money where you don't have to give way three quarters of the company at that point because you've already shown there's a market. One of the great things about crowdfunding is you can prove that there is a market. Right now guys we're proving that there's no market for a cartridge based system. I mean, this probably will never happen again. We were fortunate enough to pay $6,000 for this Atari tooling, do the math. Our minimum goal is about 6,000 people. That's about a buck a person for this tooling. [...]

We've done everything that we can to get it to this point and we feel that we're being very transparent. We're letting everybody know exactly where we are, where we need to go. It's spelled out right in the campaign and we're really to the point where we need the money to do a proper prototyping of this thing."

Gamester81: "We didn't talk about this but what's included with the further $300? You get the system, you get the AC adapter, the AV cable, the HDMI, controller with USB."

Mike Kennedy: "Yeah, and the pack-in game."

Gamester81: "Yeah, and the pack-in game, Adventures Of Tiny Knight, which is a game that I'm a part of, which I'm honored to be a part of."

Mike Kennedy: "Yeah, The Adventures Of Tiny Knight, we're really excited to have this game and from the start I always thought this game was sort of, I felt some sort of connection with this little knight going out there, you know going after all of these dragons. I didn't know that there'd be so many dragons though. The dragons in my mind were Sony, Microsoft, Nintendo, and these Android systems and mobile."

Gamester81: "The price of a normal game is between 30 and 60, correct?"

Mike Kennedy: "Yeah, 30 to 60 bucks. Most of them would be 30 to 50."

Gamester81: "I, for one, think it's kind of a fascinating system. I think there is a market. I wanted to ask you Mike, what do you think your market is, who do you think would be interested in the Retro VGS, is it the older crowd, the younger crowd?"

Mike Kennedy: "You know it's a really great question. At the Game On Expo, we had kids that came by that would pick up our prototype controller and kind of start trying to play and play with it, hitting the buttons and stuff and would look at our video and we'd explain to them and a couple of them even saw your show where you had originally mentioned our system and I think in conjunction with your game. These guys, they were asking some really intelligent questions and I tell you what, kids these days are very smart even down to 10, 11, 12, 13 years old, we talked to some that were very intelligent, asking us questions about this and would even impress us by saying that, "These are cartridges. This is really neat." and we still play my dad's Super NES and we love these things and I collect cartridges.

We've been approached over the last six months by somewhere between 150 to 200 developers. I mean you can see them on our Facebook page even as of this morning somebody chimed in like, "Can you send me an SDK or some more information?" This is all going to be pending. This is all stuff we have to build and do and so we will have all of this coming within a couple of months. I think probably two to three months after this we'll start having SDKs and tool chains for people. People are wondering who wants to make games for this, well, lots of people do because they're not making money anywhere else."

Gamester81: "Well, I think, Mike, here is my take. I think people have been very positive for the system. I see a lot of, you know, like the first couple of days, your campaign was great. It's levelled off right now but you still have over 40 days left. I think there are a lot of positives to be said but I also think a lot of people were unclear as far as what the system is, why it was $300. I mean, I think people were taken back by the fact there's no prototype. So hopefully this interview will help clear some of those."

Mike Kennedy: "Yeah, I hope so. We're ready, willing and waiting to continue on with this and not be bogged down with all of this side line stuff we're having to kind of deal with now. I mean we're losing time as we speak that gets us even further down the road."

Gamester81: "It's fascinating too because it feels like there are some people who just want to see this thing fail."

Mike Kennedy: "Yeah, from the start. From the absolute start and I can't explain that."

Gamester81: "Okay, if you don't agree with it that's great and that's okay, then leave constructive criticism, but then why bash it? Why make it personal in some cases too? I just don't think that's cool but you know it is what it is.

... having done my show for years I get that too on what I do. You get critiqued and you put yourself out there. Look, I tip my hat to you, Steve and John for putting your guys out there. You've put literally thousands of hours into this project. You put your time into it. You put yourself out there and I'm curious to see how this does, there's still plenty of time left. And I really wish you guys the best of luck because I think this is something that has a lot of potential and it sounds like to me from what you said and you have an A Team of people working on this, and it's not like you guys are just some Joe Schmoes who are looking to make a quick buck. This is something that you've put together. You have to establish a business like you said, and so like a third of your cost that you're putting into it or you're getting, goes in operating costs. So it's not just salary, I think a lot of people think like, "Oh, a third.""

Mike Kennedy: "Leases, legal and accounting, benefits, 8% is, you know, 5% is going to Indiegogo and 3% is going to credit card processing." [...]

"8% is coming right off the top so there's going to be unforeseen costs we don't even see yet that may come out. There's deterioration of our tooling, we've got a little bit of money in every system sold that, because you've got deterioration. Sooner or later we're going to have to replace that, years down the road. We want to be around for years to support this and to keep awesome games coming out on it."

Gamester81: "Absolutely, absolutely. Well Mike I really appreciate your time and I wish you guys really the best of luck. I appreciate being a part of it on the developer side of things as far as the games go. I'm curious to see how this goes and we'll see and I really hope people who do leave comments here in this video and who see this video be respectful, I guess."

Mike Kennedy: "You shouldn't even have to ask that but you do, right?"

Gamester81: "... it's okay to have a point of view and I really think the point of this Mike isn't really to sell people. I don't want us to make it sound like a sales pitch like you should have to go and buy it, right? It's really to educate people and if they're for it, support it and help spread the word and that's it."

Mike Kennedy: "That's all we're asking."

That might have been all they were asking, but it wasn't all they got as critics rounded on the video and found it somewhat disingenuous from somebody involved in the campaign, albeit on the periphery. Some described it as *"softball"* like a *"staged interview"* or an *"overnight infomercial"* where the interviewer just sets up the PR person to deliver their lines and sales pitch. Of course, there was still nothing new to come out of it and Mike just repeated many of the things he had already said and offered nothing new, other than more name dropping, ideas and dreams. It was also noticed that rather than focusing on their strengths and showing people a system and what it could do, they instead chose to attack the detractors and what they called the *"haters"* and some found that *"disheartening"* and *"intellectually dishonest."*

Willie Culver was, at this time, still in Camp Mike and showing his support for his friend, though he was honest enough to disclose that fact:

> *"Yes, a great guy he is! ... I was with the team at Game on Expo last month and the general excitement of the crowd was significant that visited the Retro Magazine booth. It is a shame all this is going on, I would really like to see something like this come out. I still am a backer, going to ride it out to the end. Disclaimer – Mike co-hosts ColecoVisions podcast with myself and Gamester81."*

Mike needed all the friends he could find at this point and again took to Facebook:

> *"No PR campaign could fix the undermining of this project (from the beginning) from the haters in the world in this hobby.*
>
> *One thing PR people would do is ban people and keep these public attacks at bay, and that is one mistake we've made in the beginning to show transparency. Big mistake and one we are learning from."*

How they were being transparent is not clear as they had literally shown nothing. No hardware, no prototype, no working system, no games running on an actual system. All they had done was talk about what they wanted to create rather than what they had created.

John Lester also had negative comments to deal with on the back of his video and again, Facebook was the venue for his reaction:

> *"I have a love for the gaming community like no other, however when I see ignorant comments like this left on my videos, it makes me facepalm. I'm clearly am (sic) in the minority with my thoughts about the RETRO VGS, but should people lose respect because of this? I certainly don't respect people less for not agreeing with me. Everyone is entitled to an opinion, and I also believe that there are two sides to every story, and that people should hear both sides before lashing out. I wanted Mike to have an opportunity to address the criticism for the RETRO VGS, and I felt that I asked questions that address these concerns."*

Another media outlet that was covering the story was the CUPodcast (Completely Unnecessary Podcast) hosted by Pat Contri and Ian Ferguson. Though they were discussing publicly available commentary, they were also being fed information by Scott that they were able to verify elsewhere, in fact Scott insisted that they do so.

> *"I was in constant communication with Pat and Ian over at CUPodcast so before many of their shows Pat and I would get on the phone and I would tell him about all the dirty deeds that Kennedy was pulling and give him information he could verify and so most of the discussion on CUPodcast was stuff that I had fed to them. I mean certainly they did innovative and original content ... but a large*

amount was stuff I had sent to them and they used, and I'm not saying that they were an unwitting mouthpiece, they were genuinely interested in the scam and its trajectory and I happily spoke with them behind the scenes and fed them"

Pat and Ian discussed a few points about the console including the campaign itself, the cost of the consoles having risen from $150 to $299 for the cheapest system, the shipping costs quoted for the units and the ridiculously high pricing for the different colored limited edition consoles. They went on to have a good discussion about the wisdom of bringing cartridges back, especially for games that were already available elsewhere much more cheaply but mainly because of games being released with bugs in them. The example they gave was that even The Legend Of Zelda on the NES had bugs in it, so what chance did the Retro VGS team have of releasing bug free games?

As he often does, Ian was drinking a beer during the show and Mike seized on this to try and discredit everything they had said.

"... their drunken commentary was filled with disinformation beginning with our shipping costs and going on from there. Very little of what they discussed had anything to back it up and they did little to no research. And their opinion there is no market for cartridge gaming and that games these days can't be made without bugs is their opinion nothing objective. Cartridge gaming thrived and we all loved it for nearly 20 years. It can happen again. We feel there is a need for this product and a market for this even though it will cost gamers a bit more to actually "own" the games they love to play. They could have easily invited me on like Gamester81's upcoming video and we could have had equal ground. But they didn't afford us this benefit even when Pat has my email address and could have asked me."

Mike did email Pat a couple of times about the saga but Pat explained to him that they did not do interviews and they don't have guests on the show, besides, even had Mike appeared he would not and could not have been completely truthful with them and would have likely dodged questions as other podcasts had allowed him to do. They also felt that they had all of the information they needed, which obviously they did, as a large part of it was given to them by Scott and then verified. They even withheld some of the information that they had as they felt that some of it could have been fabricated and they wanted to remain as professional as possible.

Campaign update:

September 21, Day 3: 172 backers, $60,041 total pledged
September 22, Day 4: 186 backers, $66,188 total pledged
September 23, Day 5: 187 backers, $65,956 total pledged
September 24, Day 6: 193 backers, $67,580 total pledged
September 25, Day 7: 192 backers, $65,970 total pledged
September 26, Day 8: 188 backers, $64,920 total pledged

With things apparently stalled, the team went into action and John posted an update on Facebook.

> *We've promised regular updates on the progress of our product development. I see no reason to wait until after our funding campaign ends. So here we are, nearly a week after our funding campaign began ...*
>
> *I'd like to start my first update by giving a heartfelt thanks to our many loyal fans--especially our backers--and also an apology.*
>
> *We haven't been showing you our best work, and there are many reasons why.*
>
> *The true visionary behind this project is Mike Kennedy. He's also a marketing person with a big heart, and he wants to reciprocate the enthusiasm our followers show us by being totally open and sharing everything. I get it, and I admire him for that. But he talks, and he talks about everything I show or tell him. Again, he's a marketing person, and that's what marketing people do.*
>
> *Knowing this about Mike (and about marketing people in general), causes me (as an engineer) to be very cautious in choosing what I share with him. The reason for this is very simple: our inventions are valuable, and premature public disclosure of our inventions would cause us to lose the ability to protect them with patents.*
>
> *For most of this year I've been working crazy long startup hours on this project. I've drained my own savings to pay for both my living expenses and building prototype circuits. I have invested a lot of time and money, I have a lot to show for it.*
>
> *The problem is: I can't patent what I share publicly. As a result, I've been protecting my inventions as if they were my own children....*
>
> *Through announcing stretch goals, we have tried to convey that our FPGA can grow in capacity and capability as our funding exceeds our minimum goal. Unfortunately, this seems to have caused some confusion, which we will attempt to clear up as soon as possible....*
>
> *We have working prototypes. For software, our game developers already have working prototypes and many even already sell finished products that run on classic platforms. For hardware, I just shot a quick video showing a little bit that won't risk our patent rights. It isn't much, but it shows our processor communicating via USB and driving simple high-resolution digital and analog video output. Most of our circuits are already in our enclosure, but I still have lots of ribbon cable and hand-wired circuits hanging out the back. [...]*
>
> *We didn't switch to Indiegogo at the last minute. We had all agreed to use Indiegogo at least two weeks before we launched our campaign. (We mention Indiegogo in a video we shot more than a week before launch.) [...]*
>
> *We didn't switch to Indiegogo because we didn't have a working prototype.*
>
> *Kickstarter publishes a rule stating that "Projects that involve the development of physical products must feature explicit demos of working prototypes. While you can run a project focused on the creation of a prototype, you can't offer the product that is under development as a reward."*

Kickstarter clearly lets many current projects slide past this requirement, and they granted us an exception, too. Getting a private exception to this publicly-stated policy seemed deceptive toward backers, and we called them on it. Kickstarter welcomed our project, but wouldn't change its policy statement to match. [...]

We don't need an outside vendor to supply FPGA cores.

An FPGA is a large programmable logic device. The first time I contributed to the design of a consumer product that shipped with programmable logic was in 1989. Over the next few years, I created many more circuit designs in and around programmable logic devices of increasing sizes. [...]

We thought we had a good vendor to delegate some of our work to and/or from whom we could leverage existing work. Clearly it didn't work out. Although I'm disappointed by his apparent lack of professionalism, he does good work and I wish him luck in his future endeavors. [...]

We are going to make adapters that let you play cartridges from older systems. Mike let the cat out of the bag early on this one.

(Again, Mike talks about everything.) Yes, it's true, and it's going to be awesome....

For example, our "Expansion Module #1" plugs in like a regular cartridge, but it has switches at the top and a slot on the front that will accept and play game cartridges that were made for the Atari VCS (2600/2600A) or Sears Tele-Games system, with potentially enough room under the slot for a wood-grain sticker. When an Atari VCS cartridge is inserted into the front of the adapter, the Atari VCS cartridge sits over the top of the RETRO VGS dome so you can read the end label and the top label, many of which were printed with important information including which number to select for which game and which controller(s) to use. Atari VCS games can be played using RETRO VGS USB controllers or classic 9-pin controllers.

We hadn't yet posted this on our campaign page, and the word is already out.

With that, I end my first public status report, and thank you for your continued support.

- John Carlsen

People were still discussing the Retro VGS Lab video and speculating about the hardware specifics, Kevin Horton for one:

> *I think it's fairly difficult to be informed if no one from the RVGS crew is giving us any real clear information. The latest video from John had him going into detail about the bench supply and stuff.... and zero at all on the actual hardware that matters. "Look over here! Don't look behind the curtain!". If I am going to show off a prototype, I show off the prototype and don't cover it up with a textured translucent plastic case to blur out and hide what the hardware is. He might as well just have shoved it into a shoebox with wires coming out of it and a hole so the blinkenlites can shine through instead.*

When I was in talks with them, I was mostly in the dark too. Thinking back on it, I'm fairly sure I was "let go" months ago when I started talking about how much I wanted for the cores I had finished already. Guess I shouldn't have asked for any kind of payback on the thousands of hours of time and the money I put into prototyping and developing them. I certainly wasn't going to work for free on the project "until it got funded", or take a lot of time to target my cores to their platform. I figured out before the IGG started I was "let go" when Mike told me they probably weren't going to even have an FPGA on it after all.

As far as I recall I didn't misrepresent anything about the price increase. I knew from day one that for the hardware they wanted to add to the board it was going to be extremely expensive.

An AtariAge member believed they had identified the circuit board that was used in the video and posted a link to it, then Kevin explained some of the performance details and specs for it:

> *"Everything on the board matches from the silk screen to the chip locations and the holes for the headers. I'm pretty sure this is the green board.*
>
> *If this is their "FPGA" it's no wonder it can't run my cores. This is simply a 256 macrocell CPLD. A CPLD is kind of like a "baby" FPGA. 256 macrocells is big enough to emulate an NES cartridge mapper, but you'd need 4 or 5 of these at least to emulate a 6502 CPU, and even more to do an entire videogame system. I am not sure why you would need a chip like this in the first place, except for "glue logic" and similar to tie stuff together.*
>
> *The FPGA I have been developing on has 25 thousand logic elements (roughly equivalent to a macrocell), and the one on my new design has 49000. Only 100 to 200 times bigger than that CPLD."*

John again posted on Facebook in response to a comment to try and clear up some of the confusion.

> *Please note that we'll have a minimum of 16,000 DMIPS, not 1600. The monitor I use is a Sony PVM-1342Q; in the demo I feed in only composite video, which would be the lowest quality of all outputs from my circuit, and it still looks beautiful.*
>
> *I'm glad to see that you understand the hardware development process well. Thank you for helping to explain it.*
>
> *Even when I was at Sony, as the principal hardware engineer on a project that was budgeted to bring in a billion dollars in revenue, I started the project the same way: building the rest of my circuits outward from an eval board.*
>
> *You have a good eye for the market. Keep in mind this is just the "minimum" configuration that we will use in a final product: The processor is indeed a Rockchip RK3188. I'm using it on a module supplied with 1 GiB mounted to an eval board. (Our finished product may have more RAM, but we don't need a lot of RAM to load into because the cartridge interface is pretty fast.) This allows*

me to quickly build up a circuit around it with the least amount of cost, effort, and risk. (Why re-invent the wheel, right?) It's a great part, but the best part of RETRO VGS really is what goes around it.

Those Gonbes GBS-8220 units aren't used in this demo; I use them with another product I make and already sell worldwide (a specialized video DAC).

The three-man team once again hit the interview trail and recorded a Skype interview with Carl Williams of Retro Gaming Magazine, during which it became clear that this was not much of a team at all, they were very disorganized, continually interrupted each other and showed that they really weren't sharing very much information between themselves, let alone with the outside world. Mike began by reminding everybody about the idea behind the console in the first place.

"We are trying to come up with this system that from an architecture standpoint that we know we can plug in a game and it will boot up and there it is and in theory 10, 30 years from now you should be able to do it again and not wait for some update or be having to be hooked up to the Internet. That's kind of how this all started."

He then went on to discuss the funding target only to be interrupted by John, not once, but twice:

Mike Kennedy: "Sure, sure, at that two million dollars, Carl, as we have said, two-thirds of that goes to parts and assembly and so again, you can take that two million ..."

John Carlsen (interjecting): "It is actually much more than two thirds, we don't want to disclose our margins and expose ourselves quite that much. It is definitely more than two thirds, so our margin is really very thin."

Mike Kennedy: "The bottom line is that it is a thin margin, and so to yield enough operating capital after the cost of goods come out to run the business and lease a small, inexpensive, building and to pay legal and accounting fees ..."

John Carlsen (interjecting): "And to pay our development costs."

Mike was also back in name dropping mode:

Mike Kennedy: "You know, we have seven or eight developers on board this thing with us that are looking at all of this negativity and, like "What is going on?!?" These are real people that want to bring games to this thing. We have got Wayforward looking at this, we got Yacht Club looking at this, we have got DotEmu looking at this, NG.DEV is looking at this ..."

John Carlsen (interjecting): "Heck, they are not just looking at it, these are companies that have signed on."

It was also re-affirmed that it was Steve Woita who wanted the FPGA chip included and how much friction that had caused in the team as they bickered about how much it had added to the costs, the confusion about the stretch goals required to include it and exactly why it was in there in the first place.

Mike Kennedy: "Yeah, John, explain the three levels of FPGA and why we want them."

John Carlsen: "We can actually bring those down a little bit. You know, what we are trying to do is make sure no one has sticker shock. Unfortunately, it is one of those things where you are damned if you do, damned if you don't. So, we can actually bring those down a little bit, but the idea there is that we have these small margins, in order to cover our development costs, we have got to sell a certain number of units at a certain configuration to make that margin and cover our development costs. After we have reached more than a certain number, we can afford to put more into the box and still cover our development costs. The idea all along is to deliver a maximum configuration as much as we can possibly afford to put in the box. So we start off with a very small FPGA, enough to do the basic functions. At our first stretch goal ($3.1 million) that, that's the point we can start doing hardware-based emulation and actually do a lot of these fun functions that can extend what we can do with the system. Kind of like having an enhancement chip on a Nintendo cartridge. Then at our second funding level ($3.8 million), that's where we get to the FPGA that we really wanted all along, and that is so huge it is kind of twice the size ..."

Mike Kennedy (interjecting): "Carl, we are not increasing people's prices for those. What we are saying is, for us to put those in, it decreases our margins so what we have to do is allocate that lower margin across a bigger quantity to cover, you know, [funding of the operation] ..."

John Carlsen (interjecting): "We amortize our development costs over a larger number."

Mike Kennedy: "Ultimately, if we left that in there, we would have to start with a $3 million or a $3.8 million dollar goal which we all know is even more ludicrous and high than what we have got. So again, we have tried to engineer a system that, first of all, is going to play all of the games that we are saying it is going to play on the [Indiegogo] homepage. Right, it is going to play Gunlord, it is going to play all of those games, through the ARM. It is great. Ultimately, Steve wanted to put this FPGA in it, not just to do old hardware replication but to also give developers ... Steve, kind of explain what that does for developers moving forward, not just looking at the hardware replication aspect but also the benefits this brings to developers, this FPGA."

Steve Woita: "It allows them to make their own, I mean, they can have their own sprite engine in hardware done on the FPGA in hardware and I have seen stuff where it is amazingly fast. You can write your own parallel processor that you can use on your own hardware if you will.

If there were some hardware that you wanted to have, to a certain degree, as a software engineer you could actually write this hardware using a high definition language, a hardware definition language, and create some cool things. If you wanted to just dedicate stuff to particle effects or whatever, you could just offload a lot of that to the FPGA."

John Carlsen: "The FPGA allows us to do this massively parallel processing in real time that you can't do even with the fastest ARM cores that we are putting in the CPU because that is all sequential processing.

This is not intended to be an emulation machine. This plays new games off of new cartridges. To try and do emulation on it would be trivial with what we are putting in the box, but that is not our purpose."

Carl Williams: "There is talk of cartridge adapters. These will support, say, Super Mario World, right?"

John Carlsen: "Yeah, yeah. Whether we need to do hardware or software based, or a combination of both or either, we can do that trivially through a low-cost cartridge adapter."

Steve Woita (interjecting): "Basically the nature of the FPGA can allow that to happen."

John Carlsen: "We don't need the FPGA to do it."

Steve Woita: "My choice for wanting the system to be based on that was to allow developers an easy path to go in that they were already developing 8-Bit titles, Intellivision titles, all of these homebrew things that were going on,

'Hey, as we are developing this hardware, here is a path for you guys, you just keep doing it the way you are doing it.'

That was the initial impetus of the architecture with the FPGA part. I was thinking, 'What kind of processor do I want in this thing right now that was easy for developers to get their heads around?' I was like, this can allow us to replicate as close as possible to some of these hardwares provided we have licenses for it. It was a development path for software people so they can keep making their game while we are figuring out exactly how to build this thing within a reasonable price. That has been a huge education for me the whole way on this, current-day parts and stuff. That was initially the reason for the FPGA.

I mean, [Mike] has sent me e-mails from developers that explain to me their tool chain of operations and I am going 'Boom! That lines right up with what we are doing, that will work.' There is (sic) no huge speed bumps in the way that has a clear path to it. Obviously all development paths have some bumps but it looked like a pretty clear one. So, you know, another developer could come at us from left field with, here is the way they build stuff and we have to look at that, and it is very complicated because everyone likes to build things different ways."

The topic of Unity came up again and there was a great moment where it showed that John was actually perhaps the most professional, and certainly the most informed, man on the team where he seemed to be directing Steve, and certainly correcting him, around the issue of where some of the campaign finances would go. In particular, he seemed to be nudging Steve into not giving too much away, as Mike was known to do.

John Carlsen: "Well, we provide the API so if someone wants to write for Unity, you go ahead and you write for the Unity interface and we provide the library. That also comes out of our development costs."

Carl Williams: "Will you be developing these plugins and SDKs internally, or will you be outsourcing them?"

John Carlsen: "A combination, we've got some industry contacts that we will probably be outsourcing a lot of this to. People that specialize in, say, just Unity or just Game Maker."

Steve Woita: "Yeah, and they are going to want money for it, right? Like, that is how we allocate this. It is an unknown amount."

John Carlsen: "No, we know."

Carl Williams: "It is not public."

John Carlsen: "Exactly, that is what Steve means."

Obviously it wasn't long before the subject of Kevin and the cores came up and it became glaringly obvious just how little communication there was among the team as they dropped a bombshell on Steve.

Carl Williams: "I know everyone is wanting me to ask about Kevin."

Mike Kennedy: "Mmm hmm."

Steve Woita: "Kevin, who?"

John Carlsen: [Chuckles]

Steve Woita: "Kevin who? No seriously."

Carl Williams: "Kevin Horton."

Mike Kennedy: "Yes, we know who you are talking about."

John Carlsen: "Yeah, we know."

Steve Woita: "I didn't know which Kevin."

Mike Kennedy: "Here Carl, so again, not to stoop to everybody else's level, I mean, this is where we are at on this thing. We have been talking to Kevin for the last four months, or longer. You know, we identified him quickly as being kind of one of the foremost kind of gurus in the FPGA world. We knew he had already created some solid cores for the 8-Bit systems. We didn't want to reinvent the wheel, so we reached out to Kevin and had some great conversations about, you know, paying him what his asking price was for each individual core, and then also letting him know that we would be happy to help fund the development of any new cores. Right now, there are no 16-bit cores, no Neo Geo cores out there. He had indicated that he wanted to do that but time and money and effort wasn't there. So we said, if we helped fund this, is it something he would be willing to do for us? It wouldn't be exclusive to us, Carl, we would let him use it for anything he wants or anybody else wanted or whatever. We were just like, we would be happy to help you fund this because we want to use it and we would like to use you. That is where it was all left up until last week."

Steve Woita: "Wait, he doesn't want to work with us? I don't get it"

John Carlsen: [Chuckles] "Yeah, I don't know."

Steve Woita: "No, no, I am not reading the forums. Carl, I want you to understand, Carl, I don't understand these forums at all. It takes too much to process. So, did he leave it at a state that he was not working with us? I thought he was."

Mike Kennedy: "Yeah, uh, he threw us under the bus and that was it."

Steve Woita: "But did he say he didn't want to write the cores?"

Mike Kennedy: "No, Steve, he is saying that he is going to come out with a competing product and that was the gist of it."

Steve Woita: "Whatever, that is fine, but he doesn't want to license any cores to us? That is money he is ... he could have done both."

There was also a clear demonstration of the lack of discussion around key issues, or just the fact that Mike did not understand it, clearly John did, and that was the issue of "bug free games" and what would happen if they sold a game that did have a bug. Mike had earlier answered this question on Facebook where he used one of his favorite phrases: *"Simple as that."*

"... first off, developers will be instructed to give us bug free games, meaning they will have to test them diligently before bringing the code to us to make the cart. We will also have game testers that will play the games beginning to end as a double check. In the rare case a bug does make it out into the wild, and if the bug completely makes the game unplayable versus something insignificant, then we will have to get the games back, fix them and send them back out. Simple as that. And we will have a mechanism in place for those rare occurrences"

This time he answered it slightly differently before being interrupted:

Mike Kennedy: "Here is the deal, so, you know, the whole idea is to release games that have been tested. They are going to go through two levels of testing. When they come through the developers, you know, we are assuming we are getting a bug free game and yeah, I did say 'assuming' but, I mean, that is part of the contract with them …"

John Carlsen: (interjecting): "And then we test the heck out of them."

Steve Woita: "See, that is another part of the cost. I mean, the test group I am running are going to be heavily beating on this. These are people I worked with a long time ago. Industry testers in the game business that just thrash the hell out of this stuff …"

John Carlsen (interjecting): "This is exactly the Nintendo model. Back when Nintendo was publishing for the NES, SNES and N64, you know, they would have the developer submit a gold master that the developer has already tested and said yeah, this is going to pass Nintendo's test, Nintendo's requirement. Then Nintendo's testers, they go through and they do complete play-throughs, and they are looking for bugs. Anything that is going to significantly affect gameplay and that's exactly what we are doing here. That is how we manage it."

Mike Kennedy: "Another thing is that a lot of the games, many of the games, we are bringing out have already been released on other formats. Whether it be Steam or the PlayStation Store or whatever, and by the time they get to us, you know, all of the bugs should be worked out. Now, we will have, we hope to have, first-party developed games that we do in-house that we do eventually. We hope to have …"

John Carlsen (interjecting): "Again, we have the two levels of testing: developer side and publisher side."

Mike Kennedy: "If a catastrophic bug does get out, which again, we are certainly going to try hard to stop that from happening. Then at that time, we will have some sort of program to get those games returned and fixed and sent back, without a doubt. If it happens."

John Carlsen: "Games replaced. We would be on the hook to replace those games." …

Carl Williams: "Who would foot the cost if a catastrophic bug did get through?"

Mike Kennedy: "Well, obviously the developer would have to …"

John Carlsen (interjecting): "What? No, no, hold on. Ultimately, if we are the publisher, we are responsible for that first round of costs. Certainly we are going to have some clauses there where we are sharing the profit with the developers but we are also sharing some of the risk here as well. That is something we will work out with the individual developers but ultimately our consumers have to know we are on the hook to replace those games and we are going to make it right."

Mike once again explained their lack of a prototype by repeating that the Ouya campaign didn't have one either:

> *Mike Kennedy: "Not bringing Ouya into this, but they used crowdfunding and that is where the similarities stop. Right off the bat. They didn't show a prototype either, she said they had one and they showed a dev board.*
>
> *I know, we are not going there, but we are being compared to that so I wanted to quickly say, go watch their video.* ***No prototype, it was smoke and mirrors."***

Even Sean Robinson had been warning Mike about not mentioning the Ouya when talking about the Retro VGS:

> *DATE: Sep 16 2015 at 12:42 PM*
> *TO: Mike Kennedy*
> *FROM: Sean Robinson*
>
> *"Hey Mike,*
> *I've been following along with the RETRO VGS stuff on Facebook and other forums and wanted to help you out... the Retron 5 can play new games on new cartridges and remember, new games on cartridges are being produced, complete with boxes, manuals and shrink wrap today in 2015... right here in the USA.*
> *Also, with you saying the RETRO VGS is not like the OUYA because that's Android based and needs to be connected online to update is partly incorrect...*
> *(1) Android is Linux based, and from what I know, the RETRO VGS is also Linux based, especially since according to John you are using Open Source technologies...*
> *(2) You can update the OUYA with the update files loaded to an SD Card... and SD cards are technically a cartridge... they have memory storage and an edge connector...*
> *I hope the console takes off... especially with the amount of time that Clay and I put into things (hardware, software and cartridge security concepts and ideas) before we stepped down in February...*
> *but you really need to stop saying that the RETRO VGS' "main focus is playing this new wave of retro games coming out ..... On cartridges" because this is and has been happening for many years already... new games coming out on brand new cartridges with complete packaging...*
>
> *Anyway... lets do lunch and catch up."*

To which Mike had responded:

> *Hey Sean,*
> *Sure, let's grab lunch and discuss.*
> *Maybe next week sometime?*
> *I believe normally I mention the RETRO VGS as the first "New" console to play new games on cartridges.*

I know clone systems can play new homebrew carts but I want this to be more mainstream, not underground if you know what I mean.

This IS the first system to play new indie style digital and/or streaming and modern day console games on cartridge :)

Mike"

In closing out the interview with Carl, Mike used some of his classic sales speak by intimating that bad publicity is still publicity after all:

> *Mike Kennedy: "We really want to say we appreciate everybody, again, whether they are the haters, I mean, we struck a chord. People are passionate. We don't want to fault people for that. People want this system. We want to deliver it to them for the best price that we can. Again, we are very appreciative that there are seventy-five pages of discussions over on AtariAge about this. Even if they are terrible and dragging me through the mud, and everything else, people are talking about this. I think that is very important, you know, people are passionate. [...]*
>
> *You know what, Carl, maybe there is no market for this, maybe that is what we are seeing. Maybe that is what we are seeing, but I don't think so, and I would hate to write off this, I think people need this, I think the industry needs a shot in the arm."*

Something that definitely did need a shot in the arm was the campaign page, as day nine, and all of the day's events, brought in just three more backers.

Campaign update:

September 21, Day 3: 172 backers, $60,041 total pledged
September 22, Day 4: 186 backers, $66,188 total pledged
September 23, Day 5: 187 backers, $65,956 total pledged
September 24, Day 6: 193 backers, $67,580 total pledged
September 25, Day 7: 192 backers, $65,970 total pledged
September 26, Day 8: 188 backers, $64,920 total pledged
September 27, Day 9: 191 backers, $65,145 total pledged

It's not exactly clear what the chain of events were that happened after this interview and on the following day, September 28th, but during that period, John Carlsen stepped down from the team and resigned from the project. He and Mike had agreed that this would be done without fanfare and that it would not be announced so as not to cause problems during the Indiegogo campaign, which was already in enough trouble, and without adding more fuel to the fire. Unfortunately, Mike went back on his word to John and announced his departure, while at the same time calling an end to the Indiegogo campaign, when he posted on the Retro VGS Facebook page on September 29th.

"Hey Everyone! It's clear, in its current state the RETRO VGS Indiegogo campaign is dead in the water and thusly will be shut down early. Once the Indiegogo team explains to us how we can do this, the plug will be pulled and all of you who have contributed will receive a refund post haste. Or you can go in and request a refund from Indiegogo right now.

The good news is we aren't giving up and have made some adjustments to our hardware team, which includes the involvement of other hardware gurus who were part of our venture in the very beginning. We will also be lowering the price while maintaining most of the cool features you all want.

We will be back in the near future with a prototype RETRO VGS system, front-and-center playing our games on our cartridges and with our USB controller. Sit tight, be patient, RETRO VGS will return.

Thanks again for your support, patience and understanding while we regroup and prepare for the relaunch of a crowdfunding campaign on Kickstarter."

He also posted on AtariAge the next day.

Folks, a lot has happened in just one week.

All we ever really wanted was to make a new old school console. Founded on the same core principles as a lot of the old systems you already love.

We've since learned what seems like a simple idea is actually quite complicated.

But it's not impossible. It requires careful planning, laser focus, and the proper mix of talented individuals.

We honestly thought we had all that. Clearly, we didn't. While we take some time to reflect on the road that got us here I want to also make a few things right.

I apologize to the retro community for overhyping this project early on. I was just trying to give it the momentum I thought it needed to push through to completion.

I want to apologize to Kevtris. Your public forum comments caught us totally off guard. In hindsight we should have included you more and treated you more like a key partner and less like an interchangeable vendor.

I want to apologize to Pat, Ian, and the other media outlets I criticized simply because they dared to point out our vision for the product didn't quite match up to the resources and information that we ourselves were willing to put forth to back up our claims. It was hard to hear after all the time and energy we've sank into the project to date.

We've learned a lot. Mostly that we need a bit more humility and proof than "trust us" and possibilities. Especially if we're asking you the community to believe in our project enough to front load the cost and risk of making them a reality.

I sincerely hope to address you all again in the future with happier news and a functional prototype that shows you our vision in action and sparks your own imagination to wonder at the other possibilities."

Campaign update:

September 21, Day 3: 172 backers, $60,041 total pledged
September 22, Day 4: 186 backers, $66,188 total pledged
September 23, Day 5: 187 backers, $65,956 total pledged
September 24, Day 6: 193 backers, $67,580 total pledged
September 25, Day 7: 192 backers, $65,970 total pledged
September 26, Day 8: 188 backers, $64,920 total pledged
September 27, Day 9: 191 backers, $65,145 total pledged
September 28, Day 10: 192 backers, $63,825 total pledged
September 29, Day 11: 191 backers, $63,546 total pledged

In addition to John Carlsen's now announced resignation, Mike also made a couple of his own. On September 29th he resigned from the ColecoVisions podcast and also from the podcast he had helped to found, Retro Gaming Roundup:

"Hey Guys,

I am going to resign from the Top-10 for the time being while I focus all my attention on getting this console back on track. We are going back to a couple guys that came on board after Curt Vendel said he didn't have the time to devote to this back at the start. We will have more info on that for everyone in a few weeks.

Thanks again and I hope we can all stay in touch. I am also stepping down from Willie's podcast as well while I get things worked out.

Mike Kennedy, Founder & President
RETRO Media Network"

Disappointed at Mike's U-turn in announcing his departure, on September 30, 2015, John Carlsen deleted his YouTube account and made his own announcement.

"As Mike had alluded yesterday, after about seven months of hard work I have recently decided to leave the Retro VGS team.

Before I go, I would like to thank every one of our loyal and vocal fans, including our critics, for showing us that you care about our project. I would especially like to thank our backers for their willingness to fund our massive development project and to wait a year to be the first to play our new video game system.

I have enjoyed reconnecting with Steve Woita, who was my colleague at Mediagenic 25 years ago, and getting to know Mike Kennedy, whose warm hearted enthusiasm for retro gaming brought our team together and built a community around it.

Together, we learned a lot, both good and bad. We learned how to offer high-quality, modern games on high-performance cartridges for reasonable prices. We learned how we could offer a system that performs more like a PlayStation 3 than a Raspberry Pi 2 for only a negligible difference in price. (By the way, I don't mean to knock either of these two great products by making these comparisons.)

We learned the costs of shipping complete systems individually to nearly anywhere in the world, and that it costs significantly more than stuffing tube socks into a flat-rate box. Although we already knew we would save massive up-front development costs, we learned how much re-using the former Jaguar case adds to the price of each unit. Over time, we learned each other's strengths and weaknesses. Unfortunately, we also learned that outsiders would fraudulently claim to be part of our team and accept credit for our work, sometimes while defaming it and us in the process.

Despite all this, I still believe that video games can once again be reasonably free of defects before they are released, just as Nintendo did with its Seal of Quality program, and that cartridges can extend the maximum size of physical distribution media beyond what has remained stagnant for nearly a decade. As we've seen through a recent patent, Nintendo appears to be on the right path.

I have enjoyed working and solving many of the unique and interesting problems this project has presented, and can only hope that I'm granted a similar opportunity in the future.

Although I am saddened that this work has not yielded a viable product, I take pride in knowing that we created a good design and offered it at a fair price through an honest campaign, and made many friends in the process.

Sincerely yours,
John Carlsen"

John would later be interviewed again by Carl Williams and separately by the author, on his own this time, and would shed some more light on the internal problems that the team had and why things may have turned out the way they did. Speaking about the disorganized and revealing interview they had done previously as a team, John commented:

"Our interview with you came at a particularly bad time after that design change, as it affected much of the software development path and I wasn't prepared to talk about the issues that I was still resolving. Mike insisted that we do the interview, but we were totally disorganized at that point."

He went on to elaborate about the lack of hardware details and why all of the team were not aware of the current state of play, largely because he had kept information to himself.

"Mike seems to share information freely (even too freely) when it appears to be in his interest. As I had mentioned, I learned that I couldn't trust Mike to keep anything secret.

Mike caused me to distrust him. When I first joined the project, we had agreed on a timeline, which of course slipped; I had promised six months and put in seven. At the end, Mike, Steve and I had agreed to quietly let the crowdfunding campaign fade as I left the project, but Mike announced only a day or two later that they were making changes to the hardware team; Mike's announcement caused me to make mine, clarifying that I had left on my own accord. Along the way, Mike had let out that I had been researching putting micro drives into the cartridges, only days after I explicitly got him to promise not to, and that I was developing low-cost adapters to play cartridges from other systems."

"At one point, I had to tell Mike and Steve that I would create a design that met their requirements and quote them a cost, but share no technical details because I didn't trust Mike not to publicly disclose everything and blow my chance to patent my work."

It is well known that Mike could not keep information to himself and in fact John had not wanted him to show pictures of the cardboard mock up that they had made. John felt it would be misleading to do so as there was a chance that their board would have a heatsink that would drastically change the way it looked. Mike would also again demonstrate this trait in fine fashion later by revealing e-mails that he had been specifically asked not to reveal and posting them publicly. John Carlsen then took down his YouTube account and the Retro VGS Lab video with it and explained the reason this way:

"I noticed that Google was advertising on my channel some of the other YouTube videos I had been watching. By that point, I had already left the project and just found it easier to kill my YouTube account."

So with the video gone and the team broken up, all that remained was to close the campaign down but unfortunately that proved more difficult than it seemed. Mike was in talks with Indiegogo about closing it early but the way their system worked meant that they were unable to do so as it had active pledges from people who had been charged for them. Mike publicly requested that anybody who had pledged should request a refund and they would be able to close the campaign, but not everybody did so which meant that the campaign ran and ran and ran. Funding fluctuated as people requested refunds and other new visitors found the campaign and pledged so it became a long and drawn out mess.

While it floundered and kicked like a dying fly, others who had been connected in some way to the project spoke out. Knowing they could no longer harm the campaign, which was all but over, they presented their thoughts on the fiasco. One such commentator was Ben Heck, or Benjamin Heckendorm to give him his full title, who is well known for his own hardware projects and an engineer who had been approached by Mike early on.

"Heard about this crowdsourced project and remembered I had it pitched to me about a year ago. Checked my email to confirm... it was these guys! I recall thinking it was a very strange concept at the time, but seems like they went for it?

Here's what I've learned about collectors and nostalgia, both from my game console mods of old and more recently pinball design and manufacture:

People will pay good money – stupid money even – for things that remind them of the past, but it has to be THINGS FROM THEIR PAST.

If I nostalgically play Duck Tales, for instance, I'm reminded of being 13 years old and not having to pay taxes or work 60 hours a week. The Twin Towers are still standing, gas is 90 cents a gallon and the Berlin Wall just came down -yahoo! Nostalgia is about the longing for things that are gone. Games (or movies, or songs...) are simply a tangible link to that memory, persistent evidence and a reminder of a past that is gone.

RVGS has no such history. It's not "taking us back to the past" because it didn't exist in the past. It's more of an impression of the past, like myself trying to imitate Sean Connery. Sure 8-bit graphics are the "hot thing" on Steam, but that's mostly because it's an affordable way for indie developers to make games.

I'm not nostalgic for cartridges. I don't even like swapping out Metal Gear V in order to watch a Blu-Ray. It is a less convenient way to enjoy media. One could argue (correctly) that Blu-Ray is superior to streaming but with games? No difference at all.

Cartridges – like a horse and buggy – were a product of their time. Couldn't download a game because there was no internet. Even if you could, you wouldn't be able to afford the RAM to hold it. Disks are cheap right? Sure, but the disk drives themselves cost as much as the computer. In that world, a mass-produced ROM mask on a PCB made sense.

Oh gee what else to complain about...

Jaguar shell is an insane idea, again, going back to nostalgia, you want to remind people of the console that killed Atari?

Save $X by using that mold, but how much does it cost to mod in all those ports that weren't on the Jag? (and on the front too)

Jag cartridges with weird handle were pretty lame, AVGN (Angry Video Game Nerd) does a pretty good job explaining why.

Nobody is going to write games (or even port them, ask the Wii-U) for a system with such a small install base.

Also, have a working prototype. Crowdfunding should be 1) develop it with your own money 2) ask for the money needed for manufacture. When the money intended for manufacture gets used to finish development you always end up in a hole and have to seek additional funding to fulfil the materials. This is where most projects truly go off the rails.

KevTris system looks great. Get a stuffing quote from a fab house, Kickstart that cost + 20%, and release files for buyers to 3D print their own custom cases.

Boom, done!"

"I believe Mike wanted my help with industrial design but yes, I didn't think it sounded like a good idea and never really followed up.

The Ouya has poisoned the well for any project crowdfunded like this (and even that was a much better concept) It failed for the same reason – lack of original content and what content there was didn't sell very well at all, driving developers away.

There are loads of homebrew games already being made (and sold here!) that work on consoles you already have. RVGS was a classic "solution in search of a problem."

Mike was back in talkative mode and it was about to get busier under that bus as he was preparing to throw John under it to join the others already there.

"I said I was not going to come back into this thread, but as you all can agree, AtariAge and this thread are a hard habit to break. Anyway, I wanted to chime back in on a few things in light of our current situation. Unlike the SoCalMike from the past, I will try and be a bit more concise:

1) As you have heard (and discussed) in our most recent team interview there was discord among the team. Since bringing John on board this product started becoming incredibly expensive. It was actually up to $450-$500 (selling price at one point). Obviously, that was NEVER going to fly so Steve and I did what we could to try and work with John to understand why the cost and selling price became to excessive. Once we decided to eliminate the need for RVGS to "handle" Neo Geo size cores/games (coming through the FPGA), the price then lowered a bit, but not nearly enough.

We then went back and forth amongst the team to include or not include an FPGA big enough to handle the existing 8-Bit cores thinking without it the price would come down even more, but at the expense of losing the magic of the FPGA. But even after removing the FPGA or using a small one for other "housekeeping" applications (John's words) the price just never came down to a price point Steve and I were comfortable with (it bottomed out at the $299-$350 you saw on the IGG campaign).

2) Regarding Kevtris (and PIKO too). Honestly, since we had been waffling on whether or not to include the FPGA leading up to a crowdfunding campaign, I didn't want to waste any more of their time. In the end, Kevin did understand that we would contract with him to license his existing 8-bit cores and also help finance his creation of 16-bit cores for our use and the community's use ONLY if we had a successfully funded campaign that included a capable FPGA. We didn't toss him out in any way, shape or form and I apologize to Kevin for how I handled his comments, which took our team by surprise and were a bit out of the blue. And, should RVGS have a successful ending, I hope we can work with him to license his cores in the future. In the end, I do believe our products will be two completely different kinds of machines and can exist together if the two of us are able to make our machines a reality.

3) Regarding PiperCub (Scott Schreiber). Yes, he was a confidant, friend and podcast co-host with me for years when I came to him with my idea to create a new cartridge based console. I valued his input and advice and he also knew Curt Vendel, someone who I initially wanted to design the hardware. Scott hooked us up and Curt and I discussed this very early on and he indicated he didn't have the time (and was also battling for his life) so he had to bow out of the running as lead engineer. I then moved on to two other very capable hardware guys who worked with Steve and I in the beginning, even to the point of having an operating prototype. This was all before Steve had the idea of integrating an FPGA (and also before a few other additions like the various output methods and 9-Pin controller ports (all things we are striving to include should it not break the bank).

4) Fast forward to the present. Yes, we pulled the IGG campaign and agree it should have NEVER been turned on in the first place. Prior to pulling the campaign John took it upon himself to light up his famous table prototype video (without any heads up to Steve or myself). At first, Steve and I were taken by surprise, but his attempt at showing a prototype did garner some positive sentiment among the natives so I thought we dodged a bullet there. In the end, I think it did more harm than good and wish it never got posted. But John is a very good guy and very capable engineer.

But somehow this product grew into a three headed monster with him at the hardware helm. And I am not saying this was all his fault. John did his best to engineer the machine Steve and I had envisioned from the start. It just got completely out of hand on many accounts and we all take the blame for that.

5) Steve Woita. Steve is awesome (I hope you can all agree with that) and he and I are on great terms and want to see RVGS to a positive end, whether that means a successfully funded campaign with a cool product you all might want OR if it dies out gracefully after given a true chance to succeed. Only time will tell where this story will end.

6) Back to #3. The good news is that our team all still agrees that having the FPGA in its fullest form is a good thing and are doing what we can to continue to include that bit of hardware in the design. We are hard at a work to complete the prototype that was begun early on in this venture and I am trying to stay out of the hardware side of things at this point so they can do their job and engineer some cool tech that doesn't cost you all an arm and a leg. That was never our intention with RVGS. If and when you hear from us again it will be with a playable prototype in hand.

7) Apologies. Hey, I think we can all agree this thread had both constructive criticism, which my team and I welcomed and also personal attacks which we didn't. I didn't mean to group everyone into any negative comments I made with regards to AA or its members. But there were a few comments that really rubbed me the wrong way and I let my emotions get the best of me. For what it's worth, I am sorry and certainly didn't mean any ill will toward the majority of the people here or on any other forum (or on Facebook) for that matter. Much of the criticism was valuable and I think we now know how to bring a viable product to market with a price point that most will agree with. But again, it's a balancing act trying to please as many people as possible while also trying to keep the price affordable.

Now all I ask is that you give my team a fair shot to win back your trust with our second effort that will go long way to address the concerns from the final weeks leading up to the IGG campaign. We will have a playable prototype and it will be on Kickstarter. Will there be some changes to the game line up? Sure, we will be working on fleshing out the initial game launch list once we have all agreed on the hardware and the price point.

Carry on . . . . .
- Mike

EDIT: Oh, one other thing. I've discussed with our campaign rep at IGG about ending the campaign and they said they would look into it but for now it's still live. If you happen to still have your money tied up there, please go in and demand a refund asap."

"I don't recall lying or being misleading when talking about developers. Earlier this year I did have a two-hour face-to-face meeting, at Konami's El Segundo HQ with Michael Rajna, Konami's Director of Marketing & Licenses.

He is a big retro gamer and liked what we were doing. We discussed brining back some old Konami arcade IP in the form of new games (like Resogun did with Defender) on RVGS. He was all for it but indicated they would like to wait it out until the product got more fleshed out. He did kindly ask me to not discuss Konami's involvement until we a had signed deal. As I said this was early on and I was gauging interest and there was and is some legitimate interest here. I recall a post here from someone stating that "some people consider emailing a company PR person as being in discussions with ....." And that was certainly never the case with any of my contacts with any of the developers I said we talked with.

We also met with Mike Mika and his team at Other Ocean up in Oakland a few months ago (Thank's Mike, btw for chiming in here a few pages ago). Mike is also a very big retro gaming fan and collector and liked our idea. I knew Mike was tied in with all the big publishers and always said, he could be our inroads to the bigger devs/pubs and that was all true. And, we discussed having them possibly work on some of the Konami arcade sequels as he already had a good relationship with them. They were also in discussions with SEGA on other business and thought they could help us make inroads there to bring back some of their 8/16 bit IP like Alex Kidd, Streets of Rage, etc. All real and legitimate.

Oh, and we discussed having Mike himself create a RETRO game maker cartridge for RVGS and that is all still something that can happen if we are able to bring RVGS to market.

All along, I've said many times, that I feel if we as a community can all show there is a market for a machine like this, then we have the contacts and believe we can get the larger devs/pubs on board. Heck, we already had WayForward (and they/we were going to announce Shantae Pirates Curse half-way through the campaign as a purchasable title if the campaign was on the road to success) and DotEMU (Met Cyrille at GDC after having many emails directly with him (They are in France) very interested in porting/making games for this IF they were to see a successfully funded campaign coming together. We were going to start with Double Dragon Trilogy. But early on I mentioned having a SHMUP arcade compilation on RVGS -- that was going to be Raiden Legacy. But DotEMU decided after I revealed that teaser they would like to start with DDT instead. Again, all real but things have been a moving target throughout this process. I will try and not get anyone's hopes up anymore with any sideline discussions we are having that aren't 100% nailed down. That was my fault and it won't happen again.

I am sorry to see NG:DEV.TEAM go, but again, believe they will be back if there is a market here. They really saw RVGS as a replacement market for the declining/pirate ridden Dreamcast market. And I was excited to get their cartridge games down to a manageable price so that all of us who can't afford to game on the Neo Geo AES could have an opportunity to own and play their games on cartridges. Again, they were really on board and I believe they will be again IF we are successfully funded the second go-around.

As far as having over 150 dev's interested in making games for this. All true. We have been inundated with inquiries from dev's around the world since we leaked this all out a few months ago. Many small and just starting out devs to more established devs. We have been shown dozens of early game screen shots and some video footage and have been sifting through them slowly. As I've indicated before, we aren't in a rush to launch with more than 6-10 titles until we see what kind of demand there is and what type of first year install base we might garner. We don't want to over saturate the games as that is not good for anyone. The great news is, we will be able to pick the cream of the crop to bring onto RVGS and have plenty of quality games and developers to choose from. This is going to be Steve Woita's task to identify the games that will be brought onto the system and he is also going to lead a small team of experienced game testers that he's worked with in the past to QA our games before going onto cart. And there are future plans to begin developing first party games exclusive to RVGS (thus our discussions with David Siller, a platform game designing genius, who I am talking with again this week). Again, we needed to first get the console officially launched and funded before adding this component which will take tons of additional effort and resources.

Again, I apologize if any of you felt misleaded (sic), but everything that I said revolved around something that actually happened and were more than just a few emails to PR people.

With John Carlsen well and truly blamed for the disaster and Mike escalating costs given to him by John being increased by 3 to 5 times in an Ars Technica interview, Mike went on to drop the names of developers again, including Konami, where he had specifically been asked not to. Unfortunately, some of them were not quite as keen as Mike claimed. First was David Siller whose name Mike had dropped several times.

"I have never agreed to develop for this console. Aero and Zero were developed at Iguana with my assistance but not Crash Bandicoot and Maximo and a whole lot more. This console is an emulator at best."

"A couple of brief talks and no conclusion is not enough to have been mentioned by them. It sounds like an endorsement that I did not agree to. Mike was supposed to call me back but never did."

Mike had also been dropping Mike Mika of Other Ocean into interviews and posts, and his partner Frank had the following to say:

> *"We never agreed to any kind of partnership, but I wouldn't exactly say this is misleading either, as we told Mike and Steve that we're totally open to providing software support if and when the numbers make sense (aka, we have reason to believe we'll make money). We gave them some ideas for cool things to do and wished them luck, is how I remember it going down.*
>
> *Just wanted to throw that out there because while I think this campaign had a lot of issues, I have never believed Mike to be a scammer or an outright liar, and it's kind of upsetting to see people take that stance."*

After a busy September, things were relatively quiet through October but there was a little excitement to keep the watchers entertained. Pat and Ian were back on October 8th and mentioned in their podcast under the title "Retro VGS Follow-Up" that they had got *"a considerable amount of grief"* for their dissection of the Retro VGS Indiegogo campaign. Jokingly apologizing for being *"####ing hammered right now"* Pat commented on the fact that they hadn't been called *"drunken podcasters"* in a private email or a private message, but publicly on the Retro VGS Facebook page and he continued that people had seen that and;

> *"fought back against that, and they did, calling it very unprofessional because if you are selling a product you can't do that. You need to present yourself in a professional manner because you need people to think that you are going to be selling a professional grade product."*

What seemed like the longest campaign in history came to an end on November 4, 2015, having fluctuated at around $60,000 for the most part. In total it raised around $81,000 of its intended $1,950,000 goal but its impact was much larger than the numbers would suggest.

A week later on November 11th Mike Kennedy and Sean Robinson were at SC3 in Los Angeles and an incident took place which would come back to haunt Mike later, though he had no clue at the time. Another man present was BTB (Brian Thomas Barnhart), a video producer from Los Angeles who runs a YouTube channel called "The Jag Bar" where he has guests on the show, sometimes enjoying a glass of wine, and talking while they play an Atari Jaguar game. Brian was a member of AtariAge and had seen talk of a guy who had bought the Atari Jaguar molds and was selling clear shells. Brian was very interested in owning one and felt *"wouldn't that be really cool for the show"* and he could shoot some of his videos using the clear Jaguar case.

Brian tried to get hold of Mike who *"never got back to me, never returned any emails or anything like that"* so he said, *"All right, maybe they're all sold out and I missed it."* Then, in October of 2015, there was an SC3 event which Brian describes as *"like a backyard arcade event hosted by this guy named Steve Hertz."*

Brian was talking to Sean Robinson who had a booth with Commodore 64s set up for play and as they were talking he asked who Brian was. Brian explained that he did a show called the Jag Bar and was told *"Well, you need to talk to this guy right over here"* and *"lo and behold, there he was, Mike Kennedy and he had a whole table out and he was doing raffles."* They talked for a while about what they did and what had brought them to SC3 and it became clear that they could both get something out of their meeting, Brian could get a clear Jaguar shell and Mike could be a guest on the Jag Bar for promotional purposes and he might be talking to somebody who would be willing to shoot their promotional videos.

Mike gave Brian a clear case, despite him being willing to pay for it, and he threw in about five copies of RETRO Magazine and they had a picture taken together. Brian told Mike *"Listen, if you're ever in town, you should come on the Jag Bar, that would be really cool, and so he did and the next thing I know, we're playing Ruiner Pinball together."*

It was five days later on November 16, 2015, and the show started with the two of them chatting while drinking red wine and they talked about who Mike was, the websites that he ran and what he was hoping to build in the community. Brian knew all about the Retro VGS debacle but didn't bring it up as he felt that *"the information is out there, I'm not going to bring anything new to the table."*

Mike was however very enthusiastic about his new system and explaining that the new system was going to do this and the new system was going to do that and how he had learned from his mistakes and was going to move on. Brian asked Mike *"Well, who's doing your marketing because I'm a freelance video guy and so I'm always looking for my next paycheck."* He thought: *"Hey, if I could help this guy out with marketing, he's in Orange County. He's like 45 minutes away from me. This thing might turn into something and then I might be doing videogame marketing for the next five years."*

The day after the filming, Mike emailed Brian and asked him to take out any footage that showed him mentioning a new console or about turning the Jaguar shell into a new console. Brian agreed and edited the footage over the next couple of weeks. On December 3rd he emailed Mike to let him know that he was almost done with the editing and told him that he had *"a ton of material on the Retro VGS"* but that it would not be included in the episode. He didn't get a reply and later that day emailed Mike a link to the video for review. The video was about 35 minutes long and if Mike was happy with it, Brian would release it the next day. Mike said that he was happy with it and it duly went live.

Two days later, Mike emailed Brian and asked him not to use any footage that he had where Mike was talking about the console. Brian replied and assured him that he wouldn't as *"it would have been extra work anyway."* Mike no doubt had something up his sleeve and his console idea was far from dead. Brian was sworn to secrecy and Mike assured his former Retro Gaming Roundup co-hosts that everything was under control.

"Seriously hope you guys are doing well. Looking back at the last couple months I can laugh at it all. We are back on track and addressing all the issues and complaints with our first mess and having lots of success with the prototype and lowering our costs significantly. Did a lot of things right up until we did everything wrong. Live and learn.

Then it went downhill and John Carlsen got involved. It did make for some funny moments though :)"

This type of email would end up being very telling as to how Mike saw the world and woefully misjudged his ability to charm people into forgetting his misdeeds. Scott had already made his terms and conditions clear to Mike who had flatly rejected them: *"Negotiations failed and it was now a wartime footing."*

While Mike spent his time typing up a *"Have a Coke and a smile"* email, Scott, UKMike and others were actively gathering intelligence and making preparations to ensure that he didn't get away with his scheme. As informed and prepared as they were, none of them could have expected the twists and turns that the story would follow before it reached a conclusion.

10: The Podcast Years – Part 3: Surf Dogs

There wasn't any single definable point where Mike went "off the rails" or where his commitment to the podcast and his co-hosts suddenly changed, it was more of a slow burn process and that made it much more difficult for Scott and UKMike to notice, but notice they did. Mike's priorities and his commitment to the show changed and Retro Gaming Roundup slipped further down his list of priorities.

The show segments tended to be recorded at 14:00 EST because the three hosts were each in different time zones: UKMike is in GMT, Scott is in EST and Mike Kennedy is in PST. That means that there is an eight-hour difference between the two Mikes with Scott somewhere in the middle. 14:00 EST was the afternoon for Scott, 19:00 for UKMike and 11:00 for Mike Kennedy which meant that he would have his work day interrupted, but as he worked from home, he was able to do that without too much issue. Occasionally they would have to pause the recording as Mike took a work call (which the other two usually heard) but it was a small price to pay for what worked out to be the most convenient recording time for all of them. They did use other times as necessary, sometimes if Scott was working nights or if Mike wasn't able to interrupt his work day, but 14:00 EST was their most usual time for recording.

As Mike began to put work into launching Retro Magazine they noticed that it was more and more difficult to schedule a recording date for the Top Ten and that for the Live News recording, he simply would not show up, leaving Scott and UKMike to do it without him. In a twelve-month period, he missed more than half of them at one point.

During the Top Ten recordings it was becoming more and more clear that Mike wasn't putting in the research necessary beforehand and would show up unprepared and was often reading directly from Google searches or from Wikipedia rather than his own notes.

Hi co-hosts prioritized the show very differently. They were all busy people with busy lives and families and it was clear that Mike held the show in less regard than both Scott and UKMike did. Scott worked a shift pattern of four days on and four days off then four nights on and four nights off and he would often get home from a night shift at 08:00 EST, do some errands, then go to bed until 14:00 when he would get up and be there for the recording session which would usually run until around 16:30 EST when he could then go and shower, eat and leave for work again.

UKMike would not break a family commitment to record the show, but if he had arranged a recording date and then a subsequent family commitment came up, he would always try and honor the show recording, and if an alternate recording wasn't available, he would be there to record the show as arranged. On occasion they recorded the show at odd times, for example, once when it was 02:00 in the UK and once when it was 05:00 in the UK but this didn't happen very often. Mike Kennedy however would be able to arrange a recording date and then if a subsequent commitment came up later he would just not show up for Live News and this of course led to the infamous "Surf Dogs" incident.

The three of them continued to record the podcast as normal while working with Mike and his now increasing absence from the Live News segment, so much so that even while he was still a part of the show they were discussing possible replacements for him, initially just for the Live News segment and later for the Top Ten debates as well.

Frustratingly around this time, while Mike seemed to be going under due to his number of projects and limited time, he was also appearing on another podcast called The ColecoVisions. This podcast was hosted by Willie Culver, John Lester and Brett Weiss, but at the time, Mike was the third host on the show before Brett came on board. In a particular episode during the summer of 2014 they had Robert Ferguson (Ferg) on as a guest and it was during this particular episode that Mike inadvertently signaled that there may be problems ahead.

Willie does all of the editing and production on the ColecoVisions Podcast, and after one of their recording sessions they had a discussion among themselves about Mike and his projects and his feelings toward Retro Gaming Roundup. This was meant to be off the record, and indeed in the audio Mike is heard to ask Willie if this is off the record, to which Willie replied that it was. Unfortunately, Willie left the segment in the final edit and it was published to the public.

The audio predated CGE 2014 but UKMike only heard it after the expo as it had been sitting on his iPod in his playlist for a couple of months. Willie was told of the error almost immediately and that the audio had gone out so he edited the show again, removing the offending section, and then uploading the trimmed down version. Unfortunately, the original version had been downloaded around five hundred times, including of course by UKMike and it sat waiting on his iPod.

The removed audio made interesting listening but before we get into it, both Scott and UKMike want to make it perfectly clear that neither of them have any issues with Willie or the ColecoVisions Podcast. Willie is a personal friend of theirs who made an honest mistake and they have no problem with him at all. What Mike Kennedy said in that audio is his own opinion, nobody else was dragged into it, and it was simply an oversight of Willie's to leave it in the final show.

In the audio Ferg asks Mike if he is still doing his Retro Gaming Roundup segments called "Atar-Rewind" and "Mike'd Up." Atar-Rewind is where Mike covers all things Atari and Mike'd Up is where Mike goes around the California Swap Meets wearing a recording camera built into his sunglasses and you can hear him talking to sellers and making deals on the retro items that he buys.

Mike replied that he would like to do them but he feels that the show is getting a little long in the tooth and in his opinion it sounds like even the hosts are tired of it, and he certainly is tired of doing it. He goes on to say that he *"doesn't put a lot of effort into it and doesn't think"* and that it *"takes a long time,"* time he doesn't have. He then goes on to say that he thinks the Live News segment should be dropped from the show as nobody likes it (in his opinion).

In actual fact, the Live News is one of the more popular segments and some listeners fast forward to that first or listen to it more than once. The reason that Mike felt it should be dropped is that this is where the hosts tend to tell most of their off-color stories, call Las Vegas hookers and of course it is where Mike had both got drunk and fallen off his chair and where he had put a joystick down his pants live on camera. This is why Mike had a problem with Live News as he had already previously asked that their behavior be cleaned up so as not to tarnish his serious business reputation.

> *"Also, in the context of creating our own expo it might be in our best interest to "clean up" a bit in future podcasts.*
>
> *For the most part we are clean and down to business, but the live news is where I think we tend to fall off the wagon. Maybe we change it up a bit. Just a thought."*

UKMike sent a copy of the audio to Scott and they put together a few plans for a worst-case scenario when they confronted Mike about it. They had to play things carefully because Mike had registered the domain retrogamingroundup.com for them when they first started, their forums were hosted under Mike's own GameGavel forums, their e-mails went via Mike's hosting account at Network Solutions and he had the keys to them all. UKMike had access as well but if he had wanted to, Mike Kennedy could have disabled their access to the whole show. They didn't think it would come to that but they made plans for that eventuality.

The three of them were due to record a Top Ten on September 25th 2014 and they messaged Mike requesting a meeting for the three of them to sit down and to discuss his absence from the show of late, what they could do to help him out and to address his statements on the ColecoVisions Podcast.

Even though they were planning for the show to continue without him, and this is with the idea that he would walk away rather than be fired by them, they knew that Mike was a popular part of the show, had a good following among the listeners and would be missed if he were to leave. The bottom line is that neither Scott or UKMike wanted Mike to leave, they just wanted the SoCalMike of old to return and put in the commitment to the show that he had previously shown. They still considered themselves the Three Musketeers, even then, but things were to take quite a sudden and unexpected twist.

On Wednesday September 25, 2014 the three of them sat down together on Skype for a show meeting and then they would record the "Top Ten Things At CGE 2014" once the meeting was finished. They asked Mike to talk about the reasons for his absences and lack of commitment and he explained that with his other projects and the fact that we had been doing the show for over five years at this point, he had begun to see the show as something that he didn't look forward to doing.

In contrast, he enjoyed doing the ColecoVisions Podcast because he had little or no preparation to do for it and Willie did all the production, so literally all Mike had to do for the show was to play whatever game they were talking about and to join the chat on Skype and sign out when he was done. That was much easier for him and he saw his Retro Gaming Roundup segments as something of a bind. Scott asked him if he wanted to leave the show and he said no, he didn't, so they asked him what could be done to help him out, to give him some more free time and they discussed some possible options.

One of the options was for them to recruit a new host to take part in the Top Ten debates and the Live News segments as they were the longest and needed the most preparation. That would then give Mike more free time to do his shorter segments, Mike'd Up, It Came From M.A.M.E. and Atar-Rewind, but Mike said that he enjoyed doing the Top Ten and Live News because he enjoyed the banter and the laid back atmosphere.

The next option was for them to drop the additional segments and he could just focus on the Top Ten debates and Live News but he also wanted to carry on producing some of his other segments when he had the time. It would also mean that they would have less content in each show.

The three of them discussed this option for a while because actually, it meant that nothing would really change. Mike would still need to find time to do the longest segments that he was finding a bind and he would still be doing his additional ones as well. After throwing the ideas around for a while they all decided that it would probably not work as a long-term solution.

The option that was settled on was for Mike to continue to take part in the Top Ten debates and Live News, and then, as and when he was able, he could do an additional segment but there would be no onus on him to do so as they would recruit a new guest host to record a new, as yet undecided, segment to fill the gaps left by Mike.

As far as the new host was concerned, Scott and UKMike already had some ideas for potential new hosts to bring in and of course they had actually already discussed it because they were making plans for a worst-case scenario if Mike were to walk away when confronted.

Finally, before the meeting ended, they decided on a date for the September 2014 Live News and that date was just days away, on Sunday September 28, 2014. All three of them made a commitment to be there and they specifically asked Mike several times if he was happy with the outcome of the meeting and if he was OK with that date for the Live News and he assured them that he was.

That Sunday was much like any other for UKMike and he was ready at the appointed time and waited for Scott to join the chat. Scott had been working on nights and had got home late after his twelve hour shift at about 09:00 and had to do a couple of jobs before going to bed at around 10:00. His alarm went off to wake him up just before 14:00 and he arrived at the mic sounding a little tired. UKMike already knew that Mike Kennedy was not going to be there as he had emailed them both the day before but Scott had not yet read the email.

> *"Well, now I have a conflict for Sunday. Normally, weekends are pretty much Tricia time, but I didn't think we were doing anything this weekend. Now she wants us to do this Sunday 8:30-1:00 which is right during our show. I would like to say that normally, I want to be there for the news but there are times where it becomes impossible. I would say future if we could eliminate the weekends that would be great. I can normally wiggle out or schedule my weekly work meetings around the show. Looks like I will miss this go around."*

When UKMike told Scott that Mike Kennedy was not showing up he did not take it well, and outlined in no uncertain terms the level of commitment that he had shown to make it to the recording session. What made this even more unbelievable is that literally days earlier they had a very constructive meeting with Mike about his commitment to show and he had assured them that he would be committing to the Top Ten debates and the Live News, specifically that he would make this Live News as he had no plans that day. When Scott found out where Mike had gone, he flipped. Mike had broken his promise to be there for the Live News to go out for the day with Tricia, to watch an event at Huntington Beach called "Surf Dogs."

This was an event that Scott described in his sleep infused anger as *"gratuitous!"*

For a few minutes, the only words that Scott could say was *"Surf Dogs"* hence the title of that episode and the now infamous term. Despite the tone and circumstance, it was still good radio.

For the first time on the show they went public about Mike and his behind the scenes shenanigans. Most of their listeners were already aware of the leaked ColecoVisions footage and were already questioning Mike's commitment because he had missed so many Live News sessions already. Scott then gave an angry, yet quite eloquent, rant about why somebody would make a commitment with them just days earlier when they were trying to help him and find ways for him to stay on the show, and then break it for such a ridiculous reason.

It perfectly outlined Mike's level of commitment to the show. He had made plans with them on Thursday but at some point over the weekend either he or Tricia had the idea of going to "Surf Dogs" and he had placed that higher up the list of priorities than a commitment he had made, and confirmed, several times.

The problem with the Live News segment is that it does require a commitment to be there, simply because it is done live and people show up in the chatroom to take part and hear the broadcast in full and unedited. It is announced as early as possible to give people notice and allow them to plan their schedule to be able to show up and participate. This means that it can't easily be rescheduled and once it is committed to, the date is pretty much locked in and they are stuck with it. It had never been a problem for Scott or UKMike but had been, on many occasions, for Mike Kennedy and this time was no different.

This really was the last straw and Scott and UKMike were chatting live to the listeners in the chatroom and also privately to each other about what to do. Due to his tiredness and anger, Scott was not willing to continue with the broadcast and wanted to fire Mike Kennedy on the spot. Being slightly less tired and slightly less angry UKMike was the voice of reason, possibly incorrectly, but he was of the opinion that they could in no way rely on Mike to show up for Live News ever again and they should replace him for that segment if nothing else. If Mike wanted to continue doing the Top Ten then they should let him as The Three Musketeers really did not want to lose him from the show or lose the banter that they still had, even then.

They apologized to the listeners but they would not be continuing with the Live News and Scott was going back to bed for a couple of hours before he went back to work for another twelve hours.

Ironically it was Willie (who had been in the chatroom waiting for the Live News) who informed Mike that they had not recorded the segment and had ended it prematurely. Mike contacted his co-hosts by email and said:

"Hey Guys,

It got back to me that Live News didn't happen and that Scott was griping about me the whole time you were on the air. Sorry I had to miss on Sunday, all I can say is family comes first and I wasn't going to tell Tricia to go to that thing alone. That was not going to happen."

UKMike responded with:

"Hey Mike,

Yes, News didn't happen. We just didn't feel motivated to do it after we all committed to it and you didn't show.

Nobody knows better than me that family comes first but we did all confirm we would be there, and if I had made that commitment then a family thing came up I would honor my commitment as I'd made it first.

Obviously your commitment to the show is not what it was, and to have the discussion we had on Thursday, and then just days later to do it to us again was too much. The chat room was full of people asking if you'd quit and my Skype was going crazy as you hadn't shown up again. I think what made it worse was that it was Surf Dogs that became more important than the show.

With that in mind Scott and I think that it would best if you stepped down as a co-host of the show and just took part in the Top Ten. The Top Ten is much easier to schedule than the Live News and we have a whole month to do it. If any of the 3 of us can't make it, we can reschedule but with Live News that isn't possible as it has a fixed time once we announce it. We can then get either a regular host for News or even a different Alumni each month. The show may even become something you enjoy listening to again.

I'm sure this arrangement would work for the best and free up a bit more of your schedule for your other projects and family. That way you can hopefully look at the Top Ten as something you can commit to and hopefully enjoy.

We also think that it would make sense to transfer the domain name and hosting to my account as you are paying for it each month, and as the 2 main co-hosts Scott and I should cover those costs."

Scott added:

"Surf Dogs could be the most gratuitous thing that could have been picked as a reason not to attend the news. Yes, Mike was disgusted and I was furious.

We accept that between the show and anything else you will choose anything else so I agree with Mike, we want to continue the show and schedule guests that will show up with enthusiasm and place the show as a priority. It is clear that the show isn't your priority but it is ours so I agree you should resign as co-host and continue to participate as a top ten guest host.

This is the way it has to be and is going to be, please let's make it a smooth transition and not bring a bad light to our project or your projects."

Mike Kennedy seemed to be happy with this arrangement and he replied:

"Sounds like a plan. Let's work on making the transfer, not sure where to start with that. Are we thinking of just dropping the GameGavel part of the forums or separating the two? I am not entirely sure I need forums for GG at this point."

After this discussion, Scott and UKMike were really now the owners of the show with Mike Kennedy in a lesser role than before but still they saw him as an important part of the show. They had started this together, had recorded the show for five years together, and would go on with the show together. Or so they thought.

With the plan in place and with Scott and UKMike now in control of the show and with the show's web presence fully under their control, they were ready to reach out to the new hosts that they had been discussing privately. Mike had already mentioned that he had a plan to close down the GameGavel forums anyway and migrate them over to his new venture, Retro Magazine, and he would have his main web presence concentrated over there, with GameGavel then being a sub forum on the Retro Magazine forums. He also wanted to close down his Network Solutions hosting account which was only being used for the podcast and had initially been used for the first Chase the Chuckwagon site.

All of the transition of ownership went smoothly and it was only the forums that took a long time to migrate, simply because they chose the slowest person in the world to do it, and it had all been done without any fuss or risk to the continuation of the show.

Once they had control of all elements of the show they added Simon Butler to the podcast. Simon is an industry veteran of over thirty years and was perhaps best known for his work during his time at Ocean Software though he still works in the industry to this day. He had worked on the design for games such as Hunchback: The Adventure (1986), N.O.M.A.D (1986), Cosmic Wartoad (1985), Shadowfire (1985) and Gift from the Gods (1984). He was primarily a pixel artist (or pixel monkey as he describes himself) and had done the artwork for games such as Worms (1995), The Addams Family (1992), Navy Seals (1991), Total Recall (1991), SimCity (1990), Army Moves (1987), Boot Camp (1987), Leader Board (1987), Highlander (1986), Hunchback: The Adventure (1986), It's a Knockout (1986), The Legend of Kage (1986), MagMax (1986), The Neverending Story (1985) and his first game Pedro's Garden (1984).

He has worked on over 300 individual titles for companies such as Ocean, Team 17, Vicarious Visions, Probe, Magnetic Fields, Atari and many others, and he would record a monthly segment for the podcast called "Dinosaur Pie" to fill the gaps left by Mike. They also recruited Mark Kaminski as a guest host to join in the Live News segment with them.

The Top Ten debate also needed a replacement host and they needed to recruit one quickly because the Live News could have been done, and was done for the most part, with just the two of them but the way that the Top Ten debate worked, they needed three of them to do it properly and Mark was unable to make the commitment to be there for it every month. What Scott and UKMike wanted was consistency and they did not want to have a different host for Top Ten debates, they felt that they needed a consistent line up which felt familiar to the listeners and helped build up the rapport that they had enjoyed with Mike Kennedy.

The last Top Ten recorded with Mike was in September 2015 and during October 2015 UKMike travelled to the U.S.A. to attend one of Scott's arcade parties and they discussed their options with each other in person. They had planned to record the October 2015 Top Ten with Willie of the ColecoVisions Podcast as he was penciled in to be at Scott's party. Unfortunately, he was unable to make it to the party and, with one thing and another, they found that they did not have the time to do the recording over Skype with Willie so they released the October 2015 show without a Top Ten debate while they considered their long term options.

They decided to recruit one of their long-time listeners, Ben Lancaster, who was already a regular with them at expos and who would help them run their expo booth. Ben, known online as Random Dave, is the man who converted their video game CGE Adventures to run on a Raspberry Pi and several other platforms, and he was also the man who wrote two games for them on the Sega Dreamcast; James And Watch: Arm and James And Watch: Tooth Cracker. In fact, it was while they were at Ben's house that UKMike had accidentally cracked Scott's tooth and the idea for that game was created.

With the gaps in the show now filled in they moved onwards and upwards but one slight annoyance for Mike Kennedy was that he now had no access to the free publicity that he had been getting on Retro Gaming Roundup and he needed to fill that void to be able to promote his other ventures. He did that by joining another podcast called Stalking The Retro. This is the man who didn't have time to do a podcast and could not commit to recording a podcast, yet here he is taking part in more podcasts.

As with the ColecoVisions podcast, this was an easy one for Mike to do. He did no prep, no production or recording and he simply logged into Skype, joined a conversation and signed out again when he had had enough, usually when he had finished going through all of his promotional talk about his various projects.

If you listen back to the episodes of the now defunct Stalking The Retro podcast, Mike makes no valuable contribution at all. He talks about how the auction site GameGavel is going, how Retro Magazine is coming along and how he hopes to get his new console idea off the ground. Once he has finished talking about his own projects, he makes his excuses and signs off. Scott and UKMike had earlier seen this for what it was and reigned in his promotional abilities on their show, even editing them out altogether, but it was taking longer for others to figure him out, but figure him out they would.

There were some questions raised by listeners at the time that he disappeared from the podcast, and these were answered incorrectly by Mike Kennedy in the show forums, and the questions centered around whether he had been fired or whether he had resigned. The truth of it is that Mike was given a choice to make.

Things could not go on as they were with his lack of commitment and preparation and his continual absence from the Live News and something needed to change. Mike painted the picture that he had been ganged up on and thrown him off his own podcast, but this was far from the truth. It was Mike himself who had inadvertently, yet publicly, spoken out about his lack of enthusiasm and effort for the podcast and it was his co-hosts that asked for the meeting to try and iron it out and help him cope with his workload. Both Scott and UKMike had wanted him to stay on the show and had tried to make that work but it came down to this:

Mike was told that things could not continue as they were and that essentially gave him three possible courses of action:

1. He could refuse to leave and continue to deal with the situation.
2. He could fight to stay on the show, outline how things would change and move forward.
3. He could resign and walk away, relieving some of the pressure he was under.

He chose the third option.

He claims that there was a fourth option, and technically there was, that he was fired, but this is not the truth and that is confirmed by his email to his co-hosts on September 29, 2015:

"Hey Guys,

I am going to resign from the Top-10 for the time being while I focus all my attention on getting this console back on track.

I am also stepping down from Willie's podcast as well while I get things worked out.

Mike then took to the forums to claim that he had been fired and had not been given a chance to say goodbye to the listeners and he felt very aggrieved about that.

On January 4, 2016 he posted:

"As far as RGRU that was something the three of us started to be something fun and ultimately they forced me out without even giving me a chance to say goodbye to our listeners."

UKMike responded, again in the forums:

"Come on Mike, you know I still have every recording we ever did, in full, unedited.

"After resigning, you emailed me to say you wanted to say goodbye and I asked you to send me the audio of you doing so in an email, to which you replied.

I did not get that audio.

There's no need to drag all this up again, especially when your memory of it is not accurate and cannot be backed up, unlike mine."

Mike had no further response and his time on the show was at an end. It would be far from the last we would hear of him though. The show continued without him and has continued to grow, even though its effects are not always intentional:

"The minute I heard our 6-year-old girl in her bedroom, re-enacting RETROGAMING Roundup, I knew our lives were changed forever. That's when I truly loved RGRU. Our marriage has never been healthier, AND we've even incorporated it into our lovemaking.

THANKS Mike James and Scott Schreiber!"

11: Remember When? Here We Go Again

With Retro Gaming Roundup being incorporated into its listeners' love–making and Mike gone from the podcast, things were about to ramp up. After all, GameGavel had spent $6,000 on the Atari Jaguar molds and they were never going to sit and gather dust on Mike's watch. In its first iteration as the Retro VGS the console had to stand on its own merits, of which there were few, but if it had a name behind it, it could potentially gain some traction and have perhaps some instant appeal.

Mike had earlier tried to license a recognizable name via his friend, the late Keith Robinson, who had access to the Intellivision brand and potentially Mattel, but nothing had come of it and the system had remained as the Retro VGS. The ace up Mike's sleeve this time was Coleco and River West Brands who owned it.

River West Brands is a *"brand acquisition and enterprise development company,"* which means that they acquire and hold on to dead brands and intellectual properties so that they can hopefully license their use at some point in the future. They do not necessarily manufacture or develop products themselves but sell licenses to others so that they can "officially" do so in a mutually beneficial arrangement.

Mike's failed attempt at an Intellivision license had leaked out and it was felt that the Intellivision license would have been much more viable had it been approved. Intellivision after all were still making their own products such as the Flashback console launched at CGE 2014. River West Brands was the easier option then, and while not without potential benefits, the Coleco name no longer carried the same weight as it once had. Also, it should be noted that the license Mike obtained was for "Coleco" and not "ColecoVision" which was a different brand and would have been a much bigger name.

Coleco was also a safer option for Mike as Intellivision would have surely required some input on a product bearing their actively used name whereas River West Brands required no such partnership, they lent their name only, not their expertise. Name aside though, it was still Mike at the helm and no amount of branding alone would fix that problem. As Scott succinctly put it:

> *"SoCal's ability to build a console began and ended with an idea, that was the extent of his ability. Everything else came from people who worked with him to*

give him a roadmap to turn his idea into an actual product, were stakeholders, and those people were all shed as soon as he thought he had enough info to move forward without them."

"This is a great parallel to the story of Atari where Nolan had the idea but Ted and later Al made those ideas into results. An idea man has value, but an idea man needs to have loyalty to those who turn it into reality unless you're clever enough to screw them after you have all the contributions, some are and some aren't."

The Coleco brand had recently been in the public eye with the launch of their Flashback console, which did sell, but not in the huge numbers expected. Some thought that it was overpriced or that AtGames didn't really understand the market for it and thought that it would be a big seller like the rest of their Flashback range, but it just didn't have the same appeal as the more familiar and more popular retro console models. Had it been released at a lower price point it may have been more of an impulse purchase but as it was, they had a brand that was familiar if not a huge draw. The Coleco branding also brought no funds with it, it was purely a licensing deal where Mike would pay them a percentage on every unit sold if he got a product to market, so he still had his cash flow problem and would have to go the crowdfunding route again to make it happen. His problem the first time around was the lack of a prototype to meet the requirements to use Kickstarter, so that had to be a top priority, a provable, working prototype. Unfortunately for Mike, that required a hardware engineer but since John Carlsen was now gone and distancing himself from the project, and actually now saying that had the campaign not been halted, he would have felt the need to report it as fraudulent himself, Mike needed somebody else.

John was never told about the previous designers that came before him and likely was also unaware of the transfer of assets between businesses, but now that the Retro VGS had been such a public fiasco, any new hardware engineer would be all too aware of the projects' history. Even if they had been living under a rock prior to coming on board, a quick Internet search would bring up more than enough reading material for them to peruse before committing themselves to bringing Mike's dream to fruition. It would also give them a glimpse of how they would be treated afterwards, whether they did valid work on the project or not.

Mike was still adamant that he had done nothing wrong and described Scott as a *"small minority owner of GGLLC"* with *"little meat in the game"* which had bothered some of his former fans on the podcast:

Originally Posted by TripHamer
"My only real issue with buying one would be if there's any "bad blood" (so to speak) between Socal and Scott and UKMike.
I would be kinda uncomfortable crossing that line, so I would factor that in to my decision."

UKMike appreciated the sentiment but calmed those feelings:

> *"You shouldn't.*
> *The product should stand or fall on its merits and I believe it will, either way."*

Scott was somewhat more pragmatic when he predicted *"I think this latest attempt will bomb bigger than the first one."* but Mike forged ahead with the announcement of his license on December 17, 2015:

> *Trabuco Canyon, CA (PR) – December 17, 2015 Video-game industry pioneer COLECO re-enters the market, partnering with Retro Video Game Systems, Inc., to introduce a new, modern-day video-game system called the COLECO Chameleon.*
>
> *COLECO Chameleon is a versatile new video-game system that serves as a modern day take on the classic game console and will accurately play classic games from the past. The COLECO Chameleon also has the ability play brand-new games in the 8, 16 and 32-bit styles, a growing and popular genre in today's game scape.*
>
> *Chris Cardillo, a partner in COLECO said, "Mark [Thomann] and I are excited to work hand-in-hand with Retro Video Game Systems, Inc. in the launch of the COLECO Chameleon. It's ironic that a new 'retro' video-game system would actually revolutionize and revitalize the COLECO brand."*
>
> *And, for the first time in nearly 20 years, the COLECO Chameleon will once again play brand new games on long-lasting, durable cartridges that can be played, traded, and collected for a lifetime. And all game cartridges will include high quality, plastic clamshell cases with illustrated instruction manuals and game developer liner notes.*
>
> *Retro Video Game Systems, Inc. President Mike Kennedy adds, "The COLECO Chameleon is a love-letter to all the classic cartridge based gaming systems that came before it and we love the fact it will succeed COLECO's successful Telstar and ColecoVision product lines. It will take gamers and their families back to a simpler time where games were all about great gameplay and fun factor."*
>
> *The COLECO Chameleon will launch in early 2016 and will also be demonstrated at Toy Fair New York 2016, February 13-16.*

He posted a follow up announcement on Facebook which partly addressed some of the concerns from before and promised to handle the development process more professionally as well as promising a playable prototype and a lower price.

> **"RETRO VIDEO GAME SYSTEMS INC**
> *Hello everyone. You have all seen the announcement we will be branding our new console under the COLECO name. We are excited to be a part of the revitalization of a great American brand and are working hard to build a system that will live up to the reputation of the original company and their gaming products. Many have mentioned they are still awaiting actual prototype hardware and wondering what is inside COLECO Chameleon.*

As we've said before we have made great progress over the last two months, but are waiting until we have the prototype 100% buttoned up before going public so we avoid the issues from before, talking about things, making changes, etc. So please, continue being patient with us while we do what you all want, making and demonstrating a playable prototype. Once we have this, all will be revealed. And rest assured, it will be at a very inviting price point. Thanks again for all your support, comments and questions."

The following day, Pat and Ian were back with a show titled *"Retro VGS Rebranded as Coleco Chameleon"* and they made a breaking announcement. They felt it was so pertinent that they couldn't wait two weeks until their next scheduled show and covered the story as it happened, with Pat telling everybody that Christmas had come early.

> *"It's here folks, Merry Christmas, and Christmas comes early. It's a ColecoVision and a Jaguar shell [...] Happy Hannukah, Merry Kwanzaa [...] It's the Atari Jaguar Retro VGS you knew and loved branded with the ColecoVision font and hologram color rainbow scheme on the controller and on the console. What the #### is this? [...] I can't make this up."*

They did promise to *"give it a fair shake for now. Maybe we'll hold off until they redo the Kickstarter before we go all in or not about this."*

Mike's announcements of course stirred up lots of discussion from accusations of lazy journalism to admiration of clever marketing. Coleco were being touted as being back in the game but they were far from that, the long dead license was being used, Coleco were not even an entity at this point. The branding was good enough to fool the general public though as they knew nothing of River West Brands and its brand acquisitions. News coverage did nothing to explain it either so, to the masses, Coleco were indeed back in the game, but more ardent fans were not convinced and questioned Mike's use of the phrase in his announcement, notably Carl Williams.

> *"Hey Carl,*
>
> *That "COLECO is Back" title was added at the last minute by our PR firm. And I guess we can all debate what "Back" means. In a sense it is back. Even if in name only. The future of what that means remains to be seen. If this product, with the COLECO name on it, becomes a success at some level, then what will that mean? Is it "back" then? Is there a future in that brand to bring out or lend their name to other "new" products? I really don't think most are reading much more into it other than, "Hey, it would be cool to see that brand name back on a new product." The Chameleon will be the first "new" forward thinking product to adorn that brand name and none of us know where it could take the brand. It was never our intention to indicate this was anything but a licensing deal."*

Carl responded:

> *"So, a PR firm that you hired made an unauthorized last minute addition to your press release without your approval? Forgive me, but if that really happened, it just proves that the same incompetence you showed with the first failed attempt at Retro VGS is still in full effect here."*

The truth came out, as it usually does, and Mike had indeed lied about a PR firm adding the comment, it was his own work, and his own lies to try and cover it up. As with so many of Mike's cartoon type episodes where something blew up in his face, the cover up was a bigger mess than the original lie.

The Chameleon part of the name also ruffled a few feathers, not those of UKMike who mused:

> *"The problem isn't that it is not a Coleco, or that the original was a Retro VGS. The problem, for me anyway, is Mike chasing the dollar at the expense of all else, be that friends, reputation or common sense."*

Some had more to say about the name:

> *"They should be calling this thing the Honey Badger instead of the Chameleon, because no matter what rational point you make about the futility of the project, Honey Badger just don't care."*

Others took it far more seriously and questioned Mike's mental stability:

> *"Just as someone with BPD (Borderline Personality Disorder) struggles to stabilize a coherent, reliable identity, the clinician contends with establishing a diagnosis which may be as elusive. The chameleon disguises of BPD implicate various illnesses. Could mood swings suggest Major Depression or Bipolar Disorder? Does destructive impulsivity infer Attention Deficit Disorder or cover over drug abuse?"*
>
> *"BPD is so difficult to accurately diagnose because it intersects with other disorders in several ways. Most often, it may coexist, but be submerged, in the wake of a more prominent disorder, such as Depression. Borderline symptoms may not become discernible until after treatment of the other illness is mobilized. Secondly, BPD's chameleon disguise may mimic another syndrome and induce an incorrect assessment. In such a way, a cursory evaluation of "mood swings" may initiate a misapplied label of Bipolar Disorder. Alternatively, BPD may camouflage another illness, and be installed inaccurately as the primary diagnosis."*

Mark Kaminski had earlier questioned whether Mike had ADHD or was *"puffin on a meth pipe"* but joking aside, there were still those coming to Mike's defense. Two days after the announcement, Willie Culver, Mike's co-host on the ColecoVisions podcast, was of course more than enthusiastic about the Coleco tie in.

"There were several mistakes made with the RVGS campaign. Mike took the brunt of it unfortunately. There is a new engineering team behind it now (not the same one that did the RGVS), changes have been made but functionality is still there. They did listen to the suggestions and criticisms and are working towards a more affordable solution based on that.

The new owner of the Coleco Brand, Chris Cardillo was looking for something for the brand to relaunch it and the RVGS fit the bill, so it got the Coleco Brand.

Being part of the team, I am privy to quite a bit but there will be much more info released soon through the official channels.

If I am to be accused of drinking the Kool Aid, then so be it. I have faith in Mike and what he is trying to do.

Coleco invited me to the toy fair in New York to be there with the working prototype of the Coleco Chameleon , so I am very excited about it!

I only hope RGRU listeners remember who Mike is and give him the benefit of the doubt, he has a good heart."

Scott and UKMike had maintained their friendship with Willie despite Willie's loyalty to Mike as he claimed to be part of the team, but they knew all too well what that meant. Willie had no official standing, no income from his association and was one unmade phone call away from not being on the team. There were none of the regular hard and soft products that would accompany such a product development other than the cursed injection molds, in fact nothing more than huge volumes of words and more 3D renders were ever created, it was still smoke and mirrors. On multiple occasions Scott tried to explain to Willie what was going on, but Willie was committed to the wild ride. At one point Scott threw his hands up and told Willie that he was just going to have to learn the hard way and when that moment finally dawned on Willie it would prompt him to make an effort to set things right, something that was perhaps the key to the downfall of the whole scheme.

Mike needed friends like Willie right now and he was taking him along for the ride as long as he was considered a part of the team and he was invited to the New York Toy Fair. This was a huge event in the calendar for the toy market, remember it was where Atari had taken their home version of Pong 40 years earlier to show it off to the industry when they felt they could get a better deal than the one Sears had offered them. Mike also now needed to be more mindful of his public image, and that of his project, as he was responsible for the reputation of the Coleco brand as long as his console bore its name. With that in mind he decided to address a few concerns with one of his wall of words style posts on December 23, 2015. There was something in Mike's perception of his ability as a salesman, or perhaps in his perception of his own charisma, that made him think that the right combination of words in sufficient number could explain away anything.

"Hello Everyone.

It is the end of a very tumultuous year for me and in the spirit of Christmas and the holidays I wanted to come in here and ask those of you who will listen to let the past be the past as it relates to this (ad)venture. RETRO VGS is the past and COLECO Chameleon is the future. The Chameleon is not just a rebranded Retro VGS. Despite sharing some of the same internal components the hardware has been completely redesigned to lower the cost while maintaining much of its ability to play a wide variety of games in a variety of ways. To boil this all down to its essence we just want to produce a product that is different, affordable and will bring joy to people's lives. The market will ultimately decide if we are crazy enough to believe a cartridge console can stand its ground in this age of digital delivery. There are clearly lots of people on both sides of this fence and ultimately it will all come down to the games that can be played and if they are compelling enough to vie for peoples hard earned money.

The COLECO branding was a business decision I made to bring instant brand recogniiton to the Chameleon. But I did not enter into this licensing agreement lightly, knowing that if done so, we have a lot to live up to. COLECO made some very influential, high quality and fun video gaming and electronic products during their time and we will try endlessly to carry on that tradition with the Chameleon. The recognition of having the COLECO logo on the system and the (game and console) boxes will make the Chameleon immediately identifiable by millions of people right from the beginning. In the end this is a good thing for all involved including us, our customers, our suppliers and distributors, our contract manufactures, potential retailers and probably most importantly to game developers. Mark and Chris at River West/Coleco Holdings are also very behind this product and will be helping out in a variety of ways, beginning by inviting us into their booth at Toy Fair which is where they want to officially begin rebuilding this brand in more concrete ways.

We know we have a mountain to climb and are prepared to do what it takes to plant a flag at the top. I will once again apologize to all of you for at times dissing some individuals and this community but it was hard being criticized by a group of my Atari and classic game lovin' peers. I let it get to me on occasion and I do regret all of it. I am aware that we gave you all plenty to poke fun at and criticize but in the end, I believe the product will be much better for going through all of this. In my mind, the best way for me to apologize once and for all is to ultimately create a game system that will make most of you turn a 180 and win over your support and positive influence. And given the chance that is what I will do.

All I ask is moving forward into the New Year is you try and give the Chameleon a fair chance to stand on its own, and again forget about the past. Let it speak for itself when we reveal it to you all early this New Year. And finally, let's respect one another and our opinions (some advice I am directing towards myself) and that goes for both believers and non-believers of what we are trying to do. In the end, we all love and are passionate about video games and sometimes this passion causes us to do uncharacteristic things.

Merry Christmas, Happy Holidays and I hope you all have a very Happy New Year!
- Mike"

That same day he was also responding to questions and promising to reveal the inner workings of the console.

> *"Once the prototype is complete we will reveal what's inside. It shouldn't be too much longer."*

Carl Williams was fast becoming a thorn in Mike's side though and began to question his incessant name dropping again, to which Mike responded on Christmas Eve, rather foolishly by revealing private emails where he had specifically been asked not to.

> *"Hey Everyone.*
>
> *First off, this post isn't pointing fingers at anyone in this community whatsoever, but will single out one Carl Williams.*

The nonsensical nature of his opening statement was apparently lost on him and he continued;

> *This is directed at him and asking him why he seems to have it out for me? I think you can agree that his 30,000 words accusing me of everything has tons of holes in it after you read further. I too, have mastered the art of copy and paste.*
>
> *I think it is safe to say that Carl is a bit obsessive in trying to ruin my reputation and character. Take a look at what he is saying in all his rants and he goes way out of this way to create mountains out of molehills in everything he writes about me. And, yes, I've banned him from our Facebook page so he can't spread his deceitful tabloid written crap over there.*
>
> *He says that I never had any "real" discussions with Konami? Well, here you go Carl!*
>
> *"From: Michael Rajna*
> *To: Mike Kennedy*
> *Hey Mike,*
> *A couple of things:*
>
> 1) *Just wanted to follow up on the below – could you please let me know your feedback?*
> 2) *Regarding the following link that we were directed to by a journalist: [LINK WITHHELD]*
>
> *Please not that we have not agreed to anything yet regarding this offer. While we may be interested in this down the line (based on the feedback you provide), we are still very far away from making any announcements about this yet. We'd like to ask that you don't bring this up in a public forum until an agreement has been made.*
> *Thank you*
> *Michael"*
>
> *Note the email from Mike Rajna to me kindly asking me not to discuss our internal discussions until some sort of official deal is made. I then kindly asked Carl Williams to remove any mention of the Konami mentions in his stories,*

at the request of Mr. Rajna. Here you will also see some original discussions beginning with Howard Phillips and Owen Rubin. Two of the other people I am accused of name dropping.

Guys, in the pursuit of opportunities to successfully bring this product to market I have tapped deep into my contacts and friends of contacts which are all legitimate contacts in the industry."

As the email above shows, Mike had indeed contacted Konami, which wasn't really in question, but he was clearly using their name to lend legitimacy to his projects. Asked not to do so in on February 26, 2015, he did just that on May 30th when he appeared on The Retro League Podcast. Unwittingly he had also now publicly posted something which he had been specifically asked not to publicly share.

As can be clearly seen, Konami were a million miles from agreeing to be on board with Mike and were waiting to see if his console was a success or not before committing to anything beyond a few pleasant emails., and even some unpleasant ones.

Carl had also followed up on some other companies whose names Mike had been touting, such as Bandai Namco, Capcom, Double Fine, John Romero, Sega and Watermelon Games. All said they either are not, or were not contacted about, working on games for the Chameleon. NG:DEV Team tweeted that they are not interested in the Chameleon and will not be supporting it in any way.

What must have been going through Mike's mind as somebody like Carl called him out, and was deadly accurate in doing so, yet he labelled the reporting as *"deceitful tabloid written crap."* Carl had done something quite simple, he had contacted the names that Mike had dropped and asked the simple questions. Did Mike never expect that? Other journalists like Pat and Ian or Stop Drop and Retro uncovered portions of the truth and presented their findings to the public so what kind of thinking results in the conclusion of going on the attack when caught red-handed?

As 2015 transitioned into 2016, Willie was speaking up for Mike's good nature as others were trying to figure out who his new hardware engineer might be. On January 8th, though it would only emerge later, Mike wrote his new engineer a cheque for $2,500 for Hardware Design. That new engineer was none other than Sean Robinson, the man who had earlier worked on the Retro VGS and Mike's web sites. This was the same day that Mike posted a request for game developers who might be interested in their games appearing on cartridges. Had he scared away the 250 or so that had been interested in working with him earlier?

With the New York Toy Fair looming Mike knew that he had to have something to show, he couldn't turn up at one of the premier events of the year in the toy industry with a series of 3D rendered images and a sales pitch. People would visit the Coleco booth and expect to see something that they could touch, something that they could play and something that would be a viable product for them to bring to market.

"We are seeing different versions of cases over a year now. What about the hardware?

It's what's inside that counts."

With the hardware side in the hands of his new engineer, Mike was still on the hunt for games to launch alongside it and he reached out again to Eli from Piko Interactive who gave us an update on the same day that Mike wrote the $2,500 cheque.

> *"First of all, I think this time around they have a better chance to make the console happen with the Coleco Brand and the slash of costs.*
>
> *Anyways, Mike has approached to us again, first time he wanted game(s) from us and then after he never posted them on the indiegogo (thank God actually)*
>
> *He reached out again, and we are going to give him another chance as we believe the project, if successful, could be cool.*
>
> *I think they want to target more the general audience that appreciates retro games. But who knows who is going to respond more this time around. It seems that the retro gaming scene feels very speculative which there is nothing wrong with that.*
>
> *Anyways, I've decided to go to NY for the Toy show and actually see the hardware; I've orally agreed to some stuff for the Coleco, but will not give final yes until we have it all signed in paper. I've seen their contract and (it) is solid.*
>
> *I will report back with pictures and my insights after the NY trip. I already have the passes for the Tradeshow, just need to get my flight and hotel room.*
>
> *For what I've heard from Mike, if they follow the plan they have, it would be very likely to be successful on the Kickstarter scale. After that of course, Content will rule; No new/exclusive content, will eventually kill the console. So they really will need to lure developers and offer them very good deals + cash to have them develop."*

While Eli seemed confident, others were questioning the relative silence from the previously garrulous team who had stopped updating their website and social media feeds.

> *"...the eerie silence from these guys the last few weeks is actually quite scary and unnerving [...]"*
>
> *"Nothing from them on their Twitter since January 9th"*
>
> *"Nothing on their Facebook page since December 18th except the occasional reply to comments"*
>
> *"Nothing new at all on their webpage except the same 3D renders of their console"*
>
> *"...everyone involved directly or indirectly seems to have gone underground"*
>
> *"Well, the guys behind it claim that they will be unveiling a working prototype at the New York Toy Fair in February. They also claimed back in December that they would be unveiling games for it throughout January but so far we've seen nothing of the sort and it's the 21st today."*

While it must have been killing Mike to be so publicly silent, maybe he had learned his lesson of sharing too much too soon but he was working away diligently behind the scenes securing launch titles to release with the system and preparing for a launch on Kickstarter rather than Indiegogo. With the change in crowdfunding platform and a change in name he would need a new launch video to show the system off to prospective backers so on January 19th he sent a text message to Brian Barnhart to ask if he would be interesting in shooting and producing the video. Presuming that Mike had been impressed with the Jag Bar and how the episode had come out, and of course seeing all of his filming equipment, lighting and green screens around the place, Brian assumed Mike had been thinking *"I could use this set for something. I could use it for the video."* and they agreed to shoot the video there.

A few days later, on January 30th, he messaged Brian by text again asking him to capture some footage of Intellivision games and Coleco products for a montage. This was off the back of an announcement of the launch titles that would be available:

> *Posted Tue Feb 2, 2016 12:40 AM*
> *The complete list of 8-bit launch titles includes:*
> *Choplifter – ColecoVision*
> *Frenzy – ColecoVision*
> *Jumpman Junior – ColecoVision*
> *Venture – ColecoVision*
> *Pepper II – ColecoVision*
> *Montezuma's Revenge – ColecoVision*
> *Gateway to Apshai – ColecoVision*
> *Armor Battle – Intellivision*
> *Astrosmash – Intellivision*
> *Frog Bog – Intellivision*
> *Shark! Shark! – Intellivision*
> *Space Armada – Intellivison*
> *B-17 Bomber – Intellivision*
> *Night Stalker – Intellivision*
> *Thin Ice – Intellivision*
> *Thunder Castle – Intellivision*
> *Tower of Doom – Intellivision*
> *Utopia – Intellivision*
>
> *16-bit offerings include:*
> *Dorke and Ymp*
> *Legend*
> *Iron Commando: Koutetsu No Senshi*
> *Jim Power: The Lost Dimension*
> *Battle Brave Saga*
> *Sydney Hunter: The Caverns of Death*
> *Apocalypse II*
> *Water Margin*

Brian had asked Mike for a script and when it wasn't forthcoming by February 3rd, he reminded Mike that he needed some direction and that he needed the script. He also enquired what inputs would be required on the TV they were using for the footage. The following day Mike sent the script to Brian who read through it and noticed that it was devoid of any technical data, no specs of what the system is. He described it as *"... nothing, it's just a dream. It's just an idea of the glory days of retro coming back."*

SCRIPT

[MIKE KENNEDY LEAD-IN] *Hi everyone, I'm Mike Kennedy and we are very excited to introduce you to the Coleco Chameleon. The Coleco Chameleon is a new cartridge based video gaming console that is designed to play both a variety of classic games from the 80's and 90's and also new retro inspired games coming from today's homebrew, indie and mainstream developers. We have spent the last few months creating a working prototype as well as seeking out launch games that will scratch that retro itch in all of you. We hope you will consider backing our campaign and help to spread the word of our campaign to your gaming friends and family.*

[STUDIO SET KIDS PLAYING GAMES WITH FADE TO GAMEPLAY VIDEO MONTAGE – Montezuma's Revenge, Pepper II, Astrosmash, Night Stalker]

Remember when video-games looked like video-games? When colorful, imaginative sprites popped off the screen and into your living room. When games were more than an impulsive download; they were highly prized, magical transports into a fantasy world all delivered inside plastic cartridges.

[GAMEPLAY VIDEO MONTAGE – Iron Commando, Dorke & YMP]

Remember when games were hard but you still couldn't tear yourself away from playing? When they didn't include lengthy tutorials or unlimited continues or saves? Remember when games came with instruction books that you actually wanted to read cover-to-cover?

[TRANSITION TO LIVING ROOM SET, KIDS ON COUCH PLAYING CHAMELEON]

Remember that feeling you had buying a game in the store and bringing it home and playing it for the first time with your friends and family, all in the same room? We want to bring those magical times back with the introduction of the COLECO Chameleon. The COLECO Chameleon is the first new home console in nearly 20 years that will play new games on cartridges and once again give today's gamers something to buy, play, trade and collect for a lifetime.

[TRANSITION TO COLECO MONTAGE]

It also marks the return of the COLECO brand name, a brand synonymous with the history of electronic handheld games and video games. COLECO was a pioneer bringing some of the first PONG systems into the home in the 1970's followed by the hugely successful ColecoVision in the 1980's, the first system to bring near arcade perfect graphics into over two million living rooms. And it was the company that made Nintendo a house-hold name when Donkey Kong was packed into every ColecoVision retail box sold.

[TRANSITION TO CHAMELEON CONSOLE MONTAGE]

The COLECO Chameleon is designed to be the ultimate retro gaming system. It has the ability to accurately play a variety of your favorite classic video games, available as compilation cartridges, while also being an outlet for many all-new, classically inspired games being programmed by some of today's best homebrew, indie and mainstream game developers. Now recognized as art form in of itself, retro gaming is once again a mainstay in today's gaming landscape as developers are realizing classic graphics and gameplay mechanics are still entertaining even in this age of triple A, big budget cinematic titles. The COLECO Chameleon is the best way to experience this new wave of RETRO. Get ready to Play Again.

[MIKE KENNEDY CALL TO ACTION]

If you're as excited as we are after viewing this, you have a chance to be one of the first gamers to have a Coleco Chameleon before it's introduced commercially. Now, you can play the old games you loved when you were younger, help your friends and family make memories of their own, and enjoy the new games from our collection.

On behalf of my team at Retro Video Game Systems, Inc. and Coleco Holdings we ask for your consideration to help us bring the COLECO Chameleon into homes around the world. This is a product that needs grass roots support to grow as it is so completely opposite of where the video-game industry is heading. Help us change the future of gaming by bringing back the RETRO.

[TRANSITION TO FADE OUT OF LIVING ROOM. ADULTS 30's NOW ON COUCH HAVING FUN PLAYING CHAMELEON]

[TRANSISTION FADE TO BLACK SCREEN. POP IN COLECO CHAMELEON LOGO + REMEMBER WHEN. PLAY AGAIN. TAGLINE]

The children mentioned in the video were going to include Brian's son and daughter and a few of their friends from school and the music would be original tunes created by Paul Nurminen (Nurmix). On February 5th Mike sent Brian a few sample tunes that he liked and asked Brian's opinion on them and to ensure that he credited "Music by Nurmix" in the video. That same day he also introduced Brian to John Lester (Gamester81) by email, explaining to John that Brian was doing the video. John said *"Hi"* and Brian replied:

"Hey John you were an influence in me starting the Jag Bar.
I also do the lynx Lounge.
Going through my Jag and Lynx collection 1 game at a time.
Glad to be involved.
Love to be on your show sometimes and you're always welcome at the Jag Bar."

He never got another response from John, but Mike was in contact by text again, asking for the address of the Jag Bar and Brian gave his parents' address as the show was being produced there at the time. At 7pm that evening, Mike texted Brian to cancel the filming for that day:

> *"Cancel for tonight get voice overs tomorrow and send the latest script"*

Brian said OK and that they should aim for 5pm the following day but Mike later changed that to 7pm. When the next day came around, February 6th, Mike was getting non-committal again:

> *"Hey Brian, still touch and go our end with proto(type) will check in with you 1pm"*

When he heard nothing more, Brian texted Mike back at 15:57:

> *"How are we looking?*

Mike asked if he was:

> *"OK to do it?"*

Brian replied that he was but he felt that they should film the sequences using the children first as he was eager by now to just get it done. He had to organize the logistics of the shooting as well as try to organize setting up families to be filmed playing on the system and if there were going to be children used in the filming, Mike couldn't keep them waiting all day and keep them out late at night. They would arrange to shoot at 5 and then it would be 6 and then 7 and then 8 and then 9, and all the time Brian was telling him *"Mike, I've got these kids over here. I can't have these kids up at 9 and then if you get here at 9:30 then what? Are we shooting at 10? There's no way that I could have these families come in at 10 o'clock at night and shoot this thing."*

Mike's excuse for cancelling again was down to his hardware guy who said there was a problem with the board. Apparently, he had plugged in a USB controller and it had *"fried a piece of the board."* Brian was curious and said *"Huh"* thinking, *"Well, isn't your controller USB? Don't you think you should've had that ironed out like maybe four months ago?"*

It could have been either Sean or Mike who wanted to do the video without the actual console being used and to just show game footage, but either way Mike assured Brian that his hardware guy was getting a part and it would be sent by priority mail so he would have it in the morning. He was also going to put a fuse box on the board so that if he plugs something in again and anything was wrong then the fuse would blow and wouldn't ruin the board again. The next day the part didn't come in the morning as Mike had promised and it was now supposed to arrive at 2pm which duly came and went, then it was set to arrive at 3pm and then 4pm.

"So, we're playing this game again and then we go all the way up until 9 o'clock and I said, "Hey, I'm going to have to call it. Let's call it, because it's not going to happen.""

Feeling that this all sounded a little dubious, Brian was left thinking *"Give me the product so I can shoot this."* while trying to figure out the best ways to shoot it and light it and have the kids having fun with it. Finally, Mike told Brian that his hardware guy wouldn't let him use the prototype for the video. He said:

"I can't do it because my hardware guy is not letting me have anybody play it because he's afraid that we're not going to make the deadline for the Toy Fair."

Resigned to the fact that it wasn't happening Brian told Mike

"I get it, your life is on the line right now because you've got to deliver this thing to the Toy Fair. You've got to do what you need to do. I'll be here."

Mike thanked him and asked if he would do the voice overs and Brian said that he would try and get them done but he was busy with other things. Later that evening Mike was in touch to ask if the voice overs had been done but, as he had been warned, Brian had been busy all day and hadn't had a chance to do them, so Mike told him that he might just do them himself.

When he heard nothing further Brian thought simply that Mike was busy in the run up to the Toy Fair and that he may be waiting until afterwards to shoot the video. He checked in with a text on February 9th asking how Mike was holding up and Mike replied:

"So far so good hope to get demo unit tomorrow. Sweating."

Brian tried to calm him a little:

"Getting down to the wire. It will be great and you will have a great show."

Not everybody was wishing that Mike would have a great show though, a fake website and Twitter account had been set up and Tweeted:

"Coming to #kickstarter soon $150 FPGA goodness #retrogaming"

Mike saw it and responded:

"The @ ColecoChameleon Twitter and ColecoChameleon.org are unofficial and were set up a week ago. We have been working very hard to rope this all back in and have worked miracles the past few months to get to where we are today. We will be revealing a lot more over the next couple weeks and stuff like this stoops to a new low for "someone". Pressing forward!"

While trying to co-ordinate the video, Mike was also trying to confirm the launch titles and a pack-in game that would be included with every system and he had to have something he could show running at the Toy Fair. Luckily for him, he got the long awaited prototype from Sean the day before he left for New York with Tricia, and the day before the show began he tweeted a picture of a close up of the Coleco Chameleon with a cartridge inserted and a TV behind it showing the title screen of the game Sydney Hunter and The Caverns Of Death, a 2016 game by Collectorvision. The picture was shared on Tumblr by John Lester with the comment:

> *"One of the games we're working on, Sydney Hunter and the Caverns of Death running on the new upcoming Coleco Chameleon prototype system. It plays great on it! #collectorvision #colecochameleon #sydneyhunter!"*

There was no mention of the fact that it was displaying on an old tube type TV where previously it had been announced that the Chameleon would be HDMI only, a feature found on newer flat screen TVs.

Earlier pictures of the Retro VGS had shown games on screen and the controller being held in front of it as though it was showing actual gameplay footage, and similarly with this picture, the cables could not be seen going from the console to the TV, so it was equally plausible that this too was faked. Scott commented that in absolute certainty it was impossible that an FPGA based board had been developed along with the necessary cores in the short hiatus between the end of the Retro VGS and the public showing of the Coleco Chameleon at the Toy Fair. They could not do in a few weeks what others had failed to do in months to years. It was very unlikely that buyers and marketing types would question what they were seeing to that degree and it was feared that somehow the deception would be digested as a real prototype and those same buyers and marketing types would lend an air of credibility to the Chameleon.

John Lester had hoped that with the Coleco license the project would be taken more seriously and Mike had actually wanted the Collectorvision game "Tiny Knight" but John was against that idea as he wanted to release it first on the Super Nintendo and then on modern platforms only. It was also doubtful whether it would be ready in time for the release date that Mike had in mind. Mike wanted to crowdfund in March 2016, have the games completed by August and be in time for a December release to make the Christmas market. John felt that a better option would be their game "Sydney Hunter and The Caverns Of Death" as they were almost ready to release it and it was also a Super Nintendo game, meaning that the FPGA in the Chameleon would be able to run it. The deal was organized and they had verbal confirmation from Mike that it would be the Chameleon's pack-in game but they eagerly awaited a written contract, which never came. As well as tweeting the picture of the game title screen next to the Chameleon, Mike sent the picture to Collectorvision who posted it on their Facebook page.

Collectorvision were also dealing with Sean, who Mike introduced as the programmer for the Chameleon, and they discussed the system's ability to run games from different platforms as Mike also wanted to have the ColecoVision game "Light Grid Racing" on it. He told them that it would be able to play ColecoVision games through an ARM processor but the only unofficial agreement that they had was for Sydney Hunter And The Caverns Of Death. From memory, they were set to receive $10 for every copy of the game sold and if Mike's touted potential sales figures were accurate, it could make them a lot of money. Either Mike or Sean told them that the Chameleon would play Super Nintendo games through an FPGA/ARM processor which was great for them as all they had to do was provide the game ROM and Mike would handle the manufacturing of the cartridge with Quality Control being handled by Collectorvision.

The next day, February 13th, the first day of the Toy Fair, was a very busy day in the saga with lots of different parts of the story being woven together later, but the day began with Scott resigning himself to the fact that he would never see his investment in GameGavel amount to anything and he publicly offered to sell back his shares in exchange for a Stunt Pilot arcade game delivered to his door. He was of course referring to the one that Mike had in his garage/home office. The offer was made mostly in jest and posted as Scott settled in for the long weekend watching all the avenues of information that were flowing through. There was of course the official Coleco Chameleon channel and also the back channels of the people that Mike was in communication with and who would happily forward any and all news immediately upon receipt. Scott spent most of the weekend in his garage tending to some projects while checking in on the activity.

Mike was far too busy to notice Scott's offer as he made a Facebook announcement that the Coleco Chameleon Kickstarter campaign would launch on the morning of Friday, February 26, 2016. Keeping in touch with Mike and still hopeful that he would get to work on the launch video, Brian sent Mike a picture of himself and his son playing Coleco games.

It turned out that Willie had been unable to make it to New York. He had been sitting in the airport, but the weather had affected his flight and he didn't make it. One who did make it was Eli and he eventually found his way to the Coleco booth where Mike, Tricia, Stephen from Coleco Addict and, of course, Chris Cardillo awaited him. Eli was keen to see the system running as it outwardly seemed like a great platform for the type of games that he was releasing and their business relationship could be a good one that might prove profitable for both sides. Typically, one of his games would sell 200 to 300 copies, which was fine, but here was Mike telling him that he could provide the pack-in game for the system and he was quoting early potential early sales numbers of 2,000, of which Piko Interactive would get a cut for every console sold. That sounded like good business to Eli and he had paid for the trip to New York in good faith, using funds that he allocated each year to go to conventions. The previous year he had blown it on a trip to E3 to talk to Hyperkin about a deal which didn't eventually happen, but he was cautiously hopeful about this one.

> *"I'm going to check it out. I'm going to see, hopefully try to build a business relationship there in a way that they get our games and sort of like sell copies, but also, I'm going to check it out because they already have flaked on me, Mike had on the Indiegogo, because he announced Super Noah's Ark as a launch title and then he just didn't add it on the Indiegogo."*

Others had warned Eli that he had dodged a bullet on that occasion but still Mike had contacted him the next day and told him *"Dude, I'm going to add your games tomorrow"* but Eli was wary and had declined, telling him that they were going to hold off.

Now though, Eli had gone to the Toy Fair armed with two cartridges, one was a Nintendo game that he wanted to give to Nerdblock to try and get his games into one of their subscription boxes. He had forgotten to post it to them so he had told Ron from Nerdblock that he would hand it over to him in person at the Toy Fair. The other was a Super Nintendo multicart that he had done for the E3 Hyperkin deal that had fallen through but he knew that Loot Crate were also going to be in New York and he intended to give it to them with the hope of getting a game into their subscription boxes.

Sometime during the morning Mike had been taking pictures of the Chameleon running games in the booth and he shot some video footage of it to use for promotion. The system itself was on the table but it was sitting underneath a clear Perspex box. On top of the box was a flat screen TV and in the front of the box were two round holes where the controller leads passed through so that passers-by could play on the system. The controllers were using some kind of extension lead, either to just make them longer or so the console wouldn't get jolted if they were pulled on, or possibly because they were allegedly hard wired in to the prototype.

Sean had warned Mike that the prototype was delicate and should be handled with care, and it was. Mike had nursed it to New York and had set it up in the booth carefully. Sean had also warned him not to show any pictures of the rear of it but, foolishly, Mike had done exactly that as he took pictures of the console from several angles, including the rear, and had shared them online in response to sceptics questioning if the console was even connected to the TV. With great confidence Mike posted the pictures to quiet down the sceptics but while they did show that it was indeed connected to the TV, they also revealed far more than he intended. Not only could the ports on the back be clearly seen but also that there was electrical tape either holding it together or covering something up. Not for the first time, Mike caused the Internet to go crazy.

There was still no official announcement about what hardware was inside the shell, just that it would be able to run Super Nintendo games, as well as other systems, due to its FPGA chip. As it sat in the booth it was indeed running a Super Nintendo game, which was of course Sydney Hunter, though Mike was also showing off several other games as well, all of them Super Nintendo games, and all of them on the one cartridge that he had.

AtariAge members who were watching the updates from the show floor began to try and decipher exactly what the system was. Obviously, it was housed in the Atari Jaguar shell, a black one so that nothing could be seen through it, but it was what was inside that was important. Favorite on the list of possible candidates, in addition to a newly designed console running SNES cores, was a Super Nintendo Mini. Had Mike really had his engineer produce a brand-new product, even in its current fragile state? Even if it had picked up where the Retro VGS left off and continued with the basis of that system, it had to be running Super Nintendo cores to run the games. Ever since Kevin Horton had withdrawn from the project and they no longer had access to his cores, they must have written their own, so were these the most quickly developed cores in the world? As one astute commenter put it; perhaps they had simply popped down to the *"core store."*

The SNES (Super Nintendo Entertainment System) began its life in Japan as the Super Famicom in November 1990 before appearing in North America as the Super Nintendo in August 1991. It later underwent a redesign which is commonly referred to as either the SNES Mini, SNES Jr, or its model number SNS-101 which was released in Japan in March 1998 and North America in October 1997. The redesigned unit was smaller than the original and was cheaper to produce.

It didn't take long for people to compare Mike's pictures of the rear of the Chameleon to those of a SNES Jr and indeed it looked like the ports on the rear of the unit lined up exactly with each other. The cartridge slot had also been photographed and shared and people were comparing the distance from the rear of the unit to the slot and looking at the pins in the slot itself, as well as the connector inside the cartridge that Mike had. It all seemed to suggest that it was indeed a SNES Jr. Examining the photos and comments Scott knew what it wasn't but was not yet sure what it was. There were lots of ways that it could be faked, the question was which one did they choose? Very quickly the pictures were being examined and zoomed in on, reflections analyzed, and it wasn't long before two pictures appeared that told the whole story. The first was an isometric view that showed a corner not covered by electrical tape and there was no doubt that it was the same color and shape as a SNES Jr rear panel. The second, showing the connector spacing, made it all too clear that it was without a doubt a SNES Jr inside a Jaguar shell, a *"SNESinaJag"* as it would become commonly known.

Scott snatched the two key ingredients from some spares that he had and there was no doubt about what he was looking at. What Mike had was a SNESinaJag and he had taken it to the New York Toy Fair. Almost equally certain was that nobody at the Toy Fair was likely to lean over and notice the details and raise the alarm. As idiotic and audacious as it was, the turducken of a console might actually fool the world.

As for the cartridge, of course the original Super Nintendo cartridges contained just one game (or sometimes more but usually one) but modern day alternatives such as the Everdrive, are available which have a slot for an SD card inside them, allowing multiple game ROMs to be copied to an SD card, inserted into the Everdrive and when turned on, the software on the Everdrive presents the player with a menu where a game can be chosen from the list and then run. Games can be played and then reset to return to the menu allowing a different game to be chosen, without ever having to remove the cartridge except to add more games to the list. It was one such similar cartridge that Mike was using, rehoused inside an empty Jaguar cartridge case and with the front of the cartridge held on with black electrical tape. It was the connector on this cartridge that allowed it to be identified as a Super Nintendo style cartridge, again suggesting that Mike was running a Super Nintendo inside his black Coleco Chameleon Jaguar shell. A smaller detail that would arise later was the lack of a power light on the console when the unit was running, it didn't seem to have one, or at least not one that was visible.

Brian Barnhart was in Las Vegas shooting a commercial with a friend and saw none of the events unfolding but Mike was clearly monitoring the situation and had responded to some of the questions and had stated that they were indeed running a custom SNES FPGA core to play the demos, so yes, apparently it was the most quickly developed core ever! He was also deleting comments from detractors on their Facebook page again, reverting to the behavior he had shown during the Retro VGS debacle.

Eli's phone began to light up from around 11am as he was making his way to the Toy Fair, where he arrived at about 11:30, and began looking around for over an hour with his wife who was keen to look at everything. He told her that he was going to skip ahead and go to the Coleco booth to look at the Chameleon and he headed off saying he would meet her later if she went to get something to eat.

As he made his way to the Coleco booth he checked his messages and he saw that one of his developers, Chiro, had sent him a message telling him that there was a rumor that Mike had a SNES Jr inside his Jaguar shell. When Eli reached the booth, Mike greeted him and introduced him to some of those present including Tricia, Stephen and of course Chris Cardillo. As soon as the introductions were out of the way Mike told Eli *"Well, they're saying that it's a Super Nintendo but it's just a connector"* and Eli assumed he was just referring to the cables and asked Mike if he could try it out. Mike told him that he was having some problems with the cartridge as it kept resetting randomly, he would be playing a game and it would just go off and reset. Something was wrong clearly.

Eli could see that it was using some type of flash card with the demo games on it and he was familiar with the one that he used for his own games, the Super UFO, but he was only vaguely familiar with one called the SD2SNES and he asked Mike if they had made their own and Mike said *"I think Lee did. He built it"* and that it was *"[...] developed in house by our hardware guy."* This is the first time that Eli had heard the name "Lee", but it would certainly not be the last, and in fact, Lee had not made it. What Mike was using was a type of Super Nintendo flash cartridge called the "SD2SNES."

When the menu was on screen Eli had spotted that at the top of the screen was the name "IKARI" and it was a name that he recalled as he had seen it previously on a forum being used by a member who produced homebrew items for retro consoles. He was now convinced that they were using an SD2SNES as everybody suspected.

Mike was familiar with the SD2SNES, though of course he denied it, as Scott had purchased one which was reviewed on Retro Gaming Roundup. Supplied by a company called Stone Age Gamer, Scott discussed the cartridge during his Hardware Flashback segment and with Mike and UKMike during the Live News on RoundUp 52 from September 2012. He had tested it using a Hyperkin portable device called the SupaBoy, a handheld version of the Super Nintendo. As he was using it he found that occasionally the cartridge would indeed reset itself and, as he was using a battery powered device, he thought that it may not be getting enough power because of the FPGA on the multi cart that was used to emulate the SNES cartridge FX chip (in a grand sense of irony) so he plugged the SupaBoy in to a wall socket to supplement what the battery could supply and the resetting issue went away. A power supply that was insufficient for the cart's needs would cause the resets to occur more or less frequently depending on how close to the limit it was running.

Stone Age Gamer confirmed with Scott on AtariAge that the SD2SNES contains an FPGA chip and several other additional circuits inside the cartridge in order to be able to read the SD card, load the ROM to the SupaBoy and configure the FPGA to emulate the FX chip as needed for that game. The battery in the SupaBoy was not sufficient to do that and would cause the cartridge to reset.

The power supply that Mike was using for the Coleco Chameleon at the Toy Fair was a third party multi adaptor which typically have three different connectors on them so that you can use the same power supply for different things. Not all at once, but Mike had one of these multi adaptors and it was not supplying enough power to the SNES Jr and the SD2SNES inside the Jaguar shell, where an original Nintendo power supply would have had sufficient capacity to run them.

Eli was unaware of the power issues that the SD2SNES cartridge could have when not using an original Nintendo power supply, and he thought that the random resets could have been caused by a faulty SD card, but he could see that the whole Operating System on the flash card was resetting, not just the game, so he realized that it was most likely the flash card that was at fault.

Mike asked him *"Eli, can you say something online about the whole SNES Mini?"* Eli asked him if he could see what was inside the Chameleon but Mike told him that he didn't really want to mess with it, so Eli said *"Okay, let me talk to your engineer. Let me talk to him over the phone and let him tell me what he did."*

Mike dialed the number on his phone and handed it to Eli who spoke to Lee and told him what people were saying about the Chameleon, that it was a SNES Jr, a fact that Lee was only too aware of having "built" it. Lee told Eli that:

> *"Oh, no. Well, we were delayed and we needed to get this done for the Toy Fair. So what I used, I had a scrap Super Nintendo Mini in the office and we used the back with the connectors, the AV-out and the AC adapter and I used the pins and that's it. The inside is just a board and the cables are wired in, the controllers are wired in and it's just the pin connector, the cart connector and the back."*

This was an absurd explanation as anyone involved in developing an actual video game console would have the basic components on hand and would never cannibalize a SNES Jr to use its power and audio/video connectors, especially one that was reported to be HDMI only. It would be far more work to incorporate such a thing than to use new, purpose specific connectors. The cartridge slot was another bridge too far, it would have been far more trouble to de-solder and use it, and much more trouble to use the slot on the PCB and hack the circuit traces when there are readily available new connectors built specifically for that purpose.

Trusting what he was being told about the cobbled together prototype board with the rear end and cartridge slot of a SNES Jr, Eli asked Lee *"Would you be comfortable if I could see the insides? Let me show it. We just pick it up. I want to see the inside, then you'll get rid of all these rumors and I'll say it, a third party, it's not an SNES Mini."* Eli of course had his own SNES Jr and his had the top removed, so he knew what the inside and what the circuit board looked like, but Lee wasn't happy for him to open the Chameleon up. He told Eli *"No, I don't feel comfortable, it was just taped together, it's too delicate. I don't want it to be broken on the first day"* telling Eli that he couldn't fix it over the phone or I couldn't fix it from over there, Eli can't remember which phrase Lee used, but either way, he wouldn't let him see inside the Chameleon Jaguar shell.

When he got off the phone from Lee, Eli was suspicious, he had his developer telling him that they were using an SD2SNES, AtariAge members were telling him that they were using an SD2SNES and Lee had told him that they had used parts of a SNES Jr, including the cartridge slot, so he knew that the SNES cartridge slot would properly read the cartridge that he had with him, so he told Mike to try his game and see if the Chameleon would continue to reset. He already knew that it would work properly of course.

Mike had somebody hold up the Perspex box and somebody else hold the controllers while he reached inside and swapped the cartridges over. They turned the Chameleon on and it didn't work. Turning to Eli he looked confused and Eli told him that he had not inserted the cartridge properly, he had been too gentle with it, so they repeated the process and Mike inserted it more firmly the second time. This time they turned the Chameleon on and Eli's cartridge booted properly and the television screen showed the list of games that were on it.

Eli saw the cartridge that Mike had been using and he explained to Mike *"Okay, dude, this is not your board, you can buy this online."* Mike argued and repeated that they had made it, but Eli assured him *"No, this is a flashcard. You put ROMs on it and you place it in your Super Nintendo."* Mike didn't seem to grasp the implications of what he was being told but Eli was now almost certain that they were using a SNES Jr. Seeing what would happen later, he became 100% convinced, but he was still willing to publicly appear to give Mike the benefit of the doubt. If Eli had come out at this point and said publicly that the prototype was a fake, he could have killed the project there and then. If he had said something to the effect of "Yes, I saw it, it's a SNESinaJag, he could have saved Mike any further embarrassment, and also several thousand dollars, further down the road.

He couldn't fail to notice that they were using a Super Nintendo controller and he looked at the cabling, knowing that they were talking about the Chameleon supporting USB controllers. The SNES controller was connected to an extension lead that passed through the Perspex box and into a hole in the front of the Jaguar shell. He asked about it and was told that their controller wasn't mapped yet, i.e. the console and the controller weren't configured to work with each other at that stage, so he assumed they had possibly hard wired the other end of the extension lead straight onto their circuit board, perhaps to the USB connectors they had talked about. Again, a blatantly absurd claim, it would be more work to hardwire the SNES controllers which would have to be connected to a USB adapter which is readily available, or easier yet, SNES type controllers that are natively USB are available from many sources. Hardwiring SNES controllers would have been a completely unnecessary step compared to these readily available solutions.

Eli's cartridge worked flawlessly and did not reset, not that he expected it to, as it was a cartridge that he had previously tested on different hardware types before offering it for sale. He had tried it in an original Super Nintendo, a SNES Jr and also a Retron 3 and all of them had been able to run it without issue. The only one that had a slight problem was his own SNES Jr which would show a small glitch on one of the games where the copyright symbol is. He suspected that was due to a fault on his own SNES Jr as nobody else had reported that issue, nor did the Chameleon at the Toy Fair show the same font glitch. Eli's of course was in his workshop with the top removed so he thought that perhaps some dirt had got inside his own and was causing the isolated issue. He was well aware that different hardware can run the same game slightly differently which is why he tests his games on different platforms before selling them.

For example, the Atari VCS had no operating system, all of the code that ran in the original machine was inside the game cartridge, but when Curt Vendel created the Atari Flashback 2, all of the integrated circuits of the original Atari VCS were contained on a single chip. When this single chip was being manufactured, the engineers found some hardware errors on the original Atari hardware and corrected them in the new chip. This meant that some of the games no longer worked because when they were programmed *"close to the metal"* they worked around these hardware errors, so when the errors were no longer there, the game code didn't run properly. Curt had to put those original hardware errors back in which meant that the games started working again.

This slight change in hardware also applied to the Chameleon, had it been a new design from Mike's engineer, Lee, and their own flashcard it would have run the game code slightly differently and could have produced a glitch that Eli could spot. Unfortunately, there was no such glitch which again suggested that there was an issue with Mike's cartridge, now known to be the SD2SNES.

Eli told Lee and Mike that all he could do was pass on what he had been told but he couldn't say for sure that it is not a SNES Jr.

> *"I wanted to remain neutral. I'm not going to be speculating or anything [...] just claiming stuff that I didn't see, even if it smells like a duck, and it walked like a duck and sounded like a duck, I'm just going to say, I give them the benefit of the doubt and say it might be a chicken. You never know."*

Others, including Scott, were feeling less charitable and set to work reconstructing a replica of the Coleco Chameleon prototype. Scott had already done a quick sanity check of the dimensions of the SNES board and the Jag shell and what he wanted to do was build a full replica with all of the extras shown at the Toy Fair. There was an idiotic debate over what Mike or Eli saw and what they knew and when they knew it but anyone looking at the Chameleon would know in seconds what it was. Scott placed orders for the same controllers, the same power supply and the other parts and a few days later when it all arrived, he cleared his schedule to complete the build.

He took an empty Jaguar shell and put the circuit board from a SNES Jr inside it and when he placed the top of the Jaguar shell in place there was an "Ah ha" moment. The cartridge slot on the circuit board lined up perfectly with the opening on the Jaguar shell. The controller ports were some way inside the shell which explained why the Chameleon was using extension leads that were not hard wired in at all as Lee had said, they were just ordinary extension leads connected to the front of the SNES Jr board. At the back of the replica was a gap which is why electrical tape had been used to cover it up and the back of the replica now looked exactly like the Toy Fair prototype. There could be no doubt that what Mike had at the Toy Fair, the toy industry's premier event, was indeed a SNESinaJag. If that is not amazing enough, what's even more amazing is that they hadn't tested it properly. If they had, they would have spotted the cartridge resets. They must have literally set it up, taken the picture of it running Sydney Hunter, tweeted it, and put the unit away to take to the Toy Fair. The first time they noticed the glitches was on the show floor in the Coleco booth, or if Sean had noticed them earlier this could be why he had told Mike and Eli that it was so delicate, mistakenly thinking that he had an issue with the SNES Jr or the SD2SNES rather than it simply being a power issue.

Eli went for dinner with the Coleco booth team that evening and spent most of it discussing action figures with Chris Cardillo but by the next day he was getting a lot of pressure to reveal what he knew and what he had seen. As he waited for his flight on the Sunday, he texted Mike.

> *"Mike, you've got to get rid of these rumors. Just send me the pic or video of the inside of the console. Send me the picture right now. You're just going to lift up the top panel, the top of the case. Send me a picture. I'll confirm it and then remove a little bit of weight."*

The responses were somewhat predictable: We don't really want to risk it, we won't do it, we'll do it later or we'll show pictures of everything on the Kickstarter. Mike was clearly reluctant to open the console at the Toy Fair, in front of everybody, but the moment the show closed on the Saturday, if you were Mike, wouldn't you want to know what was inside your system? Wouldn't you want to know what you had paid $2,500 to your engineer for? Was a SNESinaJag all he had to show for his $2,500?

Mike assured Eli that as they were only two weeks away from launching on Kickstarter when they would have to show their prototype off, he would reveal the insides of the final revision of the system then. He offered Eli the courtesy of showing the pictures to him before they went public. Of course, Eli received nothing.

Collectorvision were also monitoring the Toy Fair and when they saw Eli playing the prototype at the Toy Fair they were initially confident until, like everyone else they saw the back of the system.

> *"I then noticed it was the back of the SNES Mini, and I then became very skeptical like everyone else. We were told by Mike that it was just the back part of the SNES, but the actual hardware prototype was indeed unique. The fact Mike never opened it up to show people then, certainly was telling. Sean explained that he specifically told Mike not to take a picture of the back of the system because he had borrowed parts of the SNES, but Mike did that anyways...he's his own worst enemy.*
>
> *I immediately contacted John (Lester) and asked him if Mike could provide us pictures of the inside of the system etc....*
>
> *Instead, we were re-directed to his hardware guy.*
>
> *The hardware guy told us what he used to build this prototype and yes it was using some SNES parts and the reason they were showing this "SNES Prototype" was because they didn't get the latest board revision in time.....*
>
> *Okay.... shit could happen, I guess.....? ..... But still......suspicious......*
>
> *So they told us to wait till the Kickstarter and we are going to be blown away by the latest prototype*
>
> *This is where I've mentioned online to wait till the Kickstarter and it's going to be awesome (stupid me, I should just have shut the f&$@ up!)"*

The Toy Fair came and went, and Mike seemed to be in real trouble. Mike *was* in real trouble. He had either asked his engineer to build something that would get them through the Toy Fair and on to Kickstarter to get the crowdfunding money or he had asked his engineer to build him a prototype for $2,500 and he had been sent a SNESinaJag. Neither scenario was good but Mike was still chasing the dream and still defending his Coleco Chameleon from those who were criticizing it and calling it out for what it was, smoke and mirrors. However, some of those who appeared to be genuine were anything but, a new member of the online forums named "Janus" was having a little fun at Mike's expense:

> *"I don't understand all the haters! SocalMike is trying to create something awesome for the gaming community and everyone just keeps giving him a hard time. I met him at Seattle Retro Gaming Expo and he clearly knows his stuff. If you listened to his show or read his magazines, you would know the guy can rip apart arcade machines, so making a system would be easy for him. The guy should be praised for buying the jag cases and having the great vision to come up with a revolutionary product. He has single handily redefined Classic gaming. Look how awesome GameGavel.com ReadRETRO.com are. He was the best part of Retrogamingroundup.com as well."*

Not all those with a good word to say were disingenuous though, others really were watching out for Mike:

YouTube video:
The Coleco Chameleon is Unintentional Snake Oil

> *From: Paul Scott*
> *Sent: Thursday Feb 18, 2016*
> *Subject: Slanderous Video*
> *To Mike Kennedy*
>
> *Hi guys. Love your product. However I came across a video slandering all of your hard work.*
> *The disgusting man who made the video has 465,230 subscribers on YouTube so many people seen this.*
>
> *Hi Paul,*
> *Yes, we are aware of this and attempting to get it taken down J Thanks for your support.*
> *Mike*

Attempting to get it taken down? Based on what? Certainly not the truth. The video was on the channel "ReviewTechUSA" and the opinions shared were those of Rich, the host, and Snake Oil seemed an apt title for the video, which, at the time of writing, is still available on YouTube. In fact, Rich was allowed to keep his video online and gave an update on Twitter to say that they (Mike) had agreed not to pursue the matter as long as he released a follow up video once their Kickstarter launched and they had released their specs.

The topic of videos was back on the agenda following the Toy Fair as Mike still needed his launch video for the campaign and Brian Barnhart was now on his way back from Las Vegas after shooting his friend's commercial. On the journey home he spoke to Mike on the phone but Mike was either ignoring what had happened or was seeing it very differently to everybody else. He told Brian:

> *"You know, Brian, we had a really, really great showing at the Toy Fair, and all of these people want to get a piece of it. Toys R Us wants to sell it and Atari is going to give us 300 of their library games. So it's getting bigger than I thought it was going to be and I need to have a professional do this video for me and I don't know if I could have you doing the video for me."*

Brian told Mike *"Okay, well you've got to do what you've got to do."* and he thought about the conversation for a little while before calling Mike back but he couldn't get hold of him and texted him instead.

> *"You know what Mike, I am a professional, dude. I've done many videos for many companies. If you like I can send you my resume. I know you have to do what's best for your company but I would like to be a part of this, it would help my family out. Will talk when you get back."*

Once Brian got home, he caught up with the events from the Toy Fair and could see just how bad things were and predictably, on February 16th, Mike was back in touch by text wanting him to do the video again.

> *"Yeah, let's talk tomorrow. We're good. Still want you to do shoot."*

The next day he followed up with:

> *"Hey Brian, can we talk about shoot tomorrow? What's your schedule?"*

Brian was stalling amid the controversy and at 5pm on February 19th he told Mike that he was busy and would call him when he can. At just after 10pm Mike responded, again asking if he could go over and do the voice overs, but by this time Brian had pretty much made his mind up that he was out, thinking *"Oh, boy, this is not something I think I need to be getting involved in at this point,"* and he called Mike out. *"Mike, that was a Super Nintendo in there, man. Tell me that wasn't a Super Nintendo in there."* and Mike replied that it was the back of the Super Nintendo, explaining that they just needed the back of the Super Nintendo for the AV out and that the board was their board but they're getting a brand-new board that's coming in.

Brian was thinking *"I know a little bit about video games. I mean, listen, if my video games break, I know how to replace capacitors. I'm pretty handy that way, I'm not a pro but I know and I'm just thinking, "How are you using the back of the Super Nintendo?"*

Mike continued to assure him that it was just the back of it to which Brian responded *"Well, I'm glad that I spent like all this money on HDMI cables and an*

HDMI splitter for the prototype shoot that you wanted me to go out and get, so we could play and record at the same time. I thought this was supposed to be HDMI? How did this happen?"

Finally, Brian offered to help him out by telling him that it shouldn't even be about a Kickstarter video, it should be about wanting to prove everybody wrong.

> *"It should be about, "I need to open this thing up for everybody and show them what the board does and what it looks like and plug it in." and I said, "Mike, let's shoot all of that." I said, "Let me shoot every single angle of this thing, of you plugging in the HDMI cable and putting it into my TV and recording us playing the game. Let's do it all."*

Of course, Mike declined:

> *"No, I don't.... let's not, it would be good if we could just do the Kickstarter video."*

His refusal to use anything but game play footage and voice overs surely showed that he knew he had no prototype, and that anything he did have was nothing more than smoke and mirrors. Brian gave it one last effort and told Mike;

> *"Dude, I'm giving you a forum to come clean right now. I don't think you know anybody else that's going to shoot the video unless you want to do it yourself."*
>
> *"Look, man, I'm going to be straight with you, I don't want to get involved with this. This is really bad. You're in trouble, Mike. You're in big trouble. You are so beyond your Kickstarter video right now."*

It was around this time that Scott came up with one of the great quotes on the whole affair:

> *"The train wreck is occurring. The train has gone off the side of the bridge, is plummeting towards the bottom of the canyon. Meanwhile, the engineer is still tugging on the whistle and the fireman is still shoveling coal into the thing. This is insane."*

Pat and Ian were back again on February 17th and began by declaring that they were drinking water before recapping the story of the Retro VGS Indiegogo and the ill will that Mike had created before *"throwing his engineer John Carlson under the bus as many times as he could, not only ran him over, but then backed up and ran over him again."* They then moved on to the Toy Fair story and the fastest development of a SNES core in history. As Scott said, it was indeed insane, but Mike continued with announcements of games that were coming to his system and on February 18th he went public with an Atari deal for 300 of their games.

The Coleco Chameleon from Retro Video Game Systems won't land on Kickstarter until the end of the month. However, it did hit Toy Fair earlier this week to give the public a little taste of its retro-gaming goodness and score a few deals. And score it did, landing the rights to the Atari 2600 library. That's over 300 games, as well an option for the company to develop new games based on all that classic IP. (Update: We've gotten in touch with Atari; see comments at the end of this post.)

Sure, it's not like games from Atari and other old consoles aren't available elsewhere -- over the years it's been possible to buy compilations of old titles, as well as retro-styled systems that have hundreds of games built in. What makes the Coleco Chameleon different is that it imitates the hardware too.

The Coleco Chameleon's hardware emulation is made possible using an FPGA (field-programmable gate array) chip. That means the chip can be reconfigured to match whatever system it's meant to be emulating -- hence the console name "Chameleon."

In addition to the Atari games the company's already gotten ColecoVision, Intellivision and even SNES games running on the hardware. The Chameleon is also promising unreleased '90s Genesis games like Battle Brave Saga and Water Margin, as well as more recent 16-bit titles like adventure platformer Sydney Hunter and the Caverns of Death.

Eagle-eyed viewers will note something familiar about the system's design as well: It looks like an Atari Jaguar. But it isn't a case of simply copying an old design. The Chameleon's chassis was actually machined using the original Jaguar mold. Retro Video Game Systems president Mike Kennedy told us Atari released the designs and specs for public use years ago. The physical mold itself was bought and sold between various companies over the past two decades, before finally ending up with Retro Video Game Systems.

Fortunately, the Chameleon will not be using the Jaguar's 17-button controller. The system will include its own dual-thumbstick gamepad, with the four button array on the right resembling the layout from the SNES. But, since the Chameleon uses USB, players can connect any controller they want to the system for a real "retro" feel.

If the idea of accurate game emulation is something that appeals to your old school gamer heart, the Kickstarter will launch on February 26th with the standard retail edition going for $150, while early birds can snag one for a slightly cheaper $135.

The next day, February 19th, Mike appeared on the Sega Nerds podcast which had previously been advertised in Retro Magazine and the host, Chris Powell, was credited as a magazine contributor. This was a fairly easy interview for Mike without any tough questions before he was allowed to go into sales mode again and Mike answered a few questions about the SNESinaJag accusations.

"...this one has composite out ... we're still working on wrapping up some of the HD stuff. It was our easiest way of getting composite out [...] they did use an SNES cord [...] it just didn't occur to me that it would turn into such a big thing. [...] it happens that all the games we have are SNES [...] So our first development path for this was to create a SNES FPGA, so we could play those games. [...] we had a company create that for us [...] to create a Genesis core was a whole other thing [...] I mean, we know we can do it, but again, the first one we did was SNES, and Piko has these SNES games and John's got some games, so okay, we'll show SNES games at the show, so that's what we did but we're gonna open it up [at the Kickstarter launch]."

Mike gave some details of the upcoming Kickstarter campaign and revealed that the funding goal would be in the region of $400,000 to $500,000, and the unit may no longer be produced in the USA. In order to keep the costs down they may turn to China to produce the PCBs and perhaps even the Jaguar case as well, but still using their original molds of course. He also announced that at that time they had still not determined what the pack-in game would be.

Two days later, the Talk RETRO podcast, hosted by David Giltinan, was released. This podcast fell under the GameGavel LLC umbrella, and guesting on the show was the former RETRO Magazine editor-in-chief, Daniel Kayser. Kayser claimed to have been at the Toy Fair and to have seen the Coleco Chameleon running and he asserted that it was definitely not a SNES Jr being used but a genuine prototype of their own running on an FPGA. Hardly surprising coming from a podcast under Mike's umbrella and hosted by Mike's staff. Mike had also been a guest on the short-lived podcast but it seemed that people were willing to put their reputations on the line for him, even now. Another was a collector and writer for Retro, Michael Thomasson who asked detractors, particularly Carl Williams, to stop spreading conspiracy theories and to *"just talk with some teams developing for the system instead."*

Thomasson had always been known for his good character and nice-guy personality and Scott reached out to him to fill him in on the back story and that a team was trying to make sure the scam was revealed for all to see. When presented with such totally overwhelming evidence, Thomasson did the most bizarre thing ever, he told Scott that it was probably best if they pretend that their conversation hadn't take place.

"How in the face of such damning evidence could anyone, including Michael Thomasson, not see what was going on? How could podcast hosts have Mike on their shows and not tell him that his story was total BS?"

If they could not be made to think, they must be made to feel, and harsher lessons were coming. Thomasson went on:

"Mike and his peers have put out a fine magazine and have accomplished other fine things for the classic gaming community. Why not give them the benefit of the doubt? Why is everyone always so cynical? Just enjoy the ride, appreciate

that fellow fans and hobbyists want to do good and discover where it all ends when the pieces land. Retro gaming is to be enjoyed. I've never understood why we can't rally around our successes for what they are?"

Supporters like this though were becoming fewer and further between, and now Janus was back again to stir the pot, referring to Giltinan's fluff piece:

"The only name that matters in Retro Gaming Journalism. He is the co-host of the wildly successful talk retro podcast, and reviewer of RETRO magazine. Inside tip is that this is being privately funded, so no need for Kickstarter nonsense. Hate on haters! If you want one you will have to line up like everyone else on Black Friday... Good luck getting one when this is the hottest thing in gaming this year!"

There were indeed rumors of being self-funded but this two-week period following the Toy Fair and leading up to the Kickstarter launch was to be defined by a series of phone calls between Lee and Eli and between Mike and the two companies he had promised could supply the pack-in game.

Eli told the story in his interview with Retro Gaming Roundup in March 2016 on RoundUp 99, titled "Lawyers and Showers", and he described speaking to Lee a few times over the phone at the Toy Fair and quite a few times in the days following, but he noticed that Lee always used an unknown number or did not use caller ID, explaining that *"Oh, something is wrong this T-Mobile number."*

Lee was enthusiastic about using the menu system that Eli had used on his own cartridge, the one that Mike had tried successfully in the Chameleon at the Toy Fair, and Mike had asked Eli if he could keep the cartridge. Lee had convinced Mike that they needed that menu system on the cartridges that they would produce and he wanted to put the Coleco branding on it. He also said he needed it ready in time to show it off in the launch video.

Eli explained that there was an issue with doing that as he didn't know exactly how it worked, how it mapped each game that was on the list and ran it. What he had done in 2013 was purchase a multicart from some Chinese bootleggers and then dumped the information from the cartridge to try and reverse engineer it. They weren't able to recreate the system from scratch but they could produce cartridges that were based on that original multicart, but it was going to take some time. Unfortunately, time was something that they didn't have as Lee was asking for it by Monday or Tuesday. Eli told Lee that he could do it but they would have to pay for an engineer's time to have it ready and they agreed on a fee of $400, all of which would go to the engineer and Eli wouldn't charge anything additional.

Lee was calling Eli every day and sometimes several times a day chasing up on the cartridge but Eli explained that it was difficult as they wanted all of their launch titles on the multicart. Eli had only ever produced cartridges with games up to 4MB and totaling 32MB so they may hit problems trying to put all of the games on it, but they would try it. Lee checked whether Eli would mind doing this as he was going to be putting Sydney Hunter And The Caverns Of Death on the cartridge, and that was a Collectorvision game, which belonged to a competitor, but Eli assured him that he didn't mind, and he would do it and try to get it working.

As the calls continued throughout the week the topic of conversation strayed from the cartridge and the menu system to the project in general and how it was being managed. Eli shared his opinion that Mike had really messed up but Lee told him that he couldn't share information with him. Lee did however tell Eli that he worked for a large company, he wasn't just a guy, he had a boss, and Mike had come to them saying that he needed a prototype developed quickly so that he could show something at the Toy Fair and his boss had agreed to do it using scrap parts.

Eli was a little perturbed by how much and how many times Lee tried to stress that he worked for a company, and it seemed that every time he shared an opinion about something he would stress that it was his opinion, his own personal opinion, not the opinion of the company that he worked for. Lee also repeated that the scrap parts they had used were just the back and the cartridge slot from a SNES but the rest of the board was their own. He also repeated that they had specifically told Mike that he was not to show a picture of the back of the unit and all of this could have been avoided if Mike had not done that.

Lee continued to elaborate on the company that he worked for, making it clear that his opinions were his own, not those of the company, but the company itself had employed him for years and he had two other employees on the console project with him called Eric and Jon, spelling out J.O.N. for Jon. Mike had hired the company as a contractor to get the console done despite them never having done a console before but they had, according to Lee, worked on some big contracts before with companies such as Boeing on aerospace, government, medical, military and tech projects, including an LED flashlight that could survive being thrown or being run over by a car. It was perhaps ironic then that the Coleco Chameleon was so delicate that it couldn't survive being opened at the Toy Fair.

Eli's engineer was having trouble getting the Collectorvision game working on the multicart and John Lester states that Collectorvision were never given any specs for the Chameleon, just that it would *"play similar to the SNES"* and Mike and his team would burn the cartridges which would work if they were programmed in C+ but it was not going to plan over at Piko Interactive.

Still, Lee was talking about his employer and that they had insurance if there was a problem with the cartridges, *"[...] like one kid could eat a cartridge and they sue them, they have insurance that will take care of that."* He would never divulge the name of the company (which Eli thought sounded like a cool company) because he said that their contracts and the lawyers wouldn't allow him to. Eli told him that they could really help out their client, Mike, if they came out as this large company that they were and say that they had built the prototype and that it wasn't a SNES Jr, it was their own work morphed with parts of a SNES and they could show pictures and videos of it to dispel the rumors but, despite Eli asking several times, they were never forthcoming.

What was forthcoming was much more information about the company campus which had showers that the engineers could use when they were working long hours on projects, lawyers and showers, and Lee was working long hours on the run up to the Chameleon Kickstarter and he was eating at their on-site cafeteria, comparing their campus to Google. They also had various rooms set up for meetings, testing and watching movies after hours and these rooms were given movie related names like the *"Goldeneye"* room. It's ironic that he chose that name as the organization that James Bond goes up against in the film Goldeneye is called Janus and of course the bond villain in the film is played by an actor called Sean, Sean Bean.

Janus is perhaps better known as the Roman God of, among other things, duality and endings, and is often depicted as having two faces as he looks both forwards and back. He is also the initiator of financial enterprises and according to myth he was the first to mint coins.

All this talk of lawyers and showers and Goldeneye rooms belied the work that Eli was being asked to do though and he questioned it. Why was this huge company that had contracts with Boeing, lawyers and showers, a cafeteria and a Goldeneye room not able to build a menu for a few SNES games? Lee explained:

> *"Well, right now we just don't have anything to look pretty. We're just a developer. We're not designers so everything is command line."*
>
> *"For the Kickstarter video, we don't want to be changing carts for those SNES games [...] It would just have a menu with all the games and we just go through them and show the gameplay without taking carts out."*

Eli had now begun to smell a rat and he was still getting heat over the Toy Fair prototype that he had played. Thinking that enough was enough he needed Mike to come out and do something, to show something to prove that he had a real prototype unit that worked. He pleaded with Mike to tell people who the company was that Lee worked for. He advised Mike that if he ever wanted to get something like this done, or at least be credible online (because he already had a pretty bad reputation) this large company needed to come forward, but Mike told him they wouldn't do that as they *"want to remain anonymous."*

Venting his anger at Mike, he was given an email address for Lee which wasn't a super-duper company address, it was an @retrovgs.com address. Feeling even angrier, he emailed Lee at his retrovgs.com address and told him to call him back.

Lee called him, again from his withheld number, and Eli exploded at him.

> *"You know what? I'm done. We're out of this thing if you don't address the issues, if you don't show pictures of them or playing or a video!"*

He emphasized video because he knew they could fake pictures more easily, but Lee was adamant that they wouldn't do that and what Eli found slightly odd was that Lee seemed more intent on calming him down and getting him to stay on the project than addressing any of the concerns that were out there. What particularly angered Eli about this call was that Lee told him that;

> *"As Piko, you're just a guy that works from home, I'm a contractor man, they have been with me since day one. We struggled but we're here. If you go out of this project, you're going to lose the opportunity to make the most money that you're ever going to make in your life."*

Eli responded:

> *"Well, tell me something, tell me something to convince me that this project is not going to go down in flames and there's a prototype working because I haven't seen anything, tell me something."*

Lee assured him

> *"Well, I know there's some third party checks ready to drop and get this finished. We're going to make something work until the Kickstarter day and that's when we'd finish and then when we get the funds we'll get to finish it up. We'll have this done.*
>
> *... there's some investor cheques [...] a big check coming in and you're going to lose all this money and then we'll already have the PCB and the prototype and we're going to have it working."*

Eli thought about his options and told Lee:

> *"You know what, Lee? I'm just going to stay in this project because of you. You're going to be responsible. I'm telling you because you work for a legit company that's why I'm staying, that's why I'm believing that this is real."*

Lee assured Eli that he had made a good decision and he was glad that he was staying on the project, which Eli found a little odd because, why should a contractor care so much about Piko Interactive staying on board? Without Eli they still had Collectorvision to provide a pack-in game but without Eli they really had nothing, they had no menu system for their cartridges. As a contractor building the console that shouldn't matter as they would still get paid, but Eli put it down to the fact that they didn't want the Kickstarter to fail and not get the funding to finish their work.

Lee was now beginning to put the pressure on as it was already Tuesday and they still had no cartridge with a functioning menu that would launch the games and he kept calling and asking for it. By Wednesday Lee had lost patience and told Eli that he was informing Mike that Piko Interactive were not going to be able to deliver it on time which panicked Eli as he thought Mike might no longer pay his developer which would mean that Eli would have to pay him the $400 out of pocket. Then, he had a brainwave, *"You know what? I have an idea. Let me send you this."*

> *"Oh my God, that PCB that Mike had, worked on the so-called prototype [...] because the PCB has a little microchip that has information on the mapper and tells the console what to do. Now on the video, they're going to do their own board, their own cartridge board and this board does not have the mapper, so they have to add support for the FPGA, for the mapping information because it's not going to work. So, with all this work that we're doing, we're wasting time."*
>
> *"No, it's not going to work, your port does not have the mapping information. Let me send you an old ROM of another multicart that we've done that I have here in this computer. Get this ROM to work. If you get this ROM to work on the console with your cartridge board, then the main menu that we're finishing up is going to work."*

While they were on the phone, Lee tried what Eli had sent him, though Eli didn't know how he faked it, but Lee told him *"Okay, I got the ROM. Let me burn it into the card."* Within thirty seconds he told Eli he was plugging it in and Eli could hear the menu music start so he assumed that he had a prototype there in his office. Eli told Lee that the games wouldn't work because they weren't mapped correctly and indeed when he tried to launch one, all he got was a black screen and then the menu relaunched, which Eli could hear again.

Eli told him, you have to make the menu work on the console first and then when his engineer had built the final cartridge with the launch games on it, they will work as well. Lee asked him how to do that and Eli sent him a link to the Nocash SNES documentation so that he could work through it.

That same morning, Eli had received a copy of the contract from Mike and he had read through it and recommended a few changes, one of which was that he noticed it didn't have a clause precluding him from suing another third party involved if they somehow caused a delay in the project. As it stood, Piko Interactive would not get paid until the end of a successful Kickstarter and once the orders were fulfilled. It wasn't such a huge issue for Piko Interactive as their games were already finished and the Chameleon team were producing the cartridges meaning he wasn't going to be out of pocket, he would just have to wait until he got paid his royalties but with no work upfront.

Eli saw a potential problem if they weren't to get paid, if the project was funded and released for sale with other developer's games, not his own, the team would have the funding, not fulfil the orders if the pack-in game wasn't ready and they wouldn't have to pay Piko Interactive until it was ready. There was no risk for the Chameleon team at all, the risk was entirely on the developers. Eli told Mike that he could potentially sue Collectorvision if they did not have the pack-in game ready and delayed the project, meaning that he didn't get paid on time. This obviously sent Mike into a panic because he called Collectorvision and spoke to them before calling Eli back around 30 minutes later, telling him:

> *"Eli, CollectorVision came in and they said that they cannot finish off the game, the pack-in game. So, I was wondering if you want to do a pack-in game?"*

Eli said that he would do the pack-in game as he had previously thought that the only developer that would make any serious money from the Chameleon would be the developer that supplied the pack-in game. Every other developer may or not may not sell games for it in the aftermarket but providing the pack-in game meant guaranteed sales with every console that was sold. They discussed doing a multicart and what games would be on it and verbally agreed during that call that Piko Interactive would supply the pack-in game(s).

Within 30 minutes of that call, Lee called back and told him *"Hey you know what? I was able to make it work, it's mapping now. I just had to read through the documentation and then change three lines of code."* Once this was working, they were able to finish up the menu for the Kickstarter video by Wednesday and send it over. It was still buggy, but largely functioning.

As Thursday arrived, Collectorvision were back in touch with Mike, angry that they were not providing the pack-in game. Presumably, Mike hadn't told them about the issues with the contract that Eli had highlighted, he had just told them that somebody else was providing it. Unsure if Mike was using this as a ploy to negotiate a lower royalty rate or not as they had not even received a contract to sign, and not certain if they wanted to continue their involvement with the project, they told Mike that they would no longer be interested in being a part of his project.

This was a project that they were very interested in of course, and had been promoting and defending quite stringently, in particular, Jean-François Dupuis:

> *"No matter what people says (sic), the Chameleon is REAL!*
> *Once you'll (sic) see their Kickstarter, you'll change your mind.*
> *The Chameleon is a whole lot different than what the Retro VGS was.*
> *Now, need proofs? (sic)*
> *Be patient, you'll soon have it"*

Jean-Francois couldn't say too much though as he had signed an NDA (Non-Disclosure Agreement) with Mike:

> *"Let's just say this.....*
> *I know what tons of people wants (sic) to know.*
> *Thing is I'm under NDA , so I just can't reveal anything.*
> *You'll probably all get your answers this week."*
>
> *"Let's just say, from what I know, it's going to be awesome!"*

Mike called Eli and he was angry, he explained that John Lester had told him that if Collectorvision don't get the pack-in game, they're going to be out of the project. Eli was confused as he thought that they were using "Tiny Knight" but Mike told him no, they wanted to use "Sydney Hunter And The Caverns Of Death" instead. Eli reminded Mike that they had a verbal agreement in place and told him that he had spoken to people regarding the licensing of the games they were including on the multicart and they had those agreements in place so he needed to fix it. Mike asked Eli if he would leave the project if he didn't get the pack-in game and Eli thought about it for a moment before saying that he wouldn't walk away but he would have some requirements that would need to be met if he were to stay on board. He didn't know what they were yet, but he would be in touch when he did and Mike told him that in the meantime he would speak to John Lester again.

Eli went home and opened a Michelada beer while he considered his options. With his beer finished he tried unsuccessfully to call Mike and emailed him instead, thinking *"Okay, well if they want to make demands and they can say they're delayed, I can do that too. I have more games."*

> *Okay, you have this problem with the pack-in game with CollectorVision and I only see two options for this. Either you don't give them the pack-in game and they leave, or you meet my requirements, and these are my list of requirements. If you don't meet these requirements and you give them the pack-in game, I will be out of the project.*
>
> - *Show at least two or more different platforms running on the system in the Kickstarter launch video, changing carts, showing that there's more than a Super Nintendo in there. If you are not ready or cannot show that in the launch video, push back the Kickstarter.*
> - *Step down from the front and go to the idea board or business relations or anything else, but just not upfront.*
> - *Raise our royalty by 20% at least. ("Although honestly I could have been okay with a 5% raise").*
> - *Show the Toy Fair prototype, the insides of that prototype, that same prototype playing a game at the same time that it is showing the insides in a video.*
> - *Make a board which will include Mike, developers (either us, CollectorVision or any other major developer), the Coleco license owners, the hardware company and very importantly a **new** third party consultant.*
> - *Hire a community manager.*

After sending this email, Eli then sent the finished ROM for the Kickstarter cartridge menu and all he got in return was a brief email saying *"Let's talk tomorrow. A lot of changes have been made in the past few hours."*

The following day, Friday, the day before the Kickstarter was due to go live, he got a phone call from Mike who told him:

> *"You know what? We're going to be late at Kickstarter. I think we're going to do it ourselves. We want to keep the Kickstarter option open but we want to probably push it to retailers and self-fund it and maybe sell direct to retailers."*

Eli asked if they were going to sell games directly to the public and Mike told him that they might do it via the website and perhaps take some pre-orders and there was an announcement to this effect, well two actually, but they didn't exactly make the situation clear. Mike was still hopeful that a big buyer like Toys R Us would come in and buy units, but he had nothing thus far to sell to them and without crowdfunding where was he going to fund the prototype development?

Retro Magazine tweeted:

> *"Plan has changed actually. Got the call that we won't need to go the crowd sourcing route. More info will be @RETROVGS and FB page."*

Soon after, the Retro VGS page was indeed updated:

> *"We're delaying the Kickstarter for the Coleco Chameleon to make it even better!*
> *Last week during the Toy Fair in New York, we had the opportunity to demonstrate the Coleco Chameleon to the industry, gamers and retailers for the first time. Their response was beyond anything we'd imagined. Major retailers provided feedback on the product and expressed real interest in carrying the product for the 2016 holiday season. And, very importantly, major game companies expressed interest in providing games for our system, which meant we'd need more time to solidify those partnerships and maximize the content.*
>
> *Our team's overriding goal has always been to deliver the best possible system and experience for gamers. If there's ever anything we can do to enhance the product, we believe the extra time is worth it. Therefore, we have decided to delay the pre-sell, i.e. Kickstarter, campaign in order to finalize our prototype and work with developers on having the best possible content. This delay will not affect our overall launch date for the Coleco Chameleon.*
>
> *There has also been a whirlwind of interest, speculation and curiosity regarding the insides of the Chameleon. We are delighted by this and happy to confirm that we will be releasing photographs of the system now on our Facebook page, and we'll focus on turning our prototype into a production-ready product.*
>
> *We'll keep you posted on any major news on our Facebook page and will let you know when we launch a pre-sell program leading up to the Christmas season. Stay tuned, and thanks for your continued support."*

If there were any truth in the statement that they were being self-funded, this could well have been Mike's biggest nightmare. UKMike noted at the time that the recent post about the cancellation of the Kickstarter *"suggested an external sugar daddy and no need for crowd funding but who in their right mind would do that?"*

> *"Let's say that somebody did. As the money man and the organ grinder behind the project the first job would be to see what everybody involved brings to the table. You're gonna have to pay them after all. The only conclusion from that*

resume review would be to write a cheque to Socal to buy the molds from him and relieve him of his duties.
The only thing he brings to this party is those molds."

Eli felt that even if they were attempting to self-fund the console, they should have used crowd funding as a great marketing tool but his main concern was whether or not they would still be needing a pack-in game. Mike assured him *"No, we need our killer app, we need our game. That sells consoles."* Eli told him to keep him updated and reiterated that they really needed a community manager to co-ordinate all of these announcements as the tweet suggested that they would not need crowd funding but the post to which it referred said that they may still crowd fund in the future. Not to mention all of the other conflicting posts to come from their organization, or rather, lack of organization.

That same Friday brought another development, a series of pictures of the Coleco Chameleon, presumably taken in the Goldeneye room, and this time in a clear, but cloudy, Jaguar shell so that the insides could be seen, albeit vaguely as there was a watermark over the pictures. Once again, the Internet was sent into a frenzy as people tried to fathom out what was inside and began by removing the watermarks and tried to identify the chips on the circuit board and examine the connectors and the outputs that seemed to be hooked up to the flat screen television.

The image in question showed a wooden TV stand style unit with a large flat screen Sony TV on top and the Chameleon console sitting to the right-hand side of it. The rear of the Chameleon could not be seen and if any cables were coming out of the back of it, they were hidden by the TV. The USB controller was sitting on the unit in front of the TV and a USB connector was shown going into the front of the console and into a USB slot that appeared to be connected to the board inside. However, none of the cabling could be seen directly connecting the unit to the TV. The cables appeared to come out of the rear of the Chameleon, if at all, and disappear behind the back of the wooden unit that it was sitting on and there was an image on the screen, but no proof that the Chameleon was outputting that image. There was also an unexplained white cable visible that may or may not have been connected to the TV or the Chameleon. However, very bright and very visible was a bright red power LED, a thing that had been notably absent, and commented on, from the Toy Fair prototype.

The on-screen image showed a menu with a list of games including Iron Commando, Jim Power, Legend and Sydney Hunter. It also had a Coleco Chameleon logo on the left-hand side. This was the menu that Piko Interactive had created and sent to Lee, as confirmed by Eli in his Retro Gaming Roundup interview.

Scott: So, Eli, let me just make sure if I understand something. Is this multicart menu that you were doing, is that the one pictured in the Facebook post that has Coleco Chameleon written sideways?

Eli: Yeah.

Scott: So, you did that?

Eli: Yeah, they asked me to get it done. I didn't do it directly. I told Mike and Lee, I'm not going to charge you any money. You're just going to pay my developer.

Scott: No, I just want to make sure that that is the same, it was displayed on the screen, okay, so it is, and that is a SNES?

Eli: Yes, it's a SNES. You put that in a board and plug it in, it's going to work on an original Super Nintendo.

Scott: Okay, so it's absolutely, 100% your usual multicart boot menu, 100%?

Eli: Yeah, that's it.

If these pictures were the evidence and the proof that Mike was looking for to dispel rumors of lying and trying to cheat his way on to Kickstarter with a fake prototype, then they fell some way short and, as usual, seemed to ask more questions that they answered.

- The power supply could not be seen connected to the Chameleon.
- The Power LED did not seem to be connected to the board and used electrical tape.
- The controller was not shown to be working.
- The cartridge could not be seen to be plugged into a cartridge slot.
- The image on screen was not definitely coming from the Chameleon.
- The USB ports did not seem to be electrically connected to the rest of the board.

Rumors soon began to spread that once again, all was not as it seemed. The bright red LED was almost literally a red flag, the positioning of it made no sense, not merely because it didn't seem to be connected, it was at the wrong angle to be connected and for a board developed for a specific purpose, it made no sense to position it there. The odds were that this was a circuit board out of something else and made to look like a purpose-built board, but what was it?

Over the weekend, some intrepid investigation work was done by some talented individuals from AtariAge as they knew it couldn't be real, so they set about identifying some of the chips that could be seen on the board to see if they offered some clues. For starters the board was blue, which is unusual for a development board as it adds an additional cost to manufacture and we know that the price point was a major issue for this system from day one but surely even Mike, by now a proven liar, wouldn't try this a third time, not another fake? Actually, he didn't, it was Lee who did, and he confirmed it in a phone call to Eli the morning after the pictures were posted.

Lee told Eli that he had seen people mocking the pictures and doubting they were genuine. He added that he had taken the pictures in the Goldeneye room and that the mystery white cable was just a power cable from a fan that was also in the room. He had sent these pictures to Mike for him to post on their Facebook page and Mike had duly posted them. By now Eli was thinking that Lee *"should be a stand-up comedian or something. I don't know. Take away the Oscar from DiCaprio."*

During that call, Lee also told Eli that his colleague had written an app that would parse the forum thread at AtariAge for key words that they entered so they could follow what people were saying and were accusing them of. The call seemed to be generally pointless though and served no purpose other than Lee planting the story that the white cable was a fan and that the pictures were real. Of course, this wouldn't be the only time that Lee contacted people to plant a story with somebody involved, hoping that they would post it or discuss it and it would spread. There were instances of people contacting the Retro Gaming Roundup hosts and planting stories with them in that same hope, that they would catch on and become the accepted narrative to detract from the lies and fake prototypes that were being posted. At the time it wasn't known if these contacts to Retro Gaming Roundup were leak tests or if they were merely planting stories, or both, but they were never repeated by either Scott or UKMike as they were just so ridiculous to those in the know.

Meanwhile, the detective work continued with people measuring their Jaguar console shells to give an idea of scale for the board and it was found to closely match a PCI card for a computer, but there are countless PCI cards for all sorts of things ranging from sound cards to network cards and additional USB slots to parallel port cards.

The chips used on the blue board were a big help and they seemed to suggest some sort of video card from 15 to 20 years ago. The fact that the board was blue also dated it to around the same era. One sleuth recognized that the markings on one of the chips were centered in such a way as to make it unusual. That enabled him to identify it as a chip made by a company called Techwell, a semiconductor company who made chips that were mainly used for video decoding between 1997 and 2010, before they were acquired by a company called Intersil.

Now hot on the trail, and within the same minute, two posters on AtariAge had found it! The user "5-11under" was the first and "Albert" (Yarusso) was the second. Both had found it to be a HICAP50B CCTV DVR Capture Card. As the name would suggest, it was used in CCTV systems for capturing the video feeds, clearly nothing to do with emulating games on an FPGA. Even with the fake revealed, Lee claimed that the real chips and the real board were in fact concealed underneath the capture card and it wasn't a fake at all.

It didn't take long for Mike to realize that another fake had been exposed and, predictably, the images were taken down within minutes, adding fuel to the rumors that Mike and Sean were monitoring AtariAge, either with an app or manually. Whether Mike or Sean took the pictures down caused some debate but it is a moot point, they had been caught red handed yet again faking a working prototype to pass the criteria to make it on to Kickstarter.

UKMike, during a particularly sober moment, emailed his former co-host and appealed to his better nature but sadly his appeals were ignored, and Mike instead addressed his reply to Scott to try and brush things over with him.

From: Mike James
Date: Tuesday, March 1, 2016
Subject: Console
To: Kennedy Mike, Scott Schreiber

Hey Mike,
Is it over now?
Three fakes is a lot dude. Sell the molds and move on.

--
d-_-b
Regards
Mike James
Retro Gaming Roundup

--

Scott,
I saw the photo you posted last night and about fell out of bed. I need to talk with you please. Can I call you in an hour?

Mike Kennedy, Founder & President
RETRO Media Network

That phone call didn't happen, but one that did was between Mike and Eli who called him at 9am the day after the DVR Capture Card was uncovered and asked him what the hell was happening, and Mike told him:

"I don't know, Eli. I'm lost for words. I don't know what happened."

Eli outlined exactly what the situation was and what was happening online, to which Mike replied:

"I know. I know. I don't know what to do. I don't know what to say."

Eli asked Mike if he had ever touched a prototype, if he had ever played a prototype but Mike told him that he had not. *"No, I always trusted this guy."* Eli explained that he had got an email from Lee that morning to say that his company were going to *"come forward with a statement to take the heat off Mike and be responsible for what we've done."* As Eli puts it:

"So, you're saying you've done something bad or what." He sort of like confirmed he had *"done something."*

This is when Eli finally learned of the grand lie that had been fed to him by Lee over the many phone calls in the days since the Toy Fair, and he asked Mike to tell him the name of the company that Lee worked for, with the Boeing contracts, the lawyers and showers, the cafeteria and the Goldeneye room. Mike told him that it was all bullshit,

Lee was just a contractor, maybe he had a couple of people working for him but there was no large company. Eli was furious. Everything he had been told over the last two weeks of his life had been a lie, a grand scheme to build an illusion that they were doing legitimate work, when really it had just been *"a guy"* who couldn't get a flash card to work on his taped together SNESinaJag and his DVR Capture card. As Stop, Drop And Retro described Mike and Lee:

> *"It's a beautiful thing. It's like two Nigerian Princes meeting each other."*

It was at this point that Eli decided to come forward and tell his story, to spill all of the gory details on Mike and his grand scheme with Lee. Mike emailed him that evening when he found out what Eli was planning and warned him that he had to abide by his NDA and Eli exploded at him. *"I told him, "What NDA? There is nothing to NDA, there is no product. Why am I going to be protecting or not disclosing a fake product?""*

The next day, Monday February 29th, amazingly, even after all that had gone on, after all the lies they have spun together, and with Mike about to claim to be the victim of a scam, he wrote Sean Robinson another cheque for $3,000 for Product Development. Quite what he expected to get for this cheque is unclear but the morning after, March 1st, he denied having any knowledge of the DVR Capture Card fake prototype as the various companies around him started to implode and the net closed in. The same day, Brian Barnhart decided to speak out about his involvement and released a video on his YouTube channel where he told the story and released the script for the video he was asked to shoot.

Brian was disappointed as much as anything because he loves retro games and the hobby;

> *"Let's be honest, at the heart of the Coleco Chameleon, at the heart of whatever this whole debacle is, it's really about this love of retro gaming that we all have. I mean that's the common thread that we all share, and there's a part of that script where you're like, "You know what, I remember those days and those were good days." I like playing these retro games with my son now, and my son is into them and I could tell him, "Hey! You know Mason, when I was eight years old, I was playing this, and you're eight years old and this is what I was playing." Isn't that cool?"*

> *"Here is my thought. When the Retro VGS was announced, being an Atari Jaguar fan, I was slightly, I don't want to say appalled but I was kind of like, "Why are you using that mold dude? That's already a system and that's my system. Okay, so you're trying to go with a little retro love of a system that failed." Let's be honest, it was a system that tried and failed, but there's nothing else that you could use? You don't have any other shell that you can use? You can't do a 3D print or something like that? I mean it was kind of crazy, and then you slapped the Coleco brand on it when you rebrand, so then now it's a failed system on a reboot of a system that didn't work and then it's an Atari shell with the Coleco sticker on the front and it's like, how crazy is this?*

Brian: *Honestly, my opinion is, I think those molds, I think they need to be destroyed."*

Scott: *"I think the only thing that could ever be put in those shells from this point on is evil spirits."*

Brian: *"Honestly, I really think they just need to be destroyed and I think they just need to just die and go away somewhere or just be melted. They need to be taken up to the mountain, Mount Sauron and thrown into the lava.*

As the fallout continued over the coming days, Collectorvision started to change tack and distanced themselves from what was quickly turning into a PR nightmare for them:

"Regarding the Coleco Chameleon system: We have remained quiet overall regarding this system, and there has been plenty of excitement as well as drama surrounding it. We have been in talks with their team about porting some of our games over to the Chameleon, but we are not a part of the development team behind this project. We anticipate seeing a video of a working prototype of the system running what they advertise soon, but until then, we will continue to focus on creating and porting our games to other platforms. We're not affiliated or endorsed by the Coleco Chameleon, and we're not going to release our games for the Chameleon, until we have a working prototype in our hands."

"Not only been deceived by Mike but all his team actually. Continuous lies, promises etc... etc...

So, I've not been deceived, but rather PISSED OFF by all those lies, when we at CollectorVision had to not say a word till the KS (Kickstarter) campaign

Yeah...right.... tsss.....

Let's just say, there's more to the picture than meets the eyes

In other words, it's even worse than it might look!"

John Lester also spoke out, citing that:

"In the end, we (CollectorVision) were fools enough to have believed in this project, so yes, we have been stupid on this. The obvious was actually too obvious for us to not believe in the project.

The most thing we are guilty for, is maybe not having followed their project more closely, as we were (still) busy working on our Wii U game."

"Mike reached out to me personally after the whole debacle and he apologized and offered a free ad for CollectorVision Games in his RETRO Magazine, which we declined. I or any of us at CollectorVision Games have not been in contact with him since."

Things were happening quickly now but Janus was keeping track and came up with another gem in response to a post by the user "toiletunes" who posted:

"Now that we're starting part 3 of the trilogy, I offer some book/movie titles:
Lord of the Consoles
Part one: The Fellowship of the FPGA
Part two: The Two KickStarters
Part three: The Return of the Carts"

Janus
"Ha ha soooo funny
SocalMike and the Raiders of the Lost Molds
SocalMike and the Temple of RETRO
SocalMike and the no need for Last Kickstarter
SocalMike Kingdom of the Crystal Case
and then...
SocalMike Swimming in a Lake of Money
Just wait and see. Hopefully when everything is properly vetted, you guys will change your tunes and support this awesome product and the games on the system and give it a fair shake."

Janus would post other "trolling" posts throughout and some of them suggested that he knew more than most about what was happening behind the scenes, posts such as:

"More sour grapes about Mike and his successful businesses. Call 911 we need a waaambulance."

"Blah Blah Blah... Coleco License, Gamester, Piko, AtariAge negative press...
Ask yourself this... does any of this matter one bit if Mike Kennedy already has a signed purchase order for over $2M from Toys 'R Us?"

"Just wait until it's revealed. What everyone here fails to realize is that Daniel Kayser and David Giltinan SAW the working FPGA board. Did you ever think maybe the DVR was just a clever marketing smoke-screen? Like I said, just wait and see, this console is a movement.

Mike will release a working console and put all you haters to shame.

Have you thought just maybe HE INTENTIONALLY ADDED DVR FUNCTIONALITY to the Chameleon, hence "Making it better", DUH!"

"We will see who is laughing when this Kickstarter goes live today! It's going to be EPIC!

I hope I get first crack at a limited-edition version and you suckers will be buying it off me for big bux in the future!"

"Prepare to get schooled haters!

Daniel Kayser is a long-standing authority on video game systems... 'nuff said!
Just wait until this Kickstarter breaks the internet tomorrow and Mike and Co. are RAKING in the cash!"

"Let's be fair, the Ouya didn't' have the dream team that the Chameleon does. You guys will be eating your words when this is the most successful Kickstarted Video Game System ever."

Finally, his fun was over as he was exposed on March 7th by Albert, the owner of AtariAge.

"I just discovered that the user Janus [...] who had been trolling in this thread (including repeatedly calling people here "haters") until I finally kicked "her" out, is actually Mark Kaminski, who works for RETRO Magazine."

Mark had of course been burned by Mike back in his days at Retro Magazine and he wasn't alone in that, another of course being Scott, who had vowed to kill Mike's console, a fact that he had warned Mike about early on when he offered him a way out of this mess, and a fact that Mike was well aware of, commenting later that all was well despite efforts to the contrary:

"As for GameGavel/RETRO it's still growing. And one of my minority owners has been doing his best to crater the company."

Cratering Mike's company(s) reached new heights when Scott had the realization that Mike had not registered the colecochameleon social media accounts and he asked UKMike to register them. That way if Mike protested, as it had been done overseas, it was just an extra headache that Mike had to deal with, if he went to court in the US and said *"Hey look they're using our name"* if it was registered overseas it's much more complex and costlier for him to fight that. *"So, I reserved that through a VPN out of Turkey or something like that, and then the big thing is Twitter."* There soon followed a website and all of them were used to rain on Mike's parade to try and ensure that he didn't make it to being funded on Kickstarter. As Scott puts it:

"I'm going to kill this thing. He is not going to get away with this, so how do you kill something? How do you shut it down? How do you stop it? Well in this case it's really easy, I just expose what he's doing, and the great thing is, he gave me more and more things to expose, which was fantastic.

The other thing you do is you create chaos and confusion. How do you create chaos and confusion? Well let's see if he reserved the website because being somewhat limited in resources, he was gonna be thrifty with how he spent money. He was going to be reckless, you know, paper flying off faster than dollar bills in a strip club when it came to offering future potential profit to people, he'd whip out a roll of Kennedy stock and tear off another sheet and hand it out in a heartbeat, but with actual money he was going to be very frugal.

So, I took a look and I was amazed, colecochameleon.org, colecochameleon. biz, none of it had been reserved, and Mark being the media savvy expert he was assured me you could get those analytics. Basically, let's say you own colecochameleon.com as the official company website, if you're doing nothing

> *to drive traffic presence to earn rankings and search engines, it's entirely conceivable and somewhat easy that somebody who does do that level of effort could have colecochameleon.org be the dominant search and you're not even coming up on the main page, so that's what happened.*
>
> *They were tweeting like they were tweeting fools, just put it up all the time and Twitter was really hot at that time too, and I thought they're using RVGS, I wonder if they reserved colecochameleon and I checked, and they didn't. I literally hopped, I was in my garage sitting on a stool in front of the computer, I literally hopped off the stool and did a little dance. So, I texted UKMike and I was like, UK, dude I know it's late, whatever, we gotta talk now, and he called me. I said "Michael, you know the thing that girls do when they have something they have to tell each other, all giddy, they hold hands, jump up and down, squeal and run off to the restroom together? We're gonna be doing that in a moment."*
>
> *I said guess what our favorite person didn't do, and he goes I'm guessing it's SoCal, I said yes, guess what he didn't do, he failed to secure the colecochameleon Twitter account, and we were on it instantly, so we got @colecochameleon."*

Before you know it, Mark Kaminski had built up a huge following of gamers, Polish gamers, opinion leaders, "celebrities" and was messaging developers about working on the system and almost all of them followed the fake account in return, they had no reason to be suspicious after all. A big following was built up before anything was done to raise the awareness of Mike and his team, and it was done genuinely by following and messaging. Scott had suggested to Mark that they beat Mike at his own game, pay for a bunch of fake Facebook followers from India, but Mark said *"No, no. Let's do this organically."*

Multiple sources had given information to Scott about what the Kickstarter tiers would be and that Mike's plan was to keep the buzz going by announcing a new one every day. This would be done through the RETRO VGS Twitter account and just days before Mike wanted to start the ball rolling while at the New York Toy Fair, the fake account Tweeted:

> *"It's official @kanyewest is joining our development team for the #coleco chameleon. #huge #retrogaming"*

This was followed by Tweeting the music video for Culture Club's Karma Chameleon and later:

> *"Offiginal Coleco Seel of Kwality Retroness"*
>
> *"We never thought to make a deal with #atari ... Maybe we should have licensed their name or games instead? #retrogaming #coleco"*
>
> *The #ColecoChameleon plays #retrogames already on other systems & exclusive crappy #homebrew games you don't want!"*

Somehow Mike was oblivious to the frenzy of activity under a Twitter handle bearing the name of his fantasy product, however it was Willie who spotted and reported the tweets to him, and commented about them being *"unauthorized."* UKMike, Scott, and Mark couldn't say much in return to Willie because they were maintaining plausible deniability about the Twitter account but eventually Mike was told that he could contact Twitter and report the account as artificially representing his product, something that seemingly had not occurred to him until that moment but he duly attempted to have the account shut down by complaining to Twitter who sent a notice to say:

Please fix your account.

> **What happened?**
> Your account has been reported for impersonation. While impersonation violates the Twitter Rules, your account might qualify as parody, commentary or fan account.
>
> **What can you do?**
> To avoid account suspension, please make the necessary changes to your account within the next 48 hours.

Of course, this message was tweeted, and much to Mike's annoyance, the account was allowed to remain active and the parodies continued:

> *"Want to learn how to destroy a brand? Message us for details! Brace for impact! #retrogaming #coleco"*
>
> *"In the Democratic Republic of North Coleco we are busy removing Facebook comments. Adventures in #retrogaming"*
>
> *"We are proud to report that the Nigerian Prince is investing $10 Million in our business via email. #retrogaming"*

On February 13th, from New York, and the complaint filed with Twitter, Mike began the process of building excitement for his Kickstarter campaign:

> *Feb 13 9:30am (pinned to top of the Retro VGS Facebook page)*
> *"We are excited to announce the COLECO Chameleon Video-Game System Kickstarter campaign will begin Friday, February, 26th 2016. Check back tomorrow at this same time to see our first Early Bird reward level. Thanks again for your support and enthusiasm."*
>
> *Feb 13 3:54 pm*
> *"Eli from Piko Interactive stopped by with one of his boards, plugged in, running both Jim Power and Legend. We are running his games through our custom written SNES FPGA Core. He said they are playing flawlessly."*

Of course, they were playing flawlessly, they weren't running on a *"SNES FPGA Core"* they were running on a Super Nintendo Jr.

> Feb 14 8:31 am
> "Kickstarter Reward #1 $135: 1500 Available. Early Bird Standard Retail Coleco Chameleon. Save 10%. Includes black Coleco Chameleon system, one Coleco Chameleon USB controller, HDMI cable, AC Adapter + the pack-in game.
> To reiterate, we will be opening up the Chameleon for the Kickstarter campaign. Look for the next Kickstarter Reward tomorrow morning at 8:30 AM ET."

Armed with all the tier information, the fake site colecochameleon.org posted them all in one go, completely stealing his thunder. The tiers were:

> Kickstarter Reward #2 $150: Standard Retail Coleco Chameleon. Includes black Coleco Chameleon system, one Coleco Chameleon USB controller, HDMI cable, AC Adapter + the pack-in game.
> Look for the next Kickstarter Reward tomorrow morning at 8:30 AM ET.
>
> Kickstarter Reward #3 $185: RPG LOVERS RETAIL BUNDLE.
> Includes black Coleco Chameleon video game system, one Coleco Chameleon USB controller, HDMI cable, AC adapter + the pack-in game + Piko Interactive's Battle Brave Saga game.
> Note, this bundle comes with two games, the pack-in game (yet to reveal) and Battle Brave Saga.
> All games purchased as a part of this Kickstarter campaign will come in an exclusive campaign only cartridge color never to be produced again.
> Look for the next Kickstarter Reward tomorrow morning at 7:00 AM PT, 10:00 AM ET.
>
> Kickstarter Reward #4 $185: PLATFORM LOVERS RETAIL BUNDLE.
> Includes black Coleco Chameleon video game system, one Coleco Chameleon USB controller, HDMI cable, AC adapter + the pack-in game + your choice of either Piko Interactive's Dorke & Ymp OR Collectorvision's Sydney Hunter and the Caverns of Death.
> Note, like the RPG Lovers Retail Bundle already mentioned, this comes with both the pack-in game (yet to reveal) AND the additional platforming game of your choice.
> All games purchased as a part of this Kickstarter campaign will come in an exclusive campaign only cartridge color never to be produced again.
> Look for the next Kickstarter Reward tomorrow morning at 7:00 AM PT, 10:00 AM ET.
>
> Kickstarter Reward #5 $210: BEAT-EM UP LOVERS RETAIL BUNDLE.
> Includes black Coleco Chameleon video game system, one Coleco Chameleon USB controller, HDMI cable, AC adapter + the pack-in game + your choice of either Piko Interactive's Iron Commando or LEGEND + one addition Coleco Chameleon USB controller -- Beat-em ups are best played with a friend.

Note, like the other Retail Bundles already mentioned, this comes with both the pack-in game (yet to reveal) AND the additional beat-em up game of your choice.
All games purchased as a part of this Kickstarter campaign will come in an exclusive campaign only cartridge color never to be produced again.
Look for the next Kickstarter Reward tomorrow morning at 7:00 AM PT, 10:00 AM ET."

Kickstarter Reward #6 $225: COLECOVISION LOVERS RETAIL BUNDLE.
Includes black Coleco Chameleon video game system, one Coleco Chameleon USB controller, HDMI cable, AC adapter + the pack-in game (yet to reveal) + ColecoVision Collection #1 (15-Game Multicart) + (correction) TWO exclusive USB ColecoVision style controllers.
Look for the next Kickstarter Reward tomorrow morning at 7:00 AM PT, 10:00 AM ET.

Kickstarter Reward #7 $250: INTELLIVISION LOVERS RETAIL BUNDLE.
Includes black Coleco Chameleon video game system, one Coleco Chameleon USB controller, HDMI cable, AC adapter + the pack-in game (yet to reveal) + Intellivision Collection #1 (15-Game Multicart) + Elektronite Intellivision Game Collection (6-Game Multicart) + TWO exclusive USB Intellivision style controllers and game collection controller overlays.

Look for our final reward tiers to be announced this week.

There were no further announcements however, the game was almost up by this point, and Mike commented that the revealing of the tier announcements was *"a new low for somebody."* Scott noted that the fake sites were;

"completely stealing their thunder, and this made Mike mad, I mean, it was great, he said he didn't know it was us for sure, but you know he strongly suspected. He was right, he said "That was released through unofficial Twitter accounts a new low for somebody." Like oh man, you just knew that really hit home."

Mike was going under, of that there was little doubt, but on a more serious note, somebody else who was glad they weren't involved was Ben Heck. Ben had been approached by Mike early on of course but had declined the invitation to be involved. Ben would have been a great asset because he is what you might call an engineer extraordinaire. Ben has worked on many game consoles, usually turning home consoles into portable systems, but he has done lots of valid and proven engineering work and could have easily designed something for Mike. He would have wanted payment for it though, one would assume, and he was pretty damning of Mike's whole project.

"As some of you may know I transitioned from retro gaming to the pinball world a while back. Been a fun ride and we've had good success so far.

But there were some major blows to that sub-culture, namely a Predator game the makers didn't have the license for, and the Popaduik games that were beautiful looking yet unplayable.

In the end around $2 million vanished off the market. Many buyers asked, "why didn't anyone warn us?" They had been warned but refused to listen.

I smell all of the same BS with this project. If they're asking for money, and there's no prototype, then it's doomed to fail. Ask yourself: Am I paying for them to manufacture something they've already designed (decent chance of success) or am I paying them to develop something they want to build? (Fail)

Paying to Develop fails because KS is all about rewards. You're paying to get a console, not to fund their research. As a backer you want a tangible item in return. Unless they've figured that into their profit (unlikely) then they'll quickly get behind and even if hardware gets designed, they'll lack the funds to build.

Hell, even a prototype isn't enough. What's the business plan? Where are the games coming from? Who is this system even for?

Cartridges are stupid, period. They were a product of their time because disk drives themselves were too expensive as a hardware item. The only reason collectors like them is because they're collectable and hold apparent value better than a disc.

Even if this is the "world's best SNES clone with HDMI" nobody's gonna to develop for it anyway. If the Ouya couldn't take off with all the support of Android, a slow-as-balls console that forces you to use assembly won't stand a chance.

Wait for Kevtris to do his thing. Then it will be done right.

Gotta say, Mike called me a couple years back asking if I wanted to be involved and it was tough finding a nice way to say "no thanks" when I was really thinking "this is pretty pointless and dumb" I especially hated the Jaguar case and the carts, called them a "poisoned chalice" if I recall.

So it's very fascinating to see what came of this and to be glad I wasn't involved."

Pat Contri was Tweeting about events and on March 1st caused something of a stir, saying:

"I'm disgusted not just by the scammers now, but by anyone who helped promote, shill, or even report on this mess without doing any homework."

He also put out a special edition of CUPodcast to address the situation of the three fake prototypes where he came up with the often-quoted phrase:

"Fool me once, shame on you.
Fool me twice, shame on me.
Fool me three times, #### you forever!"

"It just disgusts me that this stuff continues [...] unfortunately, people that are either ignorant of the facts or are just so hyped up on this knowledge that they

don't have the willpower, or maybe they believe people too much, to look into these things, and that includes, unfortunately, not just people shilling their own product, but also big websites like End Gadget, CNET and Gizmodo which acted as just PR mouthpieces, just spitting back out whatever was told to them by the Coleco Chameleon crew, without doing even the minimum amount of research to look into what was going on at the Toy Fair and what was inside that prototype.

People connected to the project at Retro Magazine, people at the Talk RETRO Podcast, Daniel Kayser, who used to be the Editor of Retro Magazine, appear on the podcast saying, "Guys just wait until wait until the Kickstarter comes, everything will be revealed." Well it was revealed before it was revealed a second time and a third time, having three fake prototypes. So enough is absolutely enough, the gloves are probably going to come off.

I would implore anyone, whether these aforementioned websites that did no homework and reporting on this, anyone associated with the project directly, anyone even on YouTube that acted as a PR mouthpiece to say "Guys wait to see what's going to happen with this Kickstarter, it could be good." when you probably knew it was not going to be good, and were not acting in good faith

You guys should come out, either apologize or own up to the fact that you were delinquent and derelict in your duties on reporting on this to the best of your abilities to try to protect the community around you and not just say "Well this is coming out it's going to bring back cartridge games. Maybe it won't but I'm going to look forward to it." because in you doing that, you now are helping someone potentially rip off hundreds, if not thousands, of people."

One man in particular took great offence to this, thinking it was being aimed at him, despite him not being mentioned where others were, and that was John Lester (Gamester81) who felt that Pat had been referring to him. Though he was not mentioned directly, he could have been included under the umbrella of *"anyone even on YouTube that acted as a PR mouthpiece"* so on the next day, March 2nd, John took to AtariAge to clarify his position and to apologize for being misled and potentially misleading his audience about the validity of the Chameleon and the pictures he had shared of their games allegedly running on it.

"First off I sincerely apologize for any troubles or ill feelings that I have caused with any of you.

I was asked by Mike and his team a while ago if we'd be interested in porting some of our games over to the Chameleon. We still haven't signed anything yet officially, and at the time when they had reached out to us, it wouldn't have cost us any more work to port our games over. It made sense at the time to get involved. I've read things about some people thinking that I'm involved with the lies and deception regarding the system. I can assure you guys that I have nothing to do with the hardware side of things, and I certainly wouldn't have got involved had I known more. I've been ignorant and wrong, and I feel bad for what happened. I have been involved publicly in the gaming community since

2008, and for those who know me, they know that I pride myself of my integrity and respect in what I do and get involved with. I'm upset about this situation, and I truly hope that you guys will accept my apology.

The gaming community is very important to me. Now in regard to the deletion of my old interview with Mike talking about the RETRO VGS. That video had been "unlisted" for months now actually, and I decided to delete the video because it covers the RETRO VGS which as you guys know is no longer relevant. I don't see the point of reliving the past and dragging up things that are over. I certainly didn't mean to come across as calling you guys "haters", and I do apologize for ever alluding to that. That was wrong of me, and again ignorant and stupid for me to say.

I realize that at this point it will take time to win back my trust for some of you. I am sincerely sorry for anything I may have done or said to upset any of you guys. The honest truth is that we were asked to port a game over to the Coleco Chameleon, and that we were not in the loop to the hardware side of things. I am humbled by this experience and have learned a valuable lesson the hard way."

The deleted video that John mentioned had not been *"unlisted for months"* as the author was able to obtain a transcript of it for use in this book, but it was now gone and would not return.

"The intent of that video was to provide at the time some clarification of Mike's intentions. At the time there were a lot of accusations (which ended up being true clearly), but there are always two sides to every story. Some people felt I was being bias towards Mike during that interview, and that certainly wasn't the intent. I deleted the video because it brought some negativity towards my channel, and my goal for my channels is to keep things positive. Why beat a dead horse? I deleted the video and I don't have that video anymore, so it won't be going back up."

Hardly surprising as John was being accused of doing a "softball" interview, maybe even shilling his friend's console project. Whichever side of the fence you fall on that, John was certainly guilty of not doing his homework, not doing due diligence and looking into the rumors that were there for all to read. Sharing images of their system allegedly playing Collectorvision games, when in truth, it did no such thing (if you don't count a Super Nintendo as "their system" that is). The biggest problem for John was that he stood to profit if the Chameleon succeeded, indirectly through Collectorvision, but as an owner of Collectorvision, he stood to profit.

Some forgave him his mistakes, others did not and the fallout spread far and wide, he does have over 100,000 followers on his channel after all. Following the deletion of his original video and his apology on AtariAge he released a video which was also touted as an apology, though others didn't see it as such and said that they had lost respect for him.

"What he posted here originally was the closest thing to an apology. What he then posted to Facebook was further from it and invalidated it.

Whatever that video was, it was not an apology and only sought to make matters worse.

So, case ####ing remaining open already if you don't mind."

The video John made was entitled "Coleco Chameleon: My Thoughts – Gamester81" and it began with a disclaimer that it may not be as child-friendly as his normal videos before declaring that it was not intended to change anybody's opinions or to defend the Coleco Chameleon as *"[...] let's be honest, just be honest. it's beyond defending at this point."* He was simply recording the video to defend his reputation and his integrity and did not want to add any fuel to the fire.

He apologized for calling the members at AtariAge *"haters"* and admitted that his comments were *"wrong and ignorant"* and Mike had clearly made mistakes, as everybody has, but then he changed tack somewhat and he lashed out at Pat Contri.

"The reason I'm doing this video is and it's really because I've been called out, indirectly called out, is by Pat.

Pat is a super nice guy ... I flew Pat, paid for his flight to come out, to Phoenix, to come out to my gaming expo that I do, called the Game On Expo. Paid for his flight, paid for his hotel, gave him a free booth to sell his merchandise, free table and gave him a panel. It was a great time, hung out, had a few beers, whatever, we had a great time. As of last week, I reached out to Pat to come back with Ian this time ... I'd love to have him come back. The invitation is always open for Pat to come in and be part of Game On Expo.

So, no quarrel with Pat whatsoever, but I do have issues with his recent video about the Chameleon.

Dude, ISIS is blowing people up everywhere in the world, kids are starving in the streets, ...he's talking in this video like it's World War 3.

Come on dude, you have a website, you know how this works when you get a press release, it's not your job, you are not accountable for the action of the company. I mean come on, that's bullshit right? Then he calls out RETRO Magazine which, again I guess he forgot to mention, is that Pat, at one time, at the start of RETRO Magazine, was a key contributor to the magazine. He worked closely with Mike, he was on the team. I don't know if he was paid or what, that's none of my business, but he was part of the RETRO Magazine.

He didn't call me out by name. He didn't say Gamester81 or say Collectorvision Games, but he didn't exclude us either. [...] So, according to Pat, we are all guilty by association because when he worked with RETRO Magazine, it was cool, and everything worked out well. It didn't, and when I worked with Retro VGS and the Chameleon and shit hits the storm, and I don't want to bring up the past because I'm not about that, but, if I recall Pat was a part of a Kickstarter that was kind of controversial and no one ever asked him to apologize and no one gave him shit for it.

Don't get me wrong, I agree that the pictures look bad and I'm on board, I agree with what you guys are saying [...] but who made Pat the ####ing Judge of the internet?

When you start questioning my integrity, which you are, and my respect and my motivations to get involved with projects, you're assuming that I'm in it for the ill will and that's just bullshit. So yes, I'm sorry if you feel that I have caused ill will, I'm sorry if you feel I've done shit wrong, I'm sorry that you feel that way, but I'm not going to apologize for ####ing trying to do the best for my company.

I don't want to fight with Pat, that's the last thing I want, the last thing I want is for you to go to his channel and unsubscribe or start a war, Team Gamester vs Team Pat. I'll tell you right now he'll probably win because I'm not going to respond much. I'm washing my hands of this."

It couldn't go unnoticed that this was anything but an apology video, and was perhaps as ill-advised as the original "softball" interview video, in fact even John's fellow owners of Collectorvision seem to have advised him against it:

"Now as for John (Lester) the night before he posted his "rant video", I told him to take a fresh breath of air and relax. I never thought Pat the NES Punk called out John or even CollectorVision (which I explained to John).

I'm cool with Pat by the way, met him last year in Arizona and he was a cool dude. I think John is going to contact Pat directly (which should have been done in the first place)."

Watching the video, and even reading the transcript, it comes across as an angry and defensive response that seeks to deflect blame and the apology was completely lost in the twists and turns that it took. Behavioral analysts will tell you what the body language throughout means but this video was probably worse received than the one it attempted to apologize for. John's fans were also commenting on the video, one noting that he warns Pat to be more responsible in his commentary because he has so many fans that look up to him, yet this is the precise reason Pat should cover the story, to warn people not to back the whole fiasco. Some noted his conflict of interest in his coverage and others went much further:

"It's impressive that you managed to put out a video that's over 20 minutes long where you managed to say absolutely nothing of substance. You talked in circles trying to distance yourself from the situation and control the damage when in reality you're just as much of a scumbag as ever, only now I've wasted 20 minutes of my life so I resent you even more."

"You say multiple times that Pat didn't mention you or Collectorvision by name, but you have no problem mentioning him by name? Classy!"

"Cut that phony bullshit that nobody should be mad about this console because there's ISIS. Maybe you shouldn't be mad about Pat's videos because there's ISIS. Maybe nobody should be mad about anything but ISIS! Cut the crap."

Not all condemned him though:

> *"P.S. Pat is also a genuine person, but he is also a bit of a knob. I think most people that watch his videos get that."*

Pat and Ian of course responded in their next video on March 9th entitled "Follow-Up on Pat's Coleco Chameleon Video" and addressed the controversy and the split that was occurring over on Twitter and YouTube between those dubbed "Team Gamester" and Team Pat."

> *"I called out certain individuals, like I said, the three websites, the people that were on that podcast (Talk RETRO), basically people that I thought weren't doing their due diligence.*
>
> *If there was random youtubers pumping this up and being willfully ignorant, them too, but some people took that video and thought I was calling out someone else. Before I go into that let me just say this, I had a conversation with John Lester, Gamester81, before this podcast, we smoothed everything over like silk. Everything's okay between us, we are still invited out to the Game On Expo if we want to go, so that's cool. John put out a response video on Friday 4th, in response to my video thinking that I was singling him out as being involved with this project.*
>
> *I think John felt betrayed by Mike Kennedy, who still hasn't reached out to him by the way, that's ###ed up! That's really the guy that's causing this problem, the problem for John, still hasn't had the decency to reach out to him to say, "Hey sorry that I put out two ####ing fake prototype systems."*
>
> *I dealt with Mike Kennedy before [...] I don't trust him, I haven't trusted for a while. When I saw him at the SoCal Retro Gaming Expo about five weeks ago, he came up to me, to his credit, he said "Guys I want to apologize for things that were said." Couldn't look me in the eye when he apologized, that's a bad sign, didn't say what he was apologizing for, didn't say "I libeled you guys." I'd like it if he'd done that, but then he goes he goes directly from this fake apology, and I know what he's about at this point, I know he's a used car salesman, but whatever. [...] He goes directly from the fake apology into the spiel about "Well we're going to be at the Toy Fair, we've got this thing coming out."*
>
> *I'm not an idiot Mike, just get away from me.*
>
> *So, when I spoke to John, again, we're cool, we're cool guys, seriously. John said he might want to do an apology video, I said it's not necessary. I knew where he was coming from, he got betrayed by Mike Kennedy, he was deceived, and he was, I guess, being loyal to him in some way.*
>
> *This isn't me trying to slam John, but he said some things I think I need to clarify. He mentioned me working on Retro magazine, said I worked closely on it. I wasn't on the team I was a freelance writer that wrote for Issues 2, 3, 4 and 5. I wasn't even in the first issue which ####ed me off because Mike Kennedy used my name to promote the Kickstarter, used my image, which I gave permission to, but I was also like one of the featured writers, along with Jeremy Parish, Chris Kohler, Pat The NES Punk and Seanbaby. It was always us four. OK that's cool but*

then they didn't have me in the first issue and I was always like, well if even two people bought the subscription thinking they're going to see me writing and I'm not even the first issue, that's bullshit, absolute bullshit.

Like I said, John was upset that I didn't exclude his name and like I said before, I didn't feel I needed to since we never included it ever and I singled out specific individuals and entities in that video I did, I called out a group of, a nameless group of individuals, and obviously mentioned names of magazines and things like that and websites that were just spitting out press releases."

Ian: "If no names are named but you feel like you're being attacked, it's probably not best to jump to that conclusion and make it public, because then you're attaching yourself to it, so you went from being a nameless person who may or may not have been intended in that group and then you went and made yourself a person in that group."

Pat: "It's unfortunate, but it happened, he did a nearly hour-long interview with Mike Kennedy on his channel back in the fall, which I think could have been a direct response to us criticizing the original Indiegogo, and Mike probably asked John "Hey John, let me be on your channel, you can interview me and we can clear up some stuff." and I think once that happened, that gave people an association there. There's Mike Kennedy, there's the Retro VGS, which was almost a Coleco Chameleon, the same shell, and there's John, and that video did not do well on his channel, it got a lot of thumbs down.

So, I think at the end of the day John is a good guy, I think he saw negative comments on his video, probably his Twitter and Facebook and he's like "#### Pat!" and just lashed out."

Pat and Ian felt they were more than justified in saying what they had said, and the fact that people were upset was unfortunate, but they were reporting on a story that was damaging the community and would do so again in the same circumstances *"In a ####ing second!"*

John again responded and thanked people for the support that they had shown him and that he had lots of messages from people saying that they were on his side, but to be fair, John said that he didn't want people to take sides:

"I want you guys to also know that I did talk to Pat, we got everything squared away so even though I appreciate the whole "Team Gamester we got your back." Let's just move on from this, guys. Let's learn from it. Please don't give Pat any hate, he got some heat from my video and I apologize to him for that and I got some from his video previously so I think we just both got caught up in this mess so I want to move forward, I want to make a public apology to Pat. Pat is a good guy, a good friend of mine, as I stated in a previous video, I've got no quarrel with him or Ian whatsoever."

Should John and Collectorvision be vilified through guilt by association? Not necessarily. If Nintendo or Sony were to try to scam people, third party developers shouldn't be tarred with the same brush, but then again, they would presumably do some research into what scam was allegedly being pulled and why there were such persistent vicious rumors and photographic evidence before saying publicly that all was well and wait for the system to come out. You need only look at the differing ways that the exact same situation was handled by John and by Eli, both of whom were hoping to profit from a successful console and pack-in game, but only one of whom came out of the Chameleon scam with their reputation intact while the other came out with theirs tarnished.

On March 3rd two more writers of Retro Magazine stepped down amid the latest controversy and they were Patrick Scott Patterson and David Giltinan, long-time proponent of the console on the Talk RETRO podcast. Another long-time supporter of Mike Kennedy was also finally seeing the light, and that was Willie Culver.

Willie was a good friend to Mike, and also to Scott and UKMike, and found himself constantly torn between the two factions while trying to be true to both. No harm in that, Willie is a nice guy and, by his own admission, too trusting sometimes. He took Mike at his word and initially, who wouldn't, but even when others were beginning to doubt the whole project, Willie stayed a true friend to Mike and sadly missed the Toy Fair because of his flight problems. It could all have turned out very differently had his flight gone ahead as scheduled, we'll never know of course, but now even Willie had had enough.

> *"I wrote an article for RETRO in issue #1 and #2 and then called it quits. Like Pat said in his video, the current editor would wait until the night before the deadline to tell you to redo your article after having over a month to tell you this. I chalk it up as a ploy to get rid of writers they did not want. Did not matter to me as they would not let me write what I wanted, they were fixated on modern games and not retro games. My original idea for my article was to talk about a classic arcade game, then discuss all the ports from the early days of videogaming up to modern consoles. Kind of like I do now on my Arcade USA channel when I cover a classic arcade game. (Scott) told me he had been told my stuff was not that good by RETRO magazine which explains the tactic to wait to the last minute to have me make changes to frustrate me into quitting. Granted, I am an amateur at writing and don't consider myself a writer, I just like to talk about my favorite subject, arcades and video games!"*

> *"I have seen GameGavel decline over the past few months and recently saw Patrick Scott Patterson leave RETRO magazine so that does not bode well either. It appears everything is crashing now.*
>
> *I am very saddened by the turn of events that have occurred, I used to hear from Mike quite often, but since this latest faux chameleon appeared, nothing....*
>
> *Nothing is harder on a person than trying to stand by a friend and then have something like this occur. I am grateful Scott and UK(Mike) stuck by me, I was a blind fool and those two beat it out of me [...] It seems now anyone and everyone even slightly connected to Mike is getting attacked. I am thankful Scott and UK(Mike) have stuck up for me though, it has helped.*

My biggest flaw is I tend to be too trusting, especially with family and friends. I also tend to try to see the good in everything which tends to get me in trouble too."

Support for Willie came from other quarters too, not just Scott and UKMike, and he wrote that for him the clincher was the *"third Fauxtotype."* He was grateful for the support and grateful that he had come out of it with the support of Coleco and River West Brands and he would focus his efforts on helping them bring this to an end and take the brand forward.

With that in mind he introduced Scott and Chris Cardillo to each other via Facebook Messenger and on March 1st they began an interesting and eventually decisive discussion. Scott had been messaging back and forth with Willie on the morning following the DVR capture card pictures and Willie told Scott *"You know who you should really talk to is Chris Cardillo."* Willie said that Chris was in a spot and that he had been talking to him quite a bit since the DVR pictures were debunked. Scott recalls the first conversation with Chris:

"I was messaging with Willie and he suggested I talk to Chris Cardillo at Coleco and I wasn't so sure about the idea. After all I was effectively squashing the console, perhaps not as effectively as Mike himself, but pretty effectively, and even though this was all in play before Chris or Coleco ever put their name to it, I couldn't imagine having a very productive conversation with Chris but Willie was insisting that he would want to talk to me, so I agreed to speak to him.

This was the morning after the DVR pics were posted and we had just received Mike's email asking us to call him because he almost fell out of bed after seeing the pictures we posted showing the DVR capture card next to the console picture posted on the Chameleon Facebook page, so I was feeling pretty victorious so why not speak to him. Willie brought Chris into the text chat and made introductions then bowed out. We told Willie he was welcome to stay but Willie felt it was best to leave us to talk in private.

After some brief typing back and forth Chris sent me his phone number and I called him. He had some initial comments mainly saying that he was trying to understand the negativity dogging this project. He was very polite and receptive, and I was very impressed by how calm he was and what an attentive listener he appeared to be, considering the circumstances. I told him that I was going to tell him the true back story of what he had put his brand name on and that he wasn't going to like what I had to tell him. I also responded to his question about the hate for the project by telling him that all of that was in motion before the console ever had the Coleco name on it.

Chris listened as I explained the details regarding the business and technical history of the console and he was shaken as this was all new information to him. He had already caught Mike in quite a few lies, and I insisted that after this conversation and before we talked again that he should verify what I was telling him. I laid out the history of the transfer of assets and the cutting out of business partners, and that if the thing ever funded there were several stakeholders ready to challenge the matter in court. I discussed the first two fake prototypes and he admitted never having heard of the first one shown in John Carlsen's video. In regard to the second one at the Toy Fair he had dismissed it and put it down to online trolls, but after hitting him with a ton of bad news we exchanged some questions and I was impressed at his honesty, humility, and forthcoming answers.

The discussion was very cordial and when I asked him some hard questions, he understood that I was trying to get a better sense of how Mike had pulled the wool over his eyes as a matter of fact discussion and that there was no malice intended. I asked him if he had done any due diligence and investigated the claims Mike had made, and he pretty much answered that he hadn't done any. I asked him why, at the Toy Fair (once the accusations of a SNESinaJag surfaced) why he didn't go down to CVS, buy a screwdriver, hand it to Mike and demand he open that thing. Chris gave an answer I had to respect, he doesn't know anything about electronics and he wouldn't know what he was looking at, and what if he had publicly and wrongly accused a business partner of fraud.

He also had a few questions for me, he asked if there could be any truth to the claims that there were other chips under the DVR capture card and I explained to him what a DVR card was and how it had no relationship to, or viable use in, a video game console. I explained in great detail just how fake the fakes were and Chris was gob smacked. I also told him that I didn't think most people blamed Coleco for much of this as it was a dumpster fire before they ever put their name on it and, so long as they handled it right, they could probably emerge with the negativity remaining focused on Mike. We agreed that we would talk again that evening when I was home and I again asked Chris to verify the information I had given him before we spoke again. During the course of that phone call my phone began ringing and it was none other than Mike Kennedy. I had not spoken to him in months and had not responded to his email that morning."

The timing of the call was ironic to say the least. Why now? Scott thought there was a chance that Willie had, inadvertently and innocently, told Mike that he had put Scott and Chris in touch and Mike was trying to either head him off at the pass or to at least see what they had been discussing, but it was perhaps a form of poetic justice, karma if you will, that Mike was diverted to Scott's voice mail just as Scott was putting the final nail into the coffin of his console. No need for the engineer to tug on that whistle any more. Scott told Chris that Mike was currently trying to ring him while they were talking, and Chris was as amazed as he was.

Later that evening Scott returned home and called Chris as promised and their follow up discussion was more of the same but in more detail as Chris had made some time during the day to reflect on the matter and to do some research and he was now eyes wide open about the predicament they were in.

Scott went into a little technical detail of what an FPGA was and how people had been trying for years to accomplish what Mike had apparently achieved in a month and outlined that this was absolutely a fake and in no way could it be real. He gave him an analogy that Chris could understand, comparing the engineering on the console to cooking a meal.

If Chris were to go to his house and shoot a video for a YouTube cooking show, then Scott pulled out a frying pan, an egg, some spark plugs, grease and a wrench he was going to wonder what the hell was going on, those things have nothing to do with cooking. That is how obvious the fakes were to a technical person, that those components in New York had nothing to do with an FPGA based video game console playing games.

Now, of course, they were up to the third fake prototype, including the John Carlsen video, the Toy Fair and now the DVR Capture Card, but Scott felt that people would be willing to forgive Coleco and not blame them too much because they had been scammed as much as everybody else. It was dumb to be so misled as a partner, but they were scammed and they had a way back, whereas Mike likely didn't at this point. Scott's advice to Chris was that he should demand, within 48 hours, that the prototypes be boxed up and shipped overnight to him. The 48 hours would give Mike long enough to get them boxed and shipped but not long enough to substitute them for something else.

All this time, Mike was still messaging Chris and assuring him that nothing had been faked and the prototypes were real, but Chris was to tell him that he had no confidence that what had been shown was real and he needed them to be delivered to him for inspection. Mike was persistent that it was all legitimate work, and he wanted to salvage their relationship, rolling out the usual Mike Kennedy catchphrases and sales patter.

Later that day Scott sent Chris a document containing what should make up the test criteria:

The articles:

- must be presented.
- must visually match photos including case markings, color, finish gloss, decals or stampings, visible protrusions, interfaces, connectors and internal components.
- must function as described in electronic, written, and verbal communications as well as interviews, trade shows and other demonstrations.
- must contain components represented as being integral to the article.
- components functional in the article's operation must be found to be so and not be inert or used as passthroughs for signals, data, or power.
- must perform as depicted in videos, photos, written, and verbal presentations.
- must work as a video game console with components integral to their function.
- Failure to submit the articles would result in termination of the relationship.
- If the articles are not as represented, it will result in a termination of the relationship.

After some further discussion Chris felt that to only give Mike 48 hours might appear unprofessional so he would give him a week, that being quite a common grace period. Then came the discussion about what would be done with them on the off chance that they actually turned up on Chris' doorstep. Chris was clearly appreciative of the effort made to level with him and possibly allow him to extricate himself from the wreckage. He was also quite adamant that as soon as the box arrived from Mike that he would drive to Scott's house and they would open and inspect the box on camera and document what they found inside.

Scott felt it would be a conflict of interest if he were to be the one to do the evaluation, so he insisted as a condition of helping Coleco that Chris reach out to one of the universities near him and approach a faculty member from the Electrical Engineering and Mechanical Engineering departments and retain them to perform an independent analysis, have them write a report on what they see presented in front of them and pay them for their time. He assured him that he would more than likely have a set of reports that matched the accusations being levelled at Mike, that his series of prototypes were nothing of the sort. Chris wanted Scott to look at them as well and Scott was happy to do so, but he was adamant about obtaining an independent verification of what he already knew.

Scott also warned Chris that he hoped he understood, that if this project had ever, or did ever, get funded and moved forward, he would have been sued. *"I'd sure hate to see this end up in that condition, but I don't think it will be if you do your due diligence, you're going to find out that they have nothing and this is all fake and then you and I aren't going to end up in court together."* Chris understood that, and it wasn't made as a threat, it was very cordial.

Chris repeatedly offered to pay Scott for his time, which Scott declined, but he did have one request. He asked for a souvenir from the Toy Fair booth and in particular the embroidered Coleco Chameleon shirt that Chris had worn in the booth. Chris shipped it overnight to Scott and he treasures that souvenir to this day, parting with it only once to loan it to Ian and Pat to wear for an episode of the CUPodcast. The next day, Chris informed Mike of the situation and posted his announcement about the arrangement on March 2nd.

> *Chameleon Product: We are thankful to have a large group of passionate engineers and retro game enthusiasts who follow Coleco and other product lines. It has come to our attention that the community has certain concerns over the prototypes involving the Retro VGS model. The team at Retro remains confident that their product is developed to the extent as described; HOWEVER, in order to confirm or debase these concerns, Coleco has demanded to inspect the prototype units within a seven-day time frame. At which time, independent engineers will review their findings and determine if those units are up to our standards. We will report some or all of those findings to the community so long as they do not interfere with proprietary information. We remain hopeful that the community's concerns are merely speculations, but if there is merit to the concerns, then we have no choice but to abandon the project rather than release a sub-par product. During this time, we ask that the community allow us time to complete these inspections. Time extensions will only be granted if requested by the independent engineer. Time extensions and results will be posted here.*

Scott had to resist the temptation that week to call Mike and say *"Hey, do you know I'm the engineer that is going to decide the fate of these prototypes?"* but he didn't because that would have tainted the integrity of the process, but he was really holding out the hope that Mike would send something for inspection, while at the same time knowing that there was no way that he could. They would have made great souvenirs to go along with the Chris Cardillo Toy Fair shirt but deep down he knew that nothing was getting shipped by Mike that week. So instead of getting to tell Mike the news, Scott had to be content knowing that he had read an email from Chris containing the test criteria that he had written, *his own words*, and come to the realization that the game was up.

There were some discussions about the seven-day deadline that Mike had been given, some calling it an exit strategy, and in a way, it was, but it was a clean exit for Coleco and with no legal recompense for Mike. He had a grace period to prove his case and if he really had something, the world would now believe him. It was a win, win if he showed a working prototype, but that was a big "if", and that week saw Mike calling Chris several times to try and salvage the relationship and keep the project alive, but his words were falling on deaf ears. Mike knew what he had to do and when he was expected to do it. There was no other way out of this, submit his prototypes or his console was dead in the water. He tried to explain that the prototypes were too delicate to mail and they may become damaged in transit so he didn't really want to send them, but he really wanted to mend the relationship. When that didn't work Mike tried to say that he couldn't let an outside party look at their proprietary technology, as if it got into the wrong hands it could be copied, even by Coleco, who could then come out with a competing product. Chris wasn't interested, he had to have the units for inspection and he expected them within the time frame set, by March 10th, or it was over.

Scott checked in with Chris through the week to see if he had received anything but obviously, he had not, and on March 8th, Todd Shallbetter, COO of Atari made a statement to the effect that they do not have, and never have had, an agreement with Retro to release Atari 2600 games on their product. Not that they had a product anymore because that same day there was another announcement made by Coleco on Facebook:

> *"The Update that you were all anxiously awaiting:*
>
> *Retro VGS has decided that the work that they have created is not sufficient to demonstrate at this time. Consequently, we can no longer proceed with the project and the Chameleon project will be terminated. This separation is amicable. We wish them luck in the future. – We thank the gaming community for their continued support, input, vigilance and trust."*

The Retro VGS Team (left to right: Steve Woita, Mike Kennedy, John Carlsen)

The Retro VGS Lab

Coleco Chameleon prototype ready for the New York Toy Fair

Mike Kennedy, Drunken Podcaster

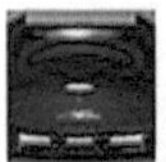

Retro Video Game Systems, Inc.

February 13 at 2:54pm ·

Eli From Piko Interactive stopped by with one of his boards, plugged in, running both Jim Power and Legend. We are running his games through our custom written SNES FPGA Core. He said they are playing flawlessly.

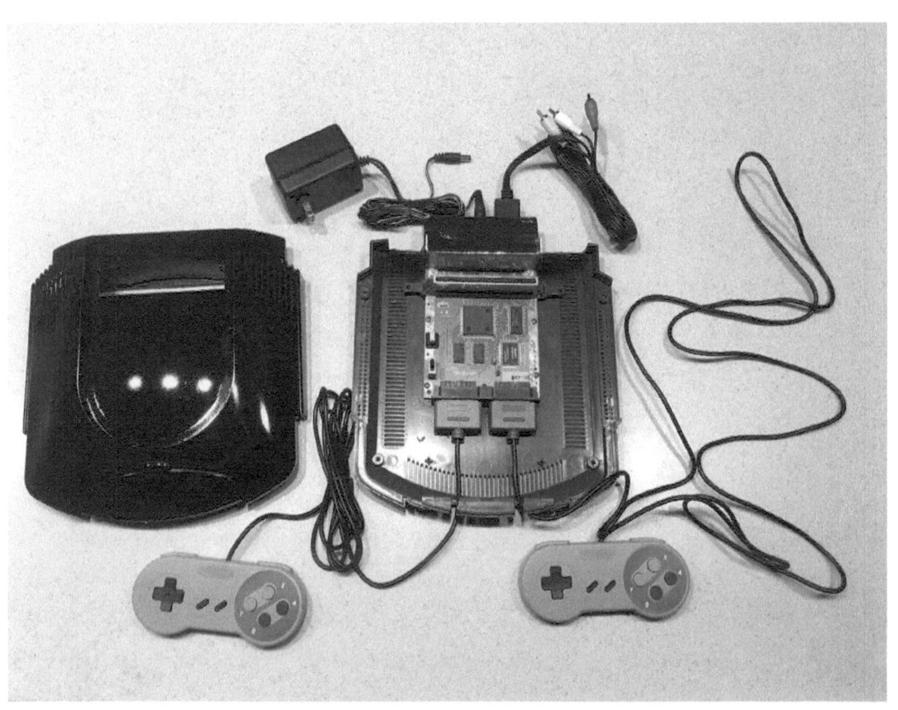

Scott's Coleco Chameleon Replica

Coleco Chameleon in the Goldeneye Room

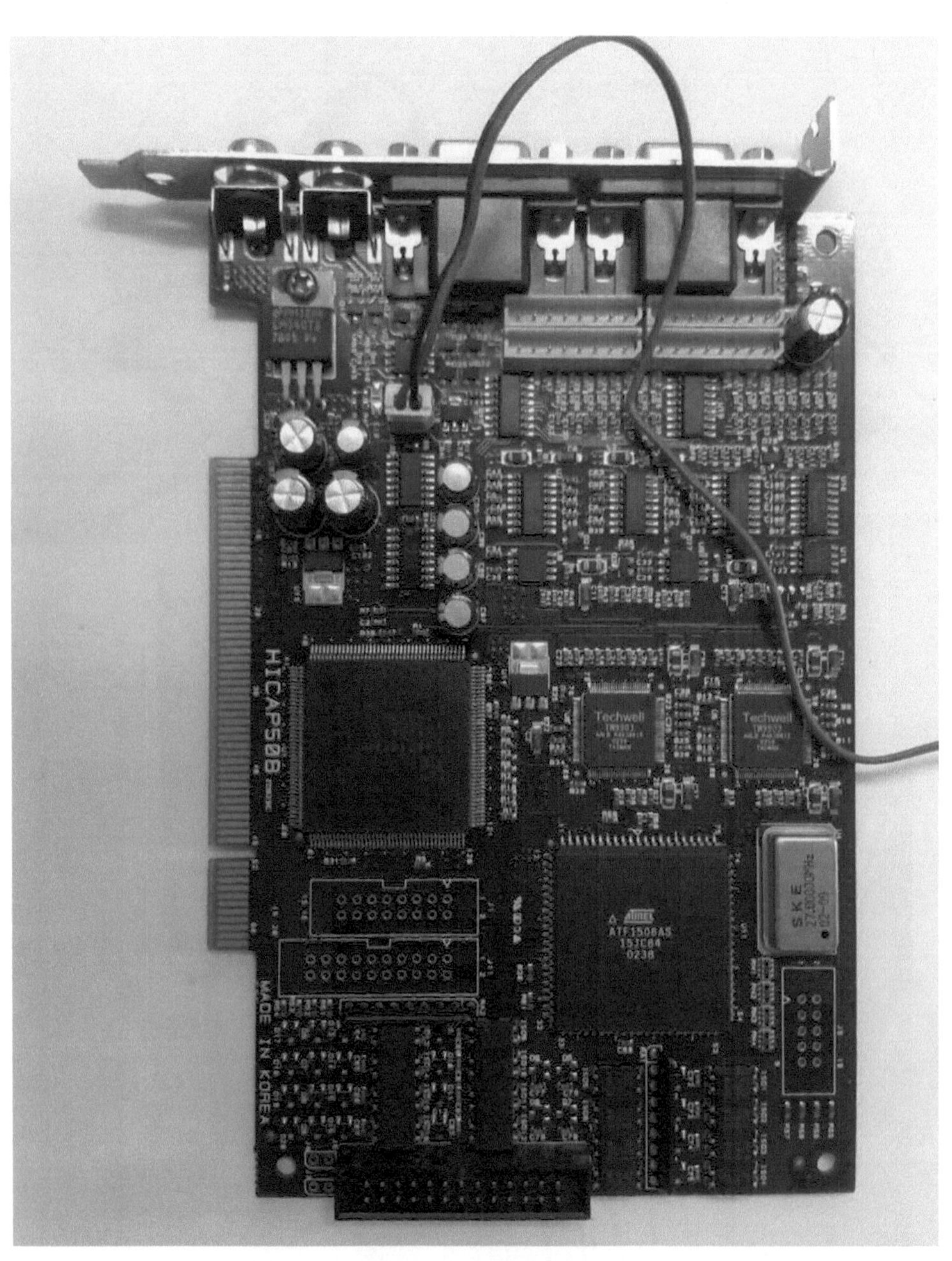

Coleco Chameleon Motherboard (HICAP50B DVR Capture Card)

12: Death Throes

So, it was over, more with a whimper than with a bang, or a crash at the bottom of the ravine, but it was over. Even Mike seemed to accept it now as he began to clean up after himself and removed the Facebook page and started taking the websites down. No announcements, just fading away, not even an update on the future of the Magazine, just a removal of anything console related.

Pat and Ian were actually quite relieved that it was over, even though it had given them lots of content for their podcast, they were happy to see it finished, as Ian posted on AtariAge and thanked those who had done great detective work and those that had fed them verifiable information:

> *"Pat and I recorded our last bits on this whole mess last night. They should be up sometime today. I have to admit I'm really happy the announcement of Coleco Holdings dropping the Chameleon came when it did, it couldn't have come at a better time both in terms of recording and my general interest and patience. We've covered this since the RVGS announcement. It's been an often amusing, always bizarre ride that became infuriating and then increasingly tiresome.*
>
> *We both broke recording schedules to signal boost info when we could, sorted through the big bursts of info and followed the quiet days or weeks after waiting for an interview or more evidence. Don't get me wrong, we weren't all-star reporters sleeping at our desks eating cold bagels and drinking stale coffee but I have a full time job, Pat has plenty of full time projects and it was honestly sort of obsessing us =D*
>
> *After almost a year on the same topic it was really nice to put a bow on it and push it out the door.*
>
> *We did as much of our own research and conclusion making as we could but it would be absolutely insane and totally unfair to not give the AtariAge forum a massive amount of credit. We put together a bunch of stone tile flooring with massive gaps and every single damn time you all came and puttied it over, filled the cracks, and sent us in new directions. Lots of times I felt we were being a megaphone. All of us together, I think, are responsible for how this rode out.*
>
> *In short: I owe a lot of ####in' beers to you out there. If you don't drink I'll provide the Martinelli's sparkling apple juice.*

That's good shit. Come say hey if you're at a convention I'm at. Would love to shake hands.

Shout outs to Brian from Jag Bar, Eli from Piko, Kevtris, Retro Gaming Roundup, and a whole bunch of others I promise I'm not omitting because I'm an asshole I just have really bad short term memory. Great info that really pushed the story along. Shout out to my cat, Spike.

In the beginning of the Chameleon era Coleco did lots of things wrong as they were towed along by Mike but in the end they did the right thing and brought it to its own inevitable conclusion, emerging from it with good grace. Certainly that's how Eli saw it, he had of course met Chris in New York and had further discussions with him about his plans for the future of the brand and the potential of working together in the future. It wouldn't be on a console project though, as he told Chris at the time "Let it die, man, just let it die."

Mike too had to let it die but he wasn't going quietly as he posted what would be referred to as his wall of text:

"Hello Everyone,
I hate to light this thread up any more but at this time I have made the decision that my reputation is worth protecting and wanted to come in here and break my silence and fill in some holes and answer some questions about the hardware "team" (term used loosely) behind the Coleco Chameleon.
This long winded response will explain:

There were only 4 engineers (or people) EVER working on this project with Steve Woita and myself (and in the beginning there were two working together) despite what Scott Schreiber has been spewing. And none were EVER working simultaneously on the project. And Scott had nothing to do with much of anything and was never considered to be "working" on this project. Has he ever produced and shown anything he was working on? Nope!

It will for the first time reveal who the hardware person was that took over after the "John Carlsen" era. And it will show that I paid him considerable amounts of money for what was essentially two fake prototypes. One that I saw (Toy Fair unit) and one that I never saw in person (clear PC card unit). I was not building that crap in my garage.

It will also reveal the shady background of said hardware person so that he can be stopped and hopefully save anyone here from dealing with this guy in the future.

And as a side note, Carl Williams IS NOT taking over RETRO Magazine nor has he ever talked with me about it. And I am not selling it or giving it to ANYONE! Carl? Explanation?

To understand how this ended, I want to direct your attention back to the early times of this venture, early to middle 2014. At this time, my first choice to design the system, Curt Vendel (who Scott Schreiber helped introduce me to thus ending his minimal involvement in the venture) decided he wouldn't have the time to devote to this venture and opted out soon and never got started. At this time I researched others that could step in and bring this product to fruition and that lead me to Clay Cowgill. Clay really took this project under his wing from Nov 2014 to January 2015 and helped us (me and Steve Woita) define the hardware and its capabilities. This is when we were considering, at Clay's recommendation, architecting something in-line with the BeagleBone Black.

It was also at this time, that another person entered into the mix, Sean "LEE" Robinson. Sean was an "acquaintance or colleague" of Clay's and it just so happened that he had moved from Washington (state) back to Southern California. He had heard that I was working with Clay on this project and offered to help. Since he and Clay were colleagues, and the fact he was local and very close to me, it seemed like a good idea to have them partner up on the project, which they did to some extent. Supposedly, Sean had a working prototype (that I NEVER saw) playing Neo Geo games in Jan 2015. This prototype was later used again when he rejoined the project explaining how we supposedly had a prototype so fast AFTER Carlsen left.

In late January 2015, Clay alerted us that he was contracted by SONY and that he would be leaving the project. At this time, Sean also decided to leave as well. Enter in the John Carlsen/Steve Woita FPGA "era". Now I am not going to go into this part of the timeline because we know how all this worked out. Fast forward to John Carlsen leaving the failed RETRO VGS project.

At the time of John's leaving in September 2015, Sean "LEE" Robinson re-entered the picture and reached out to Steve and I. He indicated he wanted to help us get this project back on track, but his condition was that he remained "behind the curtain" (his words) due to the mess he was inheriting from Carlsen. At this time I agreed to that condition and also agreed to let him and Steve work together on this without my interference. While I thought I had a competent hardware "team" working on this, and was being told early on by Sean we had games running on our hardware/software prototype and that our costs had dropped considerably, I felt confident to go ahead and continue building this venture, bringing a "go-to-market" team together and making the decision to launch this under the Coleco brand. Things seemed to be coming together. Chris from Coleco invited us to demonstrate a prototype at Toy Fair. This did pose a challenge to Sean as it expedited the process a bit to try and make the show deadline.

This is where things started to take a big bad turn. In mid-January, I had a lunch meeting with Sean and point blank asked him what he needs from me to spend the next 30 days working on the prototype full-time to get it prepared for the Toy Fair. We agreed on $4,000, which I quickly got to him via a check that he cashed with me at my bank. It was then a day before I was traveling to the show that he came over to my house with the Toy Fair "Prototype", with his instructions to NOT SHOW the back of the unit no matter what. But without any specific information as to why I shouldn't show it, other than it used an aftermarket connector that was composite-out and that was used because he didn't have the HD stable enough to get us through the show. I believed him and went to the show with that unit. My biggest concern at the time was getting this conglomeration through the TSA and on the plane.

During the show we were accused of not having that system even plugged in so I made the decision to take a photo of the back of the unit showing it was clearly plugged in. If that was true about using the composite connector, I really felt people would understand why it was used and decided to show the pics. I didn't feel we had anything to hide. Then all hell broke loose and it was identified that SNES mini parts or the whole PCB from an SNES mini was inside the console shell. I was left in a terrible spot at this point and I had a decision to make that evening at the hotel. Do I take this thing apart and see what was in it and quit the show or continue on with the show, demoing the games that were going to be on the system, and then address this issue with Sean when we got back from New York. Right or wrong, I continued on with Toy Fair and it continued to impress people and the games were very favorably liked (Thanks Eli! For stepping in with his SNES multicart in place of Sean's glitching out SD card driven demo cartridge). When I returned back home, I met Sean again and gave him the "prototype" back and he was still swearing that despite the SNES "parts" he used, the games were still running on the SNES FPGA software that he had constructed in a few short months. Again, I believed him and we moved forward. And he told me that during the Toy Fair he was preparing the next "prototype" board so I gave him the clear shells with explicit instructions from me to show "our" PCB inside the shell. This was going to be used to show the "real" prototype.

Then in a move to extract more money from me he indicated that for $3,000 paid now (2/29/16), and $3,000 paid in 60 days he could wrap this up and have a production ready prototype completed. So, again, I wrote him out a check he promptly cashed with me at my bank. Soon after this he emailed me the images of the clear unit with the PC DVR capture card in it. But, when he first emailed me the images, he indicated this was our prototype 100%. I made a comment that it looked great (in the photos) and he responded by saying something like "this is what we can do when given the proper time." Keep in mind, these pictures were to combat the criticism of the "fake" Toy Fair prototype and were given to me by him to post on Facebook to show people the real "prototype". Sean even joked about how people online were trying to identify the board in our shell, laughing and telling me they won't find it because it's our original work. He even made these comments through my car Blue Tooth speaker with my wife in the car and she heard everything. Again, I believed him.

Let's discuss the Kickstarter for a moment. So, believing I was going to have a working prototype for Toy Fair, I told Sean and Steve I was going to move forward with the Kickstarter campaign and use Toy Fair as a launching point for the campaign. A date was set. Now to Sean's credit, he played that this was not a good idea and didn't agree with me scheduling the Kickstarter to begin during the campaign was a good idea. But, at this point, I thought I had a real prototype playing games and was assured by Sean many times that our costs were now hovering around $100, so figured, let's not wait any longer. After it was learned that we essentially had a SNES duck taped in my console shell I decided to delay the Kickstarter because it was always my intention to show off *the prototype completely in the campaign video, open it up and show it running and playing games from at least two different systems. Then once I saw the clear unit was also a "fake" I made the decision to withdraw from a Kickstarter campaign altogether and reevaluate this venture.*

Back to the clear shell prototype. Since this all fell apart I have been trying to get Sean to explain to me why he would point blank lie to my face about that being "our board" and passing that two-bit PC board off as our prototype and he can't give me an explanation that makes any sense, in fact I get no explanation other than that there was more going on in there than people can see. He mentioned we had chips located underneath the board even and assured me that the cartridge was also plugged into our cartridge connector. Something was just not adding up to me and I continued to lose sleep at night wondering how this all could have happened. First, he never showed me anything in person, that he was working on. I never went to his house, nor was ever given an address where he lives or works. He subscribes to my magazine so I looked at the address the magazine is sent to, a UPS store PO Box. I have paid this guy $7,000 and have nothing to show for it. Oh, I also bought two FPGA cores from a "friend" of his (whom I never met in person) whose wife was having medical issues and needed to sell some things and just so happened his friend had made an Intellivision and Amiga FPGA core. Sean told me his friend would sell them to me for $2,500 which I, again agreed to, and wrote Sean out another check which he promptly cashed at my bank and was going to give the cash to his "friend". Did I ever get any software cores? NOPE! So, in total, with a couple other smaller checks I wrote to him, paid him nearly $10K in January and February 2016. Nothing to show for it except two fake prototypes and NO FPGA CORES! And, he swindled out my Crystal Castles Commodore 64 prototype cartridge as part of a payment as well!!!!!!!

So, trying to make more sense of all this, I started Googling Sean and this is where things get super crazy. I will just post the links that are online for all to see and you can all take it from there. There is even more stuff you can uncover if you want to all look:

[LINKS REMOVED]

In addition, I have confirmed with the Riverside County (CA) Assistant DA, Sean was charged a few years ago for 7 counts of Felony Grand-Theft and served part of a one-year sentence in jail and then got out on probation which he evidently complied with and then he made a plea to have the prior conviction AND his admittance of guilt overturned. A loophole that the DA mentioned drives prosecutors crazy.

At this point I can only hope to recover any of my money paid to him, and can no longer live by my word to keep him "behind the curtain" while his deceit led to my defamation of character and demise of the company and opportunity and also I feel I was intentionally setup to take a fall. Because why else would he give me the clear shell "prototype" photos to hang myself? Seems strange as we both knew these photos would be scrutinized like crazy based on the last "fake" SNES prototype he gave me.

I also hope that you will also wonder why I would go to all this trouble surrounding this venture with guys like Ben Herman (he was a Rockstar at Toy Fair, and had tons of legit retailer interest in this thing) and Phil Adam, Paul Wylie and eventually Steven Rosenbaum. Why would I go out and bring Coleco on board as a licensing partner? All done and then just try and pass off fake prototypes? This is just something that I would not intentionally or knowingly do. I have way more integrity and respect for this hobby to pull that shit. I did remain silent the past few weeks though while I put the pieces of this train wreck together and worked with my attorney to define my moves. And I apologize for the delay. Timed with the release of this statement here on AtariAge I have also emailed Sean a demand letter asking him to make arrangements to pay me back the money he scammed from me as well as a heads up I am going public with his participation in this deceit. But at the same time, I wonder who he might have to take advantage of to get the money to pay me back. That is the shitty part. And I am still working with my attorney and local authorities to find out what my options are.

I want to apologize to all of you for the past few months. The John Carlsen era was an honest to goodness list of mistakes. But there was never any intention to deceive or pull the wool over any of your eyes. These past few months with these fake prototypes was inexcusable and I hope you can all understand a bit more about how this all happened and why I have remained silent the past few weeks. It is not in my nature to trick people into anything. My end game has always been to give back to this hobby that I love and respect and to make and do things that people will enjoy. I've never taken one penny from anyone that wasn't genuinely earned!

You will all be glad to hear that I am officially tabling the console venture for good. I have negotiated with Albert (AtariAge) to take over the Jaguar tooling so we can all be assured it's in good hands and won't get destroyed or lost to time. And I am sure Albert will do some very cool things with the console and cartridge shells.

I want to ask you all for some level of forgiveness and I hope you all understand that I would have never gone to Kickstarter with a blatant rip-off of a prototype. That was never my intention. And please, don't let this mess carry over to the magazine. I have a great team of people working on it. We are pouring a lot of heart and soul and sweat equity into keeping the magazine going and it's only getting better.

And, I want to thank those on AtariAge (and other public forums) for opening my eyes to the craziness of all this happening right under my eyes. The fact that Sean indicated he wrote this SNES FPGA software in such a short time was questioned here and that opened my eyes. Of course, the uncovering of the fake prototypes has opened my eyes. You guys really go above and beyond to protect the hobby and it wasn't until I have had the time to reflect back on this fiasco that I saw how you all came together and your alerts spread like wildfire across the internet. Again it was never the intention of myself or those legitimate guys on my team to deceive or potentially defraud anyone. In the end, I am the only

one that has lost anything, money, potential opportunity and my reputation in this hobby.
Mike"

Scott saw the post and quickly responded with:

"Go home Mike, you're drunk."

Mike's wall of text made many points but it avoided many more, and his account of some of those addressed were clearly false, the fact that he said that only he had lost money was a bone of contention with people, from those who lost money on transaction fees when backing his abandoned Indiegogo campaign to those who had put hundreds of man-hours into it with no payment other than some shares in a worthless company. Not to mention his investors in GameGavel LLC of course and his statement was not well received.

"I don't know if it was possible for SoCal to write something to allow him a chance of recovery. But this was not that something."

"I did not want to say anything but "SoCal" Mike Kennedy you deserve no benefit of the doubt because you sir are a liar."

"Your reputation is shot to hell, because of you not because of any of us, Scott or UKMike. Not fully because of the failed Chameleon attempt but because you keep lying."

"IT IS %100 FACT YOU ARE LYING, HAVE BEEN AND CONTINUE!!
p.s. If it is not too much to ask could you please send Scott a clear Jag Shell? Thanks."

These were just a few of those posted by Mike's fans, readers and listeners but he had also named a few people that he presumably hoped would come forward and back up his story to lend weight to it. Sadly he was mistaken, mainly because he lied about their involvement or the circumstances of their involvement, Clay Cowgill for one, who had thus far remained respectably quiet:

"I've been content to take a "not my circus, not my monkeys" stance with this whole brouhaha, but since Mike decided to name drop me...

- *Mike seems to have some facts jumbled up a bit at the beginning of the project. For the record, Sean (whom I had met a couple times before) contacted me directly in early November 2014 to see if I was interested in speaking to Mike about a retro-style hardware game device. I've done that kind of development work commercially for years now, so I agreed to at least explore the possibility and agreed to let Sean give Mike my contact information. Mike and I then spoke directly by phone on Nov. 17th, 2014. Sean was already working with*

Mike well in advance of my involvement and my understanding during the call with Mike was that he and Sean were actually friends and had known each other for quite some time.

- *The project was not what I as a hardware designer would consider 'defined'. Mike wanted 'hardware' as quickly as possible, but there was nothing that I would consider a bare minimum to start designing from-- no product requirements documents, no hardware specification, no consideration of the product ecosystem. I provided some example architectures on 12/1/2014 of 'things that could be made to work in a short period of time' based on designs I'd done earlier, but there was still a pretty glaring lack of direction.*
- *By 12/19/2014 I pushed back on putting any additional time in on the hardware until we A) knew what the programmers needed/wanted for features and performance and B) knew the performance of available platforms relative to their costs. That was falling outside of what I was comfortable putting time and effort in on (all my involvement was done without compensation as spec work in return for per unit royalties should the product eventually come to market), so Sean stepped up and did a bunch of work with available generic hardware platforms and existing emulators to evaluate possible candidates. The outcome of that was that the AM3354 (based on the performance of a BeagleBone Black devboard) would probably be sufficient given the back-of-napkin type wish-list we had for features.*

  *Over the next couple months there wasn't a lot of progress on nailing down specifications (I don't know if there *ever* was an official requirements document/engineering spec generated)-- even basics like what type of video modes and outputs the device was supposed to have were still up in the air at the end of February. However, there *was* talking up the system in public when it didn't even exist on paper yet-- I took that as an excellent sign that it was time to officially part company at the end of February and "pursue other opportunities."*

Mike had Clay's involvement completely flipped around, claiming that he had originally found Clay who had in turn brought Sean in but it was, in fact, the other way round, Mike first dealt with Sean who had then brought Clay in and Clay had the impression that Mike and Sean were friends. They had certainly known each other as early as 2013 if not before. It obviously suited Mike's narrative that he wasn't responsible for Sean at that stage, distancing himself from that responsibility, and what had Sean been doing up until that point if Clay still had nothing to base a design on? Clay does say that Sean did some investigative work after his own initial input but this was nothing more than a few ideas that had been floated around, stemming from those early meetings with Ed Fries, Steve Woita, Bob Polaro, Phil Adam, Scott and UKMike. A few undefined ideas yet Mike was posting publicly about them.

Mike also posted pictures of cheques that he had written to Sean, which summarily disappeared before being posted again:

> *"Oh God. Mike posted pictures of the checks he wrote to show what money he lost. One check was dated 2-29, AFTER the capture card fiasco happened. When questioned about it, the pictures of the checks disappeared. Than (sic) they came back, with Mike saying that Sean "Mr. Lee" deleted them."*

This is plausible as we know that Mike had given Sean access to the backend of his websites when he was helping out with GameGavel and Retro, allegedly blocking code that others had put in place to falsify web stats, but who was going to believe Mike at this point? He had burned too many bridges for that.

Mike claims that Sean had contacted him about coming back on board after John Carlsen had left and this may or not be true, it could have been Mike that approached Sean but either way, Sean was, at this point, the sole engineer and he wanted to remain anonymous, *"behind the curtain"*, hence the whole "Lee" persona that he created. Mike clearly paid Sean for the work that he was doing, as the cheques show, and the money he paid Sean a month before the Toy Fair bought him a SNES Jr inside a Jaguar shell, a SNESinaJag, and a SD2SNES with some ROMs on it. Sean didn't even source a Nintendo power supply, either to save money by using a cheaper third party power supply or to try and hide the fact that they were using a Nintendo product. Clearly the power supply wasn't up to the job, hence the resetting problems at the Toy Fair.

Sean took the SNESinaJag to Mike's house with explicit instructions to be careful with it and a warning to not show anybody the back of it. There is no doubt that this meeting happened as both of them have discussed it, however, Sean later emerged again to plant the story, as he likes to do, that he had given Mike prototype A but Mike had taken prototype B to the Toy Fair, claiming that he had not built the SNESinaJag, and that Mike, or somebody else, must have built it. I find that hard to believe and we will look at this meeting, the Toy Fair and their conflicting stories in the next chapter in more detail, but for now, Mike had paid thousands of dollars for a SNESinaJag.

When Mike returned from the Toy Fair, he returned the unit to Sean, with Sean still adamant that the games were running on the SNES FPGA software that was constructed in a few short months. Are we really to believe that away from the public eye, away from the crowds and the Coleco staff at the Toy Fair, Mike didn't open it up and look? Had he done so he would have clearly seen a professionally produced Nintendo PCB in its entirety, no jumper cables connecting different parts together, no cobbled together cartridge slot and video output, no delicate components and hard-wired controllers but an entire original Nintendo produced circuit board.

Even if Mike didn't open it, it was still plainly discernible what it was as Scott's replica Chameleon showed that by looking through the openings intended for the 9-pin connectors, now occupied only by an extension cable, that one could see the

Nintendo board inside in clear detail. Similarly, looking through the cartridge slot gave a similar result. Scott's replica also laid to rest the constant claims of how delicate the unit was, the SNES Jr board was well protected inside the Jaguar shell and would have travelled and survived reasonable handling just fine. All of these details were also obvious to the general public who examined the unit once Retro Gaming Roundup took the replica Chameleon on tour and showed it in their booth at various gaming expos on both sides of the Atlantic.

If Mike did open it up, or even peered through the openings in the case, and continued to give Sean money, he was a fool. If he didn't open it up and continued to give Sean money, he was a fool. As the saying goes, a fool and his money are easily parted. How true because he was set to pay Sean another $6,000 over a 60-day period so that he could *"wrap this up and have a production ready prototype completed."* For his follow up payments, according to Mike anyway, Sean created the DVR capture card mockup and sent the images to Mike, who you would think would examine them properly before telling Sean that they looked great, because they didn't look great, they looked like what they were, a fake prototype. Unless Mike is telegraphing his thoughts that they looked great in relation to what he had asked for, a fake prototype that was convincing enough to get through the requirements for Kickstarter. History tells us that it was discovered what was really on show, but did Mike think they looked real or just convincing enough for purpose?

Mike didn't scrutinize them and duly posted them to Facebook, apparently discussing the furor over the phone within earshot of Tricia, and he also mentions Steve Woita at this point, had Steve seen them? Steve is a proven engineer, did Mike not show them to Steve at any point before posting them or even while they remained posted and were being scrutinized by those who could see that they were clearly faked? Steve would have presumably spotted something was amiss and could have warned Mike immediately not to post them and that he was being scammed, so was Steve even contributing anything at this point?

It's true that very little is known of Steve's involvement throughout, other than requesting that an FPGA be used, and he declined the offer to participate in this book, requesting that it not be written, but from conversations between Steve and the author, Steve just wanted to create a platform on which he could write games. In the early Skype conversations he was keen to get back to writing games and he wanted the best platform he could have on which to do so. His biggest mistake was believing that Mike Kennedy was the man who could provide that platform through crowd funding, having already funded his magazine using that same method. He believed that Mike knew what he was doing and appears to have left him to it. He was clearly out of the loop during the interview with Carl Williams and didn't even know Kevin Horton by name when he was discussed. Sean, on the other hand, was very involved and either had Mike hoodwinked or was providing what Mike was really asking for, a fake that would be convincing enough to meet the requirements for Kickstarter.

Mike was being economical with the truth about the delay of the Kickstarter, saying that once he had *"learned that we essentially had a SNES duck taped in my console shell I decided to delay the Kickstarter"* He surely knew what he had while he was at the Toy Fair, either on the show floor or in his hotel room that night, certainly before he returned the unit to Sean when he got home, but the week following the Toy Fair he was still announcing that the Kickstarter was to go ahead. He didn't delay the Kickstarter campaign until the very last second, when it was clear that he also had a DVR capture card and a separate red LED, and that there was no way on earth that he would get away with it. Kickstarter would have been inundated with complaints the moment he went live.

Mike paints a picture that Sean was little more than a stranger, a man he had no address for, a man who's house he had never been to and a man he knew nothing about. While some of that may be true, Sean was not exactly a stranger to Mike, as Clay states, he got the impression that they were friends and they had been working together before his involvement when Sean brought him in. They attended the same SC3 events in California, verified by Brian Barnhart, and Mike had met Sean before. In fact, all three Retro Gaming Roundup hosts had met Sean, more than once. Sean was a listener of the podcast and had met the hosts at Portland Retro Gaming Expo and Classic Gaming Expo. Furthermore, Sean had introduced himself to them and had even won a copy of CGE Adventures from one of Mike's raffles at Portland. Mike was so familiar with Sean at this point that he knew he already owned a copy of the game and challenged Sean when he won it (legitimately) and Sean told him that he was going to give it away to a friend as he did indeed already have one. Not exactly the shadowy unknown figure that Mike presents him as.

Mike had been discussing FPGA cores with Kevin Horton earlier in the process and while he didn't understand them, he knew the work that Kevin had put into them and how much he would be wanting to license them for, so when Sean offered two for a knockdown price, the same man that had built the SNESinaJag, did alarm bells not ring for Mike? Was he not the least bit suspicious before writing out another cheque and giving him a rare cartridge?

It's possible that he didn't know about Sean's criminal past, even if they were both part of a community whose members Sean had been defrauding, but he knew more about Sean than he was disclosing. It was also unfair to blame Sean for his defamation of character and the demise of the company(s) as Mike did a pretty good job of those himself, as he showed by apologizing for his behavior at times and for the total mismanagement of his "empire" with people logging into his email accounts at various times to do his job for him.

Mike also asks why Sean would give him the *"clear shell "prototype" photos to hang (him)self"*, as though Sean was setting him up for failure, but let's be honest, Mike was Sean's cash cow. Sean was extracting money from Mike left, right and center, meaning that Mike had to cash in his 401k, use money from the Retro Magazine Kickstarters, make personal loans to GameGavel and allegedly skip some mortgage payments. Imagine the funds that Sean might have had access to via Mike if they had got funded on Kickstarter. It made no sense for Sean to kill his project so why would he do it?

Mike then questions the logic of bringing in legitimate people and the Coleco brand if he wanted to scam people on Kickstarter, missing the observations that his co-hosts, and others, had made of him. They had no doubt that Mike had set out to produce a console and sell it to the public, they just knew that he didn't have the skills to do it himself and didn't have the funds to pay somebody else to do it properly. Recall his quote from the interview with John Lester:

> *"Well, there is no working prototype because we can't afford to bring a working prototype to market."*

The accusation levelled at him wasn't that he was trying to scam people and not produce a console, it was that he was trying to scam his way on to Kickstarter and then produce a prototype and a console using that funding, and that he was willing to burn family, friends, and the community to do so. An accusation that he continues to evade answering.

He also stated that he wasn't going to sell Retro Magazine, and we'll see how that goes, but for now, it was over, and he was out of the console business for good. He had a magazine to try and resurrect.

13: Post Mortem

In this chapter we will look back at how all of this saga and the shenanigans played out, who was likely telling the truth and who was clearly lying. In some instances, it will never be known for sure but in most of the key moments along the way we can make an accurate assumption of who knew what and when.

Mike Kennedy was not a technical person by any stretch of the imagination, even before he started out on his journey into the world of making a video game console, when to Scott and UKMike he was still good old SoCalMike, he would sell or trade an arcade machine if it broke, he didn't know how to fix them himself, his brain just didn't work that way. He wasn't a stupid man, he knew what a processor did, he knew what RAM did, he just couldn't open up a console or a pinball machine and tell the difference between the two. If you gave him the parts and showed him what to replace, he could probably do it if it didn't require soldering, but he couldn't have diagnosed an issue like that. So, such a man would need to surround himself with those that did understand these things, those that could design a console from the ground up, given a specification to work to, of course.

Before we get to that though, Mike had a well-known desire to work in the gaming industry, to be a public figure in the hobby that he loved, and that is where most of his schemes stemmed from. Not all of them were game related but he was always pretty much chasing financial success, not that there is necessarily anything wrong with that, but it should be measured against the lengths to which one will go in order to achieve it.

It's a matter of opinion where Mike began to go off the rails and we can try to narrow it down but the tricky part of that is Mike's personality. He was a salesman by trade and his demeanor was ideally suited to that, so how do you spot where a salesman is trying to help you out and where he is thinking about his commission? What also makes it difficult is Mike's scatter gun approach, rather than pursing that one killer idea, he would fire out one after the other in the hope that one would take off. If you throw enough mud at the wall, some of it might stick, however, you're still just throwing mud at the wall. Not all of Mike's ideas were bad ones and certainly not all of them were Mike's but did he just back the wrong horse or was he looking at a donkey all along?

First in line was Chase the Chuckwagon in 2008, and Mike launched it himself as a way to save money on eBay fees when he sold the items he picked up at the Southern California swap meets, again, no harm no foul, as you might say. He also purchased items that people listed and there were those that suspected he would look at the backend of the site to look at the highest bids so that he had an advantage when placing his own bids. There is no proof of that of course and they were only suspicions but they were voiced from time to time.

With Chase the Chuckwagon Mike was trying to build something, genuinely, he wanted this to help the gaming community out, he was enthusiastic, genuinely enthusiastic, and he desperately wanted it to work. He did make some good strides with it early on and got items listed with a fixed "Buy Now" price to show up in a Google searches but Mike was still struggling to drive traffic to his live auctions so it was always an uphill battle.

Vendazzle was perhaps not a great idea, the name is terrible and Mike was already struggling to bring traffic to Chase the Chuckwagon, so the last thing he needed was another start up based around auctions, particularly as this one was aimed straight at eBay, not just the gaming community that he was a member of. It also showed that Mike was perhaps not really giving things as much thought as he should, migrating his members' user accounts over to the new site before growing bored of it and offering it up for sale, along with all of those personal details.

GameGavel was an interesting rebrand, many companies rebrand themselves, and Mike now had a much more mainstream name for his auction site, one that stood a good chance of catching on, it described what the site was at least, and he realized that in order to help it grow, it needed financial input to pay for a redesign, auction hosting software and publicity, so he set about bringing that investment in. As most of the investors were friends and family, you would have to assume that, initially at least, he felt responsible enough to bring them a return on their investment and had their best interests at heart. He did however give out far too many free lifetime seller accounts, so much so that a lot of his sellers simply listed items at a high price time after time in the hope that one day somebody would come along and buy them. It cost them absolutely nothing to list them and they had no need to price them competitively, so why should they?

It was around this time that Mike really started to use podcasts to promote himself and his sites, not only Retro Gaming Roundup but also guesting on other podcasts to peddle his wares, such as All Gen Gamers, where he "met" with John Lester, and he would begin to use the social media feeds to which he had access to post regular promotional updates.

Mike's time on the Retro Gaming Roundup podcast was where he would forge relationships with some of the video game alumni that he would reach out to later with his business ideas and, in those early days, he came across as an absent minded but good natured guy, which his co-hosts believe was the case, initially. In the early years he would be enthusiastic about the recording sessions and would show up prepared, he would sometimes drink a little, sometimes a lot, and it was just like three friends chatting about their hobby. The phrase *"The Three Musketeers"* really was true in those early years and it was only later when he was chasing some of his hair-brained schemes that he would lose focus and even come to resent having to put in the preparation and recording time.

The promotions that he would go through for his sites, both on Retro Gaming Roundup and on other podcasts, were in keeping with what his co-hosts believed to be Mike bringing an audience in to their joint ventures and common interests, it was only later that it became proportionally unacceptable to them and they addressed the issue with him. He never did travel to an expo outside of the U.S. with them and it's likely that this was a combination of not having the funds to do it and not having the blessing of Tricia to spend that money and time away from home. Mike did pretty much everything Tricia said, even stopping a recording of Stalking The Retro in mid-session when she came into his home office and told him that he had to stop right then and come back into the house. It is likely that this had a large bearing on his lack of international travel to expos rather than a lack of funds because he would often say that he didn't have the funds to travel and would then take off in his Airstream to the wine region of California or Yellowstone or some other tourist attraction and would be unavailable while he was away, usually when some important event was happening in one of his businesses. This was either because he was in over his head and wanted to be unreachable when things went wrong, or because his own schedule had no bearing on family time and if Tricia said they were going somewhere, they were going somewhere.

GameGavel looked after itself for the most part, he either had the software vendor fix issues or his web developer add functionality, he would just do some day to day maintenance and checks, but even then, there were broken links for the most part as it got neglected from time to time. Normally though, it wasn't a time sink as he threw yet more mud to see what would stick.

Retro Arcade Radio was also completely autonomous, he took it over from Peter Hirschberg as a going concern and once his playlist and Saturday Night Party playlists were set, it never changed its track listing until later when UKMike made some changes to it. It eventually went away when Live 365 ceased business rather than through Mike's mismanagement and it was an under used but headless part of the GameGavel Network.

Next came what I think is the first incidence of Mike taking somebody else's idea and using it as his own and that was AutoGab.TV. Mike had a prior association with Shane R. Monroe of course, and after Retro Gaming Radio went away Shane started doing a podcast from his car during his daily commute, and that podcast was initially called Car Talk. Shane later had to change the name as it was already in use so he renamed it to Passenger Seat Radio. It can't have escaped your attention that Auto Gab is an appropriation of Car Talk, and Mike's promotional material for it avoided any mention of that obviously. It also showed a pattern of behavior that would repeat again in the future, that of putting the cart before the horse. Mike had not only re-imagined somebody else's idea, but he had the promotional material ready to go, he had app pricing ready to go, he knew what some of the features of the service would be such as image blurring, viewing streams, notifications, saving streams and combining streams, yet this was nothing more than a back of a napkin idea, somebody else's napkin at that. That was how his mind worked, this was a done deal, as an ideas man he had done his part and the rest was easy and would naturally follow at his predetermined launch date of *"this spring."*

Of course, it didn't.

The next site to be added to the GameGavel Network was GamerSpots, the mapping site for arcade and gaming hotspots, and again this wasn't Mike's idea, it had existed in the pinball world for several years and was still actively used. Mike had expanded it beyond the pinball world to include video game locations and even stores that sold games and gaming merchandise, and while it did see some use, it never really took off in a big way, hence him only tweeting from the account seven times.

Postal Gamer was next and was perhaps the first time that Mike really put a lot of work into one of his ventures. Postal Gamer was, again, not an original idea as there were similar services available for movies and Mike wanted to bring the gaming world up to speed. He wrote a presentation to take to the Angel Investors and he had spoken to Scott and UKMike about how nervous he was while presenting the idea to them but they did genuinely like it, they just thought that it needed more investment than they were allowed to provide.

Following a rename to Parcel Gamer after some early feedback, Mike did actually show that he had learned something from his mistakes, he did put some work into this one, looking into the numbers for processing plants that would receive incoming games and dispatch outgoing games. He had some figures from Bastian Solutions who provided a similar service for Netflix, Jack of All Games and GameStop, but he did also pluck lots of numbers out of the sky, with projected sales figures into the millions within year one, putting $500 million to the bottom line and having to *"expense that, otherwise Uncle Sam will come and take it away"* so he planned on buying a Gulf Stream Jet in year 3 as they would flying all over the world. It was an interesting idea to share his information with the publishers as they currently had no numbers on used game sales and he did get to physically meet with representatives from Microsoft and Nintendo who felt the idea merited some further talks but of course were non-committal at that stage.

A stark warning for the future though, and perhaps the first signs of the stages of a Mike Kennedy business were in play with Postal/Parcel Gamer. The idea was not Mike's, or not Mike's alone, it was a joint venture that he and Steve Sawyer had come up with and I commented earlier that with Mike, words really do matter, when "we" switches to "I" it is a warning sign that you have been used for information and you are now on your way out. In this instance we go from:

> *"brainchild of CEO Mike Kennedy and his business partner, Steve Sawyer"*

to;

> *"... part-time employee, Sawyer"*

continuing on to;

> *"two passionate gamers"*

and finishing with;

> *"Mike Kennedy, CEO of the GameGavel network, which includes ParcelGamer"*

Scott outlines the Mike Kennedy business model, of which he was a victim of course.

> *There is a very clear pattern of how things progress in one of these projects and almost anyone involved in one would have the same story. A few years ago, I was looking for a Subaru Baja Turbo and they have been out of production since 2006 and are not easy to find so that meant dealing with the used car market, I found a clean one at a dealership in Manassas and went to look it over. It was one of those buy here pay here kind of places but the truck was clean so I wrote them a check and left with it. While I was there I could not help but feel like I was on the set of some reality show, things felt scripted and contrived as if the employees were playing roles and working from a script.*
>
> *I posted about this on a car forum and someone responded that I had seen a "system store" in action. As it turns out there are consultants that will come to your dealership and teach you how to process customers to get the highest number of sales with the least effort and there is a flow chart that customers are passed along resulting in getting them into a car or out of the door very quickly.*
>
> *I think that Mike has developed a system store method for utilizing talent for turning his dreams into reality.*
>
> ***Phase 1** is that he has an idea for an entrepreneurial venture, but only that, not the means or methods to make it into a real thing.*
>
> ***Phase 2** is finding the people that can, and offering them future value in the form of stock or other benefit such as one company paying back the other. There is a lot of "WE" in this phase, you're damn near partners and it is the two of you 51% and 49% all the way baby. The "we" is also you working while he is learning what you know and then popping off for a wine tasting while you get the work done.*
>
> ***Phase 3** is looking for your replacement while you're still involved, that person is given the same deal and story and never told about you if at all possible. If needed, new promises of future profits are created, "ran out of stock to sell so I created a new company" then you're off the project. Maybe you just stop*

getting calls, maybe you're called "hard to work with." maybe the company is dissolved, but whatever method it is, your promises of future compensation are up for re-interpretation.

Phase 4 *is denial and diminishing. Any negative aspects of the project are attributed to you while your role is continually downplayed: "Yeah he wrote a few articles but wasn't really a part of it" or "He just made a few phone calls but wasn't really a part of it" etc.*

Controlling the narrative. *Big time issues here, and this is not the Mike I knew. I recall one time we made up a poster to promote Retro Gaming Roundup at Expos and part of it were quotes from iTunes reviews. Of course we put in some of the best positives but we also had a crop of the negative reviews just to be cheeky. One of my favorites is "There are so few retro gaming podcasts out there, it's a shame this is one of the biggest."*

We have never deleted posts or kicked people off our forums or Facebook, this is all new behavior, but the cause and effect is apparent.

What I am seeing is a North Korea type farcical presentation of legitimacy, so absurd and easily seen through, but clearly crafted to be presented to crowdfunding as "Look we are real, have a real prototype, and have an adoring fan following," hoping that they don't look at anything other than those sources.

Lying. *I can only factually tell you what I dealt with. When he came up with the idea for Retro Magazine, I had recently bought part of GameGavel, which, with me being in the denial and diminishing phase he has referred to me as a "small minority shareholder" also known as the only one of his friends who gave him money, and I asked him if this was a separate venture or part of GameGavel and he affirmed that it was part of GameGavel so I said "Ok".*

When he was launching it he utilized the Retro Gaming Roundup show and its media outlets heavily, on a daily basis and there was a lot of promising about how the show was going to be integrated and see advertising and representation but when the first issue came we were nowhere to be found other than in a top ten listing. UKMike and I called him up and asked where was everything we were promised. At first it was a "Yeah you know we really had to rush to put this together and maybe in the future ....." but we pressed him on why he had everything else done and pointed out that we could have prepared those things but were never asked. Finally we got the email where we were addressed in a very cold sterile and stiff manner and were told that magazines simply did not do those sorts of things and that's the way it was.

When he had the idea for the console I asked him a similar question, is this studio (which is what it was at the time, a studio to be followed by a console by that studio) a new business or part of GameGavel/Retro and he affirmed that it was part of GameGavel/Retro and as I recall the phrase was something like "Yeah, it's got the RETRO logo stamped right on the front of it" and I said "Ok" and this is what I believed right up until the Indiegogo of the Retro VGS.

I stood to make money on this system if it succeeded, at that time I was still unaware of the new company that had been created before the Indiegogo and the RETRO VGS assets transferred into that. Speaking for myself and two other GameGavel/Retro shareholders we were never told about that. When we found out and confronted him about it the response was absurd. He claimed that it was always going to be a separate venture but that GameGavel would benefit at arms-length by free subscriptions to the magazine and such."

This was standard practice for a Mike Kennedy business venture and was the source for the buzzwords that he would use, provided by his line of engineers, without knowing what they meant. For example, gleaning terms and buzzwords from Scott and passing those on to Sean and Clay and repeating the old ones and any new ones gleaned from them to John Carlsen, all lending some sense of legitimacy that this could really happen and that he was the man to make it happen.

With Parcel Gamer, there was another common trait and that was the descriptions used for current and past partners, when Mike was shown which office would be his over at Play N Trade, they were the best thing ever, a huge national company that was well respected. However, when he was told that the deal was off and they needed his things out of the office, they were just *"a small fry operation who's VP drove an old Hyundai"*

This was still during the era of "The Three Musketeers" though when Mike was still committed to the podcast and was, occasionally, a *"drunken podcaster,"* an accusation that he would later lay at the door of Pat and Ian of course to diminish the respectability of their commentary as his empire began to fall apart, but things really started to take a downturn during the magazine era. If Mike hadn't already started to chase the dollar at the expense of friendships, respectability and the community, it was a fact that he did it during the life of the magazine, and, it must be said, very early on in that process.

There is no doubt that the magazine idea was originally that of Steve Sawyer, no matter how Mike paints it, the idea was Steve's. Steve was doing some writing for GameGavel and had the idea of turning his online writing into a magazine, a retro magazine. That is not in doubt, it was Steve's idea, which Scott attested to as they drove around Los Angeles while they attended E3 together. Steve, who was a big fan of the UK magazine "Retro Gamer" felt that they could do something similar in the USA and he recruited David Giltinan who also began writing articles on GameGavel. Steve outlined the magazine idea to David and they created the first iteration of it within a couple of weeks, naturally, it wasn't great, but it sowed the seed of an idea in Mike's mind that this could be an avenue worth exploring.

Explore it they did, and Scott was a party to those early planning stages in the car and at the show with them, as they would;

"banter back and forth with their ideas on the magazine, the business operations, structure, and the content of the venture.

...if there was a take away, it was that Steve and Mike were without a doubt co-creators of whatever this publishing venture was to become, and Steve was every much a part of this as Mike was, and seemingly the greater contributor

as he was punching up Mike's ideas into something greater than Mike had originally imagined."

They put up their first copy for sale on GameGavel and it was bought by a few people, including Mark Kaminski, who liked the idea but hated the execution and offered his services to work on it with them, offering a professional layout to show them how it could look.

Mike was selling the idea, if not the magazine itself, to his co-hosts and assured them that the magazine was under GameGavel in name only but would essentially be the magazine of the podcast. While Mark was very useful, having worked on magazines before, he caused Mike something of a problem, but it was a problem of his own making. He had been promising different things to different people. Mike and Mark would define the magazine's look and most of its content, but it was the magazine of the podcast when it suited. The show was heavily used to promote it, including social media feeds as well as audio content, where Mike would wax lyrical about how it would look and what it would contain, but what he was telling Scott and UKMike, he was not telling Mark and vice-versa.

As the Kickstarter campaign for Year 1 of the magazine loomed, the promotion of it got incessant, to the point that Scott and UKMike would delete his posts unless there was a reciprocal post for the podcast on the Retro or GameGavel feeds, which there seldom was of course, though the Year 1 Kickstarter campaign mentioned the podcast specifically.

"... video game auction site GameGavel.com and the Retro Gaming Roundup. com podcast decided to team up with some of the most popular and influential gaming journalists and personalities from the past three decades[...]"

UKMike would later delete parts of the podcast where Mike had dropped into sales mode for a spell but no alarm bells rang as the Kickstarter campaign launched because it also featured Steve, and the video even included the artwork from the cover of their first GameGavel Monthly that Steve had put together. Recall Mike assuring Steve that;

"Dude, you're still going to have a stake, this is still our thing. It's just going to be better. That's all.

I'm going to be able to take care of you guys. I want to be able to pay you money, like a regular human being type money if this thing gets funded."

Of course, it didn't pan out like that as Steve was being pushed out according to the Kennedy business plan and his replacement, Brandon Justice, was brought in with Mike having found him on LinkedIn about two thirds of the way through the Kickstarter campaign.

Scott noticed that Steve Sawyer was no longer on the scene and Mike told him that Steve wasn't really involved other than a bit of writing and wasn't really a part of it. You can guarantee that Brandon was not told by Mike that the idea was Steve's at any point as he forged ahead having now cut him out while diminishing his role at the same time.

Brandon was now the best thing since sliced bread according to Mike, but things didn't exactly work out that way as Brandon was notoriously unable to produce a magazine on time, being unavailable in the mornings and being in a bar in the evenings, a fact that angered the writers who were needlessly given short notice to produce articles, articles which were, at times, badly edited.

Pat the NES Punk was used heavily in the promotion for the magazine but was absent from the first and second issues, much to his annoyance, and no doubt a surprise to his fans who subscribed based on his participation. Writers were paid vastly different sums for their articles and there was no cohesion between them.

Mike of course went AWOL as Issue 1 launched, devoid of the content he had promised his co-hosts, and following their meeting the relationship with Mike and the magazine changed forever as business arrangements took the place of friendly, verbal agreements. They could no longer take him at his word.

As things moved forwards, Mike seemed to ignore the fact that there were countless complaints of issues not being delivered and didn't follow up on email complaints. He also failed to follow up on emails for advertising leads that were sent to him, forcing others to do it for him. A lot of the magazine's problems were financial as Mike was quickly running out of Kickstarter money, not just down to his mismanagement but also because, by his own admission, he bought himself a pinball machine with the funds. In fact, he was running out of money by the time they reached Issue 4 and he was bailed out by his uncle, Lloyd Fritzmeier, to the tune of $17,000 with an interest rate at $2,000. Clearly a return to Kickstarter was needed to fund a second year.

Brandon came and went and was replaced by Daniel Kayser, but despite his efforts and enthusiastic emails, things didn't improve much. Mike's mismanagement of the whole charade was not helping of course, even before he was sidetracked by the console venture, but to him the magazine was done, it was a success, sure there were complaints about undelivered issues, the quality of the magazine and the change in direction from retro games to modern games with a retro twist, but another problem for Mike was Mark Kaminski.

During a podcast recording, Mike blamed Mark for the breakdown of his relationship with Scott and UKMike, saying that it was his fault that the promised show related content was not in the magazine and that he was backed into a corner by Mark. Mike had employed Mark and given Mark a role, which he was fulfilling, but Mike never said that to either of them. If he had been honest and told them that Mark was saying it couldn't happen, they could have addressed that, but again, they were getting the Mike Kennedy sales patter and the "have a Coke and a smile" resolution as he found himself trying to talk himself out of the position that he had put himself in.

The other problem that Mike was having regarding Mark was that he had twice removed Tricia's name from the credits, much to her annoyance despite her not having contributed. She was embarrassed by the fact that she had told friends her name was in a magazine in Barnes And Noble when it had, unknown to her, been removed. This threw her into a rage and Mike took the brunt of that rage. Told by Tricia to fix the problem, Mark had to go, but as we know, he wasn't going easily, quietly or cheaply, holding Mike to their written contract, however flimsy and flexible it was.

Classic Gaming Expo 2014 was to be organized, of course, by the hosts of Retro Gaming Roundup, it wouldn't have been as well publicized or presented without Mark Kaminski and he was a huge part of it, but as the structure was laid out, it was Scott at the helm and on the hook financially but the three directors were; Scott Schreiber, Mike James and Mike Kennedy.

As Mike was doing over at Retro, he was shirking his expo responsibilities and just not doing his job. Vendors were his domain and they were being ignored, emails were coming in but none were going out and in the end, Scott had to change the password for the email account and do Mike's job for him, a fact that Mike did not realize for a month, and only then when he was asked to check it. What was he actually doing instead? As has been noted, Mike was a fire and forget kind of guy and I think he has a very short attention span. Once he had sent a few emails to known vendors, as far as he was concerned, the job was done, and he was on to the next thing. In respect of CGE, that could have been any one of his hair-brained schemes, but not following up on emails at Retro, his own business, his own Kickstarter, there can be no excuse for that. His neck was on the line with the magazine but he had put some people in place and it was job done and on to the next thing, the console.

There was a lot of discussion about the first attempt at crowd funding for the Retro VGS and the decision to use either Kickstarter or Indiegogo. Kickstarter was their preferred option but they did not, in all good faith, have a working prototype to meet their requirements. Mike had got a pass from Luke at Kickstarter based on Mike telling him that they had a working PCB but as John Carlsen pointed out, this was false and their "pass" was not valid. For that reason, they would have to use Indiegogo and they knew it all along. John Carlsen even said that had they gone to Kickstarter he would have felt compelled to report it as fraudulent. Did this spell the end for him?

Mike was sticking to his guns and trying as hard as he could to get the team to go to Kickstarter, even requesting possible last-minute edits in their interview with Retro Gaming Roundup if they did, but he made the decision at the last minute to side with John and use Indiegogo. Far from the story he was telling publicly, that *"Indiegogo had been courting us for the last few months."*

A lot of the history of the console involves the shadowy figure that is Sean Robinson and Mike has tried to distance himself from Sean several times, as though he was a random person that he found but didn't know, classic distancing tactics, but Mike did know Sean. They had met at several expos and SC3 events and Sean was at CGE 2014 during the first year of the magazine's life, a magazine that he was involved with but not publicly. Mike had introduced him to the staff at Retro as his *"Tech Guru,"* but it was also noted that even when the Tech Guru was on board they still had to use other people for work that he couldn't do or said he had done but hadn't.

Mike gave Sean access to the backend of the website and also to GameGavel so Sean had the keys to the kingdom, the foundations of Mike's empire but what was he actually doing? Probably very little as he would usually explain it away by telling Mike that he was *"doing a bunch of database work"* which obviously Mike had no idea about and could neither prove nor disprove. It's doubtful that this "work" was done unpaid either.

Sean is described by many of those who know him as a convincing con artist, a serial liar and not to be trusted. Some came forward and posted his list of crimes and a list of people within the gaming community that had fallen victim to him. Some of them got repaid, but as one commentator put it, he was running a Ponzi scheme, using money defrauded from one person to pay off the last. Some who complained vehemently and promised action got paid, others who went quietly did not. Some of the money was for games that he allegedly had and was selling, some was for web related work that was left unfinished and some was for rare games that he allegedly had for sale. It was said that he would build trust through legitimate deals with small, low cost items or with his wife's eBay account and then once the trust was built up he would pull his scam on a larger, more expensive item and he had victims from all across the globe, including as far away as Australia.

His business "Robinson Creative Solutions" had a registered address at 6715 NE 63rd St, Vancouver, WA 98661, USA but not many people had a physical address for him and it is possible that this included Mike Kennedy of course. Throughout the story Sean displays several patterns of behavior but the main ones are:

- Building trust with smaller deals before pulling "the big one."
- Disappearing for lengths of time.
- Popping up occasionally to call somebody and see what is being discussed, usually concerning him.
- Contacting several people with a story or version of events in the hope that they will share it, making it seem to come from a reputable source.
- Having a series of conversations with the same person, over a period of time, to build up a lie and invite trust.

Sean was described by many members of various gaming groups as having used these tactics against them and he served time in prison for some of those crimes. He also contacted Brian Barnhart shortly after UKMike had interviewed Brian for this book in an attempt to plant the story that he had not made the Toy Fair Prototype. His story was that Mike had switched them. He claimed that he had taken a prototype to Mike, but that Mike had taken a different prototype to New York. A story that he repeated to Mark Kaminski much later, in fact as recently as November 2020, after the Kickstarter campaign for this book had ended. By this time though, the story had evolved somewhat and he claimed to have a video of this meeting with Mike which proves his innocence. A video which has failed to materialize in the almost five years since the event and which would have admonished him of blame immediately. Of course it is not the only example of him deflecting blame away from himself, as in this email to Scott:

> *"Who is he talking about when he says "Our". Piko is just Eli... and his storage unit. At least MK had real people to say there was a team, not that I want to give MK any credit here, but just pointing out some interesting things. Eli has asked for support in help with the spam email he sent out about his new project by using MK's Kickstarter mailing list... with a ton of AA members...*
>
> *It looks like there might be a new boogie man in town... Eleazar Galindo... aka Eli!*
> *Dun dun DUN!!!*
> *-Sean"*

Incidentally Sean was in contact with UKMike and offered to help with this book but when he was sent the list of questions, some of them awkward for him, he disappeared again. This was expected of course and UKMike already knew the answers to many of the questions asked, but Sean was told that the book was coming out with or without his involvement. He wasn't needed for it, but if he so chose, he would have the opportunity to present his side of the story and his account of events. Instead he chose to disappear again, which speaks volumes.

His other tactic, which would be amusing if it didn't have such serious repercussions, was his compulsive lying over the course of many phone calls. During this phase Sean is very convincing, telling Mark Kaminski over the course of many conversations that he was one of the first fifteen employees at Earthlink and that he was the early voice talent on Homestar Runner, even doing impressions over the phone for him. When asked by Mark to do that publicly as promotion, he obviously declined. He tried to convince others that he was a Marine, including Scott, though of course with his own military background he found this less than convincing while others were taken in by it.

One commentor put it:

> *"Sean is a terrible person and after talking with him on the phone many times I really question if he is even a sane person. I found his stories and lies could vary as often as two to three times in the same sentence."*

The two main occurrences of this behavior in the story are the series of phone calls that he had with Eli and with Steve Woita. With Eli he was building up the illusion of working for a company with a huge campus, lawyers and showers, a cafeteria, contracts with Boeing and the Goldeneye room. Eli was completely taken in by this and even when his better judgement was telling him to run for the hills, he agreed to stay on the project based on Lee's assurances. With Steve Woita, he built up the illusion that he was working on real hardware, that he had real hardware working and running games, and Steve was taken in by him, trusting him enough not to warn Mike that his engineer wasn't everything he seemed. As Mike later said;

> *"When I told him (Steve) about Sean he said it couldn't be the same guy he has been talking with all this time and that helped us early on with Clay."*

He clearly convinced Mike who continued to give him cheques, even after his fake had been exposed, and we can look at these transactions as they represent the crux of the console business and Sean's involvement in it.

Mike knew Sean and involved him with the websites and social media feeds for GameGavel, Retro magazine and presumably the Retro VGS and the Coleco Chameleon as well. He also had full access to Mike's laptop while he fixed it for him. I have no facts about this interaction but theoretically it is possible that Sean took a complete image of Mike's hard drive, could gain access to Mike's files, emails and social media accounts. Even if Mike deleted Sean's accounts on his sites, in theory, he could access them using Mike's logins if Mike had set his browser to remember the login details. Again, this is in theory and there is no proof of it, but it is certainly a possibility.

What did Sean actually do? Did he ever do anything or was it all a front? Clay Cowgill talked of his impression that Mike and Sean were friends and that Sean had been working on the project before him, a fact confirmed later by Mike after Clay had corrected him on it. Incidentally, Mike had emailed Clay a link to the thread on AtariAge after he had posted his wall of text, presumably in the hope that Clay would back him up, but Clay did not do that, Clay posted a truer account of events that contradicted Mike's narrative.

> *"Mike emailed me this thread (I assume to try to get my support on it?) I see that I'm now 'unfriended' by Mike today on Facebook, so I assume my commentary earlier today was not appreciated... *shrugs*"*

Clay talks of them coming to him and having no plan, no technical specs, no details of what the programmers would want, nothing, so what had Sean been doing up to this point if they brought Clay in with nothing to give him? Clay did some design work for them and sent them some possible specs up until the point that he was no longer comfortable working on his own time and on his own dollar. He considered this fair as spec work which may result in paid work later if they chose him to engineer the final product. However, he saw the direction of the project shift and walked away.

> *"My advice to Mike at first was to bootstrap development himself-- buy the Jag tooling, shoot some cases and sell them to recoup the acquisition cost, put subsequent 'profits' towards developing something and use crowdfunding essentially as a fulfilment channel for the product once it was ready to ship. Almost immediately the emphasis of the project shifted to 'how soon can we get this on Kickstarter' with a "smoke & mirrors" demo system for a video (well*

before a complete system architecture had even been settled on) and that 'cart before the horse' mentality combined with my past experiences in the toy/ gaming industry set off my "this isn't going to end well" alarms and accelerated my urge to exit—

How you would go from someone that's done this dozens of times telling you "14 weeks, $70K" to "30 days, $7K" and expect to have any significant chance of success... I dunno. I think enthusiasm and eagerness to get to the finish line trumped rationale thought and prudence."

Clay also mentions that Sean was Mike's CTO (Chief Technical Officer) and was *"invoicing Mike for a retainer and maximums/hourly rates 'as discussed'"* and he also mentioned that Sean did some work from December until February but what did this work actually entail? Clay had suggested some possible platforms and had done the donkey work on it and Sean came back with nothing more than a few off the shelf hardware architectures and existing emulators running on Linux or Android. None of this phase of Sean's work has been made public, everything he claimed to have was only talked about via email or by telephone and nobody ever saw anything that he allegedly had running. As Clay elaborated:

"In my ~14 years as an independent consultant (and employing others in the same capacity) I will say it's generally not 'industry standard' to keep making payments if work is substandard or not up to specification (if you still have a job at all after messing up the first time). In terms of contract engineering work, $7000 really isn't much-- that's a little shy of six days of hourly work for a hardware engineer at middle of the road hourly rates (west coast). Not sure what you'd expect to get done in a week except maybe some kind of mock-up?"

A mockup is precisely what Mike got, two of them, from Sean, and one of them from John Carlsen. The John Carlsen era is very interesting because Mike seems to go from wanting a *"smoke and mirrors"* mock up to get on to Kickstarter to having John Carlsen actually architect a system and then back to Sean for a *"smoke and mirrors"* solution again. What is key to this change in direction though, is that Mike was willing to put some money into development but not the level that was required to do it properly. Clay wouldn't do it for him and Sean seemed to be able to do nothing more than run emulators on existing hardware so he turned to John, who is a legitimate engineer, a fact verified by the well-respected Rebecca Heineman, and who was willing to spend his own money on the project. That is why he was brought in and used when the plan evolved from the Back In Time console to the Retro VGS. John burned his own savings on it rather than Mike's, right up until the point where he had none left but had architected a system that included the prerequisites defined by Mike and Steve Woita.

The system that John had architected, though certainly far from finalized, was too expensive for the market to support, having gone from the $150 level to the $350 level, hence the ridiculous $1,950,000 Indiegogo target to set up the business, rent offices, pay salaries, finish the prototyping and build and deliver a system. That was never going to happen and Mike couldn't put up another ridiculous campaign like that. He needed a more affordable system and a more reasonable crowd funding target, hence the return to Sean for the Coleco Chameleon, but again, he had nothing to show. As Steve Sawyer comments:

> *"When Mike has something good, you basically have to staple his mouth shut to get him to not talk about it. He's just not that kind of a person, and that's in everything he and I have ever worked on or done. He is the first person who, I'd be like, "Maybe we should do this and we'll wait a day or two and I'd get a phone call from him the next morning." He's like, "I wrote a thing and posted it on gamesindustry.biz and I'm like "Oh okay."*
>
> *So he loves to talk about stuff. If he had something dope and he was completely confident in the hardware and everything, dude he'd be showing you HD, 4k close-up pics of that shit.*
>
> *He should've been real honest and said, "I don't have the money to fund this prototype because despite the fact that I've raised over a hundred thousand dollars in crowdfunding, I spent it all on space cocaine and god only knows what." and so I need even more money to fund another one of my ideas that's probably not completely my own."*

So, it is clear that Mike had nothing, certainly Sean delivered nothing, but the crux of the matter lies in what was Sean asked for and what did Sean provide? As Clay puts it:

> *"If Sean was working on anything for Mike that would require compensation in addition to the terms set forth in his contract (or after it expired or was cancelled), there should be additional documentation supporting that (Scope of Work, contract with deliverables/dates/payment terms, etc.) The fact that Mike is more interested in trying to mount a smear campaign and paint himself as the victim than actually posting said contracts and demonstrating what wasn't done per the agreement(s) is suspicious to me.*
>
> *The memo lines of those checks said "prototyping", "hardware design", "product development", those are all activities, not an 'item'. If Sean was charging ~$150/hr (to use a ballpark hardware design engineering number) as "time and materials" for development even if he didn't get a single thing to work there's no recourse unless there's a contract that says the work has to meet a performance standard to merit payment (or if there was a 'claw back' should some ultimate goal not be met) -- but if that were the case it's just a contract dispute. Trying to blame everyone else is just a good way to make sure no other reputable people will ever agree to work with you again...*
>
> *There's absolutely nothing wrong with making 'mock-ups' for demonstrations, photo-shoots, etc. Stuff built in model shops (used to be with wood, now 3D prints) and displayed as "mock-up/prototype/not final design" at trade-shows, press tours, etc. is still super common-- where it gets sketchy is in *how* it's used, but that burden falls on the 'presenter', not the fabricator.*

If you don't have contracts and SOWs (Schemes Of Work) and schedules and documented deliverables and milestones and performance plans and corrective action plans, probably the last thing you should be doing is asking for other people to give you money because you have no business running a significant hardware development project in the first place.

I think Mike was lucky. Had he succeeded in getting Kickstarter funding I bet two years down the road the money would all be gone and there'd be nothing ready to ship and he'd be in FAR worse trouble when the backers came out with torches and pitchforks wanting their $2M back... Maybe he should be thanking those he blames for saving him from himself!"

If Sean had no such contract with Mike, which he clearly didn't as that is not Mike's style, and he was not supplying Mike with any real hardware, as Mike never saw, touched or played a real prototype built by Sean, what had they agreed to be the way forward? Mike wasn't going to fund a real prototype and had twice avoided doing that, admitting to John Lester that *"Well, there is no working prototype because we can't afford to bring a working prototype to market."* so what was Sean asked to do? There were really only two options to begin with:

1. Provide a real, working prototype which Mike would pay for.
2. Provide a fake mockup convincing enough to pass the criteria for Kickstarter and develop a console with the funds raised.

It was clear that option 1 was non-starter so it has to be option 2. If Mike needed an engineer that was willing to build a fake prototype he certainly found him in Sean Robinson but is that what happened? The key to understanding this lies in whether we think that Mike knew he was showing fakes or if he believed that they were real and he had been conned by Sean as he claimed.

The first fake provided by Sean was the SNESinaJag that was shown at the Toy Fair. We know that Sean took this to Mike the day before he left for New York and instructed him to be careful with it as it was delicate, and not to show the back of it. We now know why it was delicate as the cartridge kept resetting and he wasn't to show the back of it because it was a SNES Jr, but did Mike know?

UKMike could understand how somebody could give Mike some technical details and he would take their word for it as he wouldn't necessarily understand what he was being told, but he can also see a scenario where Mike was just bare-faced lying to everyone.

Mike was on the show floor showing off his prototype, and of course he showed the rear of it, which sparked the rumors that it was a SNESinaJag. He was the one on the line, his reputation, his investment, his future in the industry were all on the line as people told him he had a fake prototype. Perhaps understandably he did nothing during the Saturday of the show as he showed it off to potential customers, and of course fakes have been shown at trade shows before and by companies much larger and more established than his, but the engineers and presenters in those cases knew that they were temporarily fooling the public, the Commodore VIC-20 is a good example, but here, Mike was claiming to be ignorant and a victim of fraud. Once the show closed on Saturday Mike says:

> *"I was left in a terrible spot at this point and I had a decision to make that evening at the hotel. Do I take this thing apart and see what was in it and quit the show or continue on with the show."*

He had paid money for what people were calling a fake, what looked like a duck, walked like a duck and quacked like a duck, so Mike did one of four things:

- Opened it and discovered it was fake.
- Examined it through the openings in the shell and saw it was a fake.
- Did not open it and continued blindly.
- Continued to deceive the public, knowing he had asked for a mockup.

Whichever action he chose, he not only chose it at the show of course, but he took his prototype home with him and handed it back to Sean, who assured him that it was real. Even if we give Mike the benefit of the doubt and allow for the possibility that he didn't want to open it on the Saturday of the show when the public were there and when companies like Atari and Toys R Us were there, even if he didn't want to open it on the Saturday night, just in case it broke and he would have nothing to demo with on the Sunday. Even if we allow him that scenario, what about when he got it home? Did he really not open it or look inside it then either? Did he not have a conversation with Sean around making Sean open it up and show him what he had paid thousands of dollars for? Remember, he gave Sean another cheque after the show. With all the rumors and the heat he was getting and Eli not coming out and helping him dispel those rumors, he still gave Sean another cheque. Did he really put that much faith in Sean and ignore everybody else or did he pay Sean for what he had asked for in the first place? A fake prototype.

Even after the Toy Fair, Mike was trying to get Brian Barnhart to shoot the Kickstarter video without the prototype, to use footage of Intellivision and ColecoVision games and to do the voice overs for him while avoiding taking a prototype over to the Jag Bar to feature in the video.

Sean claims that Mike switched the prototypes and took a different one to New York, not the one that he supplied, and it's true that Mike owned a SNES Jr, as confirmed by a picture of his lounge that he posted on March 3, 2017, it is clearly visible beneath his TV. He obviously owned a Jaguar shell and he knew what a SD2SNES was but is this really a viable story? Why would Mike pay thousands of dollars to Sean and then not use what he was given in return? The only circumstance in which that could be possible was if he saw that Sean had brought something that was sub-par and was then forced to make his own mockup, but if that were true, why did he then subsequently continue to pay Sean? It just doesn't make any sense.

If there is any credence to Sean's story that Mike took a different prototype to New York than the one Sean provided, why would he not let Eli open it if his was a genuine prototype? Why did he tell Mike not to show the back of it? Why when Mike did exactly that did Sean not cry foul and say it was a different unit? Or had they both happened to build a prototype using the rear of a SNES Jr?

The fact is that after the SNESinaJag fake was exposed, he did continue to pay Sean and Sean produced yet another fake, the DVR capture card in a clear shell that Mike gave to him. According to Mike, Sean emailed him the pictures and told him that it was their prototype 100% and Mike replied to say that it looked great. It's almost certainly true that Mike wouldn't know the difference between a prototype and the fake in those pictures but did he mean that it looked great because he thought it was real or because he thought that it looked convincing? If he had been scammed by Sean in New York why would he suddenly trust Sean now? Wouldn't he want to see the system in person? Touch it, turn it on and play games on it?

Mike posted the pictures online and Sean emailed him to joke about the fact that people didn't believe that they were real and were trying to identify the board, which happened over that weekend of course. As soon as they were identified, the pictures were taken down, Mike says that Sean did it and Sean says that Mike did it. Both of them likely had access so it could have been either one of them, ultimately the final fake was uncovered and Mike posted his wall of text blaming everything on everybody else but him, including posting images of the cheques that he had given to Sean.

Mike also mentions that Sean told him they were real over the phone while Tricia was in the car with him but was Mike really going to admit that he knew they were fake or that he had asked for mockups while Tricia was there? He was in to her family for tens of thousands of dollars, he'd taken money from his 401k, and reportedly been skipping mortgage payments to push the console through, certain that he would soon be flush with crowdfunding cash, so the last thing he needed was for Tricia to know if he was in cahoots with Sean. Of course he was going to keep up the charade for her benefit if he was in on it.

Again, as soon as the pictures of the cheques were posted, they were taken down, again, possibly by Sean who was now well and truly rumbled, but then again, so was Mike, those cheques proved that Mike was still paying Sean, even after it was confirmed that they had presented a SNESinaJag at the Toy Fair. Had Sean delivered on Mike's orders or had he scammed him again? The pictures of the cheques went up at 19:22; Mike was asked why he was paying Sean after the DVR capture card was exposed at 19:30; and the pictures were taken down at 19:47. Mike explains it away as *"Sean weaseled his way as an admin on ReadRetro.com."* but Mike had given him that access as his *"Tech Guru"*, remember, words matter, Mike was at the top of this empire and he has to take responsibility for the access that Sean had.

The next day of course, Mike denied any knowledge of what had happened and that the pictures of the DVR Capture card fake had been taken down. Ignoring UKMike's comment in an email that three fakes was a lot and he should now sell the molds and move on, he instead addressed Scott about the DVR capture card being exposed as a fake and that when he saw it on waking, he almost *"fell out of bed."* Honestly, whoever deleted the pictures is irrelevant, what is important is the arrangement that the two of them had with each other. Only those two people know what deal they made and what Mike had asked Sean for, but both of them are proven liars, so who could we believe anyway? There has to be a reason that Mike did not pay Clay Cowgill or John Carlsen but did pay Sean Robinson, yet he asks for forgiveness, saying that *"I hope you all understand that I would have never gone to Kickstarter with a blatant rip-off of a prototype. That was never my intention."* which counters his previous statement of not having the funds to bring a prototype to market. He can't have it both ways.

After the final fake and the inevitable Kickstarter cancellation, Mike went on vacation and stayed out of the spotlight for a month before returning to AtariAge to post his account of events and to outline how he would try and get Sean to return the money that he had given him. This is extremely unlikely to happen, as Clay has said, the wording on those cheques is not specific and Mike cannot prove that Sean did not do what was described on them.

Mike had done some investigations into Sean's criminal past, you might say far too late, and his lawyer told him that Sean wasn't the type of man to just take the money and run, he would stay in touch with his victims and would come up with countless excuses when he was pulling a scam, describing him as a sophisticated criminal, choosing victims from out-of-state, using his wife's eBay account, fake identities and fulfilling smaller transactions. Using anonymizing tools so it was harder to trace him through an email chain but there were people who did find him and knew where he lived. Had Mike really wanted to know, he could have found him. In fact, Scott and UKMike had breakfast just round the corner from his house while at Portland Retro Gaming Expo.

Sean's ability to build and maintain a lie over a period of time is well-known and was used on many people in this whole saga, but also on his wife, as he allegedly told her for two years that he had a job at Sprint and would leave the house every day as though going to work. Mike was in for a fight though if he was going to pursue his goal of a refund as there is also the legal issue of "clean hands."

> *Clean hands, sometimes called the clean hands doctrine or the dirty hands doctrine, is an equitable defense in which the defendant argues that the plaintiff is not entitled to obtain an equitable remedy because the plaintiff is acting unethically or has acted in bad faith with respect to the subject of the complaint, that is, with "unclean hands."*

What this basically means in layman's terms is that a scammer can't sue a scammer. Mike would have to prove that he was clean in his dealings with Sean, which will certainly not be easy, as he has been proven to have, at the very least, been economical with the truth. One need only dig a little into his company finances and any reasonable judge would laugh him out of court, if it even got that far.

Even though Sean did have his convictions expunged and legally does not have to declare them to a future employer for example, even though he pled guilty and went to prison for them, the video game community, and any other community which Sean and Mike seek to be a part of must surely apply the three strikes and you're out rule. Can they ever be welcomed back to the gaming community after everything that has happened?

There is also the other scenario to consider, a scenario which Scott warned potential backers about, and that was if Mike had managed to get through the gates of Kickstarter with a fake prototype and got funded.

Scott warned backers that they would never receive a console and he was right. John Lester and Pete Dorr of the All Gen Gamers podcast were almost right too when they said that it seemed as though some people had it in for Mike from the start. They certainly did, and Mike chose to ignore the warnings about what would happen if he refused to meet Scott's terms of acknowledging all contributors and returning the assets to the original company.

This console, in any of its iterations, was never going to come to market. Shortly after being funded, Mike would have found himself having to defend a legal case and go through the illegalities of his corporate fraud and asset stripping of GameGavel. Defending cases like that are time consuming and expensive but Mike had no personal funds left to do it, he would have had to use the crowd funding money, money that he needed to use to develop a prototype, bring a final product to market and ship it. It wasn't going to happen, even if he had gone to China to produce it. *"They would have eaten him alive."*

Steve Sawyer had been watching the story unfold from a distance and the endless stream of lies and fake consoles brought to mind a Winston Churchill quote:

> *The truth is incontrovertible. Malice may attack it, ignorance may deride it, but in the end, there it is.*

The other burning question that we should ask is, was this console even a good idea? Did it have a market at all? Its main target was collectors who wanted to own physical cartridge based copies of new games so they could put them on their shelf alongside their classic collection and play them for years to come. Most of these games are available via online stores like Steam, Xbox Live or the PlayStation Network and these online stores may be gone in the years to come, along with the games that you bought of course. These games often had patches to fix bugs so in the future you would need a platform to play the games and an infrastructure to find and install the patches. What the Retro VGS was going to do was supply these games on cartridge so that you would always have access to them and could still play them in 50 years.

While that sounds fine, what is also true is that any games that needed patches to fix them had already been be burned to cartridge and would remain permanently broken. Granted, after thorough testing under Steve Woita's watch, they would likely not be so broken that they didn't work or were not completable, but a bug could cause anything from crashes and lock ups under certain circumstances to graphical glitches and broken game saves, literally anything. Cartridges would also cost much more to purchase. A game that is released on Steam that costs around $10 would cost anything from $30 to $60 on the Coleco Chameleon, with most costing $30 to $50.

As we saw earlier, most new games are traded in after a two-week period once people have completed them, so your average game player is not going to pay that extra premium for a game that they will play, complete and trade in. The trade in value for a game at a store like GameStop would not be great either because the market for them to resell it to would be tiny as it would only work on the Coleco Chameleon, so here was a system aimed squarely at the collector market, the problem was, were any of its games going to be collectable?

What makes classis games collectible is the nostalgia that we have for playing them, we loved them as children and we have a yearning to recapture those emotions in adulthood, we want to go back and play some of those same games, the advantage being that most of them can be found very cheaply either in stores or online. The Coleco Chameleon games had no collectability, no nostalgia attached to them, so they weren't collectable. Mike knew this and attempted to make them collectable by offering to put the first few copies of a game into a gold case or a silver case or any combination of colors that he talked about, mimicking the gold case of the NES Legend Of Zelda or the Nintendo 64 Legend Of Zelda: Ocarina Of Time, but those games are collectable because they are Nintendo games, in particular Legend Of Zelda games, and they have nostalgia value. You cannot say the same about a gold cartridge for Sydney Hunter or a silver cartridge for Super Noah's Ark with serial number 1, it just isn't the same.

Steve Sawyer felt that Mike had lost touch with the gaming community that he claimed to love, saying that Mike didn't play games much anymore, he was trying to make money from it instead, and he had lost his way and had lost any concept of what the gaming community wanted. He was making the console that he wanted to make, not the console that gamers wanted to buy.

Mike knew that his new games weren't collectable and he had to try and increase the market for the Coleco Chameleon, so he did that by adding the ability for it to play old games, genuinely collectable games rather than artificially collectable games. This would be done with the use of after-market adaptors which would have cartridge slots for your chosen platform. If you wanted to play your gold Legend Of Zelda you would buy the Coleco Chameleon NES adaptor. If you wanted to play your gold Legend Of Zelda: Ocarina Of Time you would buy the Coleco Chameleon Nintendo 64 adaptor. The problem with this market is that these are an additional cost in each case so by the time you have bought the Coleco Chameleon and an adaptor, you could have bought the original system more cheaply and you could play those games with their original controller instead of the somewhat flimsy EMiO controller for the Coleco Chameleon or another third party controller that it supported. Alternatively, you could just buy a Retron 5 or a Retro Freak that already has multiple slots in it for the major retro systems, again much more cheaply than the Coleco Chameleon and its adaptors. Yes, these systems use software emulation which is not perfect, but does the average player care? These systems are aimed at the mass market and not the purist, the mass market doesn't care if the color is slightly off or if the sound at the end of level 3 isn't quite right. The kind of person that does care about those things is the kind of person who will buy the original system anyway. That kind of person is also likely to still have a tube TV to play them on in their game room rather than a flat screen TV in their lounge using HDMI. The mass market uses a hybrid system through HDMI in their lounge when they have guests. There really wasn't a big market for this system.

The mass market was also completely unaware of the Retro VGS and the Coleco Chameleon, it just got no traction. While Mike was starting new companies and moving assets between them, showing fake prototypes at the premier Toy show on the calendar in New York, the media didn't care and the story barely broke out beyond the gaming sites that covered it, and covered it badly. Lazy journalism was an accusation that Pat Contri levelled at websites that covered the story and lazy journalism is what we got. Nobody looked beyond the videos of Mike going through his spiel and footage of 3D rendered models that looked nice. Interviewers didn't push him on the issues of the lack of a working prototype, the escalating cost of a niche system or the premium price for games on cartridge, they said "Hi" wound Mike up and let him go, and Mike talked and Mike talked and Mike talked, dropping names, going through the range of console and cartridge colors available for the system and adding very little of substance regarding specs and hardware.

Few reached out to cover the story properly. Stop, Drop And Retro did several great videos on it, Scott was a guest on Good Old Gamers, Pat and Ian did their homework and showed it for what it was, but this whole saga could have been stopped much sooner if anybody had paid attention to those that knew, those that were involved or those that were examining photos of the prototypes and revealing what they actually were. It may even have been stopped before Mike completely lost the respect of the community and alienated himself from the community that he loved.

The information was there for anybody who wanted to find it, Mike had initiated the concept for the system and purchased the Jaguar molds for $6,000 allegedly with a personal loan to the company GAMEGAVEL LLC (Entity Number: 201029410278), he then moved the assets one month prior to the Indiegogo campaign to the company RETRO ENTERTAINMENT TECHNOLOGY, INC. (Entity Number: C3823713) and when he rebranded it as the Coleco Chameleon he moved them to a third company RETRO VIDEO GAME SYSTEMS, INC. (Entity Number:C3850998). This is all public information, but nobody cared. Scott made multiple posts laying out these details and giving the pertinent facts such as the company creation dates and entity numbers but nobody seemed to notice those posts but the next YouTube talking head making incorrect assumptions would get posted and discussion would follow.

The money that Mike made by selling newly pressed shells made with the molds did not repay his loan to GameGavel, it went straight to Retro magazine which had been bled dry and was running low on funds by Issue 4. Once the Kickstarter funds came in, they would not go solely to the console that people had backed, they would pay for the molds that he already had, they would pay Retro magazine for sponsored coverage and they would prop up GameGavel which was costing money rather than making it. Aside from the legal case that Mike would be presented with, the Kickstarter funds would begin to disappear before you even got a prototype, and if Sean was involved you would likely never get one of those either. Again, nobody cared outside of a dedicated few who were determined that Mike would not succeed in this venture. UKMike commented on the whole idea:

> *"This is part of the reason the whole thing gets a bit ludicrous.*
>
> *To those behind the console it is a great idea and they believe in it and believe it will happen and be a competing entity in today's market. They just want you to take the risk rather than going the more legitimate and traditional route of "doing an Atari" and having 3 guys start a company with their own money and run a business as a business should be run.*
>
> *They want the success and the profits but none of the risk but I guess they're not alone in that. I just choose not to support that notion.*
>
> *There's a great saying that fits perfectly. "Put your money where your mouth is."*
>
> *It's a good song too."*

Mike's final plea as his empire crumbled was:

> *"And please, don't let this mess carry over to the magazine. I have a great team of people working on it. We are pouring a lot of heart and soul and sweat equity into keeping the magazine going and it's only getting better."*

His definition of *"better"* is interesting as most readers had noticed, and commented on, the decline in quality, the decline in the paper stock it was printed on and its slipping schedule. Things were so bad that his team of writers left, meaning that Mike was left pretty much alone to fulfil the Kickstarter obligation that he had with his backers to finish the second year of releases. He had boldly made this claim though:

> *"And as a side note, Carl Williams IS NOT taking over RETRO Magazine nor has he ever talked with me about it. And I am not selling it or giving it to ANYONE!"*

We're about to find out how that worked out.

14: The Carrion Carry On

> *"I think gaming is a close-knit community. Add to that, gamers are very passionate people and I think it takes a passionate person like myself to run a website like GameGavel, as that gives confidence to its members. We are all in this thing together."*

Mike's empire was crumbling around him, the console idea was dead and he had sold the Jaguar molds to Albert, all he had left now was a dying auction site and a magazine that was rapidly declining in quality and sales, but before the dust from the console crash had even settled, the vultures were circling with some looking to pick off parts of his fallen empire.

Carl Williams had gone public with his intention to buy Retro Magazine and he assured people that it was not done out of malice or because of any grudge with Mike. He had covered Mike's story journalistically which had angered Mike who lashed out at him, but Carl saw Retro for what it was: *"For better or for worse, the magazine is viewed as the current leader for North American based retro publications."*

By this stage though, the writing team had mostly jumped ship, advertisers were thin on the ground, particularly at the current circulation numbers, and Mike was pretty much running a one-man band. He was also under pressure to finish the final two issues that he was obliged to deliver under his Kickstarter campaign and Carl knew this going in as he told people who questioned his motives:

> *"I plan on assessing the situation when I know more as far as exactly how many subscribers there are total. How many were Year Two backers and how many "after Kickstarter subscribers" that are owed two or more issues.*
>
> *I view these subscribers as valuable members of the family. I would not move forward on this if I had no intention of taking care of those subscribers. That would be wrong, it would be ignorant of their support and it would be plain stupid of anyone assuming this mess to ignore them. That is going to be a HUGE investment of money and time to make things right with them- it is something that is priority one for me.*
>
> *Telling those subscribers I am not responsible for their lack of receiving issues would be beyond reprehensible. That is not an option to me.*
>
> *This is not a merger of the magazines as in Mike with RETRO and me with Retro Gaming Magazine. This would be a hostile takeover and Mike would no*

longer be involved with the project in any way. He may receive a complimentary lifetime subscription though."

Some thought Carl's desire to take over the magazine was crazy and considered the property in some way toxic and forever tainted, maybe it was part of a personal vendetta after his public clash with Mike, but would the magazine ever be able to attract professional writers again after earning the reputation it now had? He was also advised against announcing his hostile takeover publicly, and some thought it was a publicity stunt, but Carl posted that he was contacting the shareholders in GameGavel/Retro and attempting to attain enough shares to take control of the company, the magazine and more importantly the use of the name "Retro" for an American magazine publication. Perhaps that was the real value here. Mark Kaminski had investigated using the name "Retro" for a series of books, which Mike had tried to block, but it appeared that the property he had registered applied only to a magazine publication and not a book, so he was powerless to stop Mark if he had wanted to pursue his idea.

If Carl was attempting a hostile takeover, Mike could take steps to block it and continue to sit on the name just to prevent anybody else using it. Aside from some unsold inventory in a storage container, that's really all there was, a name. There was no company to speak of and no money in the bank but if Carl thought that Mike would give up easily, he was mistaken. Mike had every intention of reviving the magazine and fulfilling his year two Kickstarter obligations. This could have been a blessing in disguise for Carl because if he did take over the magazine and obtain the unsold inventory, he would also inherit the obligations to supply people with the issues they were owed, not only Issues 11 and 12 which were still not complete, but also the earlier issues that they hadn't received. Nobody knows for sure how many people were owed issues, but it was a lot. Some subscribers for both Year 1 and Year 2 had still not received a single magazine at this point.

There is also the question of just how viable a print magazine is in this day and age of digital distribution and eBook readers, certainly in its current guise the magazine could not sustain itself and was forced to crowd fund each year. Yes, Mike had allegedly siphoned the Kickstarter funds away into his other businesses, mismanaged his empire and paid for his pinball machine, but even some major publishers are struggling with print magazines, particularly in such a niche area as retro video games. As Mike had identified in his quote above, they are a very passionate community, but they are also a relatively small community and some of them are notoriously thrifty.

Carl claimed to have identified and been *"in talks with shareholders, other than Mike, that represented about 60% percent"* of Retro, and discovered that the magazine was *"apparently in debt, for many reasons that I was never really made clear of."* As he continued his pursuit of shares the talks proved fruitless as the shareholders failed to meet a deadline to provide paperwork and at the end of March, Carl ended those discussions. While this was going on, Mike was attempting some damage control and trying to rebuild confidence in his brand:

"Hello Everyone!

We are working very hard to try and improve our customer service. In doing so, we have seen most problems arise from missing subscriber issues. With each mailing a small % go undelivered and that has happened with both printers we've used, who also do the subscriber mailings. So we have setup a new email address dedicated to tracking and addressing this problem: missingissue@ readretro.com.

We will monitor this email address daily and handle missing issue requests within 24 hours if the request comes in during the week. We can then mail you out a replacement issue. Please help us by providing your current address in your "missing issue" email and make sure we have updated addresses if and when you move in the middle of your subscription. Thanks to all of you for your patience as we continue to grow and publish more RETRO Videogame Magazines.

Now for the fun stuff . . . .

We are on time to deliver issue #11 to subscribers and retail in early April. This issue will be celebrating 30 years of Legend of Zelda among other great retro gaming topics. We are also putting the finishing touches on our first ever 200-page RETRO Replay: Best of Years 1 & 2.

We are limiting the print run of these and they will only be available for pre-order for a limited time. Current and past subscribers will get a discount on this collectible issue. We will make sure you all know when it goes up for pre-order so you can make sure you get one for your collection. They will also be shipping in the month of April and feature a thicker stock cover with new artwork from Rob Duenas who created the awesome cover artwork for our Premier Issue (Mighty No.9), Issue #2 (River City Ransom) and Issue #10 (Star Wars).

We are also very excited to be participating in a Barnes & Noble stores videogaming endcap promotion in April. Look for RETRO #11 on these special gaming dedicated endcaps in most Barnes & Noble stores next month."

Mike was also trying to generate some revenue in order to take these remaining issues to print and get them delivered, and in order to do that he was putting out a compendium featuring the best bits of Retro from the previous issues. This wouldn't contain any new content and would be made up of material that he already had and that was already edited and had been laid out, it was nothing more than a money spinner, if it sold well, and required some simple copy and pasting but where he had been quoting healthy circulation numbers when it suited, he only had a short print run done on the compendium, but that made it more collectable, right?

Every time Mike posted publicly to try and peddle his wares and save his empire he was met with derision and further difficult questions, or difficult answers, more to the point, and finally he had had enough:

"And this is why I won't be answering any more questions. Just for the record."

To further rub salt into the wound, he was now the topic of some games written by UKMike; New York Toy Fair: The Text Adventure and New York Toy Fair: The Web Game. These were ported to iOS and Android by Adrian Killens of Gimpy Software and made available for free on both apps stores, they were simple adventure style games where you played the part of Mike and you made your way around the New York Toy Fair and collected the various parts required to build a fake prototype console to make it on to Kickstarter. The game declared itself to be bug free and outlined that your efforts would be thwarted by Mr. Lee, Mr. GoGo and Mr. Press who would try to steal the parts from you. Those parts were the Jaguar Shell, the SD2SNES Flash card, the SNES Controllers, the SNES Jr Motherboard, the Nintendo AV Lead and the Electrical Tape. The game began with the preface:

> *Your reputation is at stake and is worth salvaging and you make your way around the various locations in the Toy Fair, including locating your own booth, all the while dreaming of Lawyers and Showers and Goldeneye rooms cos, cartridges.*

Some of the location descriptions in the game are:

> *"YOU ARE STANDING ON THE STREET OUTSIDE THE TOY FAIR.*
> *YOU STEP AWAY FROM THE KERB BEFORE YOU END UP UNDER A BUS.*
> *THERE ISN'T MUCH ROOM UNDER THOSE THINGS THESE DAYS.*
> *ANYWAY. THOSE COMPONENTS WON'T BUILD THEMSELVES!*
> *YOU'D BETTER GO IN AND CHASE YOUR DREAM."*
>
> *"THIS PART OF THE EXPO HALL IS QUITE QUIET AS PEOPLE SEEM TO BE LOOKING AT RETRO BOOKS.*
> *NERDS.*
> *MAYBE ONE DAY SOMEBODY WILL WRITE A BOOK ABOUT YOU."*
>
> *"THERE IS AN SD2SNES FLASH CARD ON A TABLE. HUZZAH!*
> *YOU PICK IT UP AND PUT IT IN YOUR FANNY PACK.*
> *YOU REMEMBER SEEING ONE OF THOSE BEFORE."*
>
> *"YOU MAKE YOUR WAY OUT OF THE NEW YORK TOY FAIR AND OUT ONTO THE STREET WITH YOUR ARMS FULL OF COMPONENTS.*
> *YOU HEAD FOR YOUR HOTEL ROOM WHERE YOU CAN GET TO WORK ON BUILDING YOUR FAKE PROTOTYPE AND GET ON TO KICKSTARTER.*
> *KONAMI ARE GOING TO BE ALL OVER THIS WHEN YOU E-MAIL THEM AGAIN."*

Mike was confident that he was going to be able to salvage things and he reserved a booth at Portland Retro Gaming Expo for later that year as he came up with another way to bring in some much-needed revenue. He would use the shopreadretro site to act as a reseller for other people's consoles and peripherals rather than his own, including an NES Bluetooth Controller, Pac-Man figurines and the Retro-BIT Super RetroTRIO 3 in 1 system. Retro-Bit had been advertisers in Retro Magazine, so there was something of a working relationship already, and these weren't exclusive items as they would also be available elsewhere, but Mike was going to make commission on any that were sold through his site and he would use that commission to help fund the remaining issues of the magazine. At least these products did actually exist though, and if you ordered them through Mike you would actually receive a real console. People weren't buying it though, literally, Mike had burned too any bridges for this to be seen as making amends or even to be seen as sufficient to *"right a sinking ship."*

Mike then used a previous working relationship and his publishing credentials to align himself with a product aimed at owners of the recently released NES Classic Edition, also known as the Nintendo Classic Mini or simply the Nintendo Mini. The NES Classic is an official Nintendo product that aesthetically was a miniature version of the original NES console and was released in November 2016 before becoming a huge hit. It came with 30 built-in games that were stored on a 512MB internal flash memory chip, had HDMI output and two controller ports on the front. The supplied controllers came with the Wii Nun-chuk connector so they could be connected to a Wii Remote for use with the Virtual Console games on the Wii and Wii-U, and similarly the Wii Classic Controller could also be used on the Nintendo Classic. The list of 30 games for the US version included: Balloon Fight, Bubble Bobble, Castlevania, Castlevania II: Simon's Quest, Donkey Kong, Donkey Kong Jr., Double Dragon II: The Revenge, Dr. Mario, Excitebike, Final Fantasy, Galaga, Ghosts 'n Goblins, Gradius, Ice Climber, Kid Icarus, Kirby's Adventure, Mario Bros., Mega Man 2, Metroid, Ninja Gaiden, Pac-Man, Punch-Out!!, Star Tropics, Super Contra, Super Mario Bros., Super Mario Bros. 2, Super Mario Bros. 3, Tecmo Bowl, The Legend of Zelda and Zelda II: The Adventure of Link.

The system was soon hacked, and people found ways to add many more games to the list of 30 included, as well as emulating other consoles such as the Nintendo 64 and Sega 32X, and companies soon began selling third party controllers intended to be used with it, one of those third parties was a company called EMiO.

EMiO were formerly known as Interworks Unlimited and had previously produced a Pro Controller for the Wii and the Wii-U which had some compatibility issues, in that it didn't work with Wii-U Pro Controller games and would randomly disconnect from the system. Mike had been working with them as a potential supplier for the Retro VGS console controllers and he had covered their Wii controller in Retro Magazine. They went through a name change to EMiO and began selling a controller for the NES Classic called the Edge Gamepad that boasted a nine-foot cable and turbo buttons which they claimed worked with the unit. In fact, it didn't. There was a difference in the wiring for the connectors between the Wii and the NES Classic but EMiO had presumably made the assumption that it was the same and simply rebadged their controller as compatible. Once they were on the market and people began returning them as not functioning they investigated and realized their mistake before issuing the following email:

> *"Dear Customers who bought The Edge Joystick (batch #:110116WSJ) and The Edge Gamepad (batch:110116WSP).*
>
> *Thank you for contacting us, we know your time is valuable, and we wanted to give you a solution for connecting your controller with the NES Classic Console.*

The Edge Joystick and The Edge Gamepad are compatible with Wii U and NES Classic Edition game consoles. It was brought to our attention that a few batches shipped, failed to include the NES Classic Console adapter in the box. To make it right with you, we are offering a FREE NES Classic Edition Adapter + a FREE NES Classic Edition Extension Cable + a FREE SURPRISE BONUS GIFT (a $30 Value). This offer only applies to qualifying customers.

To receive your FREE NES Gift Pack:

1. *Do not return item to the store.*
2. *Instead Send an email to Support@PoweredByEmio.com*
   Include title: "FREE NES GIFT PACK", Name, address, and send proof of purchase receipt.
3. *Wait to receive your product in the mail.*
4. *If you wish and are satisfied with our service. Please provide 5 Star rating or edit a negative listing with your updated experience. 5 Star ratings mean a lot to us.*
5. *Thank you!"*

As the unit wasn't faulty, just not compatible because of the wiring change, they made an adaptor that would switch the wiring and make the controllers work. To cover their mistake they claimed that the problems customers had experienced were caused by a batch of controllers that were shipped without that adaptor, so they needed to send a proof of purchase and claim their "missing" adaptor. It was more likely that they hadn't tested it and had made the incorrect assumption that it would work. If that wasn't a big enough headache for them, included in the box with each controller was a cheat guide for the 30 games included on the NES Classic and that cheat guide contained numerous errors. The guide was produced by none other than Mike Kennedy under the guise of Retro Magazine and it contained an advert for shopreadretro.com. Mike was paid $8,500 for producing the booklet but as his staff had all but gone, he had to pay $5,500 to get it laid out, written and printed. Some of the errors contained in it were:

- The cover of the guide showed a picture of a Yellow Devil from the Mega Man series who did not appear in the included Mega Man 2 game.
- The inside page mentions that the original NES cartridges had 70 pins when in fact they had 72.
- The cheat code for the game Super Contra was listed as the Konami Code (UP, UP, DOWN, DOWN, LEFT, RIGHT, LEFT, RIGHT, B, A, START) when it has its own code of RIGHT, LEFT, DOWN, UP, A, B, START.
- The Super Contra code is said to give you 30 lives, in fact it gives you 10. (It is 30 in the original Contra, a different game).
- The artwork used for Tecmo Bowl is actually that of Tecmo Super Bowl.
- Balloon Fight has a tip to enable auto fire on your Edge controller and tells you to then hold the A button to float without having to keep tapping it. This completely ignores the fact that Balloon Fight has a built-in turbo function on the B button.

Mike had previously asked that any fall out from his fake consoles did not spill over to the magazine, but as Steve Sawyer pointed out, he was doing a pretty good job of that himself.

> *"I think what's really sad is that it's to the point where it affected more than just the Coleco Chameleon's chances of success or survival. It's to the point now where I think people are just going to kind of go, "Is everything that you touched kind of tinged with a little bit of snake oil," because it leaves a bad impression in your mouth.*
>
> *I'm trying to be gentle about it, but yeah, I mean if you're shit at one business, then you have to suspect that maybe you're shit at all your businesses."*

Brian Barnhart had earlier commented that the molds needed to be destroyed in Mount Sauron and Scott had added that the only thing they could now contain is evil spirts, but they were by now in Albert's safe hands, yet it did seem that Mike did indeed have the reverse Midas touch, as everything he touched was turning into a disaster. It was time for one last effort to save the magazine and, now afraid that his reputation would follow him to either Indiegogo or Kickstarter, he turned to another crowd funding platform, Patreon, in December of 2016.

Patreon is used mainly as a monthly funding option for things like blogs, podcasts and YouTube channels that release content on a regular basis but Mike had a strange method of funding going on. He had set a target of $9,500 per magazine as he claimed that was his cost to take an edition of the magazine from conception to delivery. This is besides the fact that he had earlier claimed to have legitimately run out of funds on the magazine when he had received, over the two years, $126,591 to produce 12 magazines, $75,759 from year one and $50,832 from year two. If his estimate of $9,500 per magazine were correct, he should have had $12,591 left over. Ignoring that fact, rather than a monthly target, this was just an ongoing target, though he did set a deadline of February to meet the target by. Once he had been backed to the tune of $9,500 he would release an issue, but when January rolled around and he was still only sitting on around $770 from 147 patrons, he halved the target amount and pushed back the deadline to March 29th.

What this funding model did not allow for is that patrons could pledge their money which would mean that Mike would get to work on a magazine and incur his own costs but then backers could drop out and leave him high and dry. The Patreon campaign was also non-committal about what you were receiving. It could have been a pamphlet made up of 5 pages of A4 paper stapled together and there was nothing a backer could do about it. It just didn't make sense. This was unlikely to happen though, as Scott sarcastically observed:

> *"For that to happen you would need to have angered and offended an entire community to the point that they would register and pledge-withdraw in sufficient numbe...... oh! I get that now!"*

Mike still owed backers the final Year 2 issue, Issue 12, but as he was bereft of funds and staff he would release an issue that contained just interviews, he needed no creative writing, no real editing and could just include material that he already had on tap. He was also struggling to get the layout done as Issue 8 had been laid out by Daniel Kayser and a contractor called Monique Convertito, and from Issue 9 onwards Monique had done all of the layouts, but now she was owed so much money by Mike, $8,500, that she wouldn't do any more work for him until she got paid.

Mike made a final appeal for support with another wall of words in a desperate attempt to get the Patreon funding moving:

> *"I also wanted to apologize to you all for the delays that have plagued this second year campaign. It was fraught with lots of challenges, the greatest of which was the under-funding of the campaign followed closely with my supreme idiocy with a derailed side project.*
>
> *Because of some changes inside the RETRO team early on in this campaign, the cost to produce the magazine increased after the campaign completed. And that led to the last two issues of RETRO being self-funded by myself to finish out the obligations set in motion from this campaign. So the delays were caused mostly by me waiting for the personal funds required to finish out the issues and the campaign.*
>
> *In the end, all six magazines were produced and I hope you enjoyed them all despite the inconsistent releases.*
>
> *I do have a couple dozen shirts and posters that still need to be sent out and if you backed at those levels, and are still waiting you will get what you paid for. It is just that I focused all my attention on making sure the magazines all were published first and foremost. The other awards took a backseat to finishing out the magazine.*
>
> *Moving forward, I hope you decide to continue reading RETRO Magazine and I have made an effort to change how our future subscriptions are handled so it will eliminate any risk for our readers. I realize that many of you lost faith in the magazine due to the delays. So, to remedy that risk I have made the switch to Patreon for all future issue sales. The benefit to you is that you can sign up there and only pay for one issue at a time, and only after it is complete and ready to mail. This will eliminate the risk associated with paying for an entire run of issues up front. And Patreon is the perfect mechanism for this model.*
>
> *I have seen how successful Nintendo Force [LINK REMOVED] has become using Patreon and Lucas (the Head Honcho at NF) has been a great help in explaining to me the benefits of this service for us indie magazine publishers. So, if you have enjoyed RETRO over the past couple years, please consider CLICKING TO OUR PATREON PAGE [LINK REMOVED] and continuing on the journey with us to keep print video game magazines a thing of the future. My team and I really enjoy working on RETRO and are depending on our readers to keep us going. If we can reach our goal on Patreon, then we will be able to produce RETRO on schedule, bi-monthly. All of you can help us get to that goal.*
>
> *Now for the fun stuff! As indicated RETRO #12 is mailing on Monday and it's filled with what I hope you will find to be very interesting interviews with*

a smattering of great gaming pioneers. It was so exciting to work with our interviewees and find out more about their life in the industry. We all have them to thank for the great memories we all share! This issue of RETRO is our shortest print run to date, with only 2,500 printed issues. And, then we dice it up with three randomly distributed separate cover variations featuring the Atari 2600, Intellivision and ColecoVision. If you don't get the cover you want, we will have a decent supply of them for sale on ShopReadRetro.com [LINK REMOVED] beginning mid February. And, if you haven't aleady, you can download the digital version of RETRO #12 using discount code, "retropioneers" when you CHECKOUT HERE [LINK REMOVED]. And if you want to get any of the other digital back issues from our first twelve issues you can use code "retrodigital" when you checkout on ShopReadRetro.com

You can download up to three issues at a time. It was because of all of you, these twelve issues were made.

I want to personally thank you all for your support with this campaign and hopefully your continued support moving forward with our third year of RETRO Video Game Magazine over on Patreon [LINK REMOVED]

Thank you, thank you, thank you!
Mike Kennedy"

As Mike mentions, he had spoken to Lucas about the Nintendo Force business model for Patreon and had applied his own business model of copying an idea, but without success, as the one-man band bit had by now become quite transparent, there was no "we" or "team" it was just Mike that remained, rearranging non-existent armies on a map of Berlin trying to turn the war around. By now though, his appeals were falling largely on deaf ears as he had alienated so many people, particularly those over at AtariAge, as Brian Barnhart noted:

Brian: Well you know I would imagine that AtariAge would have been where he would be getting most of his sales.

Scott: Yes, and somebody even said something to the effect of (after he had sort of told AtariAge to go to hell) "Yeah, bunch of 40 and 50 somethings with lots of disposable income. I don't need you."

He was also angering a few people with his email blasts as they had previously unsubscribed from them, sometimes as many as six times, but they still kept receiving them, prompting the meme *"Remember when, unsubscribe again"* a play on words based on his slogan for the Retro VGS *"Remember when. Play Again."* There was still a bit of the old Mike in there somewhere though as he reached out to UKMike on hearing about the sudden death of his brother Neil.

"Hey Mike,

If what I read is true you and your family are in both Tricia's and my prayers.
Mike"

Human side apart, it did finally seem to be dawning on him that his name and his businesses were toxic in the community and that he was not going to be able to salvage his reputation and turn things around. As he cancelled his booth at the Portland Retro Gaming Expo for that October, a disappointment to Scott and UKMike who had hoped to have a booth opposite him, he planned his exit strategy while, conversely, River West Brands, and in particular the Coleco brand, would look to build their presence.

Scott had commented on Mike's claim that he was the only one who lost anything in the whole debacle but Coleco had certainly lost some of their reputation as well, in particular Chris Cardillo who was managing the Coleco brand at the time. Scott had always found him to be *"honest and eager to do the right thing from understanding what he had put his name on right through taking transparent and meaningful action."*

Having done that in handling the Chameleon debacle, what Chris was about to do next was exactly the opposite and took a few people by surprise, he lodged a complaint with Facebook about a ColecoVision fan page. The owner of the page had received notification that there were a number of complaints concerning images of homebrew ColecoVision games that he had posted. He had tried to resolve the issue with Chris but had failed, so on May 19th he posted the complaint publicly.

> *Hi. My name is Robb and I run the ColecoVision Fan Facebook page. We are a page of over 25,000 ColecoVision fans helping promote and support the homebrew community and even Coleco themselves. Recently I received a number of Trademark Infringement DMCA take-down notifications from Facebook by Coleco over several photos & videos of ColecoVision homebrew games that we published on our page. We were not using the ColecoVision logos in any way other than showcase photos or videos of homebrew published games and fan-made ColecoVision projects on our page.*
>
> *I choose to run the ColecoVision Fan page for my own personal enjoyment and because I love the homebrew community.*
>
> *There is no revenue generated from the page, no ulterior motive of any kind, and in fact I volunteer to spend my own money to help the community because I *enjoy* doing so. My only agenda is to help gain exposure for the homebrewers who have spent a lot of their own personal time creating games for the fans. Due to these trademark claims, I have had to disable our page in fear of Coleco unfairly flagging more of our images at the risk of having our Facebook account permanently disabled. Coleco should not be allowed to strong-arm their fans and the homebrew community like this. [...]*
>
> *None of the products showcased in the photos were created by ColecoVision Fan and we were simply posting these photos to help spread the word to the community about these homebrew projects. Coleco claiming trademark infringement on these photos would be akin to Nintendo or Sega coming along and flagging photos found on the many fan pages, Facebook pages, websites, videos, or podcasts of their games. Think about how this would impact the fan community if you were no longer able to post a picture or video of anything that said Nintendo, Sega, Atari, etc, on it. Also keep in mind, I own the respective*

rights of the photos and videos that were removed or have the permission from the rights holder of those photos to post them.

Coleco owns no copyright on the images or videos themselves, they only appear to be claiming trademark infringement because their logo was on an item featured in a photo or video.

So why is this shady?

When we emailed Coleco about the images being marked as trademark infringement, this is how they responded:

> *I am sorry that you are having concerns with your site. It is exciting that you are working on developing new video games. Please let me know if you would like to submit products to have them officially licensed by Coleco and ColecoVision. I am sure that we can work something out that is fair. We are mostly concerned with the image of certain games being appropriate for the children who will be playing them. Secondly, it is important that all IPs (if any) have been properly cleared by the rights holder.*
>
> *It would be nice to look at what you have developed.*

What does this even mean? ColecoVision Fan is not developing any games for the ColecoVision system. Nor are we interested in licensing anything from Coleco. If there are any IP rights issues that should be taken up with the publishers themselves, not a fan site. And if third party IP is involved, that is beyond Coleco's purview. Coleco has no rights to dictate what hardware and software can be released for the defunct ColecoVision console. Nor should they have any expectation regarding editorial control, such as what they feel is suitable for children.

Publicly, Coleco, or Chris Cardillo at least, were trying to protect the family friendly image of the brand and protect the children potentially playing these titles by removing them from the ColecoVision Fan page, aside from the fact that the people buying homebrew ColecoVision games were the 40 to 50 year olds with disposable income that Mike had alienated, without the homebrew fan community, his brand would have remained dead in the water. Ironically the first ColecoVision homebrew game was released in 1996 by Kevin Horton and was a Tetris clone called Kevtris.

For the past 30 years the Coleco name had lived on only via the homebrew community and the fans that supported it, so why would Chris go after a fan page? There were rumors that Coleco were looking to run a Coleco Expo and launch products such as a revival of their mini arcade systems or even their own console, so if they wanted to protect the family friendly image of the brand, why not go after the people that were producing the adult titles in the first place instead of a fan page that was building a community around their brand, and had been doing so for some time, certainly before Chris Cardillo arrived on the scene? You would expect that they would want to work with the fan sites, the YouTube channels and the blogs that covered the brand, the games and the homebrew scene, but that is not what they were doing. What they were doing was alienating their audience in the same way that Mike had done.

Robb made a final appeal at the end of his post:

> *"If you like the official Coleco page on Facebook or other social media, unlike their page. Do not support their products like their announced Rainbow Brite game or the Expo. Instead, follow and support homebrewers such as: Opcode Games, CollectorVision, AtariAge, those are the organizations who have kept ColecoVision alive all these years. Join and support fansites like ColecoVisions Podcast, ColecoVision North, etc. Join Facebook groups like ColecoVision Lunatics and be active in discussions.*
>
> *Please stand with us and let Coleco know that you will not tolerate their shady practices and strong-arming the members of the community who have helped build it. Thank you for your time."*

Chris responded on May 19th to say that:

> *"The genesis of our complaints are the promotion of pornographic related games by an individual attempting to assert some type of authority over the Coleco Brand. Additionally, the use of other third party rights to games bearing our name. As you can imagine this may cause some concern for folks unrelated to either side.*
>
> *This individual had been warned on a number of occasions that these actions were improper.*
>
> *Over the years Coleco has embraced the home brewer, and more specifically in a number of interviews invited home brewers to submit their content in order to receive an official license to use the name. In some cases no actual dollars were requested.*
>
> *This is unheard of in the industry and something that we do in order. We wish to continue this approach.*
>
> *Additionally, Coleco typically offers game development projects first to members of communities such as AtariAge as was the case with Rainbow Brite.*
>
> *Although this individual wishes to attempt to align this battle between HIM + the Homebrew Community vs Coleco*
>
> *This is NOT an accurate depiction of what is going on here. The accurate equation is Coleco Vs. A man who promotes pornographic materials on a site that he uses for profit."*

Outwardly it appeared that they were more interested in profiting from licensing the Coleco name and the ColecoVision brand name on these homebrew games. Essentially that is what the business model of River West Brands was, to buy old licenses and revive them for profit by having officially licensed products, but that was only a valid business model if the brand held any credibility, which currently the Coleco brand did not. They had not made a product for years and they had just come through the Coleco Chameleon fiasco so you would expect that they would be looking to rebuild the trust of the fan community rather than destroy it.

What the claims were actually about was the fact that these homebrew games used the ColecoVision logo on their covers and Coleco Holdings LLC wanted to license the use of it, control the use of it and prohibit the use of it on unlicensed games. While publicly Chris was saying that it only affected 2 games with adult content, in fact they had complained about 63 games in total, most of which were not adult in nature but did carry the ColecoVision logo. This is what they were complaining about and Robb was forced to take down his fan page for fear of Facebook removing it completely with so many complaints about it. Coleco Holdings LLC were also likely concerned that some of the games used unlicensed properties such as a remake of the 1983 Namco arcade game Mappy and other licensed arcade characters and games. If Coleco were going to be bringing back their mini arcades, they would need to approach those same license holders, particularly for the active Frogger and Donkey Kong licenses, which they couldn't really do if their logo was splashed all over these games.

> *"[...] those "adult" games that you are questioning ARE STILL FOR SALE RIGHT NOW on the CollectorVision website The fact that you are going after ME about these games and suggesting you want to control the content we post, that is what I will NOT tolerate. [...]*
>
> *Please don't try to create a sub-story around this fact: Coleco removed images from our page for Trademark Infringement. Coleco did NOT remove images from our page due to "adult content." That was not the reason you gave Facebook. Once again, you removed them due to a violation of "Trademark Rights."*

What they actually filed with Facebook was a DMCA (Digital Millennium Copyright Act) complaint against the use of this logo because they felt it infringed upon their trademark. However, this was a case of the pot calling the kettle black because they were doing exactly the same thing. They were promoting their upcoming Coleco Expo on August 5th and 6th at the New Jersey Convention and Exposition Center in Edison New Jersey, but their promotional material featured some well-known video game characters, including the frog from Frogger, a Konami property, and the gorilla from Donkey Kong, obviously a Nintendo property. As soon as this was pointed out to them, they changed their website banner to remove it and replace it with the ColecoVision logo, but the artwork in question still existed on other parts of their website that they had clearly missed.

Technically they were allowed to use those images as there is such a thing as "fair use." For example, if you were writing a book about every Nintendo NES game, as Pat Contri had done, you could include Nintendo artwork and screenshots from the games that you were covering. That is fair use, and Coleco Holdings LLC were doing the same thing on their banner, just as the ColecoVision Fan page was doing by showing the box art from the games they were covering. They didn't produce the games and they didn't claim that they were licensed by Coleco, they just covered them journalistically, again, this is fair use, yet Chris would not retract the complaints. What he actually did was set up a rival fan page called ColecoVision Nation instead and edited the ColecoVision Wikipedia page to make it look as though the company had never gone away and had been in existence all along and that the Coleco name of today was the same company from over 30 years prior. It really did look like the Mike Kennedy reverse Midas touch was in full effect again as people began digging into the details of the trademark that Coleco Holdings LLC actually owned and how they had gone about obtaining it.

What River West Brands were trying to protect was Coleco and ColecoVision under the company Coleco Holdings LLC which in turn was owned by River West Brands. They had to start the Coleco Holdings LLC company so that it looked like they were an actual business, but an actual business must *do* actual business in order to be seen as active, so what had they actually done that qualified as business under that name?

They had never actually produced anything themselves, they didn't make any products and had no manufacturing facilities, they just licensed the use of the name to those that did. In 2006 they licensed 20 games from Sega and they were included on a handheld console called the Coleco Sonic. This was a rebranded version of a unit that had previously been produced by AtGames and which was also released in Canada and the UK as the PlayPal, and in Europe as the Pocket Gear, and the games could be played either on the built-in screen or on a connected TV. They didn't license some of the bigger titles, perhaps understandably as either Sega wouldn't license the main Sonic games or they would have been cost prohibitive, but Sonic did appear in some of the included games which were; on the Game Gear: Columns, Ecco II: The Tides of Time, Sonic Drift 2, Sonic Triple Trouble and Super Columns, and on the Master System were; Alex Kidd in High-Tech World, Alex Kidd in Miracle World, Altered Beast, Assault City, Astro Warrior, Aztec Adventure, Bomber Raid, Fantasy Zone, Fantasy Zone: The Maze, Global Defense, Kung Fu Kid, The Ninja, Penguin Land, Quartet and Snail Maze. If they licensed this unit in 2006, they had proved that they were a business doing actual business and they could keep the trademark alive, but that was only Coleco, not ColecoVision.

As this is public information it is possible to search the history of the trademarks and they had first applied for ColecoVision in December 2003, and then every 6 months an extension was applied for to give them chance to show their SOU (Statement Of Use) before losing the chance to register it after 24 months. On December 31, 2005, Ben Heck cropped up in the story again when he posted pictures of one of his projects, a one off unit that he built for a private individual which was a handheld version of the original ColecoVision console, complete with keypad, joystick and ColecoVision logo. Ben has made many of these handheld versions of consoles before, so this was nothing out of the ordinary, he wasn't talking it to market, he had simply produced a one off unit.

Sometime during the Summer of 2008, he was contacted by Mark Thomann under the guise of either River West Brands or Coleco Holdings LLC (he can't recall which as he no longer has the emails) and Mark had seen Ben's pictures of the unit and told him that they owned the trademark for ColecoVision so he would need to license it. They were being reasonable and would give him the license for the fee of $1, which Ben thought very odd as he had made handheld versions of consoles by much larger and more active companies like Microsoft, Sega and Sony and none of them had ever contacted him about a license. Thinking it odd but wanting them off his back he signed the license form but doesn't remember sending them the $1 fee and he thought nothing further of it, even when they asked him to supply the artwork that he had used as they didn't have any.

Ben had created his own vector version of the original logo from scratch as he hadn't been able to find one either, so he didn't find it that unusual that they didn't have one. He had formerly been a graphic artist and was used to being approached by companies who needed artwork creating, sometimes based on what they had on their business cards. He found his original source images and the Illustrator files he had used, dated March 16, 2008, and sent them off to Mark.

Following the "transaction" there was a new Statement Of Use application filed to say that the trademark ColecoVision was now being used and had been first used on December 15, 2005, just 2 weeks before Ben had posted his image. The trademark office knew nothing about Ben or his work and just saw a photo of a console bearing the name ColecoVision posted on December 31, 2005, and granted the trademark based on that unethical, deceitful transaction. As Scott noted;

> *"I think it goes further than that even, his portable as I recall, was a cut down modified ColecoVision. Let's say I take one of my cars and cut the top off and install a convertible top, change the wheels, and put on a wide body kit. I do not need to go back to Subaru, Ferrari, Chevy, or Lotus and get permission for my car to exist or wear the company badge. The car is customized but still is what it is."*

Without Ben's handheld console the 24-month period would have expired and Coleco Holdings LLC would not have been able to register the trademark for their own use, but this was not the only dubious trademark that they had registered. They registered several non-Coleco arcade games including Bump 'n' Jump, Jungle Hunt, Omega Race and Zaxxon and they had also attempted to register Burgertime but their attempt was declined by the USPTO. Bump 'n' Jump and Burgertime are both owned by the Japanese company G-Mode and the USPTO found the live registration for Burgertime but did not find one for Bump 'n' Jump. This is because in Japan the game Bump 'n' Jump is known as Burnin' Rubber and the USPTO did not know that. As evidence for their claim to Bump 'n' Jump Coleco Holdings LLC submitted the box art for the original ColecoVision game from 1984, fooling the USPTO into thinking that Coleco Holdings LLC were the same company as Coleco, a fraud that can carry a heavy fine and a possible prison sentence.

The reason that they registered these games is because they had hoped to use them on their ColecoVision Flashback in 2014 which came bundled with sixty built-in games. Those sixty games were: Alphabet Zoo, Aquattack, Artillery Duel, BlackJack/Poker, Blockade Runner, Brain Strainers, Bump 'n' Jump, Choplifter!, Cosmic Avenger, Dragonfire, Evolution, Fathom, Flipper Slipper, Fortune Builder, Frantic Freddy, Frenzy, Gateway to Apshai, Gust Buster, Jumpman Junior, Jungle Hunt, Miner 2049er,

Montezuma's Revenge, Moonsweeper, Motocross Racer, Mountain King, Nova Blast, Oil's Well, Omega Race, Pepper II, Quest for Quintana Roo, Rolloverture, Sammy Lightfoot, Sir Lancelot, Slurpy, Space Fury, Space Panic, Squish 'Em Featuring Sam, Super Cross Force, Telly Turtle, The Dam Buster, The Heist, Threshold, Tomarc the Barbarian, Tournament Tennis, Venture, War Room, Wing War and Zaxxon.

Notably absent was arguably the ColecoVision's best game, Donkey Kong, no doubt due to licensing issues, and also missing was of course another great game on the original ColecoVision system, Burgertime, which they had attempted to trademark and had failed. Based on River West / Coleco Holdings initial application using Ben Heck's one-off handheld, the homebrew community had two choices:

- Produce homebrew games and use the ColecoVision logo.
- Produce homebrew games and use an alternate logo or phrase.

If they had used the ColecoVision logo would Coleco Holdings LLC have taken it all the way to court, knowing that their fraudulent application would be revealed? As mentioned, a crime that carries a heavy fine and a possible prison sentence, or would they have conceded defeat and left the homebrewers alone. Most homebrew producers did not want the headache of a legal battle, even one they would likely win, they did this as a hobby not as a profession after all, and they could move ahead without using the logo and describe their games the way that Activision and Imagic had done when they produced games for the Atari VCS console, with words to the effect of "Compatible with the Atari VCS" or "For use with the Atari VCS" and there was nothing that Chris Cardillo or Coleco Holdings LLC could do about it. That battle had already been fought and won in the courts in 1979.

When the Atari VCS ruled the gaming world, the developers who worked at Atari were not allowed to have their names included on their games, an Atari game was an Atari game, no matter who had created it. By this time Nolan Bushnell had sold the company to Warner and had been replaced by Ray Kassar who had no appreciation for the work that the programmers were doing. He famously sent out a memo which broke down their sales figures by game to show the developers what type of games were the big sellers but it had the knock on effect of showing which developers were bringing the most money into Atari. David Crane's games had earned the company $20 million yet he was working anonymously for a fraction of that.

The programmers approached Atari management with a contract proposal that would give them design credits and royalties based on sales but this offer was rejected by management who told them that they could easily be replaced. Crane spoke with his fellow designers and what became known as *"The Gang Of Four"* (David Crane, Larry Kaplan, Alan Miller and Bob Whitehead) put their heads together and found that their combined games had earned Atari $60 million in sales in a single year. Armed with this information they went back to Ray Kassar who told them, in no uncertain terms *"You are no more important to Atari than the person on the assembly line who puts the cartridges in the box."'*

Seeing that there was no other option, The Gang Of Four left Atari, started the company Activision and began producing their own games for the Atari VCS, obviously crediting the developers for their games. Activision immediately began to sell hit games and despite this increasing the sales of the Atari VCS console, Atari sued them, claiming that only Atari could produce games for the Atari console. In 1982 Atari lost the court case and the concept of the third party developer was born and many others soon followed.

Just as Activision didn't need Atari's permission, ColecoVision homebrew developers did not need permission from either Coleco, ColecoVision or Coleco Holdings LLC, and the company that was trying to build an audience and keep their brand alive had just alienated every single one of them. They had used Ben's one-off console to get their trademark and they were now allegedly buying social media followers to build their presence in lieu of their upcoming expo. Even if that were true, they still lagged some way behind the established fan site who had almost 30,000 likes to their 1,200, and like Mike before them, they: *"Did a lot of things right up until we did everything wrong. Live and Learn."*

They didn't seem to be living and learning though as Chris dug himself, and the brand, deeper and deeper into trouble as he tried to justify his actions while refusing to retract his Facebook complaints against the ColecoVision Fan page and publicly arguing with Pat Contri who had covered the story in the CUPodcast.

> *Chris: "On that note, do you mind if someone set up a Pat the Punk fan club page. Then reprinted and sold your books? Or would that be unacceptable to you?"*
>
> *Pat: "Do you own the copyright to old ColecoVision games? If so, which games do you own the actual copyright to? Also: I produced and composed the book myself. Did you produce and put together the ColecoVision games you speak of?" [..] Disappointing and unprofessional comments, Chris – especially saying that my book infringed on a trademark when fair use for trademark exists, especially when it comes to books – look at the dozens of Coca-Cola collectible books out there. I gave you a huge benefit of the doubt when it came to the Chameleon. Good luck with your convention."*

Robb would comment that:

> *"This is not even close to being an equivalent analogy. ColecoVision Fan does not sell anything. There is no money that is made from our fan page. We produce the fan page out of passion for the classic ColecoVision system."*

As Chris argued more and more, people began looking into his hypocrisy more and more, and it started to emerge that he may not be as clean cut as he had earlier portrayed. Chris is an action figure collector and had spoken about his hobby at length to Eli in New York, and, in particular, his penchant for G.I. Joe. His eBay account was full of G.I. Joe figures that he was selling but these were not official merchandise made by Hasbro. The topic of molds reared its head again as the figures being sold by Chris were made from old molds that Hasbro had once used but no longer owned, though they did still own the rights to them.

The figures created using these old molds are known as recasts and are not approved by Hasbro and are frowned upon in the collector's market. Lots of people sell modified G.I. Joe figures after they have painted their uniforms a different color or removed parts from them and this is fine as the models were originally bought from the manufacturer, Hasbro, whereas recasts are not, they are produced unofficially and are not licensed or supported by Hasbro, even though the mold still has the Hasbro name on it and imprints it onto the models.

Chris had tried to justify his auctions by saying that he;

> *"was initially disliked by the Joe community. It was this 'bootleg' matter, in which I made a fuss that caused that initial resentment. It was that fuss that caused people to customize properly and I would imagine caused Hasbro to clarify this matter.*
>
> *If you must know, Hasbro is well aware that I have these figures and I even made a presentation to them to acquire a license to package them. The request was denied due to consumer demand."*

So, Chris claimed to be responsible for Hasbro clarifying that recasts were not allowed, having tried to license an unlicensed product which they denied as it would affect their sales. He could equally have been caught selling them and told to stop by Hasbro who then issued a statement to that effect. Either way, Chris reduced the price of all his recast models in an attempt to shift them quickly and then removed them from eBay altogether, which looked very suspicious if he was doing nothing wrong as he claimed.

Once he had cleaned up his eBay account and removed the Nintendo properties from the Coleco Expo banner, he was back again to emulate Mike in trying to control the narrative and erase any evidence of his misdeeds from AtariAge.

> *"Now that you have been made aware of these facts, I respectfully ask you to remove this 'bootleg' thread and all parts related as the information is both INACCURATE, SLANDEROUS, and detrimental to my character and business."*

In addition to the G.I.Joe thread on AtariAge, he also wanted the thread about the ColecoVision Fan page deleted as well:

> *"[...] is the community and CVF page under agreement that games which feature lewd or suggesting (sic) content not to be created or promoted on CVF, as well as games that are unlicensed with recognizable games form a third party? Is that what everyone is saying? [...] We retract the violations with these terms to FB (Facebook) and you folks delete the several threads relating to this concern?"*

He was told, in no uncertain terms, that this would not happen and what the community wanted was an apology, not a return to a stalemate with the evidence of his duplicity deleted.

> *"There are going to be unlicensed games made for the classic ColecoVision and Coleco is just going to have to deal with it. Any other games, if the publisher wants to use the official ColecoVision logos, they work with Coleco. If not, then drop the logos and everything is fair game."*

Eli had previously warned Chris that taking on the community was a very bad idea and if he did so, he would *"have a very bad time."* Eli also noted that the Trademark that they had for ColecoVision was for the typeface only, not the actual logo itself, so it may be true that it was legally possible for a homebrewer to use it anyway.

As the saga dragged on it was clear that Chris had caused much more trouble than a few adult games ever could, and he had completely destroyed any chance of being in the good favor of the community that he claimed he wanted to support so much. River West Brands was in it to make money, and if that involved licensing games, so be it, but the fact that no homebrew developer would now turn to them for licensing destroyed any hope of that. As much as he claimed that this wasn't the case, that is their business model, and in fact since 2002 they had filed 121 intent to use trademark applications but had failed to file a statement of actual use in more than half of those same applications.

Satisfied that the homebrew community could move ahead without any kind of license from Coleco Holdings LLC, one of the major ColecoVision homebrew publishers, Opcode Games, stated that he would be;

> *"removing all the references to Coleco and ColecoVision logos and names from my games and will identify my platform as the Super Game Module. All homebrewers are welcome to use the SGM logo and I will provide licenses at no costs and no strings attached under request. Please contact me so we can do this in a (sic) ordered way."*

The Super Game Module is an after-market add on for the original ColecoVision console and Coleco ADAM computer which connected to the expansion port and gave both units enhanced audio capabilities with 4 additional sound channels, expanded memory raised from 1KB to 32KB and the option to save game high scores. Highly ironic was the fact that it also added a power LED which the original unit had lacked. It was a popular add on which sold out whenever a production run was made and it supported many of the new homebrew games which were written with those expanded capabilities in mind.

The unit was first designed in 1983 by Coleco, the original Coleco, but it was unreleased. They had presented it at the New York Toy Fair in February 1983, 33 years before the brand returned to the same show with the Coleco Chameleon and, like the Chameleon, it wasn't ready in time for the show. Again, like the Chameleon, they decided not to take it to market and the company folded after suffering huge losses, although the video game crash of 1983 was largely responsible for that.

There are two versions of the Super Game Module: Version 1 was produced under public license from River West Brands and qualifies as an official Coleco product and Version 2 which was not and does not qualify, therefore it was Opcode's prerogative to license it to homebrewers with impunity. The Version 1 was compatible with the NTSC and PAL ColecoVision and the ADAM Computer and the Version 2 added compatibility with the French CBS Scart ColecoVision. Between them the first two production runs sold over 200 units with later runs taking it closer to 1,000.

Now distancing themselves from their earlier Coleco licensed work, Opcode now asked that:

> *"[...] when anyone is referring to the company that Cardillo etc. works for that they from now on refer to it by the proper name of "Coleco Holdings LLC". Referring to it as Coleco infers that they have a genuine link to the original Coleco company, which they do not. Coleco were the manufacturers of The Cabbage Patch Kids and the ColecoVision and NOT Coleco Holdings which is a pathetic shell living off the hard work and original creations of others."*

Still in desperate need of reversing their fortunes and reputation with their upcoming expo in mind and unable to control the narrative on Facebook, Twitter and AtariAge, Chris took to editing the Coleco Wikipedia page instead. An anonymous user had deleted any reference to the Retro VGS and Coleco Chameleon and had added promotional material for the Coleco Expo and the planned mini arcade machines they were hoping to bring to market, including a link to the Kickstarter page.

Coleco had previously been warned about editing the Wikipedia page, as a company editing their own entries amounted to a conflict of interest, and any such changes should have been directed to an independent editor for proof reading before being posted. Unfortunately, the anonymous editor in this instance did not realize that there was a character limit on the section they were editing and their text was cut short. They also later failed to realize that the IP address used to make edits could be linked back to Mount Laurel, New Jersey which is the home of Castle Windows, another one of Chris Cardillo's businesses.

Once a moderator removed these "anonymous" changes and restored the page to its original form, Chris returned to AtariAge to try again, only this time he appealed to the owner, Albert, citing the way that Robb (a moderator) had been acting:

> *"Quite honestly, if one of my employees of Coleco ever talked to a client, supplier or co-worker in this fashion, he would be terminated immediately. And this is just one of many attacks that were incited or carried out.*
>
> *Albert can you help us understand this a little better? Is this what you set out to create? Or do you possibly think that threads like this are a black eye on your site considering that your own moderater fans the flames, speaks to your users with such distain (sic)? [...]*

Unfortunately, as i said before, I don't plan on having someone Bully me or the people around me, or kids that I don't even know, or people that work for me, or with me. [...]

I've never backed down to a bully face to face, so I'll be damned if someone behind a keyboard is gonna make me sweat."

Eli again tried to offer some advice to Chris and have him apologize to the community rather than continue his battle them and attempt to have threads remove in order to control the narrative.

"Right now, the best you guys can do is Damage Control. If there are personal attacks to you here, it is best to ignore them;

What damage can that do to you? If the G.I. Joe comments are false and Hasbro has indeed allowed people to sell re-cast parts/figures; then good, there is nothing to worry about; no need to come and attack an already angry community."

Albert of course responded to Chris' ridiculous statement and standpoint:

"I wanted everyone to know that I have recently received several emails from Coleco asking me to remove the threads Eduardo and Robb started on AtariAge with regards to Coleco (including this thread). The first email was sent by a "[NAME WITHHELD" from a Coleco-related email address. The next two messages were from Chris Cardillo himself. I did not respond to these messages, as I've found that it's best to ignore trolls. Given that Chris Cardillo of Coleco Holdings LLC is now calling me out as being derelict in my duty to moderate the forum, I feel it's time to share the existence of these emails with everyone.

Chris believes he and Coleco are being unfairly attacked, that people are breaking various rules of the forum, and that AtariAge is obligated to take action on posts when our "Terms of Service" (Chris' words) are violated. [...]

By attacking the ColecoVision Fan page on Facebook you invited the criticism you are seeing. You are not the victim. The fact that you continue to refuse to rescind the unwarranted takedown notices on Facebook speaks volumes about your intent and your character. [...]

Do I feel Robb's actions in this case reflect poorly on AtariAge as Chris suggests? No, he and others are simply bringing attention to the bullying Chris is inflicting on the community. Coleco has now tried to silence content they don't approve of on ColecoVision Fan and AtariAge, both which have a large number of active ColecoVision fans and developers. They have also been editing Coleco-related Wikipedia pages in attempts to remove factual references that do not reflect favorably on the brand.

Chris Cardillo is not a friend of the ColecoVision community. It's this community full of true ColecoVision fans that have kept the brand alive all these years. Chris, you are a leach and a stain on the Coleco and ColecoVision legacies.

You seem incapable of comprehending that your words and actions reflect poorly on yourself and the Coleco brand. I'm not sure how you worked it out in your head that attacking the community would somehow rally people behind

Coleco, especially with the Coleco Chameleon fiasco still fresh in everyone's mind.

Fortunately, the community does not need you, and they have already taken steps to avoid having to further interact with you and "Coleco" down the road.

..Al"

The whole thing was by now beyond ridiculous and it seemed that Chris had now well and truly inherited the reverse Midas touch and was mimicking Mike's every move as summed up by Scott:

"This latest fiasco is such an unnecessary waste of the hobby's energy and resources, and totally illogical because Chris and Coleco had generated a ton of good will when they stood up and took honorable and visible action when the CC (Coleco Chameleon) scam was revealed. This feud has wiped out all that good will. At this point, I think that the smartest thing Chris can do is halt any efforts to explain or justify their position and just leave the community alone. Maybe a ColecoVision or table top arcade will get featured as a prop in Guardians of the Galaxy 3 like the Mattel handheld and that will stir up a nostalgia for a modestly successful line of Coleco shirts at Target and they can see some profit on their investment in the brand.

I have never had a problem with their stated business model, the example I have used is PBR, Pabst went from a national brand to essentially gone yet it returned as a popular brand served nationwide, you see PBR shirts now and even Stern pinball created a PBR themed pinball! Imagine if you bought the brand for a song when it was down and were able to craft that return? I think it is an interesting business idea, albeit a risky one. Buying and restoring distressed brands can be done without patent or copyright trolling.

And last but not least, when Socal played the victim card and tried to control the narrative by seeking to get videos, threads etc. removed that had almost as much of a backlash as the fake prototypes, copying this move is something that leaves me pretty much speechless, I honestly can't put the words together to explain the pointless, counter-productive and illogical nature of this!"

With no option but to forge ahead with the Coleco Expo, Coleco put out an announcement to try and raise awareness and sell tickets to what was threatening to become a massive failure, unfortunately their announcements were full of errors.

"ColecoVision, one of the gaming giants of the 80s is back with the release of Sydney Hunter, a new video game on cartridge."

CollectorVision had sold 150 copies of Sydney Hunter And The Sacred Tribe to Coleco Holdings for them to sell at the expo, including the ColecoVision logo on the box, so ColecoVision wasn't back, CollectorVision was back, not that they had been away in the first place of course.

"The release will mark the first commercial release of a video game cartridge in 15 years."

How can anybody even remotely connected to the video game industry think that statement was true?

In another move to secure vendors for their expo, two of the Coleco staff, who were mainly young girls, attended the three day Too Many Games Expo (formerly East Coast Gaming Expo) at the Greater Philadelphia Expo Center in Oaks, Philadelphia. The show ran from June 23rd to 25th and boasted around 12,000 attendees. The Coleco staff, who also featured in the Coleco Expo promotional video, were promoting their event and handing out flyers to vendors. They were not at the show in an official capacity as Coleco did not have a booth there and they were not a show sponsor, they were just walking the floor wearing ColecoVision t-shirts. They weren't the only ones doing that at Too Many Games as there were also people there from New Jersey Gamer Con but they were spotted by staff and asked to leave. The Too Many Games staff did later remove the Coleco flyers once they realized what had happened.

While you might expect Chris Cardillo to keep his nose clean before the Coleco Expo, he was actually selling the "Coleco Expo Exclusive" copies of Sydney Hunter on eBay which meant they were no longer a *"show exclusive"* yet they continued to be advertised as exactly that. So, to try and win some favor, while also taking a stab at the community that had refused to work with him, Chris announced that he would be donating 100% of the profits from sales of the Sydney Hunter game to an anti-bullying charity:

"Coleco will be conducting their first Coleco Expo in the New Jersey Convention and Exposition Center located in Edison New Jersey. At this event fans will be able to pick up a convention exclusive version of Sydney Hunter for the ColecoVision console and Adam computer with 100% of profits from the sale of this cartridge being donated to the Free 2 Luv charity."

The expo staff were planning all the usual expo style features, music, vendors, cosplay contests and panels, including one hosted by Mark Thomann, who, wisely it would seem, dropped out and cancelled his panel. This expo was only going one way, and that was down.

As day one of the expo arrived, August 5th 2017, and photos began to emerge on social media and as the panels were streamed live, it quickly became clear that the place was a ghost town. Everywhere you looked was open, unoccupied space. Some said that the vendors outnumbered the attendees and the attendees were mostly cosplayers. The special guest who was there to sign autographs and do a meet and greet was Disney Channel's Ashley Parker, but she was mostly pictured using her phone as she cut a lonely figure for the most part.

Posts and comments from those who had attended and those who watched the live streams and social media updates were mostly negative and most showed regret at having wasted their time.

"You think they would have pulled the plug on the whole thing to save face. There is no way in hell they can spin this to call it a successful event."

"This expo turned out to be a bigger farce than I thought it would be."

"They had consoles set up to play, but I actually didn't see a single ColecoVision unit!"

"I honestly feel sorry for the vendors who I'm sure have probably lost money on this show."

"They had lots of consoles set up... Nintendo, XBOX, PlayStation... but where are the ColecoVisions????"

"Waste of a 2 hour trip"

"Maybe 50-75 people. Probably more vendors than people."

"The vendors looked miserable and I felt sorry for them."

"It was so terrible."

"This was a Coleco expo void of anything Coleco!"

"The more I am thinking about it, the more mad I am I wasted a day on it."

"There was even a bathtub vendor there. What the ####. Worst convention I have ever been to no doubt."

One of the vendors gave a full review of their experience rather than a sound bite and it was quite revealing.

"Review from a Vendor. (I AM NOT SIDING FOR NOR AGAINST The promoters. This is a non biased TRUE report of the Expo)

I only recently learned of the debacle with Chris and the fanbase/ Homebrewers on THURSDAY!. But alas I had already paid for 2 booths. ($120 per booth)

Anyway here goes my report:

I was one of the Vendors that did Coleco Expo. Overall the sales weren't as bad as some would think especially for the LOW attendance. (I would say 1 in 3 people bought from me, maybe even 2 outta 3 at points.) A LOT of NES games sold, but this seems to be the usual. [...]

Friday night: Set up was a BREEZE as the place was mostly empty/already set up. [...]

Saturday: MANY VENDOR BOOTHS were still EMPTY. (up to 20%!) Now mind you this show was 1.5 hours from opening. Most cons/shows I do, 2 HOURS before and the place is fully set up and the vendors are buzzing around looking for mispriced product, variants and personal wants. NOTHING. [...]

By 9:30ish the vendors were mostly ready. The Artists seemed to still be AWOL till 10. 10 am comes and goes like nothing happened. FEW people streamed in and browsed. The sound system began to "wake up" throughout the day. By Lunch there was a crowd, but not anything spectacular. [...]

Many times the other vendors would walk around and shoot the shit as the crowd died out. Some points got so bad you could walk away from your booth and go peek at the Arcade and panels (Which ranged from a somewhat packed arcade to a ghost town. It seemed that as the day progressed, the crowd got bigger. I can't say that it was packed (I never had more than 10+ people at my booth at one time), but at times it seemed like the attendance was set to explode. Alas that did NOT happen. [..]

Sunday: I got to the Expo at around 8:30 and actually had the chance to sort ALL my inventory with no interruptions. [...]

What really saddened me was outside at 930ish. NOONE was waiting to be let in. As 10 rolled around you were LUCKY to see a FEW and I mean A FEW people walking around. [...]

Around 1ish (I wasn't really paying attention) the "crowd" started to trickle in. Few times it DID feel like it was a good crowd. Stuff sold ok with NES again being the main focus. [...]

By 5ish it was nearly DEAD though. So we packed up around 5.30ish and off to home with another convention done.

While I don't believe this was a TERRIBLE show (I've had worse MUCH worse in the past.) It was no home run or even a double. [...]

It's a REAL shame that this whole thing happened between the promoters/ Owners and the fanbase/Homebrew community. This show could have been a SMASHING success and had the fanbase and homebrewers not been alienated and shunned been invited to attend and display all things Coleco old and new, and not let bad business get involved, we may be talking amazing things about the 1st Coleco Expo. Instead things happened that were bad whether for business reasons/greed/god knows what. So now this Expo will go down as a poorly attended/handled event.

There was some more positive coverage of the show to be found, obviously on the new ColecoVision Nation fan page of course, but also an article on hardcoregamer.com who were very positive about it.

"Upon entering the building, guests are met with a full video display of the upcoming Rainbow Brite and Robotech video games. The footage shown for Rainbow Brite is fittingly colorful and quite crisp on the screen used. They weren't demonstrated at all, but if it remains as seen, the end result should be good. [...]

On the inside of the convention were all the vendors and artists with some booming businesses. [...]

Plenty of toys from the '70s to today could be found. Sellers had many Funko Pop!s, action figures, comic books and some other all-around nerdy items. For gamers, however, the selection was quite enticing. Brand new merchandise from current games were available, but the main bread and butter is for fans who absolutely love going retro. [...]

In addition to browsing the goodies of the past, there was lots of fun to be had. Attendees could meet and chat with celebrities, including Ashley Parker of Disney Channel fame. There were also authors and industry professionals to rub shoulders with. A cosplay contest was held which would net the winner a few hundred bucks. But one of the coolest parts was the arcade room. There were functional arcade cabinets from past decades like Popeye, Punch-Out!!, Rampage and many more. A raffle giveaway was even held for one lucky winner to obtain their very own cabinet. Some home console titles were also set up on monitors where you could play everything from Atari to Wii U. Rocket League, Super Smash Bros. and a few other games could be enjoyed. [...]

The main function of Coleco Expo was to bring lovers of retro video games together and celebrate everything about the crucial beginnings of the industry. New and old surprises awaited eager hearts. Hopefully more fans will travel to the next Coleco Expo to keep spreading the joy of old school games. It was a fun time and worth checking out again.

Jacob Whritenour on August 10, 2017

Who is Jacob Whritenour you may ask? Jacob's LinkedIn profile describes him as having; *"[...] copywriting and product writing experience with online retailers specializing in wholesale supplies for various markets"* and he has a *"Demonstrated ability to write creative descriptions to increase customer interaction."*

He was certainly being creative here, and even Willie, host of the ColecoVisions Podcast, now without the official ColecoVision logo of course, was happy that he gave the show a miss, saying:

"I had planned to go to represent the ColecoVisions Podcast and The Toy Tomb Podcast. Kind of glad I did not invest time and cash on this."

The general consensus was of course that *"Cardillo and friends basically ruined and eliminated any and all positive possibilities long before this colossal failure even began."* Coleco Holdings LLC were not needed by the homebrew scene and their expo was not exactly a roaring success, so they had no option but to go back to the highlights of the original Coleco back catalogue, and one of the stand out products that Coleco had made were of course the mini arcade machines.

In the early 1980s Coleco sold four different home versions of classic arcade games, they were Donkey Kong (1981), Pac-Man (1981), Ms. Pac-Man (1981) and Frogger (1982). The games were set in a plastic case that mimicked an arcade machine, complete with joystick and used a VFD (Vacuum Fluorescent Display) for their screen. VFDs were common in things such as VHS recorders, car radios and microwave ovens and the beauty of a VFD screen is that it has a vibrant, warm glow to it while not requiring much power, which was convenient as these mini arcades could run from batteries. They required more power than an equivalent LCD (Liquid Crystal Display) screen but they had a much quicker response time which made them great for games, they were resilient, relatively cheap to make and achieved color with the use of colored filters applied to the glass in the same way that some arcade machines of the era did, Space Invaders 2 (1979) for example. These original mini arcades were cut down versions of the full arcade games they were based on and were very popular at the time and are still coveted by collectors today. Coleco Holdings LLC hoped to bring the format back with two games initially, and these were Robotech: The Macross Saga and Rainbow Brite: Journey to Rainbow Land.

Robotech is a comic book series from 1984 that was made into an animated TV series from 1985 and turned into movies that same year. Essentially it is a clone of the Transformers franchise and the game would be a remake of the 2002 game that had appeared on the Nintendo Game Boy Advance, a side scrolling shooter developed by Lucky Chicken Games and published by TDK Mediactive.

Rainbow Brite, also known as Magical Girl Rainbow Brite in Japan, was a character created by Hallmark Cards in 1983 and who also starred in an animated series in 1984, the same year that Mattel licensed a series of dolls and other merchandise. A movie by Warner Bros called Rainbow Brite and the Star Stealer followed in 1985.

Neither Robotech or Rainbow Brite featured in an arcade game during their heyday which makes them a slightly odd choice for a mini arcade but to bring the games to market, Coleco Holdings LLC would turn to Kickstarter in a campaign titled "Coleco Evolved Mini Arcades". The new machines would use the same form factor as the original four but would see some internal upgrades, replacing the VFD display with a color LCD and the four C batteries with a rechargeable lithium ion battery, as the Kickstarter campaign described them:

Classic shell, new hardware

In 1981, Coleco released a line of mini arcade machines that changed the way we played arcade games forever.
For the first time, people could experience Pac-Man, Frogger, Donkey Kong, and many more classics outside the arcade.
For years, we've heard your requests to bring this classic arcade machine back to life for a new generation. Well, the wait is over!

Introducing Coleco Evolved.

Coleco Evolved Mini Arcade machines preserve the classic shape and heavy-duty plastic shell construction you remember from the 80s while updating the technology inside to create a modern arcade gaming experience.

Coleco Evolved machines feature:
Full Color LCD Display
Powerful new gaming chip set
Revamped joystick and accurate action buttons
Rechargeable Lithium Ion battery pack
Highly-detailed, colorful Rainbow Brite and Robotech art wraps

It's Retro done right!

The campaign launched on May 8th, 2018, and would run for 30 days until June 7th, 2018, with a funding target of $30,000. The risks and challenges section outlined that the prototyping phase was already complete and one of the questions in the FAQ section addressed the other elephant in the room.

> **"Is this the same company/team that worked on the Coleco Chameleon?"**
>
> *"The Coleco Chameleon was developed by a third party licensee who was responsible for all aspects of the development. We terminated our relationship with that licensee once it became clear the product was not living up to the Coleco name."*

The intended timeline for the project if it were to be successful was:

- Apr 2018 – Tooling opened
- May 2018 – Tooling finish/first shots
- Jun 2018 – Pre-production samples
- Jul 2018 – Order materials
- Aug 2018 – Production
- Sep 2018 – Ship to backers

The funding levels open to backers were:

- *Pledge US$ 5 or more*
  – Coleco Revival Fan Reward!
- *Pledge US$ 45 or more*
  – Early Bird Coleco Evolved Rainbow Brite / Early Bird Coleco Evolved Robotech
  – Retail $69
  – Estimated delivery Sep 2018
- *Pledge US$ 55 or more*
  – Coleco Evolved Rainbow Brite / Coleco Evolved Robotech
  – Retail $69
  – Estimated delivery Sep 2018
- *Pledge US$ 85 or more*
  – Early Bird Coleco Collector (2 pack)
  – Estimated delivery Sep 2018
- *Pledge US$ 105 or more*
  – Coleco Collector (2 pack)
  – Estimated delivery Sep 2018
- *Pledge US$ 200 or more*
  – Limited Edition Robotech
  – WILL NOT BE AVAILABLE IN RETAIL!

– This Limited Edition Coleco Evolved Robotech mini arcade is shot in a special gold color just for Kickstarter Backers. Ideal for the Coleco Super Fan!
– Limited to just 50 pieces!
– Item will include Official Limited Edition numbered label.
– Estimated delivery Sep 2018

- *Pledge US$ 200 or more*
  – Limited Edition Rainbow Brite
  – WILL NOT BE AVAILABLE IN RETAIL!
  – This Limited Edition Coleco Evolved Rainbow Brite mini arcade is shot in a special silver color just for Kickstarter Backers. Ideal for the Coleco Super Fan!
  – Limited to just 50 pieces!
  – Item will include Official Limited Edition numbered label.
  – Estimated delivery Sep 2018

- *Pledge US$ 400 or more*
  – Limited Edition 2-P1ack
  – WILL NOT BE AVAILABLE IN RETAIL!
  – Both Limited Edition Coleco Evolved mini arcades is shot in metallic color just for Kickstarter Backers. Ideal for the Coleco Super Fan!
  – Limited to just 50 pieces!
  – Item will include Official Limited Edition numbered label.
  – Estimated delivery Sep 2018

By May 9th, 2018, the campaign was funded, in less than 24 hours, and by the end of it, 736 backers had pledged $71,246 which showed that Coleco Holdings LLC may be able to emerge from their recent nightmares with their heads held high. The proof would be in the pudding though, once backers got the systems in their hands and played them. Most serious collectors were put off by the choice of games but if successful and popular, particularly in retail after the Kickstarter backer orders were fulfilled, it is possible that other games would be brought to the Coleco Evolved line up, as suggested by an update from Coleco on June 7th:

> *"Thank you all for helping to make this a successful campaign! Because of you, Coleco was able to reach 237% of the goal. Please continue to stay tuned for development updates and Coleco's future plans including the next titles on the first Coleco mini arcades in decades!"*

As expected with a manufacturing project like this there were delays *"We are sorting out unexpected manufacturing issues which seem to crop up during production runs"* and the shipping date of September passed before an update on October 27th to say:

> *"Hello to all of our patient backers,*
> *We know you are all curious to know the status of the minis. Here is the latest—*

We have just finished more software updates on the Rainbow Brite game. After game play, we thought it made sense to add some new intros for each level that helped make sense of the game play in addition to the manuals. (See screenshot). Notice the retro look/feel- simple and helpful. We also adjusted some difficulty settings based on player feedback.

We're just finishing some last optimizations for Robotech to make the gameplay more adapted to the minis as well. Then, production time!

Thank you all for your understanding and patience."

After some further delays and changes in hardware, the units began shipping in January of 2019, with those who ordered both units receiving theirs first. Some boxes were damaged in transit but luckily the games themselves were not. Buyers were happy with their games though there were some issues with things like dust under the screen and some other minor issues but they are to be expected with a small production run of this type.

This was undoubtedly the last chance saloon for Coleco Holdings LLC and the Coleco and ColecoVision properties under their management. Patience and tolerance for the brands was wearing thin and only time will tell if they can turn their fortunes around and salvage their reputation completely.

15: Moving Forward

Mike had been unable to salvage his own reputation and rescue his empire, and Coleco Holdings LLC had definitely been channeling him in many ways in the mistakes that they had made, but Mike had finally given up and continued with his plan for an exit from the scene.

Mike's employer, Creform Corporation, wanted him to travel more but he was reluctant to do that, his time at home was precious and Tricia was dead set against the idea so something had to give. As he told others, he owed around $20,000 to his editors, his layout artist Monique and writers like Jeremy Parish, Chris Kohler and Seanbaby. Sean hadn't asked Mike for payment in a while so he was hoping that he could write off that debt but he had finally realized that he could not be the public face of anything to do with retro and gaming any more. He would still like to be involved with a project behind the scenes but right now he was considered damaged goods and he needed a way to shift approximately 10,000 unsold copies of Retro magazine that were sitting in a container and he needed a way out. Others who had been caught up in his mess were also feeling the heat a little as an event in California would show.

The Frank & Son's Collectible Show is held in San Jose California and it is a huge event for vendors who sell all manner things from comic books to figurines and baseball cards to video games, all with free admission and parking every Wednesday and Saturday. During one such event, Armando, the owner of a retro game store in Ontario California called Pixel Vault Games, announced that he would be having an after party at his store with drinks and tacos.

Among those present was Brian Barnhart, who had previously entertained Armando at the Jag Bar, and Brian was asked about the Coleco Chameleon and began to tell the story about the Kickstarter video and the Pat and Gamester81 exchanges. This was not long after those events and just as he was finishing his telling of the story, John Lester walked through the door and the room went deathly quiet.

It was uncomfortable for a few moments, but people soon went back to their drinks and tacos and Brian had a conversation with John where they talked further about the Chameleon fiasco with John telling him that he was just trying to develop games for it and had no deeper involvement. Curiously, Brian has noticed a change in the way that he is received at these events and in exchanges ever since his tell all video about the cancelled Coleco Chameleon Kickstarter video shoot went live, he says that:

> *"Things changed a bit. When I run into anyone associated with Mike I can tell they do not want me there. I have reached out to people in our community and no one gets back to me. I know I kicked over the ant hill but my reputation was more important than fooling the community over a fake product, I don't lose any sleep over what I did."*

This alienation is confusing because Brian did the right thing when so many others hadn't, and many of those commenting and releasing video after video knew nothing about the inner workings of the Kennedy empire, yet their videos got tens of thousands of views and were taken as gospel, while others who were on the inside went largely unheard. It was over though, and Mike realized it and he set about getting out of the community and paying off his financial debts. To do that he needed to sell GameGavel and Retro Magazine, but who would be willing to buy them as they were considered almost as toxic as Mike himself? Really there was only one preferred candidate for Mike and that was Mark Kaminski. Mike had a deal in place with Mark that if he ever sold Retro, he would pay him 30% of the purchase price along with 20% going to Brandon Justice, as confirmed by Mike in his earlier email to Mark.

> *"What we agreed was that IF the magazine is sold I would pay you 30% of the proceeds from the sale (and Brandon now 20% of the sale) and the remaining balance would go to GameGavel, LLC."*

Mark had foreseen an issue following that email and it was a portent for what was about to happen as Mike emailed Mark on April 18th, 2017 and began negotiations to see if he was interested in a buyout, hinting that he was still reluctant to "work" after 5pm and that a house move was imminent when he said *"What about talking on Monday. I'd rather discuss during the day if possible. I am still PST so could call you after your work day too"* and describing the writing *"team"* as *"pretty fluid at this point."*

Was his reluctance to work after 5pm because that was Tricia time or did he just not want her to overhear him doing business when she was home? Either way, Mark appeared to bite, although his interest in anything other than potential future use of the name "Retro" for a publication was minimal, and he certainly didn't want to inherit any of the staffing problems and lack of payments that Mike had created: *"I have no interest in any work from Monique either complete or partial."*

Mike had done a deal with GOG (Good Old Games) who, starting with Issue 13, were going to promote the magazine in return for coverage in it and he offered to set up a Skype call between them, but Mark had no interest in that or in GameGavel which Mike also offered to him.

> *"gg.com or gamegavel.com?*
> *Do you own all the software and a such to run the site?"*

He did not and told Mark that it may not matter as he had somebody else who was interested in it, and indeed he did, as he was simultaneously having the same negotiation discussions with Eli who seemed genuinely keen. Mark wanted some figures for the site and its traffic and asked:

> *"Can you prepare visitor analytics (last 24 months), ad rev, TCO (total cost of ownership) and NPV (net present value) of Gamegavel.com?*
> *I need to factor that in to my offer.*
>
> *Thank you*
> *Mark"*

Mike offered to do that but was pretty honest when he said that:

> *"But for all practical purposes it's not generating any rev. No ad rev either. The stats will show you how many new members per month, the number of listings, sales, and fee rev (very little). Most the value would be future perceived value + maybe replacement cost to create a site like this from scratch. It does pop up in the top spot for the search "video game auctions."*
>
> *I was going to throw it in with RETRO but there wasn't any value put on it as I was just going to shut it down. But, I do have another person interested in possibly taking it over and I do really need to try and make as much as I can on the sale of the two properties to help me dig out a bit."*

This statement is very interesting indeed as we will see. Mike states that there is no value in GameGavel which is not generating any revenue through either ads or selling fees (aside from the monthly cost for running the software) and that he was just going to throw it in to a sale along with Retro or otherwise was just going to shut it down. In a later email he would place the membership numbers at 10,000 seller accounts which, if true, goes to show just how much he had neglected and mismanaged the site. He had 10,000 members and yet the site was not generating any revenue. He then goes on to use one of his favorite and often repeated phrases, *"Most (of) the value would be future perceived value"* in much the same way that he would hand out shares in his businesses in lieu of actual monetary payment because they would take off in the future. If GameGavel had such future value and could be turned around, why hadn't he been able to do it in the 9 years that he had run it?

The price that Mike had in mind for the sale was $15,000 and he arrived at that number based on paying off his debts rather than on any financial report or assessment of the business. Understandably, Mark saw that as far too high and the week of emails between them had gone nowhere by this point which was making Mike slightly anxious. On April 27th Mark put a number on what he was valuing the properties at.

> *"Mike, the price of $15,000 is far too high. I was thinking more like $7,000 for RETRO (all IP+documents+physical assets) and GameGavel.com URL + member list. I would not continue the auction on the current platform due to you not owning the software to run the site."*

Mike countered at $9,500 and 4 days later, on May 1, Mark dropped the bombshell that he may not need to buy anything from Mike after all.

> *"Hi Mike,*
>
> *I'm green lighted, however, we are just checking what your copyright actually covers. Since our publication will be a book, we may not need your copyright at all and can still name it RETRO. I'll keep you posted tomorrow. Some of the other assets may still be of interest.*
>
> *Thanks*
> *Mark"*

This was not exactly what Mike wanted to hear but he was still negotiating with Eli of course so there was hope for him yet, even though time was running out, and Mark was dragging his heels. Mike chased him daily before agreeing to his $7,000 offer for Retro but said that it would not include GameGavel as Eli was keen on buying that so he could use it as a market place for Piko Interactive and their games. Buying himself another day Mark replied;

> *"I'll get back to you tomorrow, I need another day. I don't want to hold you up on the other side, so you can move forward on GG, I see no value in it under the current structure for our deal."*

The next day Mark replied as promised with the question: *"Mike, on the offer letter, should it be made out to you or the company?"* and Mike asked for it to be made out to him personally, not the company. Things took an interesting turn a few days later, on May 7th when Retro subscribers (and unsubscribers) received an email out of the blue.

> *"Hello, Friends!*
>
> *Introducing nocheckpoint.com! A new project/concept to deliver retro gaming news, articles, retrospectives, interviews, and over all what is happening with the scene. You may be wondering why and how we are emailing you right now; nocheckpoint.com team is being composed by retro scene veterans, journalists, contributors and writers that have had reach you in the past.*
>
> *We are alpha-launching today with this newsletter! While we work on our website, this newsletter will be our only way of communication; hopefully we grow our reach to every retro gamer in this crazy sphere we call world! We'll pick news, rumors, and events we stumble up on in our circles; but make sure to let us know if you have any news tip, gossip, cool thing, opinion, or anything that you think us or the retro gaming community should know!"*

What was this and where had it come from? Eli had been keen during his negotiations to get access to the GameGavel/Retro mailing list and Mike had clearly given it to him in the hope that Eli would come through and buy his fallen empire from him. The email newsletter angered many of the recipients though, particularly those who had repeatedly unsubscribed from the list, and Eli had to make a public apology for the intrusion.

> *"Hey Guys before this grows like wild fire, I should probably apologize, It is a new project of mine that I'll be funding. Didn't mean to be intrusive, Mike Kennedy is not involved. I am launching that site as a project to consolidate info on best retro gaming scene projects, some retrospectives and behind the scenes info.*
>
> *Eventually I want to turn it into a yearly magazine or bi yearly magazine. I plan to have smaller free zines issues etc.*
>
> *Again, I Apologized, I tried to be the least intrusive on the email as possible etc.*
>
> *Info I got as I am buying out gamegavel (gamerspots too and hoping some other stuff) as-is I think it could be a cool tool and I plan to turn it around. As we work in Piko by Rescuing old unreleased/unfinished games, I plan to do the same for Gamegavel (and some other brands, but that is for another thread)*
>
> *Idea for nocheckpoint came when I started investigating real hard a couple of gaming giants that went bankrupt. I found all this cool and crazy information on SEC archives and the US Federal Archives office.*
>
> *Another thing I'd like to mention is that everything mentioned in the newsletter was not paid advertising (aside from our current project) I asked about 12-15 people about projects they'd like to share etc. Only featured the ones that actually gave me a who, what, when and where (I guess other people where (sic) too lazy).*
>
> *Again I apologize, but I also want you to tell me (as I ask in that newsletter) what do you think of the current state of retro gaming, your opinions, comments, ideas etc. I see the scene rapidly changing and there is a gut feeling (not good) and I really want to understand and know what is going on and what to do to keep the fire burning.*
>
> *If I bothered you, I am sorry, I'll give you a free slap in the head voucher if we ever meet in person. You may click spam if that is what you felt I sent you, let me know and I'll personally unsubscribe you."*

Eli seemed very confident about his pending deal for GameGavel/Retro and the dead GamerSpots but Mike was still negotiating with Mark who had dropped a bombshell on him by telling him that he didn't need the "Retro" name if he wanted to produce a book called Retro and he wasn't that interested in picking up the carcass of a business. Eli certainly was though and was responding to people who were questioning his sanity in wanting to pay for the failed properties that Mike was selling. Eli felt that the SEO (Search Engine Optimization) that GameGavel had, having been an established auction site for a number of years, was worth buying rather than starting a new site and having to build that up organically. There was also the issue of the negative connotations that the website had, having been associated with Mike and his fallen empire but Eli was not put off by that.

> *"The site needs massive work and a lot of time invested to make it work again. SEO has some potential, but again lots of work to turn it around.*

It will be mainly incorporated for a new concept store I been toying with the idea for a couple of years, that I think people, stores, homebrewers, developers will appreciate."

UKMike warned Eli, just in case Mike hadn't;

"Be fully aware up front that Mike can not sell the code that runs GameGavel and he pays a monthly fee to host and license it.
You will have that ongoing cost as well.
He will probably tell you the guy would take less than he currently pays but then why hasn't Mike already done that?
You should buy the name if you want it but the site as such is not his to sell completely and he has many investors who have a stake in it too, (Scott) included."

Mark had another bombshell for Mike, one that he seemed to have forgotten or, more likely, ignored.

"Last questions
How will we handle my % of the sale of RETRO?
Should I discount my offer 30% or will I pay you the full offer amount and you will in turn send a check from the proceeds back to me and Brandon for our % of the sale of the property as outlined in our original ownership agreement when I started RETRO
Are you willing to take a payment schedule, or do you need a lump sum?
What is the approximate size of the back issues? Will they fit on one pallet?
I should be able to get you the offer quickly afterward today."

Mike began to watch his words and tried to choose them carefully, completely ignoring the fact that he had agreements in place with Mark already about the sale of Retro.

"The spirit of that generous offer was to share in any windfall should the magazine be a success. As it is this is a fire sale. I need to clear $10,000 net from the sale of Retro and GameGavel to help pay some outstanding receivables. And this doesn't even cover all of them.
So, if you are going to hold me to that end of the agreement then your offer will need to be near that $15K you and I discussed initially (before I dropped to your $7K initial offer) and then you can discount your 30% off of that amount.
Or just pay the $7K and we agree to waive that part of the agreement.
If we come to an agreement I would need a lump sum payment.
Guessing it will be a 40x48 pallet stacked around 5-6' high. Weighing 500-800 lbs."

Wow! *"The spirit of that generous offer [...]"* What a great way to describe a contractual agreement that Mike seemed to think was now waived because he was in desperate need and having a *"fire sale"* Following up with: *"So if you are going to hold me to that end of the agreement [...]"* Another great way to phrase the parts of the agreement that Mike had wanted to stick to earlier when it seemed the magazine may be successful but didn't want to stick to now. Realizing that Mark and Brandon would take 50% of his sale price between them he went from the agreed $7,000 back up to $15,000, again based on the debts that he needed to pay off rather than any inherent value in the properties that he was selling. It's the equivalent of valuing your SMART car at $100,000 because you need that much to buy a Ferrari.

Mike continued his daily emails to Mark as he needed the deal wrapped up, but Mark stalled for a further week until May 15th before Mike pressed him for a final answer as *"I need to make a decision this week."*

Scott strongly requested that Mark did not make any offer for GameGavel/Retro and seriously hoped that nobody else would. The idea that Mike would get something, anything, out of this whole mess was pretty offensive and Scott was adamant that the community should not give Mike a single cent to dig himself out. Mark did make Mike a final offer of $7,000 but Mike told him that it was too late as he had already sold both GameGavel and Retro to Eli for $10,000. Mark was fine with that as he was now expecting his 30% of the sale price, and Brandon his 20%, but Mike had one final dirty deal left in him, one more scam before he was out.

Before he realized, or acknowledged, that Mark would enforce their 30% clause, Mike had agreed to a sale price of $7,000 for Retro and would either include GameGavel as it had no value or would close it down. Now though, when he did the deal with Eli he told him that he needed to do it as two separate transactions, one for Retro and one for GameGavel, one at $7,000 and one at $3,000, however, he switched the transactions around so that Eli bought GameGavel for $7,000 and Retro for $3,000. This meant that Mike still got his $10,000 but now he only owed Mark and Brandon half of $3,000 instead of half of $7,000, so $1,500 not $3,500. GameGavel was, by his own admission, worthless and Retro had assets and inventory, yet GameGavel was now somehow worth more than double what Retro was worth? As Mark put it:

> *"Of course it (Retro) was worth more, physical assets, Patreon subscribers, social media networks, a ####ing TRADEMARK, recognizable brand, IP, etc. GameGavel is a logo from 99designs.com and a URL running software Mike doesn't even own the rights to, and an outdated user base of spam email signups from 9 years ago for free accounts."*

Mark was obviously angry, but probably not that surprised, and with his new $10,000 investment Eli was looking to recoup some of his outlay as soon as he could so he asked UKMike to put him in touch with Mark. Mark agreed to the introduction and Eli reached out to him offering to license the use of the name Retro if he wanted to use it for a project. Mark already knew that he didn't need the license and could use it anyway and he certainly wasn't going to pay Eli for anything.

From: Mike Kennedy
Date: May 30, 2017
To: Mark Kaminski
Subject: RETRO

Hi Mark,

Thanks for that, but it was too late. As indicated, I had to move on this May 16th/17th to take care of a creditor that was going to turn over to collections. Can you send me your banking wire info (routing and account) for your 30% distribution. I ended up selling the RETRO portion for $3,000 so you have $900 coming your way. I will set up the wire transfer as soon as I get your banking information. I can send you the RETRO bill of sale this evening when I get home.

The new owner indicated they would be happy to license material to you for a reasonable price, if you are interested.

What a kick in the teeth, and Mark jokingly commented *"I'll offer him license to lick my sweaty balls."* He was clearly not going to be dealing with Eli who was getting some heat on AtariAge for using the distribution list and for giving Mike any money at all for what was essentially worthless and certainly toxic.

"You (Eli) are not a scammer but you put money in MK's pocket and people are going to be dead set against rewarding you for that or helping to facilitate it. There have been many posts where people have expressed their opinion about making sure not one dime goes to him and that will include it passing through you.

Same with Retro, the burned writers and contributors won't come back and the readers have already jumped ship and moved on. Patreon could barely break 300 people willing to consider one issue. Even if you staff it out with great people somehow the moment is gone.

I have liked your other ventures and been impressed by your ability to see value in things such as the faith based media, but I am certain you will be spending a lot of time and effort in the future trying to wash this stink off. Out of all the reactions to your decision has there been one positive one, how would you gauge the interest?"

Like Mike before him, Eli had seen enough:

"Alright, so I see everybody posting sarcasm comments as if I am Mike Kennedy + the Chameleon. So I am done with this thread. I am trying to be cool and transparent. I'm not asking for your support nor help. If you are going to be disrespectful I am just going to ignore you."

There were obvious echoes of Mike's earlier; *"And this is why I won't be answering any more questions. Just for the record"* and it seemed that the GameGavel/Retro properties might be haunted after all as Eli had even started to use the good old Kennedy phrase *"moving forward."* As Scott succinctly put it:

> *"New management of a dumpster fire is just that, a new guy standing next to a burning trash heap."*

Pleased with the sale, and not having to pay out more than he had to, to get Mark and Brandon off his back, Mike now had the funds to pay off some of his debts and to get rid of the immediate threat of "collections", but by no means did he have enough to cover them all, so he had to try and find more from somewhere and he began selling off some personal items. His yacht had to go because, aside from running costs, it was costing him $600 per month just to moor it, and he sold off some smaller items too, unfortunately some of which didn't even belong to him. On June 5th Willie had discovered that Mike was selling some items on eBay that were actually his and, understandably, he was not happy about it at all.

> *"I stood by that ####er through all the fiasco, took quite a bit of heat trying to remain neutral and still be a friend. Have not really said anything about the whole mess and this is how I get repaid?"*

When the two of them did the ColecoVisions Podcast together, Willie had lent Mike some of his Coleco table top machines for research purposes, specifically a Galaxian and a Donkey Kong, Mike was also selling a Frogger but Willie couldn't remember if he had sent that one to him or not. There were other systems that Willie had also sent to Mike but he didn't know what Mike had done with those, they were a Bandai Blockout and a Coleco Alien Attack.

Not only was Willie angry because Mike had sold his property, but the units were also quite delicate as he had made some repairs to them, adding jumper wires where circuit board traces were broken and he wasn't sure how resilient those repairs were. These units were fine for careful home use and for research purposes for the podcast, but unless they were treated with care they would be likely to break again. The buyers were completely unaware of this of course as the eBay listing made no mention of it, in fact the Galaxian unit was described as *"Very nice condition from my personal collection. No battery cover"* and the Donkey Kong as *"Nice condition from my personal collection. No battery cover."*

> *"I feel sorry for the people who just bought these, he knew they were repaired but said nothing in the auctions. Had I caught them while they were live I could have notified eBay or something especially with the Donkey Kong as I have the original pic when I had it to repair.*
>
> *Funny how none of these were sold on GameGavel. Oh Wait, its another Scam site to get people to list items for him to snag cheaply due to no traffic over there.......*
>
> *Needless to say I am EXTREMELY PISSED OFF!!!*
>
> *As Scott and UK(Mike) told me – "uses you then dumps you" is 100 percent true!"*

Willie posted about this and Mike saw his post and emailed him saying that he *"thought"* they had been given to him but Willie assured him that he had told him at the time that when he was done with them he was to send them back. *"I told him the only thing I "gave" him was the Coleco Alien Attack (which he sold of course) which is no big deal as I did "give" him that for his collection."*

Mike offered to send Willie the money from the two auctions and to return the Frogger and the Bandai Blockout but Willie told him that he didn't want the money, it wasn't about the money, it was about principles and those machines were not his to sell. Mike was to refund the buyers and return the loaned machines that he still had.

Willie did get in touch with the new owner of the Donkey Kong machine who told him that he was converting it into a mini M.A.M.E. machine but offered to send him something in return. Willie declined the kind offer and was more concerned about him getting his money back on an item that was not as described. Mike assured Willie that he would refund the money and did so a couple of weeks later, but Willie was still out of pocket of course and this episode won Mike the accolade of *"Scumbag Seller Of The Week"* on the CUPodcast.

> *"Mike Kennedy who just exudes vomit from every pore, who was responsible for the Retro VGS and the Coleco Chameleon [...] it was a train wreck. [...]*
>
> *Willie, to his credit or not, for sticking by Mike, was pretty neutral on the whole Retro VGS/Coleco Chameleon thing, even when it turned sour, even when it started to be like this might not be something that you want to get into. Willie didn't want to throw his friend under the bus directly. [...]*
>
> *Satan Mike Kennedy actually decided to sell these off but not only did he sell them off, he sold them as restored like new, and blatantly ####ed over his friend and did exactly what his friend, who was just trying to help him out, had asked him not to. [...]*
>
> *Willie, apparently a great guy, I'd buy Willie a sandwich in a heartbeat, was like "No dude I don't want your ####ing dirty money, I want you to refund these people, get the machines back and send them back to me." [..]*
>
> *Someone said he wanted to come on the forum to say "Okay it's time we should back off Mike and then this happened, I don't see why you'd back off of someone where this is their shitty behavior. This is who they are, there is no backing off, they're not going to change, not gonna happen." [...] I think my gloves are off, I just don't care, only when I said that, I got into trouble, the Internet came after me when I said the gloves are coming off. Don't come at me, defend this one, if you want to send some mean tweets at one o'clock in the morning and defend this guy."*

Willie updated his post 10 days later to say that the buyers had been refunded on June 15th and then the Internet showed how kind it can be when a GoFundMe page was started to buy Willie the sandwich that Ian had mentioned. Mike Kennedy was one of the donors but he used the opportunity to try and clear things up a bit.

"For the record. Once it was brought to my attention these were refurbished I immediately emailed the buyers and have since issued them both refunds. I also told Willie I would pay him for them but he insisted that he didn't want the money and to just refund the buyers. Over the many years Willie and I have given/traded many things back and forth and in addition, I've given him a platform to promote his YouTube channels and podcasts. When I give something to someone it is theirs to do whatever they please, no strings attached. Either way, this is an opportunity to make this right with Willie as I always intended once he contacted me privately about it."

It was an apology of sorts but rather passive aggressive and Willie was content to just move on having really seen Mike for what he was by this point. Once he had the funds from the sandwich GoFundMe page, he donated them to Oscar Toledo, author of the smallest chess program on various platforms called "Nanochess." Oscar's family was experiencing a particularly tough time at that point and Willie wanted to do his bit to help them out, a very noble gesture that was appreciated.

With his finances and reputation at rock bottom and Mike not willing to do more travelling in his job at Creform Corporation, or Creform Corporation finding out about his failed online ventures and letting him go, it was time to move on and relocate. There were rumors that he had been found using the company credit card to fund some of his personal costs, allegedly some of the New York Toy Fair trip, but whether true or not, he was no longer employed by them and returned his company car. Having sold off many of his possessions, the final one being the costly Los Angeles townhouse that he and Tricia shared in Trabuco Canyon, one-time LLC Central, he had no further ties to the Southern California region that gave him his alter ego, SoCalMike. Tricia's employer had a satellite office in Arizona and they had family nearby, so it seemed like the obvious choice, and that Spring they relocated.

Temporarily they stayed in a cheap motel, paying around $150 a week, though it was possibly just Mike staying there as Tricia contemplated their future at a relative's house, while their own house sale was processed and until they could get an apartment. Importantly they had halved their living costs and Mike had taken a job that didn't give him a car but did give him a stipend for a phone. Now he was in Arizona he reached out to his old friend, Shane R. Monroe, who lives in Phoenix, hoping to meet up with him, but Shane didn't follow up on it as Mike was still persona non grata.

He went quiet for a long time while he rebuilt family relationships and set about paying back the money he had borrowed from both his and Tricia's family and it was some time later, in January 2018, when he raised his head above the parapet again by returning to AtariAge. Some welcomed him, some didn't, and some explained that he had a lot to answer for and welcomed him on the proviso that he never tried to sell them anything ever again. That is human nature, you might say "horses for courses", people see things differently in life and react differently to them, and this was no different, Mike had divided people's opinions.

His attempt to re-integrate was posting about a Pac-Man suit that was on sale at Kohl's.

> *"I know you all hate my guts but I can't help but share this. $25 Clearance Pac-Man Suits at Kohls. Normally $120. Find one if you can! I found one tonight. Google Pac-Man Oppo Suits to see what it looks like. Includes Sport Coat, Slacks and Tie. Super high quality. Good luck!"*

The mixed reactions to his "testing the water" post ranged from those that were welcoming:

> *"Mike, this is the first time in many years I've seen you speak about gamey things in a way that wasn't trying to sell something. It's a good look for you, please keep it up.*
>
> *Welcome back to the human race.*
>
> *I think you will find forgiveness in the community if you can demonstrate that you've given up the get-rich-quick schemes, and always speak the truth. If you don't know something, say so or STFU. No one wants to hear any more lies.*
>
> *I'm not buying that tickytack suit, because I'm not The Riddler, nor am I Billy Mitchell.*
>
> *But seriously, it's nice to see you above ground again."*

> *"I don't think (most) people hate your guts.*
>
> *I Do think they wished you'd stepped up and been more honest with them. I think they would have appreciated more personal accountability,...They do wish you'd taken responsibility and quit throwing people under the bus etc.*
>
> *Other than that you may be giving yourself too much importance...After a snarky internet comment (or tons of pages of them, because...You know it can be fun), they move on quickly to something else.*
>
> *At the end of the day, you made a mistake, or even a series of mistakes, which seemingly get amplified as everyone anonymously weighs in...And that's the nature of the internet."*

> *"Take away the "businessman" nonsense and he's just another game dork like us. Well, maybe he talks a lot more than some of us, but it takes all kinds."*

Of course, there were some that were less than welcoming:

> *"You're a scam artist, no better than a common thief, and you deserve to be treated as such. And worse than that, you still won't even own up to what you did.*
>
> *Others here may be willing to mince words but I'll call a spade a spade. Or a lying, thieving, scamming scumbag as the case may be."*

> *"I don't have anything nice to say about him because there is nothing nice to be said. He's a scammer. Actually, he's worse. He's a failure at scamming. He's morally bankrupt AND incompetent."*

"I'm not suggesting we cut the man's hand off or lock him up for the rest of his life. But he doesn't deserve to interact on level ground with members who didn't try to run a million dollar scam."

"He lost all of his businesses because he is incompetent. That wasn't a punishment for his attempted thievery."

Godwin's law was coined on Usenet in 1990 by American attorney and author Mike Godwin when he said that:

"Godwin's rule of Hitler analogies is an Internet adage asserting that "As an online discussion grows longer, the probability of a comparison involving Nazis or Hitler approaches; that is, if an online discussion (regardless of topic or scope) goes on long enough, sooner or later someone will compare someone or something to Adolf Hitler or his deeds, the point at which effectively the discussion or thread often ends."

In this case it wasn't Hitler that Mike was compared to but OJ Simpson.

"By all accounts, OJ Simpson was a nice guy before he killed those people. And no, I am absolutely not saying that what Mike did was anywhere near as bad as what OJ did. But the point is, the bad things you do in life can't always be eclipsed by whatever nice things you did beforehand. OJ was a great football player and he was in some awesome movies, but so what? All that good will is gone forever."

The Internet can be a place of extremes at times and this was no different. It should be noted that Godwin also added: *"I wanted folks who glibly compared someone else to Hitler to think a bit harder about the Holocaust."*

Godwin makes a good point, and while Mike was being kept at arms-length, there was a way back for him should he choose it. If he wanted to be accepted though, he would have to come clean, but could he ever do that and own up to what he had attempted to do and what he had actually done? Unlikely, but while some were adamant that he should not be welcomed back, claiming that he had not lost his businesses as a punishment but through incompetency, others were more level headed:

"I think a punishment should fit the crime. Does him losing GameGavel, Retro Magazine, the Jag shells, etc. along with our trust with future attempts at similar things fit? Yes.

Does him getting a life sentence away from the hobby and community to an extent that he isn't even welcome to discuss a Pac-Man suit fit? No."

"Those of you who have already gotten your torches and pitchforks back out of the closet obviously have too much time on your hands."

Many had moved on, co-hosts, friends and listeners alike, and looked back on the situation with the same thoughts that Scott and UKMike did, Mike had done some terrible things and the SoCalMike of old, the third musketeer, was gone forever, and Willie seemed to capture that feeling when he replied to Mike's post.

> *"I was refunded by the campaign. Aside from kicking me to the kerb, it's all water under the bridge now. He did a lot of good before the CC (Coleco Chameleon) situation. He was not always like he was during the CC situation. [...]*
>
> *I welcome him back but in a guarded fashion. I miss talking with him on our latest retro finds and talking about things like friends did back before the CC situation."*

Mike addressed the mixed response that he was getting, and again it wasn't the heart-felt apology or admission of guilt that many were looking for, but there was a tinge of regret in his words.

> *"I ended friendships with some great people in the hobby. I really did this as I didn't want their friendship with me to jeopardize their friendship with others and their reputations. I was (maybe still am) toxic and wanted to remove myself from their equations for that reason. Maybe it came across as I didn't like them anymore, but that couldn't be farther from the truth. I really miss the gaming friends I had prior to that mess. Had some of my best times with them -- they all know who they are. And, I will say again, I will not be starting any more gaming businesses personally. I will not overstay my welcome here but might post occasionally if I come across something cool in the hobby to share."*

Scott feels as though it's like Mike knows full well what he is doing to people but feels not a twinge of guilt or remorse while doing it. The phases of his businesses where people go from being flavor of the month to being a minor contributor who was responsible for all the mistakes are perhaps not considered by Mike to be the dubious repeating pattern that they are, perhaps there are even some sociopathic tendencies that Mike is unaware of. As one Retro Gaming Roundup listener would put it:

> *"Scott is the man who always has an answer, ask him whatever you like and he will start talking, but the only question I have ever asked Scott that took a minute before he said anything was 'Is SoCalMike actually mentally ill?'"*

Whatever the case, it was certainly true that Mike had crossed the wrong community and that the wrong people in that community had ended up under the bus. Would Mike have had those same feelings of regret were he sitting in his new rented office, earning his $80,000 salary and burning through the $1,950,000 from Kickstarter had he been successful, or were his regrets simply due to the fact that he had lost everything? The question is somewhat rhetorical but even success can be a lonely place.

Mike had lost his home, his yacht, his car, his businesses, his game collection, his place in the gaming community and almost his family. Albert of AtariAge now owns the Jaguar molds, Kevin Horton has several successful FPGA based consoles on the market and is considered a leader in the field, Eli of Piko Interactive owned Retro

Magazine and GameGavel, CollectorVision recovered and are still selling games, John Lester has recovered and is still broadcasting, The Jag Bar continues to broadcast and Mark Kaminski has taken Mike's place on Retro Gaming Roundup.

At one time or another Mike had the right people around him, the right people in the right place at the right time, he just chose to either ignore them or throw them under the bus.

> *"As a side note, I see you added Mark K to the cast. As an FYI he was the one that spearheaded separating the magazine from the show when we were at one time talking with Play N Trade about a partnership. He was adamant about not associating the magazine with the podcast because of our language and other things. And, he bitched anytime I wanted to run a free advert for the show. The ones I did run I had to pay him commission on. Again, water under the bridge, but thought it was strange to see him as part of the show. He was a big part of the rocky relationship that started between the podcast, you guys and me.*
>
> *Wish you both well and hope to talk more again in the future. Feel free to share this with Scott if you want, too. Love to mend the fence."*

It could have ended very differently. Mike never accepted responsibility for the scam, instead blaming Sean who, in all probability, was compromised enough to give Mike a mockup, if that's what he asked for, and who in turn scammed Mike if that's not what he asked for. Either way, Mike had to know that a mockup is what he had. At various stages of the console process he had gone from not having the funds to bring a prototype to market and looking for a smoke and mirrors approach, through the stage of John Carlsen using his own savings to pay for his development work, to finally, and seemingly out of the blue, finding $7,000 out of a planned $10,000 to pay Sean for a finished prototype. Clay Cowgill had told Mike at the very beginning that it would take around $70,000 and 14 weeks of full-time work to build a prototype, but Mike had continued to tell the world that what he had from Sean, in a fraction of that time, at a fraction of that cost and running the world's most quickly developed SNES core, was the real thing when clearly, it was not. When all those around him were telling him that he had nothing, that what he was showing was anything but a prototype, he forged onwards and continued writing cheques.

Steve Sawyer had watched his former friend go through the whole process, and while he feels that Mike had set out with good intentions, his story should serve as a stark warning to others, that: *"The big lesson is, your dreams can be your dreams, but they can also end up being your undoing and your nightmare."* They were certainly now a nightmare for Mike who had lost everything, he had not done right by his friends, his business partners or his investors, and it was very clear that they were not of the utmost importance to him as he had earlier assured them:

> *"Next, GameGavel, LLC and its owners are still of utmost importance to me. I have other family that bought in and obviously I still want them and you to have an upside in that investment. It is always top priority!"*

It wasn't top priority as it took a back seat to Mike's attempt at quitting his day job and *"work(ing) in gaming, as an ideas man"* and *"cornering the market on retro."* Like Mike's dream, their investment was gone. Mike had played the victim card but he was certainly not the only one who had lost anything as he had claimed. Those who were swept up by the whirlwind of enthusiasm that was Mike Kennedy hadn't just lost their time, their reputation and their money, they had also lost their friend.

> *"I appreciate the comments and don't take them for granted. Believe me, no one wants to forget the past more than I.*
>
> *And you can be assured I won't be attempting any more gaming ventures. I woefully mismanaged things the past few years and paid the price, in more ways I can count. And, it will take a few more years for me to recover from that debacle financially. It's true that turning your hobby into even a part-time profession is a sure-fire way to enjoy your hobby less and stress yourself half to death. Especially, when you make the mistakes I did. I nearly lost all my love for gaming and regrettably did lose a handful of great friends in the hobby.*
>
> *Over the past year, I have played more video games than I have played probably in the past 9 years. I've rebuilt a small collection of consoles that are all out and playable including an Atari 2600, 7800, PS1, Timex Sinclair 1000, Apple IIc and Commodore 64 -- oh, and my original Sega Genesis I had growing up and all my original games (I gave it to my cousin way back when, he kept it and recently found it and shipped it back to me).*
>
> *In any event, I'll take what I can get but don't expect anything when it comes to being completely forgiven for what I put everyone through the past few years."*
>
> Mike Kennedy
> January 14, 2018

Afterword

by Scott Schreiber

What a wild ride, with a disjointed, sputtering, and lurching ending, but that is how it happened. There was no concise, neat and tidy ending with a single event to tie it all together and give closure. When UKMike first discussed this book, one of my concerns was that the ending was so chaotic and went through several zombie cockroach resurrections, even after it had been declared dead. I was one of those that pronounced a time of death more than once, only to have the thing spring back to life, like an alien creature in a sci-fi movie that just won't stay down, no matter how many rounds you put into it.

However, after reading the first draft of this book, I was surprised in several ways by what UKMike had accomplished. Not so much that he had managed to do it, but how well he had managed to do it for a first-time author. The book was approached more as a scholarly work than a tell all book, with original interviews, documents, business filings and other primary source material, yet somehow, he had managed to make the chaos as organized as one can. Not bad for a first book. If one added citations, footnotes, and the other formatting requirements of a peer reviewed publication it could be a doctoral thesis on the subject, but then it would also read like one, and as UKMike mentions in his Foreword, he didn't want to just write a factual documentation of events. This book represents the real story and the actual mechanisms that created and halted the whole wild ride. Any speculation or assumptions made to help connect the dots are clearly presented as such.

During what we have generally decided to call the Coleco Chameleon debacle, one of the more frustrating things is that a network of people, made up of Retro Gaming Roundup members, former Mike Kennedy "empire" participants and alert observers, had first-hand knowledge of dishonesty and fraud being committed, and yet it was an unbelievable struggle to have their voices heard. I cannot tell you the frustration of obtaining and timing the release of a key piece of evidence that we had gathered, or passed on to others, so that it would have the best chance of being noticed and have the maximum effect in hopefully halting this scam, only to see it go relatively unnoticed! More than once we had a bombshell that should have stood the whole gaming community up like meerkats, yet when we revealed it through the podcast, social media or on forums, it was skipped over relatively unnoticed but would be followed by a Youtuber, pulling hundreds of thousands of views, that said nothing of any quality or accuracy. That happened more than a few times and occurred right up until the end. I have no doubt that SocalMike was hoping and praying that the voices of those in the know would be lost among the noise and drowned out by the broad reach of his unquestioned press releases that were circulated by the gaming media without any scrutiny.

Mike expressed on several occasions that he was *"a CEO God dammit!"* with a company, a lucrative product launch with official standing and that the gaming community consisted merely of haters and trolls. I am convinced that Mike was certain that his standing and his voice, through the media channels, would see him through the gates of Kickstarter and beyond, presenting his tarted-up electronic scrap as working product prototypes.

While we're on the topic, shame on the press that covered this story, other than a few exceptions, like Pat Contri and Ian Ferguson, the Good Ole Gamers podcast, Youtuber Stop Drop and Retro, and of course Carl Williams. The games press is mostly nothing more than a cut and paste crew hoping to parasite a few bucks in ad revenue and click throughs from repeating press releases before moving on to the next one. When they could be bothered to deviate from that practice and write about the scam, after the community had done their investigative job for them and laid it bare as a scam, they did so with hastily thrown together articles, mainly citing tweets and other easily obtained information that could be gathered in minutes, and they were just as inaccurate in print as the commenting Youtubers were in video. Not once was a primary source contacted for an interview to gather evidence. In fact, until this book, nothing out there got the whole story right and relied on primary sources.

So why did SocalMike do all this? SocalMike told me that he wanted two things in the gaming world: First he wanted to have a career in the industry. This was never something secret, he was always very open about this matter. The second thing he wanted was to be a famous figure in the gaming world, and this I believe was more important than the career and employment aspect. In all the time that I knew Mike, he was never cheap or money grubbing, nor did he seem to have a fascination with money. He looked at the adulation and following that the icons in his beloved gaming industry had and he wanted that for himself. My assessment is that notoriety was his primary drive, with the career that followed being a useful and convenient secondary goal. Well, achievement unlocked!! He is certainly memorialized as a name in gaming history that will be referenced for decades to come, sadly for him, only as a Scooby Doo villain and not as a beloved icon of gaming. I don't believe that Mike started out as a bad guy, I think that his desire for success and adulation was such that it overrode his sense of right and wrong, and that family, friends, the gaming community and anything else in the way were dispensable in order to reach that end goal.

I did take personal offense that he tried to defraud me, because we were close friends that shared our triumphs and troubles, enjoyed endless hours of laughs, travelled and vacationed together, and I have a fierce loyalty to my friends. Mike came to me during those early days, cap in hand, asking for help, and later we began this console adventure together as well, and it hurt me that he would dispose of all that for the adulation of strangers.

Once the situation, and his change in character, was clear for all to see, I took even greater offense that he thought he could get the better of me. That really galled me and remained a constant motivator, almost as strong as the other motivations, for trying to put a stop to this. After I was armed with the information about the new business entity that Mike formed on the eve of the Retro VGS Indiegogo campaign, I called him and confronted him about it, though I would have much preferred to have done this in person, as I doubt very much that he would have had the balls to look me in the eye and tell me that he was going ahead. When I laid out to him everything I knew, I didn't bother asking why as I figured it was a waste of time, and we had been down this road before with the promises made in regard to Retro magazine, and when confronted on those occasions he had avoided addressing the problem statement. My goal during this call was to let him know what I knew, that he had stripped the GameGavel company and formed a new one, as well as dishonoring our agreement that the console was under the umbrella of the original company. When he started his litany of excuses, I waited for him to finish and told him what his way out was. He was to return the assets to GameGavel and he was to acknowledge the partners and contributors on his projects that had been sidelined and had their ideas taken. This was not a point of debate, it was terms of surrender.

I was honestly surprised when, instead of capitulating and ending it there, he simply said *"Well I can't do that"* which I took to mean, well I can't do that and still make this console. I was uncertain if he was too stupid to understand what he was getting into or if he really thought he had what it took to get the better of me. SocalMike knew I was a veteran and had served in the middle east, and I had faced a lot more adversity than a pitch man with a video game idea. He had seen me deal decisively with those who challenged me during the Classic Gaming Expo planning and execution, and he knew that I did not suffer fools gladly. So, did he not understand that I was not going to go quietly because of his success in previously getting the better of his magazine partner, Steve Sawyer, or did he think he could simply outwit me and go through with this thing? I couldn't decide which it was, and I didn't spend much time on it, but I was furious that he had squared off with me as an opponent. In fact, it was probably only a few seconds between hanging up the phone and me saying out loud *"This mother####er!!"*

By the end of that day, I had a solid plan in place. I was one of many in the end, but there were so many people that had fallen foul of Mike's broken promises, had signed contracts ignored or had put in hundreds of hours of uncompensated work that there was almost an army of people working to stop the deception.

If this could have gone a different way, I would have been grateful for it to have never happened. When UKMike says that he would have been there to head Mike off before boarding the bus, I have no doubt that he would have done so, and I would have been right there beside him. SocalMike made his choices though. He not only made them, but he doubled down, and then doubled down again.

In his last written words on the matter he remained unrepentant, with a Babe in the Woods style claim of innocence and clinging to story lines that have long since been disproven. I found it very fitting that UKMike decided to end the last chapter in Mike Kennedy's own words.

Appendix

Sources

Chapter 1:
Classic Video Gamer Magazine, deloitte.com, dictionary.com, LinkedIn, old-friends.co, oxforddictionaries.com, Retro Gaming Roundup, Wikipedia

Chapter 2:
AtariAge, chasethechuckwagon.com, eBay, GameGavel, GamerSpots, GamesIndustryBiz, Mark Kaminski, Parcel Gamer, PowerSellersForum, Retro Arcade Radio, Retro Gaming Roundup, tuliptools.com, YouTube, Wikipedia

Chapter 3:
Retro Gaming Roundup

Chapter 4:
Gamasutra, GamePro, IGN, Mark Kaminski, Parcel Gamer, Pixelitis, Retro Gaming Roundup, Thumb Culture, Video Game Writers, Wired

Chapter 5:
AtariAge, Retro Gaming Roundup, Wikipedia

Chapter 6:
Pat Contri, CUPodcast, Facebook, IGN, John Lester,
Mark Kaminski, Kickstarter, Retro Gaming Roundup, Steve Sawyer, Twitter, Wulf Space

Chapter 7:
cgexpo.com, Facebook, midwestgamingclassic.com, retrogamingexpo.com, Retro Gaming Roundup, Twitter, Vegas Retro Expo LLC, Wikipedia

Chapter 8:

angel.co, AtariAge, Buzzfile.com, Clay Cowgill, GameGavel, Google Groups, Rebecca Heineman, Mark Kaminski, Kickstarter, Bob Polaro, Retro Gaming Roundup, Riverside Criminal & Traffic

Chapter 9:

AtariAge, John Carlsen, CollectorVision, CUPodcast, Gamesbeat, Rebecca Heineman, Indiegogo, Mark Kaminski, John Lester, Piko Interactive, Retro Gaming Magazine, Retro Gaming Roundup

Chapter 10:

ColecoVisions Podcast, Retro Gaming Roundup

Chapter 11:

AtariAge, Brian Barhnart, CUPodcast, Facebook, John Lester, psychologytoday.com, Retro Gaming Roundup, Twitter, YouTube

Chapter 12:

AtariAge, Facebook, Retro Gaming Roundup, YouTube

Chapter 13:

chasethechuckwagon.com, Pat Contri, Clay Cowqgill, GameGavel, GamerSpots, Mark Kaminski, John Lester, Parcel Gamer, Retro Arcade Radio, Retro Gaming Roundup, Retro Magazine

Chapter 14:

AtariAge, Brian Barnhart, ColecoVision.dk, Facebook, GambitMag.com, hardcoregamer.com, hotpads.com, Retro Gaming Roundup, Twitter, USPTO (United States Patent and Trademark Office), Wikipedia

Chapter 15:

AtariAge, Brian Barnhart, Mark Kaminski, Retro Gaming Roundup

Quotes

I just want to quit my day job and work in gaming, as an ideas man.

Mike Kennedy

He is a very good salesman and he can definitely get you amped up for all kinds of things.

Steve Sawyer

They are LYING to you. Do not fall for it. It is all a bunch of lies and manipulation.

Mike Kennedy

His eyes were red, his face was red and he said he was ready to puke!

Tricia Kennedy

I want to thank my Retro Gaming Roundup Co-Hosts, UKMike and Scott. There are no two other people I would want to share an Atari 2600 game with!

Mike Kennedy

Dude, you're still going to have a stake, this is still our thing. It's just going to be better.

Mike Kennedy

You gave it to one of the most mistrusted names in this industry, and along every step of the way you tried to make me like it.

Steve Sawyer

I've never known an entrepreneur that put in so little time and resources.

Mark Kaminski

OMG do you need some ADHD medicine or are you puffin on a meth pipe over there?

Mark Kaminski

When it comes to creative design some people see things and ask 'Why?' I dream things that never were; and say 'Why not?'

Sean Robinson

I am "still" enjoying reading everyone's comments and criticism. We are really trying to be transparent about this entire process.

Mike Kennedy

This whole thing is beginning to seem like someone is having a manic episode and documenting it online...along with some 3D renders.

madman (AtariAge)

In the end, you know, behind the scenes, Indiegogo had been courting us for the last few months.

Mike Kennedy

I started a new company for the console as I don't have any stock available on the GG/Magazine side to give Steve or any other hardware person meat in the game so I had no choice.

Mike Kennedy

That's not how business works. It might be how the government works, when we ran out of money, we printed more, but the IRS gets to do that and the Treasury Department, not us. We go to jail for that stuff.

Scott Schreiber

We are just three legitimate guys who want to bring a cool product to market. It's as simple as that.

Mike Kennedy

Actually getting some of the most favorable responses yet on our FB page.

Mike Kennedy

Well, there is no working prototype because we can't afford to bring a working prototype to market.

Mike Kennedy

The facts are you cannot, nobody can make an FPGA system any cheaper than we can.

Mike Kennedy

It's fascinating too because it feels like there are some people who just want to see this thing fail.

John Lester

First off, developers will be instructed to give us bug free games.

Mike Kennedy

I know, we are not going there, but we are being compared to that (Ouya) so I wanted to quickly say, go watch their video. No prototype, it was smoke and mirrors.

Mike Kennedy

We are very appreciative that there are seventy-five pages of discussions over on AtariAge about this, even if they are terrible and dragging me through the mud.

Mike Kennedy

Mike seems to share information freely (even too freely) when it appears to be in his interest.

John Carlsen

If you want to play a SNES game, buy a used SNES. If you want to play a 2600 game, buy a used 2600.

John Carlsen

Did a lot of things right up until we did everything wrong.

Mike Kennedy

An idea man has value, but an idea man needs to have loyalty to those who turn it into reality unless you're clever enough to screw them after you have all the contributions, some are and some aren't.

Scott Schreiber

That "COLECO is Back" title was added at the last minute by our PR firm. And I guess we can all debate what "Back" means.

Mike Kennedy

Once the prototype is complete we will reveal what's inside. It shouldn't be too much longer.

Mike Kennedy

First off, this post isn't pointing fingers at anyone in this community whatsoever, but will single out one Carl Williams.

Mike Kennedy

Note the email from Mike Rajna to me kindly asking me not to discuss our internal discussions until some sort of official deal is made.

Mike Kennedy

[...] with my technical expertise services I strive to prevent and solve any technology crisis.

Sean Robinson

You know, Brian, we had a really, really great showing at the Toy Fair, and all of these people want to get a piece of it.

Mike Kennedy

You know what Mike, I am a professional, dude.

Brian Barnhart

The train wreck is occurring. The train has gone off the side of the bridge, is plummeting towards the bottom of the canyon. Meanwhile, the engineer is still tugging on the whistle and the fireman is still shoveling coal into the thing. This is insane.

Scott Schreiber

We're delaying the Kickstarter for the Coleco Chameleon to make it even better!

Mike Kennedy

The only conclusion from that resume review would be to write a cheque to SoCal to buy the molds from him and release him of his duties.

Mike James

I think the only thing that could ever be put in those shells from this point on is evil spirits.

Scott Schreiber

This is what we can do when given the proper time.

Sean Robinson

Fool me once, shame on you. Fool me twice, shame on me. Fool me three times, #### you forever!

Pat Contri

We are running his games through our custom written SNES FPGA Core. He said they are playing flawlessly.

Mike Kennedy

Not sure what you'd expect to get done in a week except maybe some kind of mock-up?

Clay Cowgill

You're not gonna get your reputation back Mike, do something else not in the hobby. I don't care what it is. I don't care if you whittle wood sticks on the porch. Please stay out of the retro gaming hobby.

Pat Contri

When Mike has something good, you basically have to staple his mouth shut to get him to not talk about it.

Steve Sawyer

If he had something dope and he was completely confident in the hardware and everything, dude he'd be showing you HD, 4k close-up pics of that shit.

Steve Sawyer

They want the success and the profits but none of the risk but I guess they're not alone in that. I just choose not to support that notion.

Mike James

Carl Williams IS NOT taking over RETRO Magazine nor has he ever talked with me about it. And I am not selling it or giving it to ANYONE!

Mike Kennedy

I'm trying to be gentle about it, but yeah, I mean if you're shit at one business, then you have to suspect that maybe you're shit at all your businesses.

Steve Sawyer

I think it takes a passionate person like myself to run a website like GameGavel, as that gives confidence to its members.

Mike Kennedy

I know I kicked over the ant hill but my reputation was more important than fooling the community over a fake product, I don't lose any sleep over what I did.

Brian Barnhart

Most (of) the value would be future perceived value + maybe replacement cost to create a site like this from scratch.

Mike Kennedy

New management of a dumpster fire is just that, a new guy standing next to a burning trash heap.

Scott Schreiber

I really miss the gaming friends I had prior to that mess. Had some of my best times with them -- they all know who they are.

Mike Kennedy

Scott is the man who always has an answer, ask him whatever you like and he will start talking, but the only question I have ever asked Scott that took a minute before he said anything was 'Is SoCalMike actually mentally ill?'

Anonymous

In any event, I'll take what I can get but don't expect anything when it comes to being completely forgiven for what I put everyone through the past few years.

Mike Kennedy

A Note from the Author

This is an official account of events that led to the evolution of GameGavel, RETRO magazine, the RETRO VGS, and the Coleco Chameleon written by somebody who was involved and had inside information that has never been published before.

It is a factual account of events, but more than that, it is a human story of the man behind the GameGavel Network and the Retro VGS / Coleco Chameleon and shows how one man's dream can quickly become a nightmare.

Mike Kennedy set out with good intentions and wanted to produce a video game console but somewhere along the way he lost control of his vision, his empire, and his livelihood. At any stage, he could have stopped the descent into madness but he chose to double down and forge ahead with one of the biggest scams in video game history.

Join Mike on his journey from hobby gamer to C.E.O. and back again and experience his highs and lows along the way.

You can find many other resources, further information and merchandise on our website www.colecochameleon.org.

www.ingramcontent.com/pod-product-compliance
Ingram Content Group UK Ltd.
Pitfield, Milton Keynes, MK11 3LW, UK
UKHW041831200726
13854UKWH00002BA/984

9 781837 910533